JAN 1 1 2012

ELK GROVE VILLAGE PUBLIC LIBRARY

W9-BGN-491

DISCARDED BY
ELK GROVE VILLAGE PUBLIC LIBRARY

DISCARDED BY
ELK GROVE VILLAGE PUBLIC LIBRARY

ELK GROVE VILLAGE PUBLIC LIBRARY
1001 WELLINGTON AVE
ELK GROVE VILLAGE, IL 60007
(847) 439-0447

Jack Kennedy

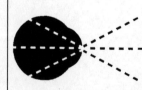

This Large Print Book carries the
Seal of Approval of N.A.V.H.

JACK KENNEDY

ELUSIVE HERO

CHRIS MATTHEWS

THORNDIKE PRESS
A part of Gale, Cengage Learning

GALE
CENGAGE Learning·

Detroit • New York • San Francisco • New Haven, Conn • Waterville, Maine • London

GALE
CENGAGE Learning

Copyright © 2011 by Christopher J. Matthews.

Thorndike Press, a part of Gale, Cengage Learning.

ALL RIGHTS RESERVED

Thorndike Press® Large Print Nonfiction.

The text of this Large Print edition is unabridged.

Other aspects of the book may vary from the original edition.

Set in 16 pt. Plantin.

LIBRARY OF CONGRESS CATALOGING-IN-PUBLICATION DATA

Matthews, Christopher, 1945–
    Jack Kennedy, elusive hero / by Chris Matthews. — Large
print ed.
        p. cm.
    Orig. published: New York : Simon & Schuster, 2011.
    ISBN-13: 978-1-4104-4357-1 (hardcover : large print)
    ISBN-10: 1-4104-4357-4 (hardcover : large print) 1. Kennedy,
John F. (John Fitzgerald), 1917–1963. 2. United States —
Politics and government — 1961–1963. 3. Presidents — United
States — Biography. 4. Large type books. I. Title.
E842.M346 2011
973.922092—dc23
[B]
                                                    2011034168

Published in 2011 by arrangement with Simon & Schuster, Inc.

Printed in Mexico
1 2 3 4 5 6 7 15 14 13 12 11

To Kathleen

CONTENTS

At the peak of the Cold War, an American president saved his country and the world from a nuclear war. How did Jack Kennedy gain the cold detachment to navigate this perilous moment in history? What prepared him to be the hero we needed?

This is my attempt to explain the leader Jacqueline Kennedy called "that unforgettable, elusive man."

1956
DEMOCRATIC
NAT[IONAL]
CONV[ENTI]ON

1

PREFACE

I grew up in a Republican family. My own political awakening began in 1952, when I was six. I remember riding the school bus to Maternity of the Blessed Virgin Mary. One of my classmates was a boy whose father was a Democratic committeeman in Somerton, our remote Philadelphia hamlet bordering Bucks County. I felt sorry for him because he was the only kid for Stevenson. It seemed everybody I knew was for Ike.

Back then, even though we kids were small, our souls were large. We had a sense of things we weren't supposed to understand. I knew that Adlai Stevenson was an "egghead." My father said he "talked over the heads of people." There was distance between us and those like Stevenson. We were regular people.

My older brother, Bert, and I spent our days fighting World War II and the Korean War in our backyard. I knew General Eisenhower had fought in what Mom and Dad always called "the war." It made him a hero. Once I was sitting with Dad at a movie theater when a newsreel came on showing Eisenhower making his return from NATO in Europe, boarding an airplane and waving. I wondered whether he was president and turned to my right to ask my father this. "No," came the answer, "but he will be."

One outcome of World War II was to offer Catholics their opening to join the American mainstream. My mother once told us how the big milk company in Philadelphia used to ask for religion on its job application. The correct answer, she explained, was any one of the Protestant denominations. "Catholic" meant you didn't get the job. What I know for sure is that in the early 1950s we were still making an effort to fit in.

Looking back, I can't count how many times we first and second graders found ourselves marching up and down Bustleton Avenue in front of Maternity carrying little flags. I don't even know which holidays we were celebrating; maybe none. But there we were, mini–George M. Cohans offering up some endless display of our American regularness. All this actually happened, this postwar assimilation of Catholics, and it's a key part of the story I'm telling.

Those were the early boomer years. And a boom it was. We had a hundred kids in our first grade, more than would fit in a classroom, so they had to put us in the auditorium.

I remember an afternoon in 1956 that's hard to believe now. What's strange about it to me is the way it marks a before-and-after moment in time. History changed. It was July, and we were listening to the radio in our two-tone '54 Chevy Bel Air.

It was broadcasting the balloting from the Democratic Convention in Chicago. The fight to become the party's vice-presidential candidate was on between Kefauver — a name I knew from listening to the news, just as I knew the name Nixon — and now, out of nowhere, this candidate named Kennedy. We'd never heard of him. It was an Irish name.

So, because he was a known quantity — Kefauver, a brand name — I was happy when the Tennessee senator won, finally, on the second ballot. The name I knew had beaten the other name. Isn't that how most voting seems to be, voting for the name you recognize, rooting for its victory, and all the time having no real idea who the person is?

Yet, looking back on this event, that Democratic National Convention of over a half-century ago, an image from it remains frozen in my mind's eye. The truth is, it's a picture that entered my consciousness and stayed there. What I still see, as clearly as if it were yesterday, is that giant hall with its thousands of cheering delegates, its chaos then suddenly punctuated by the appearance onstage of a young stranger. It was John F. Kennedy, who

13

had just lost the nomination to Estes Kefauver; swiftly he came through the crowd and up to the podium in order to ask that his opponent's victory be made by acclamation. He was releasing his delegates and requesting unity, and, in making this important gesture, he seemed both confident and gracious. It was the first look the country at large had had of him, a figure we would come to know so well, one who would soon mean so much to us, to me.

I was ten at the time.

I was becoming increasingly obsessed with politics. Two years later, on the midterm election night in 1958, I was backing the GOP candidates, among them Hugh Scott, who won his fight that night to be junior senator from Pennsylvania in an upset. In New York, the Republican candidate, Nelson Rockefeller, defeated the Democrat Averell Harriman, the incumbent governor. My father, a court reporter working for the city of Philadelphia, offered a kind remark about the patrician Harriman, saying he looked sad. It was one of those rare, memorable times when Dad would step out of his workaday world to make such a comment, or to quote from a poem he'd learned in school.

By 1960, I was a paperboy for the *Philadelphia Bulletin,* and suddenly, as I started reading the daily afternoon paper I was throwing onto people's lawns, my loyalties were challenged. Now I was following Jack Kennedy in that year's primaries and enthusiastically rooting for him. He was Catholic, after all, and I felt the pull. Yet all the while I followed his trail through New Hampshire, Wisconsin, and West Virginia, I knew that, in the end, I'd wind up supporting Nixon, his opponent.

That's because, by this time, I'd become not merely a member of a Republican family but a Republican myself. Yet here I found myself entranced by the spectacle of the glamorous JFK winning his party's nomination.

And not only was I cheering the idea of Jack occupying the White House for the next eight years, by the time of the Los Angeles convention I was dreaming of the "happily ever after" — the succession of his vice president, Lyndon Johnson, elected to follow JFK with his own two terms; then, after that, Bobby and Teddy. Momentarily dazzled, I was caught up by the romance of dynasty.

I'd lived my boyhood reading the biographies of great men. From a young age I'd gone from one to the next and been taken with the notion of leaders' destinies. For every birthday and Christmas, Grandmom had made it her regular practice to buy me a book on the life of a famous historic figure. First it was the Young American series, then the Landmark books. I remember ones on Davy Crockett and Abe Lincoln, while others told stories of iconic events such as the Civil War sea battle between the *Monitor* and the *Merrimack*.

The first book I got from the little public library next to Maternity was an illustrated biography of Alexander the Great. And so that's who I was in 1960 — a kid who had this gut interest in history and liked reading biographies of heroes.

The Democratic Convention of 1960 was in Los Angeles. Now it was the Republicans' turn in Chicago. I followed the events gavel to gavel, either watching on television or going to bed listening to the radio. I remember the jaunty, optimistic strains of "California, Here I Come!" repeatedly erupting whenever Nixon's name was mentioned. Caught up in the Republican spirit, I once again shifted my allegiance.

Nixon had reexerted his pull over me. I saw him as the scrappy challenger. I was rooting for the underdog, who was also the one who deserved it. Nixon was tough on fighting the Russians. He'd held his ground in that Kitchen Table debate with Nikita Khrushchev over in Moscow. He and his running mate, Henry Cabot Lodge, struck me as the more solid and seasoned candidates to take on the Cold War, to stop the Communist spread around the globe.

On election night, as the returns started to come in, the early ones signaling their defeat, I was overwhelmed — and I cried. By a little after seven, I was drenched in the bad news.

Yet the Matthews house was not as united as I have so far portrayed it. I remember asking my father whom he intended to vote for. When he said Nixon without hesitation, I challenged him. Weren't we Catholic? Shouldn't we be for Kennedy? "I'm a Republican" was his simple, all-explaining response. Dad stuck to his party loyalty. He was a Catholic convert and didn't feel that tribal pull the way the all-Irish side of the family did. It was simple for him, even if he was willing to go so far as to allow how Jack Kennedy had "a touch of Churchill" about him. Interestingly, he also believed that in a fistfight between the two candidates there would be no contest: JFK would easily best Nixon, he declared. I'd raised the issue, and it seemed a matter of no little importance back then.

My mother — born Mary Teresa Shields, Irish to the core — more resembled me in her responses to the political dilemma of our household. But I could tell she was keeping her sympathies to herself, as if to make less trouble in the house. One night, when I was drying the dishes alongside her as she washed them, I offered my opinion that it might be wrong to support Kennedy simply because of religion. It seemed to scrape a wound. She shot back that Grandmom, my father's mother, from County Antrim, had become a citizen *only* in order to be able to cast her vote for Eisenhower, a fellow Presbyterian. Mom said it defensively. Don't single me out, she was arguing, your dad's side of the family was right out there voting religion, too.

Mom's dad, Charles Patrick Shields, was a classic Irishman and local Democratic committeeman. He worked the night shift as an inspector at a nearby plant, and left the house every weekday afternoon carrying his lunchbox and thermos. When he had on his peacoat and cap, he could have been heading off to work in County Cork. On Sundays he wore a three-piece suit to church at St. Stephen's and kept it on all day, even when he'd come up to visit us in Somerton, which he called "God's country." He was right out of Eugene O'Neill's *A Touch of the Poet*.

A favorite ritual of mine, when he retired, was accompanying him for long walks through the old neighborhoods, then stopping to buy the bulldog edition of the *Inquirer* on the way home. Once he'd finished reading it, sitting there under the mantelpiece, he'd fold the paper, look up at me, and say simply, "Christopher John." I loved him and I always loved that moment, and we would talk politics forever.

This conflict between being Catholic and Republican was a constant bother to me over the years. Yes, a lot of Catholics had voted for Eisenhower, but the old loyalties were deeply Democratic. The vote at LaSalle College High

18

School, where I was going and where I argued the Kennedy-Nixon race at lunchtime, was 24 to 9 for Kennedy in my homeroom.

Our family divisions along these lines never actually reached the level of a right-out-there dispute, but the business of voting either Republican or Catholic did raise the whole question of what we were. We could be Republican, but we were still mostly Irish. In the end, I never actually knew how Mom voted. Because of how I subsequently came to feel — and how I feel now — I hope it was Kennedy she cast her ballot for in the privacy of that curtained booth. Still, I confess that when the inauguration rolled around, on January 20, 1961, my loyalties remained with the loser.

While my mother was ironing in our basement rec room, we watched the ceremonies as they took place in snowy Washington. She seemed upbeat, quietly happy about the event we were witnessing. I think.

As for me, I moved rightward in the days of the New Frontier. I became a fan of Barry Goldwater, lured by his libertarian case for greater personal freedom. Like Hillary Clinton, herself a Goldwater Girl at the time, I would eventually change course. But even back then, I found John F. Kennedy the most interesting political figure of the day. I wanted to meet him, be in the same room with him, study him.

■ ■ ■ ■

A half century of political life later, my fascination with the elusive spirit of John F. Kennedy has remained an abiding one. He is both pathfinder and puzzle, a beacon and a conundrum. Whenever I spot the name in print, I stop to read. Anytime I've ever met a person who knew him — someone who was there with JFK in real time — I crave hearing his or her first-person memories.

One significant opportunity to listen to firsthand Jack stories came when I spent a half dozen years in the 1980s working for Thomas P. "Tip" O'Neill, Jr., Speaker of the House of Representatives. His and Kennedy's mutual history went way back in the arena of Boston politics, that fiercest of partisan battlefields. In 1946, when young Jack Kennedy was making his first political bid, in the primary race for the 11th Congressional District of Massachusetts, Tip actually had been in his opponent's camp. Later, though, when Jack gained his Senate seat in '52 after serving three terms in the House, Tip replaced him there, serving with him companionably for the next eight years.

During the time I served as his administrative assistant — enjoying a front-row seat when Tip employed all his liberal conscience and veteran's craft against that affable ideologue Ronald Reagan — I found I could occasionally get him, when he was in the right mood and time hung over us, to reminisce about the old days. It was like talking to Grandpop under the mantelpiece.

I treasured hearing him tell how Boston mayor James Michael Curley "was corrupt even by the standards of those days" and what Richard Nixon, whom he'd helped bring down over Watergate, was like to play cards with: "talked too much; not a bad guy." I'd listen eagerly, hardly able to believe my good fortune.

Later, I got to know and became friends with Ben Bradlee, the legendary *Washington Post* editor and Kennedy chum. He quickly understood what an appreciative listener I was. And in the early 1990s, when I began to research my book on the surprising history of the Jack Kennedy–Dick Nixon relationship, with its fascinating backstory, I came to know such men as Charles Bartlett, Paul "Red" Fay, and Chuck Spalding, veteran JFK cronies all.

Yet none of those encounters were enough. I wanted to get every possible look at him, see him from any angle that would help explain him. Was he a liberal as he's been tagged, or was he a pragmatist open to liberal causes? Was he a rich boy pushed by his dad, buying into what his father had sold him on, or was he a self-made leader? Was he a legacy or a Gatsby? The hold JFK had begun to exert on my imagination and on my curiosity when I was a young boy never abated. Instead, it only increased with the passing decades.

Before he came along, politics mostly meant gray men in three-piece suits, indoor types, sexless: Truman, Taft, Dewey, Kefauver, Eisenhower, Nixon. What he did was grip the country, quickening us. From the black-and-white world in which we'd been drifting we suddenly opened our eyes, feeling alive and energized, and saw Technicolor. JFK was wired into our central nervous system and juiced us. He sent us around the planet in the Peace Corps, and then rocketing beyond it to the moon.

Most of all — and, to me, this is what matters above everything else — he saved us from the perilous fate toward which we were headed. All those ICBMs, all those loaded warheads: the Cold War Kennedy inherited was bound for Armageddon. It was just a matter of time — we thought, I thought — until there'd be nuclear war, that "World War III" dreaded in every heart.

If you were a kid you didn't have to read the newspapers to know this, for, unlike our elders, we were actually living it. Weekly drills sent us crouching under our little varnished wooden desks on command. Then, at one critical moment in the fall of 1962, a lone man, President John F. Kennedy, understood the danger clearly, pushed back against his advisors' counsel of war and got us through.

The hard-liners in Moscow and Washington, their backs up, were ready to fight. The word in the air was *escalation*. JFK found a way to deliver us.

How'd he do it? What personal capability did he have? What had he learned? What combination of nature and training enabled him to see through the noise and emotions of the Cuban Missile Crisis and allowed him to grasp the root of the matter, to understand what he was up against, and what Nikita Khrushchev, his opposite number, was thinking? How did he know to overrule the experts, the angry generals and the professional Cold Warriors, whose every instinct dictated "Bombs away!"?

It goes without saying that Jack and Jacqueline Kennedy were beautiful. But don't look at the pictures; they're a distraction. Jack understood that better than anyone, using them to divert us from his own far more complex reality.

Yet look at them we did. And it's hard, now, to grasp just how brief that moment was: only seven years from 1956, when we caught the first glimpse, to 1963, when the moment was extinguished.

Whether you're politically conservative, liberal, or moderate, whatever age you are, you probably have your own responses to and your own questions about Jack Kennedy, still today. And that includes all those questions about his personal life, the ones that linger and disturb.

I began this book wanting to discover how he became that leader who, at a moment of national fear and anger, when emotions were running high, could cut so coldly and clearly to the truth, grasping the nature of the catastrophe to be averted.

Not only has that decisive vision continued to hold me and stir my admiration, it has also fed my fascination with him. So what was it about him? What brought him into the world's hearts and hopes so vividly, inspiring such fascination, leaving it, mine included, so alive behind him?

Jack himself, also an avid reader of history and the lives of history-makers, once remarked to Ben Bradlee that the chief reason anyone reads biography is to answer the simple question, "What's he like?"

Having thought about it for so long, I believe I've come to recognize, and even unearth, key clues that help explain the greatness and the enigma of Jack Kennedy. They don't come easily, however. Those glamorous images deflect us from the answers. But if you want to get Jack, you need to look for what they hide.

Among them: He was a dreamer who found his dreams as he read voraciously throughout his boyhood, all alone in one infirmary and hospital bed after another. He was a rebel who showed early the grit that would repeatedly motivate him, launching him against every obstacle in his life, not the least of which was the one presented by his own all-powerful father. He was a dead-serious student of history. In young adulthood, while finishing college, he wrote *Why England Slept,* and never was able to forget the critical lesson he took away from it — that nations die or thrive on the ability and judgment of their leaders to stir them at perilous times.

Then there was the extraordinary rite of passage made in the waters of the South Pacific during World War II, when he gained the confidence that he, always the frail boy, could meet as a man the twin tests of stamina and courage. At the age of twenty-eight, he determined to master the unforgiving art of politics and did so, with his love of that rough-and-tumble more and more an essential part of him. Finally, there was the deep revulsion he felt at the possibility of nuclear war.

Before Jack Kennedy could make himself president, he first had to make himself Jack Kennedy. We've been led to take him as, essentially, a handsome young swell, born to privilege and accepting his father's purpose along with his wealth.

What I discovered, however, was an inner-directed self-creation, an adult stirred and confected in the dreams and loneliness of his youth. I found a serious man who was teaching himself the hard discipline of politics up until the last minute of his life.

What's hardest to see clearly, though, is often what hides in plain sight. So much of this man is what he did. His life is marked by events and achievements that speak for themselves. In searching for Jack Kennedy, I found a fighting prince never free from pain, never far from trouble, never accepting the world he found, never wanting to be his father's son. He was a far greater hero than he ever wished us to know.

CHAPTER ONE
SECOND SON

*History made him, this lonely, sick boy. His
mother never loved him. History made Jack,
this little boy reading history.*
— Jacqueline Kennedy, November
29, 1963, from notes scribbled
by Theodore H. White

Certain things come with the territory. Jack
Kennedy, born in 1917 in the spring of the
next-to-last year of World War I, was the second son of nine children. That's important to
know. The first son is expected to be what the
parents are looking for. Realizing that notion
early, he becomes their ally. They want him to
be like them — or, more accurately and better
yet, what they long to be.

Joseph Kennedy, a titan of finance, whose
murky early connections helped bring him
riches and power but never the fullest respect,
had married in 1914, after a seven-year courtship, Rose Fitzgerald. The pious daughter of
the colorful Boston mayor John F. "Honey

2

3

Lem Billings

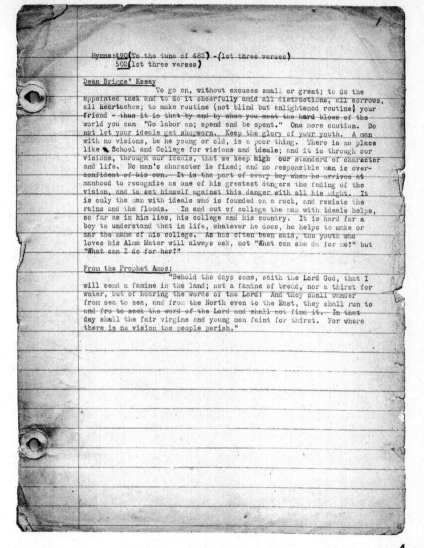

Hymns: ~~490~~ (To the tune of 482) - ~~(1st three verses)~~
502 (1st three verses)

Dean Briggs' Essay

To go on, without excuses small or great; to do the appointed task and to do it cheerfully amid all distractions, all sorrows, all heartaches; to make routine (not blind but enlightened routine) your friend - ~~thus it is that by and by when you meet the hard blows of the~~ world you can "Go labor on; spend and be spent." One more caution. Do not let your ideals get shopworn. Keep the glory of your youth. A man with no visions, be he young or old, is a poor thing. There is no place like a School and College for visions and ideals; and it is through our visions, through our ideals, that we keep high our standard of character and life. No man's character is fixed; and no responsible man is over- ~~confident of his own. It is the part of every boy when he arrives at~~ manhood to recognize as one of his greatest dangers the fading of the vision, and to set himself against this danger with all his might. It is only the man with ideals who is founded on a rock, and resists the rains and the floods. In and out of college the man with ideals helps, so far as in him lies, his college and his country. It is hard for a boy to understand that in life, whatever he does, he helps to make or mar the name of his college. As has often been said, the youth who loves his Alma Mater will always ask, not "What can she do for me!" but "What can I do for her!"

From the Prophet Amos:

"Behold the days come, saith the Lord God, that I will send a famine in the land; not a famine of bread, nor a thirst for water, but of hearing the words of the Lord. And they shall wander from sea to sea, and from the North even to the East, they shall run to ~~and fro to seek the word of the Lord and shall not find it. In that~~ day shall the fair virgins and young men faint for thirst. For where there is no vision the people perish."

Fitz" Fitzgerald, she launched their substantial family when, nine months later, she presented her husband with his son and heir, Joseph P. Kennedy, Jr. For the proud couple, he would be their bridge to both joining and mastering the WASP society from which they, as Roman Catholics in early twentieth-century America, were barred.

Such stand-in status meant, for the young Joe, that he had to accept all the terms and rules put forth by those whose ranks he was expected to enter. The idea was to succeed in exactly the well-rounded manner of the New England Brahmin. Above all, that meant grades good enough to keep up at the right Protestant schools, and an ability to shine at sports as well. In this last instance, there was no doubt about the most desirable benchmark of achievement. The football field was not just where reputations were made and popularity earned, it was where campus legends were born.

Joseph Kennedy's handsome eldest boy would prove himself equal to the task. Entering Choate, the boarding school in Wallingford, Connecticut, where he was a student from the age of fourteen to eighteen, he quickly made his mark. A golden youth, he became the headmaster George St. John's ideal exemplar. Transcending his origins — which meant getting past the prejudices St. John was said to hold for his kind, the social-climbing

Irish — Joe Jr., with his perfect body and unquestioning, other-directed mind, seemed to embody the Choate ethos without breaking a sweat.

A second son such as Jack Kennedy, arriving as he did two years later, finds himself faced with that old familiar tough act to follow. And, of course, embedded in the soul of any second male child is this Hobson's choice: to fail to match what's gone before guarantees disappointment; to match it guarantees nothing.

You have to be original; it's the only way to get any attention at all — any good attention, that is.

Jack Kennedy, almost as soon as he got to Choate, quite obviously put himself on notice not to be a carbon copy. He was neither a "junior," nor would he be a junior edition. He would be nothing like the much-admired Joe, nothing like the Choate ideal. What he brought, instead, was a grace his brother — and Choate itself — lacked. Even as a child of the outrageously wealthy Joseph Kennedy and his lace-curtain wife, Jack soon showed himself well able to see the humor in life. The wit he displayed cut to the heart of situations and added to life an extra dimension. He was fun.

Here, then, is where we begin to catch a glimpse of the young man who would stride decisively up to that convention stage a quarter century later, leaving behind the indelible image. Even though he's very much still a boy, he's preternaturally aware of the way life demands roles and resistant to stepping into one preselected for him.

There's the wonderful irony that comes with those surprises that second sons — Jack Kennedy included — are driven, and also inspired, to produce. Unlike his older brother, bound to a more conventional blueprint, Jack wasn't under the same pressure. There was a lightness to him, a wry Irishness that blended with the WASP manner rather than aspiring to it. With that combination, he could enter where his father, mother, and brother could not.

What happened to Jack when he got to Choate in the fall of 1931, by then already a victim of persistent ill health, was that, first of all, he had to find himself, and, to a daunting degree, simply survive. His brother Robert — the seventh Kennedy child, younger than JFK by eight years — later said of that period that any mosquito unlucky enough to bite Jack would surely have paid the ultimate price. Jean, his youngest sister, told me it was his bedridden youth that made all the difference. "I remember him being sick. I remember that he read a great deal, and why he was so smart was because during those formative years he was reading when everyone else was playing baseball or football or something like that."

So it was in the sickbed, it turns out, that he became a passionate reader, thrilling to the bold heroes of Sir Walter Scott and the tales of King Arthur. At Choate, he may have wound up the holder of a title he never trumpeted: the record for most days spent in the school's Archbold Infirmary.

The appalling reality is that no one — no doctor, nor any of the top-drawer specialists to which his father sent Jack — could tell the Kennedy family or the young patient why he suffered so. He'd had scarlet fever, and his appendix removed, but what continued to plague him was a knot in his stomach that never went away. Frighteningly, too, his blood count was always being tested. Leukemia was one of the grim possibilities that concerned his doctors, and Jack couldn't avoid hearing the whispers.

What seems clear to me is that, both at home and away, this fourteen-year-old — a big-eared, skinny kid nicknamed "Ratface" — wasn't marked for anything in particular, as far as his father was concerned. The succession was taken care of. There was only one dukedom.

For Joseph Kennedy, his determination that his kids not be losers counted as a one-rule-fits-all. Nor did Jack seem to be of any particular emotional interest to his mother.

Rose Kennedy kept her distance geographically as well as emotionally. Hard as it is to believe, she never once visited Jack at Choate, not even when he was ill and confined to the infirmary. "Gee, you're a great mother to go away and leave your children alone," he once told her at age six, as she was preparing for a long trip to California.

Sent away to school, Jack Kennedy was a spirit marooned. Choate, from the first, caused him to feel trapped. Chilly and restrictive, overly organized and tiresomely gung-ho, it was a typical Protestant boarding school based on the classic British model, and as such, more suited to his brother's nature than his own. Perhaps because he suddenly was more aware of his Catholic identity in that setting, he faithfully went into Wallingford to church on Sunday mornings. At night, he knelt next to his bed to say his Hail Marys and Our Fathers.

However serious were Jack's fears about his ultimate medical prognosis, he kept them to himself. There was no one yet in whom to confide his secrets. What he really needed to figure out for himself was a way to be happy there. He understood, too, the necessity of putting forth his best effort to prove himself at the sports at which he stood a chance of excelling — swimming and golf were his choices — while doing his best in the rougher ones, football and basketball. With that covered, he was free to make his name in more inventive ways.

His great success was to find ways to have fun. Jack Kennedy knew how to have — and share — good times. Watching *The Sound of Music* decades later, a classmate was reminded of him. Like the trouble-prone Maria, he "made people laugh."

But even before he'd gotten to Choate, Jack was forming and nurturing an interior self. He had survived, even thrived in his way, as a bookish boy who soon would tolerate no interruptions when reading. While at the Catholic school where he'd boarded before coming to Choate, Jack had devoured Churchill's account of the Great War, *The World Crisis 1911–1918*. Soon he was getting *the New York Times* each day. After finishing an article, it was his habit, as he once told a friend, to close his eyes in an attempt to recall each of its main points.

There would come over his face an expression of almost childlike pleasure when he'd worked through something difficult and figured it out. We all remember those kids who knew things, and cared about them, that weren't taught at school. Jack was one of them. And it wasn't the knowledge for its own sake, it was the grander world he glimpsed through it. Such habits of mind as thinking about Churchillian views of history were the glimmerings of the man he was shaping himself to become.

Yet, early on — and this habit, too, sprang from the many solitary hospital stays, lying in bed waiting for visitors — Jack had developed a craving for company. Left to himself so often for periods of his young life, as he grew older he never wanted to be alone. Even the companionship of any single person for too long never suited him. New people, and new people's attentions, energized him, bringing out the seductive best in him — all his quickness, wit, and charm.

It was close to the end of his sophomore year at Choate that he met the first person he felt he could truly trust, and this allowed the first real crack to appear in his wall of solitude.

Boys in closed-off environments such as boarding schools are caught by the dilemma of needing one another while recognizing they must stay wary. The easily popular types and their followers don't suffer; the quirkier, harder-to-classify ones are left to feel their way more carefully into friendships. Kirk LeMoyne Billings, a year ahead of Jack, would become, to the bewilderment of many, the absolute enduring stalwart of Jack's life. Their relationship was a natural affinity that could never have been described until it happened.

Also a second son — his older brother, Fred, had, like Joe Kennedy, been a Choate superstar — Lem was a big kid, a 175-pounder. His father was a Pittsburgh physician. With all the strength of his instantly faithful devotion, Lem Billings quickly began to tend to the needs of his new pal, whom he'd met in the offices of the Choate yearbook, the *Brief*. Looking at the support this friendship quickly began to provide for Jack, one could even see it as counterbalancing the neglect by his mother. He would confide in Lem that he cried whenever his mother sent word that she was heading off on yet another extended trip. He would be equally open with Lem about his health situation.

Jack was willing to divulge to Lem, a doctor's boy, descriptions of those periods he'd spent captive to medical procedures and tests — even at their most graphic. "God, what a beating I'm taking," he wrote once to Lem from one hospital over a summer break. "Nobody able to figure what's wrong with me. All they do is talk about what an interesting case. It would be funny . . . if there was nothing wrong with me. I'm commencing to stay awake nights on that."

The thought that even the experts were stymied by his symptoms tore at him, and came to haunt him. However jaunty he might have tried to sound, it was the fears they'd planted of a shortened life that he really wanted to share with Lem.

Sidekick, confidant, and traveling companion, and, above all, a touchstone, Lem was always to be a cherished constant. When his friend became Mr. President to the rest of the world, it wasn't long before Lem Billings had his own room at the White House. As Joseph Kennedy, Sr., wryly observed at the beginning, he "moved in one day with his tattered suitcase and never moved out."

Lem's loyalty changed Jack's notion of himself. It taught him he could have followers, which he soon did.

Jack had entered Choate a vulnerable and often lonely boy, a seemingly negligible younger brother with no constituency. He would depart four years later a practiced ringleader. If his adventures before then had been vicarious ones, enjoyed among knights and princes in the pages of books, when Jack left, fealty had been sworn to him much as it would have been to Robin Hood or King Arthur.

His Merry Men were called the Muckers.

To begin with, there were just the two of them, Jack and Lem. Their chemistry was the center from which the circle grew around them. Next came Ralph "Rip" Horton, the son of a wealthy New York family. The rest followed, until there were thirteen in all. Credit, or blame, for the way the Muckers chose that impudent name must be laid directly at the door of the very authority figure to whom they were setting themselves up in opposition.

It was during one of his daily sermons in

evening chapel that headmaster George St. John had gone on the attack against those students displaying what now would simply be called "bad attitude." The background is this: It was Jack and Lem's final year. Lem, a class ahead of his best friend, had elected to stay on in order to graduate with Jack, and they were uproariously, and very chaotically, rooming together. The instructor overseeing their dormitory wing was not amused by their shenanigans. Fed up not only with their mess but also with the noisy gang of disciples who gathered there each day to listen to Jack's Victrola, he complained repeatedly to the headmaster.

St. John, when he went on the attack, was clearly directing his words at Jack and Lem's little band, and it was one of those you-know-who-I'm-talking-to moments. What the headmaster couldn't anticipate, though, was the way one expression, in particular, that he chose to use — to refer to the "bad apples" he pegged as a small percentage of the student body — soon would come back to haunt him.

Mucker, the label he hung on the Kennedy-Billings gang, has several meanings. A mucker can be someone who takes important matters too lightly, who mucks about to no particular purpose — in this case, the sort of boys unwilling to uphold the time-approved, gold-plated Choate standards of decency, cleanliness, sportsmanship, piety, politeness, and, above all, respect for the powers that be.

In short, the kind exemplified by Jack's and Lem's older brothers.

Yet there is another, secondary definition of *mucker* that would have been well known to a Boston boy of Irish extraction. That meaning addresses itself directly to those who traffic in muck, which is to say, mud. And in Boston, this sense of *mucker* had evolved from being a derisive term applied to Irish-Americans put to work shoveling up horse manure from the city streets during the era of carriages, to becoming an all-purpose epithet for their immigrant countrymen.

Without realizing it, then, George St. John had thrown down a gauntlet. Sitting in front of him was Honey Fitz's grandson, whose own Irish ancestry was a source of pride to him and for whom the insult hit home. But the headmaster's choice of words also, Jack realized, provided an opportunity for a memorable stunt, perhaps the cap to his career at Choate.

Troublemaking by kids at school escalates. They compete to come up with outrageous schemes, each trying to top the other. Strategically astute, Jack and Lem — already known as Public Enemies Number One and Two on the Choate campus — had recruited their followers, the ones who now were the regulars in their room, from among the "wheels." That is to say, their pals were the sons of rich fathers upon whose deep pockets the school's endowment and building programs depended. That night, after chapel, back at Jack and Lem's room, they agreed to be henceforth known, as dubbed by Jack, the Muckers.

It was a thumb in the eye to old St. John.

Then Jack was clever enough — when further inspiration struck — to conjure up a reality out of the metaphor. Here was the plan: The dining hall had been decorated for an important school dance. Just imagine, he proposed, the faces of their classmates if a large quantity of manure, imported from a nearby field, suddenly got dumped in front of them and their dates. Cue the Muckers, shovels in hand, to scoop it all up and save the day.

Glorious a prank as it was, it didn't happen. What kept it stillborn was the killjoy who'd caught a whiff of what was going on and ratted them out to St. John. All thirteen would-be culprits were instantly called from their classrooms and onto the carpet of the headmaster's office, where they were reminded the punishment for forming an illegal club was expulsion. They were told they could count themselves as Choate students no longer; they would have to pack their bags and arrange for transportation home.

Almost as quickly, Joseph Kennedy, Sr., was also summoned from his office in Washington, where he was chairing Franklin Roosevelt's new Securities and Exchange Commission. Jack's fifteen-year-old sister, Kick, alarmed at hearing the news from Lem — he adored her and stayed in close touch — telegrammed her support: DEAR PUBLIC ENEMIES ONE AND TWO ALL OUR PRAYERS ARE UNITED WITH YOU AND THE ELEVEN OTHER MUCKS WHEN THE OLD MEN ARRIVE SORRY WE WON'T BE THERE FOR THE BURIAL.

However, Jack's father, a ruthless rule-breaker in his own right, seemed far more impressed than angry once he heard the story. Pretending to share the headmaster's anger, he waited until he had his son alone to tell him that if *he'd* founded the club, its name would *not* have begun with an *M*.

For the first time, I imagine, Joe Kennedy was forced to take a good look at his second son. He'd devoted a great deal of his attention to imbuing Joe Jr. with the style he wanted, but now, I think, he saw in Jack essential qualities that he recognized only too well. Just as he, Joe Sr., had been a corsair defiantly mapping his own way, now Jack was revealed to be similarly audacious.

When the furor died down and, somehow, they weren't expelled after all, the failed stunt only left Jack and Lem with a zest for defiance. On the night of a different dance, they and their dates drove off campus, chauffeured in a convertible by a friend who'd already graduated. Such behavior was strictly forbidden: no students were to leave the grounds, *ever,* during a Saturday-night dance.

Off they went — Jack and Lem in white tie and tails, the girls in long formal gowns, the Connecticut country lanes opening invitingly before them. But to their shock, just as they confidently assumed they were getting away with it, they glimpsed a car following them. Panicky, and sure it was campus security, they swerved into a farmhouse driveway, leaped out, and scattered. Jack, Lem, and one of the girls sought cover in a barn. Lem's date stayed in the car and pretended to neck with the driver. When the coast seemed clear, Jack suddenly was nowhere to be found, so the others headed back to campus without him.

A half hour later he turned up at the dance. In the end, it was all a false alarm: no one from Choate had been after them, and they were never found out. The tale is a fine example of the sort of risk Jack Kennedy enjoyed taking — dangerous on the downside, with very little on the up, except for the tremendous sensation it gave, short-lived but long-savored. It offered the promise of deliverance. It was his way of coming alive, and it would never change.

As Jack's time at Choate was drawing to an end, he and the Muckers changed course. Legitimate concerns now occupied them: directed by Jack, they began to invest their wit and energy in securing for themselves the "Most" tags featured in the senior yearbook.

Jack wanted "Most Likely to Succeed" for himself, while Lem would get "Most Likeable." The rest would divide the allotted spoils. However they managed it — and the historical record persists as a bit murky about whatever vote-swapping went on — Jack's budding skill as a strategist-with-defined-set-of-goals successfully came into play.

This exercise may have involved only prep school popularity, forgotten in the crumbling album of time — except for the identity of the intelligence masterminding it all. In this long-ago microcosm, Jack, the leader, created the first of what Tip O'Neill later dubbed the "Kennedy Party," a political faction united by a personality. Their success sharing the yearbook spoils, as JFK might later say, had a hundred fathers.

Speeches do, too.

Perhaps the most significant legacy from Choate was his likely memory of a familiar refrain of George St. John. As with all the other well-loved mottoes, maxims, and homilies the headmaster delivered into the ears of his youthful charges during evening chapel, he expected this one to sink in. It's a portion of an essay by his beloved mentor, Harvard dean LeBaron Russell Briggs. "In and out of college the man with ideals helps, so far as in him lies, his college and his country. It is hard for a boy to understand that in life, whatever he does, he helps to make or mar the name of his college. As has often been said, the youth who loves his alma mater will always ask not 'What can she do for me?' but 'What can I do for her?' "

Though Jack Kennedy had rebelled against that call to higher duty in his youth, it would come to define him.

CHAPTER TWO
THE TWO JACKS

Adversity is the first path to truth.
— Lord Byron

The self-made rich man forever remains the poor kid he once was. The short boy, no matter how tall he grows, never stops measuring himself. Jack Kennedy, for all his apparent vitality as an adult, projected the shining image we remember mostly by an extraordinary force of will. We now understand that he was beset by lifelong pain in his stomach and back. What's also clear, if you listen to those who knew him best, is that this deeper Jack, who spent so much time as the vulnerable youngster struggling toward sound health, endured over the decades.

It's this bedridden child behind the man who transcended it all to become a war hero, congressman, senator, and president.

The burden of that effort gives us insight into John F. Kennedy.

From an early age, there were *two* Jacks.

He'd had to learn, from necessity, to separate his life into compartments, ones that eventually grew greater in number and more intricate in their interrelatedness as time passed and the number of his relationships increased.

At Choate he seemed to most of his classmates a sunny boy, full of good humor, always ready for fun. That was the picture he chose to present. But there were also, at school, the first signs of seriousness, and with it ambition. The young Jack revealed what would later be known as his "charisma," and also, along with his risk-taking inclination, his leadership instincts and his innate political talent. When he reached Harvard in the fall of 1936, this Jack comes into sharper focus.

The standard take on Jack Kennedy is that he never intended a political career for himself until his brother's death in World War II changed everything. But Jack was always ambitious. He was headed, one way or another, into public life. Even his father was starting to take notice of him as a leader, a kid exhibiting his own defiant spunk.

When summoned by the Choate headmaster, Joe Kennedy hadn't quashed Jack's Mucker spirit so much as honored it. You don't get to be a tycoon, one of the richest men in the country, by saying "please" and "thank you" and sticking to the script.

Despite the fact that his dad had been a Harvard man, as was Joe Jr., Jack planned to

We're puttin' on our top hat,
    Tyin' up our white tie,
        Brushin' off our tails,
In order to
    Wish you

A Merry Christmas

    Rip.   Leem.   Ken.

*Princeton
1935 with
Ralph "Rip"
Horton and
Lem Billings*

*Jack, Bobby,
Torbert Macdonald*

Harvard swim team

7

spend his first year after Choate at the London School of Economics. While the LSE was known to favor a socialist point of view, Joseph Kennedy was a capitalist who liked being ahead of the market. He wanted his sons to have an edge on what he saw coming in the world.

But as fate would have it, Jack's chronic stomach problems sent him reeling back to America after hardly more than a month there. Rather than return to London when he recovered, he chose to break a second time with Kennedy family tradition and, still shunning Harvard, entered Princeton. There were several good reasons for this decision, the main one being that his closest friend, Lem Billings, and another Choate pal, Rip Horton, were already there. It's easy to see what such friendship meant to him, and how he was learning to have — to make, to keep — the kind of friends Lem and Rip represented.

Quickly moving in with them, he began attending classes. Then, once more, illness overtook him; standing six feet tall, Jack now weighed a puny 135 pounds. The blood-count roulette he was forced to play started up again, and, as his complexion went sallow, he resembled nothing so much as a scarecrow.

Back he went to Peter Bent Brigham Hospital in Boston for two months, and then, suffering also from asthma, he spent the remainder of the school year trying to recover under the dry desert sun of Arizona. Finally, facing the inevitable, he arrived in Cambridge that September to take his room in Weld Hall. He was a Harvard man.

Scrawny as he was, he quickly went out for freshman football. Whatever illnesses dogged him, he was doing his best not to let them define him. You couldn't be the "sick kid" and still be popular the way he wanted to be. Interestingly, he followed his older brother's lead in making a football star his best pal; three years ahead of him, Joe Jr. quickly had bonded with the quarterback, Timothy "Ted" Reardon. Jack's new friend was Torbert Macdonald, his own class's football hero, and Torby, like Lem before him, would come to know both Jacks. By sophomore year they were roommates.

One thing had changed. At Choate, he'd operated outside the system. Now at Harvard, his father's and brother's school, he seemed to be looking to succeed from within it. He ran for student office in both his freshman and sophomore years, falling short of success both times. Yet he continued to emphasize his quest for campus leadership over academic excellence.

"Exam today," he wrote Lem at the end of his first semester, "so have to open my book & see what the fucking course is about." But then he chalked up a social victory when he managed to get named chairman of the freshman "Smoker," just as Joe earlier had been.

51

Traditionally the class's most elaborate party, the Smoker was considered a hot ticket, and expectations for it ran high.

Taking his responsibilities to heart, Jack didn't disappoint, producing not one but two jazz bands for the occasion. "No matter who you were or what you did as a freshman . . . everybody went to the Smoker," one of his classmates recalled. "It was a leadership activity at Harvard . . . a big deal. It was his first political success. So by this, Jack Kennedy had made his mark."

Still, he had yet to outdo his brother. When he did, it would be a matter of beating Joe at his own game. During his sophomore year he was asked to join Spee, one of Harvard's top final clubs. With that coveted invitation, the second son now possessed entrance into circles closed to both Joes. Demonstrating what we might call his "crossover appeal," Jack, with his easy charm, had moved beyond the self-circumscribed orbit of the equally ambitious but unimaginative Joe Jr., who seemed unwilling to stride beyond the local Irish comfort zone. According to Joe's tutor, John Kenneth Galbraith, the older brother was "slightly humorless, and . . . introduced all his thoughts with the words 'Father says.'"

Quickly becoming both well known and popular, Jack didn't give off the impression that he was trying too hard, and he made good use of what his older brother never seemed to have, namely a light touch. And more than that, his conversation, friends said, ranged more widely than that of anyone else their age.

As Jack started to make a name for himself on campus, his energies at first were directed to such pursuits as arranging to meet Lem at the Stork Club in New York. Only in his "Gov," or political science courses, in which he would eventually major, was the unexpectedly serious side to him glimpsed. Before an injury sidelined him — his congenital back troubles made worse by one leg's being shorter than the other — Torby patiently threw passes for hours to help improve Jack's skills as a receiver. Undaunted, Jack, who'd competed in backstroke at Choate, transferred his hopes for varsity success to the Harvard swim team.

Just as Lem would always be, Torby turned into a Kennedy constant, there when his friend needed support. Lem and Torby were the first recruits of what would one day grow to be an unofficial reserve corps of steadfast compadres always game for the next adventure. What Jack required from any of his new best sidekicks was one thing above all else, and that was rescue: from being alone, from being bored, from being *stuck*.

After spending Jack's freshman year apart, in the summer of 1937 he and Lem crossed the Atlantic to embark on a traditional grand tour. Such an exciting trip was a way to try to erase the memories of Jack's hospital stays that February and March. Sickness continued to be one specter he couldn't charm his way past.

For two months they hit the road, having fun but also making sure they saw the best cathedrals and historic buildings. Jack showed himself willing to stay in the cheapest pensions to help keep down expenses for his friend. Being two high-spirited young Americans, they couldn't help having a terrific time. It was nonetheless a moment when Europe's dark political realities were visible even to the most fun-loving of tourists.

In France, where they stopped first, Jack wrote in his diary: "The general impression also seems to be that there will not be a war in the future and that France is much too well prepared for Germany." Later, Lem would recall that his friend "was beginning to show more interest and more of a desire to think out the problems of the world. . . . He insisted, for instance, that we pick up every German hitchhiker. This worked out very well because a high percentage of them were students and could speak English. In that way, we learned a great deal about Germany." Jack and Lem couldn't resist making fun of the Nazis they saw: "Hi yah, Hitler!" they'd cheerfully call out.

The threat of war, in fact, was now less rumor than fact. The Third Reich had been rapidly rearming, and possessed an army and air corps that couldn't help but cast a pall over Europe. When Hitler first showed his true colors and remilitarized the Rhineland, in total violation of the Treaty of Versailles, which had ended World War I, neither Britain nor France rose up to challenge him. Thoughts of war, to most Europeans, too vividly brought back the devastation wrought by World War I, when masses of young soldiers were thrown against one another in a conflict that left the continent in carnage.

Returning to Cambridge for his sophomore year, Jack soon faced an array of familiar, disturbing physical setbacks. As always, he fought against them in his own way. To remain on the swim team — as freshmen, they'd gained glory by being undefeated — was one of his goals. Thus, when he found himself in Stillman Infirmary, he relied on Torby, who brought him steaks and ice cream to tempt his appetite and build up his strength. His friend even snuck Jack out to the indoor swimming pool to get the practice time he needed. Swimming for Harvard was serious business, after all, and team members were expected to sandwich in four hours a day between classes.

Then, just before the year drew to a close, Franklin Roosevelt, now in the first year of his second White House term, threw a joker into the U.S. international diplomacy game: he named Joseph P. Kennedy, Sr., ambassador to Great Britain. It's impossible to figure out exactly what mix of motives inspired this maladroit appointment. Certainly domestic politics played a major role, for Irish-American voters made up a huge faction of the Democratic constituency. Also, given his background and connections, Joe Kennedy's presence in London might help resolve the tricky situation between Ireland and Britain. However, if Roosevelt imagined that his new envoy would act as his surrogate in trying to stiffen the spine of the British when it came to facing down Nazi aggression, he was, sadly, wrong.

The choice of Kennedy, who'd been an early, generous FDR supporter, for this ultimate plum offered the wily Roosevelt the satisfaction of making him into a retainer — a well-rewarded one, but a retainer nevertheless. Both men were well aware the job had to be entrusted to someone able to foot the extravagant costs its social traditions demanded. Ever the bold striver, Joe wanted badly to go there and was ready to spend whatever it took. Until the consequences of sending him to London would prove too large, FDR, too, was ready to weather them.

With his credentials ready to present at the Court of St. James, Joe arrived in London in early 1938, just eleven days before Hitler demanded acceptance of *Anschluss* — in effect, annexation — from the government of his native Austria. Such a relationship between the two countries had been forbidden by the allies at the end of World War I, but the Führer ignored it. Bent on expanding the borders of the great German-speaking state he envisioned, he signaled ever louder his disdain for those who considered themselves Germany's masters.

The Treaty of Versailles for him was no longer worth the paper it had been written on, and so the next territory he looked to grab was the German-speaking part of Czechoslovakia, the Sudetenland, taken from Germany by the allies in 1919.

He had only a simple goal, Hitler told the world — acting the perfect wolf in sheep's clothing — and that was to see all Germans united into one country. Hearing this, Germany's old European and British antagonists managed, hiding their faces in the sand, to justify tolerating it as a means to preventing the continent from again morphing into a bloody battlefield. Meanwhile, to the newly arrived American ambassador to Great Britain, a new war was out of the question. In late September 1938, British, French, and Italian diplomats fatefully met in Munich and there gave in to Hitler's demands for the Sudetenland. The British delegation was led by Prime Minister Neville Chamberlain, whose reputation would ultimately be destroyed by this concession to the Germans.

Returning to Britain, he announced, "We regard the agreement signed last night and the Anglo-German Naval Agreement as symbolic of the desire of our two peoples never to go to war with one another again." Later that day, he stood outside 10 Downing Street and this time said, "My good friends, this is the second time in our history that there has come back from Germany to Downing Street peace with honour. I believe it is peace for our time."

Events would swiftly prove him wrong.

Ambassador Kennedy, as soon as he'd arrived in London, formed a close relationship with Chamberlain, and it wasn't long before they were in almost daily contact. After the Munich capitulation, Joe made widely known his approval, and gave in October a Trafalgar Day speech that spoke of the need for "democratic and dictator countries" to focus on their similarities and not their differences. "After all, we have to live together in the same world, whether we like it or not," he declared. It could hardly have been worse timing. Only three weeks later came *Kristallnacht,* or Night of Broken Glass, when across Germany and Austria state-sanctioned violence against Jews and Jewish property raged for two days, shocking the world.

Repugnant as appeasement strikes us today, Joe Kennedy wasn't that out of sync with the prevailing temper of the British Establishment. Events were moving swiftly to force the democracies to make a stand, but the reluctance of the ruling class to engage with the Third Reich died hard. Four years earlier the Oxford Union, the legendary university debating society, after hearing arguments pro and con, had notoriously resolved *not* to fight "for King and Country," and that remained still a popular, if increasingly indefensible, position in London's drawing rooms.

Only the politician and ardent historian Winston Churchill — who was a hero, through his writings, to Jack Kennedy — had steadily been speaking out, from his backbench in Parliament, against the pacifist temper of the times. And people were beginning to listen to him.

It's very hard, looking at this now, to accept that Jack's father never seemed to feel any shame about backing appeasement. Joe's detachment from the sentiments of the times had always been his strength in business, as he invested or divested against the popular current. However, after *Kristallnacht,* when it was starkly evident that there could be no accommodation with Nazism, Ambassador Kennedy was out there on his own.

For a twenty-one-year-old American, the thought of war carried personal meaning. It brought with it both excitement and dread. Young men of Jack Kennedy's age had died by the hundreds of thousands in the century's first great European war. Now the daily press clamored the drumbeat of a second. Young Jack Kennedy was about to enter the very theater in which the question would be decided: Would Britain stand another Nazi demand for territory?

He had come to visit his family that summer of 1938, joining them on vacation in the South of France. It was decided that he'd figure out a way to spend the coming spring semester of his junior year working as his father's secretary in London; it meant he'd have to get permission to double up his classes at school in the fall term, but this was an opportunity to witness history.

Jack knew the valor Britain had shown in the Great War. He was powerfully affected by Winston Churchill's description of the willing courage of an upper-class Englishman, Raymond Asquith. Son of Herbert Asquith, the Liberal prime minister under whose leadership the British entered the Great War, Raymond was four years younger than Churchill and a much-admired, much-loved role model for his generation. His brave death on a French battlefield stood for all that was fine, and the tribute Churchill had written to him struck for Jack a resonant chord: "The War which found the measure of so many never got to the bottom of him, and when the Grenadiers strode into the crash and thunder of the Somme, he

60

went to his fate cool, poised, resolute, matter-of-fact, debonair." In later years he would quote this passage from memory.

However, the poignancy of young death for a noble cause seemed far removed from the moral climate Jack began to sense around him as he spent more time in England beginning in February 1939, when he took up his post at the embassy. Arriving primed to enjoy the perks of the ambassador's family, he found himself distracted not just by the predictable flood of society invitations but also by the debate being waged.

By March, it was clear Hitler was looking to take more land beyond the chunk of Czechoslovakia ceded to him at Munich. All at once, with no warning, Hitler fulfilled the watching world's worst fears and defiantly laid claim to all of Czechoslovakia. Immediately, the issue turned to neighboring Poland's sovereignty. Would the British take their stand now?

Despite the increasingly alarmed warnings of Winston Churchill, the Chamberlain government had been hugging the belief that a second major war could be avoided. It knew that neither the British public's memory of the human devastation of the trenches of WWI nor the traumas of the returning survivors had lessened; a generation had been lost, with the country, overall, remaining shell-shocked.

For the first time in his life — as he learned the ways of a country not his own but mattering greatly to him — Jack Kennedy found himself seeing men and women wrestling with national principles. Quickly pegged as a highly desirable bachelor and invited everywhere, he grew increasingly sensitive to the atmosphere around him — and soon began to feel the disharmony unbalancing it.

On the one hand, his father continued to support Chamberlain, in direct opposition to the position fiercely held by Churchill. Churchill's assessments of German capabilities, Jack was aware, had proved — and continued to prove — startlingly accurate. He couldn't help but respect Churchill's arguments, despite knowing that his own father and the ruling-class parents of his new friends openly dismissed the former cabinet minister as a warmonger. And while Jack was intellectually open, he was still a son with a powerful father.

Jack was also convinced, as he grew to be at home in the continual round of parties and pleasures, that something vital was missing in the character of those privileged young English whose company he was so enjoying. Charming they were, and always delightful hosts, yet he found himself doubting the current state of their mettle — their fighting spirit. Even in front of them he didn't hesitate to share his observation that the once-valiant English elite seemed to have turned "decadent" over the two decades since the last war.

How could they ever rally themselves and prevail against such a threat as the Third Reich?

In short, they were no Raymond Asquiths.

Mulling over what he was hearing and seeing, he began to form for himself a notion of where Britain's elected leaders had failed. He began to work out his ideas on the subject of leadership, the ones he would continue to consider for the rest of his life.

When the Nazis invaded Poland on September 1, 1939, Jack was still in Europe, having been touring again that summer, this time with Torby. Three days later, he sat with his parents and sister Kathleen in the Strangers' Gallery of the House of Commons and witnessed Prime Minister Chamberlain declare war against Germany. Returning to college at the end of September, by which time the Luftwaffe had begun dropping its bombs, he seemed a different person.

Certainly, in the opinion of Torby — who *was there* — his friend "had definitely changed. I don't think he really got interested in the intellectual side of academic life until perhaps his junior year when war seemed to bring a lot of us, especially Jack, a recognition that it wasn't all fun and games and that life was about to get very real and earnest."

But what was happening to Jack continued as an evolution. Then, in early June of 1940, he took a visible stand, writing a signed letter to *the Harvard Crimson,* implicitly renouncing his father's position. Even in 1940, once the war was under way, Joe had hoped the British would soon find a way to make peace with Hitler. He spoke disparagingly of Britain's and France's prospects, in a letter to Roosevelt, giving them hardly "a Chinaman's chance" of prevailing.

In his letter to the *Crimson,* Jack noted sharply: "The failure to build up her armaments has not saved England from a war, and may cost her one. Are we in America to let that lesson go unlearned?"

He'd chosen this for his Harvard senior thesis. "Appeasement in Munich" was its title, and it shows how Jack's thinking was diverging from that of his father. Reading it today, what you recognize is that it's actually a masterful political compromise, reconciling the views of his dad with the growing American consensus. Soon to be retitled *Why England Slept* and commercially published that same year, what Jack's analysis argues, to begin with, is that Britain simply had been unprepared in 1938. Had the British gone to war then, they would have lost badly. Most crucially, their defense capability was short the trained fighter pilots needed to keep at bay the Luftwaffe, the fearsome German air force.

The two years between 1938 and 1940, then, were critical, he contends, because, had the war begun at the earlier date, Britain would have been naked to its enemies. The beauty of this argument is that it mitigates the moral failure of giving away a country and its people to Adolf Hitler. Joe Kennedy, one assumes, wouldn't have forsworn appeasement based simply on a shift in the balance of weaponry. He didn't believe in fighting Hitler under any circumstances. But, while Jack makes the case that Chamberlain had no choice but to parlay and retreat, the real issue now, for him, is that the United States, his own country, must take the lesson and do better.

"I do not believe necessarily," he wrote, "that if Hitler wins the present war he will continue on his course to world domination. . . . But, in the light of what has happened in the last five years, we cannot depend on it."

In other words, America needed to get its act together and stop blaming Chamberlain, and therefore his own father, for not doing what it still needed to do. It was a masterful exercise in intergenerational politics. Here was the son, taking on, without condemning, the father's indefensible position on what would soon be revealed as the worst horror of the century. He was doing so with such a deft touch that his father took no apparent offense. In truth, he was saying that Britain should have been *morally prepared* to fight, and his father was saying Britain should still *avoid* the fight.

What Jack now proposed was that America be prepared to fight, not repeating Britain's error. "England made many mistakes; she is paying heavily for them now. In studying the reasons why England slept, let us try to profit by them and save ourselves her anguish." *Why England Slept* quickly became a best seller on both sides of the Atlantic, and Jack donated the royalties from the British edition to the fund to rebuild war-scarred Plymouth.

It is yet another manifestation of the two Jacks: the young American drawn to Churchill's mind and fearlessness on the one hand, and the son whose father was equally fearless but to a different purpose. To reconcile the lessons of these two figures was a task for which he had needed to make the effort.

Again, it was masterful politics. If Joe Kennedy had been paying strict attention, he would have spotted the end run his son was making around him here. Jack was arguing that Britain didn't fight because it hadn't rearmed. But wasn't that tantamount to saying Britain should have been ready to fight? And wasn't that a subversion of his father's own position? Jack had done more than find a middle ground with his father; he'd subtly taken that ground right out from under him.

That fall, the senior Kennedy would be forced from his job in London, a victim of his poor judgment. He had been quoted in a *Boston Globe* column saying, "Democracy is finished in England. It may be here." Jack's career would go on to be a continual balancing act between the nobility of valiant death on the battlefield, so admired by Churchill, and the horror of war itself, so understood by Chamberlain and backed by the hardnosed Joe Kennedy.

Jack felt deeply the emotional weight of the valor, commitment, and sacrifice demanded by war. Nothing makes this clearer than his beloved *Pilgrim's Way,* the autobiography of John Buchan, famous for writing *The Thirty-Nine Steps.* Published in 1940, it immediately became a favorite and would remain the best-loved book of his life. Most significant, in its pages he again encountered the widely mourned figure of Raymond Asquith, about whom Churchill had written so movingly.

"He loved his youth," Buchan wrote of Asquith. "And his youth has become eternal. Debonair and brilliant and brave, he is now part of that immortal England which knows not age or weariness or defeat."

Jack loved courage, hated war. That conflict would define his view of history's leaders. As we will see very soon, it will define how he viewed himself.

CHAPTER THREE
SKIPPER

He had never found a circle where he was so much at home and his popularity was immediate and complete. He was an excellent battalion officer.
— John Buchan on Raymond Asquith,
from *Pilgrim's Way*

Up until he went to war, Jack Kennedy had the luxury of living two lives. There was the often bedridden young man, who, loving books and loving heroes, greatly admired Winston Churchill. Twinned with him was the popular bon vivant son of the wealthy Ambassador Joseph P. Kennedy. One lived in the quiet world where history looks back and looms forward, where tales of majesty mingle with dreams of glory. The other lived in the divine, fortunate present of Mayfair addresses and country estates, of titled hosts and society hostesses.

War, for a time, joined the two Jacks as one. Called upon in 1943 to be a leader of men, he shouldered willingly the burden that comes with taking others into harm's way and then getting them back alive and whole. His experience in the waters of the South Pacific was to be the most searing event of his life, the one that transformed him into a figure like those who previously consumed his imagination.

It would make of him a hero like those he'd read about. There is nowhere to hide any part of yourself when you face death. What's more, Jack Kennedy now would be what he'd never been before: a regular guy. He was about to enter a world where he'd be accepted for the man he was. It didn't matter where he'd come from, or what he'd done before. Finally, for the first time in his life, he was moving on to a level playing field. He proved more than up to the challenge, and the confidence that came of it would stay with him.

Look back at Raymond Asquith. Comparing the pair at this moment — two men poised on the brink of different wars — offers clear parallels. Both had been born to privilege and attended the most elite of schools. Both were tall and handsome. Both seemed, effortlessly, to gain the loyalty and devotion of friends. Both volunteered at the outset of world war. Both were assigned cushy, safe postings in intelligence — and, in each case, in locations far from the front. Both, on their own, rejected that safety and sought aggressively to get to the action, wanting to be in

8

9

Inga Marie Arvad

Raymond Asquith

10

Red Fay

11

*Chuck Spalding
saluting*

PT 109

12

the thick of things, in front-line combat units. And the fact that Jack identified with Asquith — who lost his life after being shot by a sniper at the Battle of the Somme, where the British casualties were 420,000 men — was never any secret from his friends.

Jack and Lem Billings were playing touch football on the Washington Mall the Sunday Pearl Harbor was attacked. It was December 7, 1941. They heard the news on the car radio as they were heading back to Jack's apartment on Sixteenth Street. Jack had managed to join the navy earlier that fall after being rejected by the army for obvious health reasons.

In fact, the navy had turned him down, too, but he stubbornly went all out for five months, exercising to overcome the bad back problems that had caused him to flunk. Strengthened by the training regimen, he passed the physical on his second try, but he also benefited from the support of a naval captain who'd been attaché at the London embassy and was now the director of the Office of Naval Intelligence, the outfit to which Jack was immediately assigned in Washington. It was a no-sweat job that had him knocking out routine bulletins and briefing memos. While Jack considered the paper-pushing a waste of his time, it left him enough leisure to enjoy the distractions of the city's buzzing social life, to which the threat of imminent war added an extra charge of intensity.

His specific distraction at that moment was a Danish beauty he'd met through his sister Kathleen and was dazzled by. Inga Marie Arvad, or "Inga Binga," as Jack liked to call her, was working as a columnist at the *Washington Times-Herald,* where Kick was a research assistant to the executive editor. Four years older than he and European, she had just enough experience on him to be exciting. She'd acted in a couple of Danish films, and had married the director of one of them; in fact, she was still legally married to him when she was living in Washington.

Chuck Spalding, a Yalie Jack had met through Torby Macdonald the previous year and who now was one of his closest pals, watched the relationship heat up with fascination. "Her conversation was miles and miles ahead of everybody," he was to explain. "There was something adventurous about her. She'd done so much, been involved in so much. She was a fictional character almost, walking around. Of all the people that I ever saw him with I'd say she was the most compatible."

She cherished the memories of their wartime love affair for the rest of her life. "He had the charm that makes birds come out of their trees," was a description she would give.

Unfortunately, he wasn't the only one paying close attention to her. Washington was a

hotbed of spies, obviously, each one masquer-
ading as something else, and the FBI, led by
J. Edgar Hoover, was keeping a close eye on
all resident aliens. The Bureau's dossier on
Inga contained enough to make her of serious interest to it, including one very explosive
item: a photo of this gorgeous blonde in the
company of the Führer himself.

That snapshot was a legacy of a stint she'd
spent as a freelance reporter in Denmark,
during which she'd gotten a tip, in early
1935, that the high-ranking Nazi Hermann
Göring, a widower, was about to be married
for the second time. Based on her scoop, she
was assigned to cover the wedding that April,
where she found herself being introduced to
Hitler. Struck by the beautiful young Dane's
embodiment of the perfect Nordic physical
ideal, he invited her to come back to Berlin
the following August to be his guest at the
1936 Olympics.

The FBI didn't like the looks of it. They
refused to clear Arvad, suspecting her of
being pro-Hitler or, worse yet, being a spy,
using the *Herald-Examiner* job as a cover.
They maintained surveillance of her comings
and goings, being quite concerned about the
company she was keeping, especially the time
spent with the son of the rich former ambassador who backed appeasement.

Hoover's agents bugged Inga's rooms, and
made voice recordings, with Jack clearly audi-

ble, which soon were in the files, testifying to the long weekends the couple spent together and Jack's love of risk-taking. Before long, Ensign Kennedy was given a new assignment and dispatched to a Southern naval base, more than four hundred miles away. It's likely the FBI had a hand in the transfer to Charleston, Hoover hoping to get him out of harm's way by removing the immediate temptation. At least, JFK thought so: "They shagged my ass down to South Carolina because I was going around with a Scandinavian blonde, and they thought she was a spy."

Away from the excitement of Washington, Jack quickly grew bored. Now, more than ever fed up with a desk job, what he wanted, above all, was to be where there was action. His pulse quickened by war fever, he could think only of getting to the front. Inga, who visited him, took his grand, if still unclear, ambitions seriously. "If you can find something you really believe in, then, my dear, you caught the biggest fish in the ocean," she wrote. "You can pull it aboard, but don't rush it, there is still time."

The FBI, still on Inga's trail, found the pair sharing a February weekend at the Fort Sumter House hotel. Its agent reported the two left the hotel only for late-night meals and to attend church together Sunday morning at the Catholic cathedral on Broad Street; young Kennedy was keeping up with church even as he shared a bed with Inga Binga.

Jack Kennedy, being a man of his times, felt the patriotic pull of service. His older brother had experienced the pull, too. Though Joe Jr., as in all things, had previously followed his father's lead, identifying with the isolationist America First movement, by the summer of 1941 he was training to be a navy pilot. It was truly a time of testing for such elite young men, suddenly having to square their belief systems with their consciences.

I talked to one of Joe's Choate classmates, Paul Ferber, then in his nineties, who'd never forgotten being at naval aviation school in Jacksonville, Florida, and running into young Joe there. He was deeply taken with his words. "I want to go over there and bomb the hell out of those Nazis!" Ferber, after all, was familiar with the antiwar sentiments of Joe's dad.

In July, Jack transferred to midshipman's school at Northwestern University, and from there applied to the Motor Torpedo Boat Squadron Training Center in Melville, Rhode Island. The essential conditions being looked for in the Melville recruits were exactly the ones he possessed, he told Lem. "I have applied for torpedo boat school under Lt. Bulkeley. The requirements are very strict physically. You have to be young, healthy and unmarried. As I am young, healthy and unmarried, I'm trying to get in."

Bulkeley was looking for hotshot junior officers used to handling high-powered speed-boats and to the rigors of long sailing races. Fast thinking, teamwork, and endurance were everything. What this meant, then, was a group disproportionately Ivy League, ones who'd grown up summering in such places as coastal Maine or on Long Island Sound, where their families and friends belonged to yacht clubs. In other words, young men like Jack Kennedy.

Joining the PTs gave Jack the chance, finally, to command his own boat. His love of the sea is one of those things most people associate with him. Jack was proud of the Nantucket Sound sailing championship he'd earned. He and Joe had even been together on a victorious Harvard intercollegiate sailing team in '38, but now he was ready to be the skipper.

There in Rhode Island, he shared a Quonset hut with Torby Macdonald, who, with a little help from Jack's father, happily arrived to keep him company. After they completed their training and had their sights on the South Pacific, a snag arose when Jack received orders to stay stateside as an instructor. This time, political rescue came from on high in the person of Senator David I. Walsh of Massachusetts, chairman of the Committee on Naval Affairs.

Yet barely was that issue resolved when another crimp appeared in Jack's plans. It was his bad back and the pounding it could expect to suffer aboard a PT boat. While he got past muster, his health condition was precarious. No one knew this as well as Jack himself. Even going at half-speed, standing upright on these boats was as tough as riding a bucking bronco. One person this worried was Jack's father.

"Jack came home," he wrote Joe Jr., after Jack stopped for some R & R at Hyannis Port while at Melville, "and between you and me is having terrific trouble with his back." His son, ignoring all the danger signs, chose to make the best of it, preferring to get into the action rather than worry over its certain consequences for him.

He feared as much for what his sensitive gut would have to take. "I'm rather glad to be on my way," he wrote Lem, "although I understand that this South Pacific is not a place where you lie on a white beach with a cool breeze, while those native girls who aren't out hunting for your daily supply of bananas are busy popping grapes in your mouth. It would seem to consist of heat and rain and dysentery + cold beans, all of which won't of course bother anyone with a good stomach. If it's as bad as they say it is, I imagine I'll be voting Republican in '44."

Kennedy's first taste of the hazards of war came even before he reached his assigned PT base in the Solomon Islands, when his transport ship, an LST, was attacked by Japanese airplanes. A pilot, shot down and swimming off the side of his ship, was about to be picked up as a survivor. Then, just as the American crewmen prepared to begin the rescue, the flyer threw off his life jacket, pulled out a revolver he'd been hiding in the water, and fired two shots at the bridge, aiming for the ship's captain and other ranking officers.

Describing the scene to Lem, he wrote: "I had been praising the Lord and passing the ammunition right alongside — but that showed me a bit — the thought of him sitting in the water — battling an entire ship. We returned the fire with everything we had — the water boiled around him — but everyone was too surprised to shoot straight. Finally an old soldier standing next to me — picked up his rifle — fired once — and blew the top of his head off. He threw up his arms — plunged forward — and sank — and we hauled our ass out of there. That was the start of a very interesting month — and it brought home very strongly how long it is going to take to finish this war." What he'd now witnessed for himself was that the Japanese they were fighting were not only willing to risk their lives but to sacrifice them.

Lieutenant (JG) Kennedy found for himself a new world in the navy. His fellow officers posted to the South Pacific were, by the fact of their commissions, college men, and many from the Ivies. Yet there were also self-described "weed leaguers," young men from state universities. What united them all was merit; each had earned his place there. It was Jack's first time in such a company of dedicated equals, all facing the same discomforts and, of course, the same danger of getting killed.

"It's not bad here at all," he told Lem in one letter from Tulagi Island in the Solomons. "They have just opened up an Officers Club which consists of a tent. The liquor served is an alcoholic concoction which is drawn out of the torpedo tubes known as torp juice. Every night about 7:30 the tent bulges, about five men come crashing out, blow their lunch and swagger off to bed."

Soon he was collecting around himself new lifelong friends, just as he had at Choate and Harvard. One was Paul "Red" Fay, a Stanford grad whose father ran a San Francisco construction company. The two met when Fay, being instructed by Jack, ignored orders and got on the wrong PT boat. Kennedy dressed him down in powerful language Red Fay never forgot: "Do you realize that if what you did was compounded by every single person in the United States coming through training the war would be won by the Japs inside of three months!" Trust a pair of Irishmen to start a good friendship with a good fight.

One day Bill Battle, another officer on Tulagi, noticed that all the Catholics, including

Jack Kennedy and Red Fay, seemed to head off each afternoon to visit the chaplain, Charlie Webster, who'd played football at Princeton and was now a Franciscan. It turned out that Father Webster was doubling as a bartender, complete with his own stock of medicinal alcohol of some kind. Kennedy, who hardly ever drank, would join them for the ritual but spend more of his time reading and writing letters. "Jack was a big letter writer," one of his crew members attested. But Jack would join other Catholics on a boat trip every Sunday to nearby Sesape Island for mass.

"Getting out every night on patrol," he wrote his parents in May 1943. "On good nights it's beautiful — the water is amazingly phosphorescent — flying fishes which shine like lights are zooming around and you usually get two or three porpoises who lodge right under the bow and no matter how fast the boat goes keep just about six inches ahead of the boat."

He had found an unexpected comfort in the South Pacific. "That laugh of his," Red later recalled, "the laugh was so contagious that it'd make everybody laugh." Jim Reed was another friend Jack made for life out there. "There was an aura around him that I've never seen duplicated in anybody else. He had a light touch and a serious side," said Reed. He once tossed a book onto an officer's bed. "Get acquainted with this damn war," he told him. "Read my favorite book by my favorite author." It was *Why England Slept*.

Kennedy loved mocking the brass that made occasional visits to the front lines. "Just had an inspection by an Admiral," he wrote Inga. "He must have weighed over three hundred, and came bursting through our hut like a bull coming out of chute three." He went on to satirize the flag officer's recent trip: the absurd questions, the vain jottings down of the obvious, the "inane" comment before he "toddled off to stoke his furnace at the luncheon table . . . That, Binga, is total war at its totalest."

Finding comedy around him always enlarged the picture. "His back was troubling him, he wasn't well," Jim Reed recalled. "But I can tell you this about Jack — he never complained. He always had a terrific humor — a really acute sense of humor. He was very self-deprecating. He claimed to me once that he'd never had an unhappy day in his life. Now, whether or not he'd had an unhappy childhood, he'd come to fall back on his inner resources. He loved to read. He was curious — he had a natural curiosity about anything." Jack Kennedy often slept with a plywood board under him or, sometimes, even stretched out on a table. In another officer's most vivid memory, he recalled a day when Jack paced worriedly, holding his torn sacroiliac belt and looking for someone who could lend him a needle and thread. He would rely on that corset for much of his life.

When he did beef, he reserved his sounding-off for the officers above him and the orders they issued. Such predictable behavior eventually won him the nickname "Shafty." If he got handed a crappy assignment, he'd say, "I've been shafted" — although, with his accent, it came out as "shofted."

Out there in the middle of nowhere, talk was one of the only entertainments, and Jack preferred political discussions. "What's the purpose of having the conflict," Red Fay recalled him asking during one of these sessions, "if we're going to come out here and fight and let the people that got us here get us back into it again?" He was constantly asking questions. "We'd sit in a corner and I'd recall all the political problems in New Jersey and Long Island where I come from," the PT commander at the Russell Islands base would recall. "He did that with everybody. He had a way of really picking your brain if you knew something he didn't," recalled another officer. "He loved sitting around talking with a bunch of guys, and he'd come out with these remarks — remarks like you'd never forget."

There were twelve crewmen aboard Jack's command vessel, *PT 109* — the same number as the Muckers. The job of the PTs in the Russell Islands that August of 1943 was to patrol the Blackett Strait and attack Japanese

83

convoys passing through. His trial by fire would come at 2:30 a.m. on August 2. It was pitch black. There was no radar. Only one of the three engines was running, standard procedure because the propellers stirred up the water, creating that phosphorescent light that Jack had told his parents was so beautiful, signaling their presence to Japanese planes patrolling overhead.

Barney Ross, one of his crewmen, thought he saw a shape out there in the darkness. Jack pegged it as another PT boat, and got consensus. But as it grew larger, the skipper became concerned. "Lenny, look at this," he told his executive officer. "Ship at two o'clock!" a crewman shouted. Ross, who'd believed the oncoming vessel was running parallel, now saw it turning toward him.

"Sound general quarters!" Lieutenant Kennedy ordered. He spun the wheel to the left in preparation for firing their torpedoes. But, operating on just the single engine, it was sluggish. Before a thirty-degree turn could be effected, a Japanese destroyer, heading at 40 knots, suddenly rammed them through. Jack was thrown hard to the deck, where, lying there, he thought to himself, *This is how it feels to be killed.* He then watched as the Japanese ship passed him, only a few feet away.

All this had happened in less than fifteen seconds.

In the darkness now, the only sound was

the burning gasoline. Jack began to call out, "Who's aboard?" Only five crewmen answered. Spotting fire just twenty feet away, he ordered them all to abandon ship.

Pappy McMahon, the chief engineer, now in the separated stern of the plywood boat, found himself in far worse trouble. The flaming gasoline all around him had burned his face and hands, scorched his shins. Burning fuel continued to collect as he sank deeper into the water, the orange glare now above him.

Jack, having taken a place with the five others in the bow, realized what was happening and instantly headed to Pappy's rescue. Removing his shoes, shirt, and revolver, he dived into the water, wearing his rubber life belt, to search for the rest of his crew. Finding McMahon, he saw at once that his engineer was unable to use his badly burned arms. "Go on, Skipper," McMahon mumbled. "You go on. I've had it."

Jack grabbed McMahon's life jacket and began towing him to the floating bow, which had by this point drifted a fair distance away. Another crewman, Harris, was also losing heart. His leg was badly injured, making it difficult to swim. He wanted to stop trying, but Jack kept rallying him. "Come on! Where are you, Harris?" The crewman swore at his skipper, finally all but giving up. "I can't go any farther."

"For a guy from Boston, you're certainly putting up a great exhibition out here, Harris." Jack was not going to leave him behind. "Well, come on!" he kept at him, purposely ignoring Harris's bad leg. He then helped him take off the sodden sweater that was weighing him down, and that made a big difference. Harris could now move through the water.

When the two reached the part of the boat that was still afloat, Jack took roll. Ten answered this time, all but Harold Marney and Andrew Kirksey. Could anyone spot them? For the rest of the night the crew called out the two names, to no avail.

When dawn came, the hull flipped over on its back, becoming turtlelike. Slowly, it began to sink in the water, making it clear it wasn't going to last through another night. By midday, Jack announced they'd soon have to abandon what was left of *PT 109* and try to make it to land before too late in the day. He didn't want the hull to sink in the middle of the night, and knew it would if they stayed. By two o'clock in the afternoon, they were ready to go.

Each man was well aware of the gruesome stories about Japanese treatment of prisoners, which included horrific torture. The problem was, many of the islands around them were known to be occupied by the enemy.

"There's nothing in the book about a situation like this," Kennedy had told his crew that morning at daybreak. "A lot of you men have families and some of you have children. What do you want to do? I have nothing to lose." Jim Maguire, a fellow Catholic who'd gone to church regularly with Jack, found this hard to believe. The skipper, he felt sure, had a lot to live for.

There was also the question of Pappy Mc-Mahon, with his terribly seared flesh. And half the crew members couldn't swim. Their skipper's solution was to order nine of them to hang on to a floating eight-foot plank they luckily found nearby. Not only would this keep them together, but it would increase the nonswimmers' chances.

Lieutenant Kennedy then calmly pulled out his knife, cutting loose a strap of McMahon's life jacket and taking it between his teeth. He intended to tow him that way. The engineer never forgot his matter-of-fact manner. To him, the skipper seemed almost casual, as if he did it all the time. "I'll take McMahon with me," Jack told them. Next, he issued the order "The rest of you can swim together on this plank." Lenny Thom was put in charge.

When one seaman expressed aloud the fear that they'd never get out of this, Kennedy disagreed. "It can be done!"

For four hours they were out there in the water, their skipper pulling his engineer by his teeth and all the while keeping watch on his crew. Fortunately, the Pacific water was warm. For four hours Jack Kennedy plowed on, halting his breaststroke only occasionally to rest. The man he was pulling, meanwhile, hadn't a clue his rescuer suffered from a bad back, slept on a sheet of plywood, and wore a corset for support. As McMahon floated on his back, he had nothing to do but look up at the sky. He was always aware of the rhythmic tugs of the skipper's arm strokes. He would remember most the sound of Jack's hard breathing.

Plum Pudding Island, named for its shape, was the length of a football field and two thirds as wide at the middle. It had a few palm trees on it, like an island in a *New Yorker* cartoon. When he finally made it, Jack could only lie panting on the sand. And when he went to stand, he vomited from swallowing so much seawater. Soon his crew also reached the beach, all clutching the plank.

Back at base, a very sad Red Fay was writing his sister: "George Ross has lost his life for a cause that he believed in stronger than any one of us, because he was an idealist in the purest sense. Jack Kennedy, the Ambassador's son, was on the same boat. The man who said that the cream of a nation is lost in war can never be accused of making an overstatement of a very cruel fact."

Jim Reed would recall: "The next morning we heard that *PT 109* hadn't returned and they'd seen an explosion and a fire. I

88

was very sad. I couldn't believe it." Of Kennedy, he said, "He had many friends here, almost everybody knew him. He was very well liked."

Meanwhile, on Plum Pudding Island, Kennedy was conferring with Thom and Ross. "How are we going to get out of here?" he wanted to know. But, in fact, he already had a plan. What he intended to do, Jack told them, was to swim out on his own into Ferguson Passage that night to try to signal a ship.

Hanging his .38 pistol on a lanyard around his neck, he wrapped a flashlight in a life jacket to keep it afloat and headed off at sundown, knowing the PT boats went out on patrol then. Since no one had yet come to get them, he was thinking aggressively and taking matters into his own hands.

There was little point in just camping out there on that island, waiting for the Japanese to butcher them. If and when he spotted a PT boat, he'd try to draw attention by firing three shots in the air and signaling with the flashlight. There was no other choice.

Kennedy reached his destination at eight o'clock and stayed in place four hours. When no PT boats had appeared, he began the long swim back to the island. Unfortunately, he was caught in a powerful current that swept him past Plum Pudding. Drifting south, and after passing out several times, he stopped to sleep on a sandbar. The next morning he awoke and found his way back to his men. He arrived at noontime, looking scrawny and exhausted, with yellow skin and bloodshot eyes. He vomited again, and passed out.

Opening his eyes, he saw Barney Ross. He managed to say only, "Barney, you try it tonight," before, a second later, conking out.

The next day, Kennedy decided they needed to move to a nearby, larger island. Again, he assembled his men on that eight-foot plank. Again, he swam on, dragging the badly burned Pappy by the strap held in his teeth. Still there was no sign of rescue, and all they had to drink was the rainfall they captured in their mouths as they lay in a storm. The day after that, Kennedy and Ross swam to yet another island, Nauru.

There, they came upon some very welcome surprises — a dugout canoe, a fifty-five-gallon drum filled with freshwater, and a crate of crackers and candy. Exhausted, Ross fell asleep for the night, while Kennedy took the dugout back in the dark with the water and candy, supplies presumably left by the Japanese, to his crew.

This time he was greeted not just by his men but by two islanders who'd unexpectedly arrived and had gotten a fire going. They were helping the Americans. Jack used his pocketknife to scratch a message on a coconut shell: NAURO ISL NATIVE KNOWS POSIT HE CAN PILOT 11 ALIVE NEED SMALL BOAT

KENNEDY. Handing it to them, he told the islanders where they must take it. "Rendova . . . Rendova," he repeated.

When the *PT 109* crewmen awoke the next morning, a large canoe was just arriving on the beach. From it stepped eight islanders, who presented Lieutenant Kennedy with a letter that read: "On His Majesty's Service / To the Senior Officer / Nauru Island / I have learned of your presence on Nauru Island. I am in command of a New Zealand infantry operating in conjunction with US Army troops on New Georgia. I strongly advise that you come with these natives to me. Lt. Winscote."

Their friends waiting for them on the base at Rendova were so happy to see them they cried. Jack became angry when a fellow officer said he'd had a mass said for his soul.

"Kennedy's Son Is Hero in Pacific as Destroyer Splits His PT Boat," read the *New York Times* headline on August 20, 1943. The *New York Herald Tribune* told its readers that John F. Kennedy had written a "blazing new saga in PT boat annals."

A more personal commendation would come from a fellow officer, Dick Keresey, writing years later. "As a captain, Jack Kennedy was a man of courage, a good PT-boat man, and he was good company. Ranking the virtue of good company on a level with the other two may have been peculiar to those on PT boats.

We were almost always on the front lines. We knew it was time to pack when the base got showers. When the movies showed up, we were long gone. So we were highly dependent on conversation to divert ourselves, and Kennedy was a good listener and an amusing talker. Our conversation was seldom deep and never about future plans, for this brought bad luck."

Jack had his own account, which he mailed to Inga, and it wasn't what made it into the headlines and news stories. It's a testament to his writing ability — but also to his heart.

He typed it in block letters on a navy typewriter:

The war goes slowly here, slower than you can ever imagine from reading the papers at home. The only way you can get the proper perspective on its progress is put away the headlines for a month and watch us move on the map. It's deathly slow. The Japs have dug deep, and with the possible exception of a couple of Marine divisions are the greatest jungle fighters in the world. Their willingness to die for a place like Munda gives them a tremendous advantage over us. We, in aggregate, just don't have the willingness. Of course, at times, an individual will rise up to it, but in total, no . . . Munda or any of those spots are just God damned hot stinking corners of small islands in a group of islands in a part of the ocean we all hope to never see again.

We are at a great disadvantage — the Russians could see their country invaded, the Chinese the same. The British were bombed, but we are fighting on some islands belonging to the Lever Company, a British concern making soap. I suppose if we were stockholders we would perhaps be doing better, but to see that by dying at Munda you are helping to secure peace in our time takes a larger imagination than most possess . . . The Japs have this advantage: because of their feeling about Hirohito, they merely wish to kill. An American's energies are divided: he wants to kill but he also is trying desperately to prevent himself from being killed.

The war is a dirty business. It's very easy to talk about the war and beating the Japs if it takes years and a million men, but anyone who talks like that should consider well his words. We get so used to talking about billions of dollars, and millions of soldiers, that thousands of casualties sound like drops in the bucket. But if those thousands want to live as much as the ten I saw, the people deciding the whys and wherefores had better make mighty sure that all this effort is headed for some definite goal, and that when we reach that goal we may say it was worth it, for if it isn't, the whole thing will turn to ashes, and we will face great trouble in the years to come after the war.

I received a letter today from the wife of my engineer, who was so badly burnt that his face and hands were just flesh, and he was that way for six days. He couldn't swim, and I was able to help him, and his wife thanked me, and in her letter she said, "I suppose to you it was just part of your job, but Mr. McMahon was part of my life and if he had died I don't think I would have wanted to go on living."

There are many McMahons that don't come through. There was a boy on my boat, only twenty-four, had three kids, one night, two bombs straddled our boat and two of the men were hit, one standing right next to me. He never got over it. He hardly ever spoke after that. He told me one night he thought he was going to be killed. I wanted to put him ashore to work. I wish I had. He was in the forward gun turret where the destroyer hit us.

I don't know what it all adds up to, nothing I guess, but you said that you figured I'd go to Texas and write my experiences. I wouldn't go near a book like that. This thing is so stupid, that while it has a sickening fascination for some of us, myself included, I want to leave it far behind when I go.

Inga Binga, I'll be glad to see you again. I'm tired now. We were riding every night, and the sleeping is tough in the daytime but I've been told they are sending some of us home to form a new squadron in a couple of months. I've had a great time here, everything considered, but I'll be just as glad to get away from it for a while. I used to have the feeling that no matter what happened I'd get through. It's a funny thing that as long as you have that feeling you seem to get through. I've lost that feeling lately but as a matter of fact I don't feel badly about it. If anything happens to me I have this knowledge that if I had lived to be a hundred I could only have improved the quantity of my life, not the quality. This sounds gloomy as hell. I'll cut it. You are the only person I'm saying it to. As a matter of fact knowing you has been the brightest point in an already bright twenty-six years.

"Now that I look back," he ended, "it has been a hell of a letter." He promised to visit her in L.A. when he got relieved of duty.

Jack Kennedy had endured an extraordinary rite of passage. Now there was a kinship with those he admired that went beyond just reading about them on the printed page — Churchill, for example, as a young man had escaped from the Boers, and then there was Hemingway, who'd been badly wounded driving an ambulance for the Italians — and so, in a real way, this linked him with them.

He was a young man who'd "proven himself on foreign soil," as an excited booster would soon declare. But for all that his courage and fortitude came to mean to others, it counted most with Jack himself. No other challenge he might face, he knew, would ever be as hard as had getting his men back to safety. He had met fear head-on, and it had changed him.

"On the bright side of an otherwise completely black time," he wrote his parents, "was the way that everyone stood up to it. Previous to that I had become somewhat cynical about the American as a fighting man. I had seen too much bellyaching and layout out here. But with the chips down — that all faded away. I can now believe — which I never would have before — the stories of Bataan and Wake. For an American it's got to be awfully easy or awfully tough. When it's in the middle, then there's the trouble."

And in a letter to Lem that downplayed his individual heroism, he said: "We have been having a difficult time for the past two months — lost our boat a month ago when a Jap cut us in two + lost some of our boys. We had a bad time — a week on a Jap island — but finally got picked up — and have got another boat. It really makes me wonder if most success is merely a great deal of fortuitous accidents. I imagine I would agree with you that it was lucky the whole thing happened —

if the two fellows had not been killed which rather spoils the whole thing for me."

At the same time he got off a letter to Lem's mother. He expressed his pride in what her son was doing with the American Field Service Ambulance Corps in North Africa.

Before leaving the South Pacific, Jack Kennedy made it his final task to ensure that all his crew members got back to the States. When he arrived there, too, he quickly found himself in familiar surroundings: another hospital room. The physical harm that had been done to him was immeasurable. Not only had he contracted tropical malaria, but the orthopedic diagnosis of "chronic disc disease of the lumbar area" was followed by the first of what would be many back operations. There was a second back surgery also that year, but neither that nor any subsequent one would provide the relief he sought.

Those who visited Chelsea Naval Hospital in Boston saw him lying there wracked, alternately, by chills and fever. Torby Macdonald offered his impression of Jack's case: "His skin had turned yellow. His weight had dropped from 160 pounds to about 125 pounds. When I came into his room, he raised a bony hand and gave me a shaky wave." Jack insisted he felt "great." When Torby refused to believe him, the patient amended it to, "Great, considering the shape I'm in."

In June 1944, while still in Chelsea Naval Hospital, Jack was awarded the Navy and Marine Medal for "extremely heroic conduct." But medals don't mend bodies. Chuck Spalding, who visited him a little later after he'd gone down to Palm Beach to rest in the sunshine, gave this graphic account: "That wound was a savage wound, a big wound. It went maybe eight inches or so down his back. It would never heal and it was open and painful. He had to fight to get his back healed and I would walk up and down the beach with him with the back still open and he'd say 'How is it now?' or 'Is any stuff running out of it?' It was severe pain."

Spalding, who was himself a navy pilot, said, "I'll never forget Jack sitting at our table watching the 'home front.' All he felt was cynicism — everybody dancing, the lights, the women. It was the only time I ever saw him reacting like a real soldier. It was the rapidity of his move from the Pacific to Palm Beach, the juxtaposition."

That August, Joe Jr. was killed. He and his copilot had accepted a mission to fly a plane packed with 20,000 pounds of TNT toward a V3 site on the French coast, then parachute out before reaching the target. The idea was to create a guided missile, but before the two men could bail to safety, the deadly cargo detonated.

Jack, up at Hyannis Port when the telegram

came, went out walking alone on the beach right after he heard. His brother had been the family standard-bearer and, in matters of politics, the prospective heir. The rivalry between the brothers, especially for the father's colors, had always been a part of their lives and endured right to the end.

There was a revealing story Jack heard about a farewell dinner for Joe, occurring just before Joe was sent to Britain as a naval aviator. It had taken place soon after accounts of Jack's Pacific ordeal were splashed across the front pages. One of the guests at the party, trying to do the right thing, had raised a glass to toast "Ambassador Joe Kennedy, the father of our hero, our own hero, Lieutenant John F. Kennedy of the United States Navy." However, Jack was absent. Joe was very much there.

Later that night, as it was reported to Jack, Joe was seen on his cot "clenching and unclenching his fists," saying to himself aloud, "By God, I'll show them." Jack understood that it had been his brother's desire to match, or even top, his own courage in the South Pacific that drove him to volunteer for the high-risk mission over Europe. In fact, when Joe Jr. perished in the line of duty, he'd already flown twenty-five combat missions, enough to permit him, honorably, to fly no more, but his fraternal competitive spirit was too deeply rooted: he simply couldn't stop trying to beat the younger brother who'd managed to pull ahead of him.

A month later, another terrible blow was dealt the Kennedys. In the spring, Jack's sister Kathleen, his beloved Kick, had married Billy Hartington, the elder son of the Duke of Devonshire and a major in the Coldstream Guards. Now he was declared a casualty in Belgium, causing Jack to write his grieving sister that Billy's death reminded him of Raymond Asquith, that other privileged Englishman whose promise was cut short on the battlefield.

Despite Jack's own triumph, the loss of a brother and a brother-in-law, each an aspirant to a career in the public arena, of necessity pushed his celebrated heroism into the background, at least for a time. It would soon be again prominent, however, for Joe's and Billy's deaths left him a legacy he was ready now to accept and the public would be ready to endorse. As one of Jack's supporters, himself a veteran, would later observe, World War II was Kennedy's "greatest campaign manager."

Jack fixed his sights on the 1946 U.S. congressional election. In this race, as in the British "khaki election" of 1900, civilians got the chance to reward the gallant service of the returning soldiers and sailors with their votes. The man who'd made his reputation saving men in wartime was about to test his mettle in a different theater — equally demanding but entirely different, one that would call on all the democratizing experience he'd gained in uniform.

The fun-loving Jack and the serious Jack would now find a mutual pursuit: politics.

CHAPTER FOUR
WAR HERO

It has been a strange experience and I shall never forget the succession of great halls packed with excited people until there was no room for a single person more, speech after speech, meeting after meeting — three, even four in a night — intermittent flashes of heat and light and enthusiasm with cold air and the rattle of the carriage in between: a great experience. And I improve every time. I have hardly repeated myself at all.

> — Winston Churchill, from a
> letter to Pamela Plowden, 1899

The biographies of all heroes contain common elements. Becoming one is the most important. With the physical courage of which he'd shown himself to be capable, Jack Kennedy had turned his years of frailty and private suffering into a personal and public confidence that would take him forward. In mythic terms, he'd also challenged his father's point of view on the war and bent it to his own. He'd experienced the loss not only of comrades in arms, but of the family's prince, his brother. Now, ahead of him loomed new ways for him to demonstrate the man he was becoming — and the leader he would be.

If Jack Kennedy didn't see at first the change he was undergoing when he was discharged from the navy in 1944 and then directly afterward, many around him certainly did. "It was written all over the sky that he was going to be something big," recalled one of his fellow officers.

Yet, as he was starting to look to the future, he couldn't let go of what he'd witnessed and what he'd learned. War marks you forever, and so there was one crucial idea he had grasped, which was that it was wrong. In conversations with other officers, he urged them to take the life of their country seriously when they got home, to prevent another war.

For his own part, he spoke as if he, himself, was on the brink of coming to grips with big decisions, of preparing to face them. His commanding officer, for one, commented on the changes in Lieutenant Kennedy that started to be evident at this point: "I think there was probably a serious side to Kennedy that started evolving at that time that had not existed before."

Now came the fortuitous: his secret illnesses could now be worn as public honors. His

13

Billy Sutton

14

Charlie Bartlett

Bunker Hill Day, 1946, with Dave Powers

15

chronic bad back would from this era on be attributed to his war injuries. When the noted writer John Hersey, who chronicled Jack's South Pacific exploits for *the New Yorker,* made the assumption it was the result of the *PT 109* collision and all those hours spent hauling a helpless man through the water, Kennedy let it pass.

All of the other old troubles continued to plague him, especially his serious stomach problems, but they were now morphing into part of his new biography, or new image, just as the bad back was. Scarily thin and still sallow of complexion, Jack met new people and made new acquaintances who immediately chalked up his strange appearance to the malaria and other lingering effects of the PT-boat ordeal. What had been the hidden facts of life were now a statement to the man on the street — especially those meeting him face-to-face for the first time, as soon they would — of his very real heroism.

Everyone has written that Jack Kennedy needed to be dragooned into running for Congress in 1946. Everyone, that is, except the people who really knew him. The solitary walk he took on the beach at Hyannis after getting the news about Joe Jr. must have involved, along with the grief, recognition of a coming swerve on his life's path. The personal landscape he'd long taken for granted had rearranged itself around him, and so, too, had the expected demands. He was ready, it turned out, to welcome them.

Many aspects of the man were coming together. Jack had run for student office, majored in government. The reading interests that he'd maintained so steadily — memoirs and history, news stories and political currents, world affairs — had culminated in *Why England Slept,* his thesis-turned-best-seller. It had shown his skills as a firsthand observer of history. He'd been planning to go to law school, specializing in international law.

I should add that he liked poetry — Tennyson's "Ulysses" was a favorite, as were the poems sent from the front in World War I by a fellow Harvard man, Alan Seeger, who died on a French battlefield. Yet Jack, despite his childhood built on books, resisted the artistic sensibility. Though he was comfortable with the arts, the poetry that drew him was about mission and dedication, courage and overcoming obstacles. A great example are these several lines from "Ulysses" —

I am become a name;
For always roaming with a hungry heart
Much have I seen and known, — cities of men
And manners, climates, councils, govern-
    ments,
Myself not least, but honour'd of them all;
And drunk delight of battle with my peers,

Far on the ringing plains of windy Troy.
I am a part of all that I have met;

Even in the far-off Solomon Islands — where, like Ulysses, he'd "suffer'd greatly" on a "dim sea" — he'd kept up lively conversations with his messmates about all the subjects that most fascinated him: indeed, "cities of men and manners, climates, councils, governments."

When he returned stateside and was required to put in more hospital time, with everything else on hold, the idea of attending law school continued to be his operative plan right up through early 1945. "I'm returning to law school at Harvard in the fall," he wrote Lem Billings, "and then if something good turns up while I am there I will run for it. I have my eye on something pretty good now if it comes through." That "something good" may well have been the seat for the 11th Congressional District of Massachusetts, a district that included Cambridge.

In the pre–Civil War nineteenth century, that seat had been held by John Quincy Adams, also a Harvard man, and the country's sixth president; it was the only time a president had served in the House after leaving the White House. At the moment, the seat was occupied by the old-style Irish pol James Michael Curley, now nearing the end of a legendary career that would, by its close, include not just four terms as Boston's mayor but also two stints in prison.

Curley, now, was about to abandon his congressional post to run again for mayor. Jack knew this because Joseph P. Kennedy, Sr., freshly involved in local political matters, was bankrolling the rascal. His son knew it but he kept it to himself, as he took one last try at another career possibility.

His father wrangled him a job stringing for the Chicago *Herald-American,* a Hearst paper. His assignment was to cover the founding conference of the United Nations in San Francisco. He'd be reporting the historic event "from the point of view of the ordinary GI."

The city was hopping when he got there, with men and women on hand from all over the world. Fifty nations sent delegates to the conference, which began in late April 1945 and lasted two months. FDR had just died, leaving his vice president, Harry Truman, in the White House. Everyone knew World War II was nearing its close. Out in San Francisco the politically connected of every stripe were there to see and be seen, to hobnob and network amid the carnival-like atmosphere.

For Jack Kennedy, the U.N. Conference was the right place at the right moment, offering as it did an irresistible mix of high ideals and high life. It gave him a view of the political arena that now beckoned him. The atmosphere he found himself immersed in was electric with the sounds and sights of a new world being born.

Wherever he went, Kennedy worked contacts both old and new, honing his skills at making professional allies out of social friends, and vice versa. You never knew where you'd see him, but he seemed to be everywhere. For instance, when he hosted a briefing on Russia by the diplomat and Soviet scholar Charles "Chip" Bohlen, he found himself in distinguished company that included the British foreign minister, Anthony Eden, and the U.S. ambassador to the Soviet Union, Averell Harriman.

Along for the ride in San Francisco were two of Jack's pals: Red Fay and Chuck Spalding. For the former he'd wangled the boondoggle of acting as his aide at the conference, while Chuck Spalding somehow was hanging out on the strength of a best-selling book he'd cowritten, *Love at First Flight,* a memoir of his wartime training experience. Young men home from the front, they managed to share laughs despite all the speeches and earnestness, including one memorable moment that occurred in the midst of Bohlen's deadly serious analysis of Soviet intentions.

It was Jack who first noticed the elegant Harriman had slipped away from the room in the Palace Hotel where the briefing was taking place, and out onto the balcony with a young woman. "I give him about two more minutes, and then he's going to hang himself," Jack whispered to Fay. Focused on Bohlen, Fay wondered why his pal would say such a thing.

"I'm not talking about Bohlen," Kennedy shot back. "I'm talking about Harriman!"

Also in the group with whom Jack socialized at the conference were Cord Meyer, another young veteran with big political hopes, and his attractive, vivacious wife, Mary. Meyer, at this time, was an aide to the Republican presidential candidate Harold Stassen, but would go on to join the CIA.

For Kennedy, the business at hand was not just about filing stories or making the scene. As always, it was his curiosity that drove and excited him. He seemed particularly intrigued by the Soviet delegation, led by the coldly robotic Vyacheslav Molotov.

Along with the rest of the world, he'd seen President Roosevelt concede the territories of Eastern Europe to Josef Stalin at the Yalta Conference that February, only weeks before his death. Critics saw this concession of important strategic and autonomous lands to the Soviets as an unconscionable giveaway to a soon-to-be enemy.

FDR's failing health might have been a factor in the outcome at Yalta; there on the shore of the Black Sea, he was pushing himself hard and losing the battle with his own body. But equally at play were other factors that Kennedy, with his growing fascination with the way nations behaved, saw and grasped.

But if he didn't like the agreement Roosevelt had signed off on, he was able to assess it from more than one perspective. He knew his history, and saw clearly the unyielding strength of Russian nationalism. Napolean had invaded her in 1812. To repel the Grand Army, the Russians had been forced to burn Moscow. Now, in the middle of the twentieth century, the Russians, once again invaded, were facing the harsh fact that they'd lost 20 million people fighting the Germans mostly on Russian soil, with their Allies slow to open a second front.

Jack Kennedy was displaying an ability to regard an adversary's situation without emotion. In one of the pieces that ran in the *Herald-American* under his byline, he offered his own take on how the Soviets thought, and he ended it by reminding his readers of "the heritage of 25 years of distrust between Russia and the rest of the world that cannot be overcome completely for a good many years."

Also, true to his mission, he held the perspective of the fighting American home from the front.

When Victory in Europe Day came — on May 8, during the conference's second week — Jack responded by writing eloquently in the *Herald-American:* "Any man who had risked his life for his country and seen his friends killed around him must inevitably wonder why this has happened to him and most important what good will it do. It is perhaps normal that they would be disappointed with what they have seen in San Francisco. I suppose that this is inevitable. Youth is a time for direct action and simplification. To come from battlefields where sacrifice is the order of the day — to come from there to here — it is not surprising that they should question the worth of their sacrifice and feel somewhat betrayed."

In a letter to one of his war buddies, he phrased his message more bluntly: "We must face the truth that the people have not been horrified by war to a sufficient extent to force them to go to any extent rather than have another war."

Chuck Spalding, keeping an eye on his friend as well as on the tone of his articles, was starting to draw his own conclusions. "Either wittingly or unwittingly, he began to write as a politician." Just as in the South Pacific, he was acting more as a leader than as an observer. "The war makes less sense to me now," Jack wrote, "than it ever made and that was little enough — and I would really like — as my life's goal — in some way at home or at some time to do something to help prevent another."

While still on the job in San Francisco, Jack learned his next assignment was to be London. There he'd be reporting on the fierce political struggle taking place as the British home-front coalition broke down. The opposition Labour Party was going all out to contest Prime Minister Winston Churchill's Conservative government in the first postwar British general election. For Jack, it was a chance to see his most enduring hero fight for his political life, and yet he was stunned. How could Churchill, whose indomitable leadership had meant so much to his nation in wartime, now be in such serious trouble?

What Jack was about to learn is how quickly economic concerns replaced wartime loyalties. The war had been hard on the British working class and, suddenly, voters were remembering how the Conservatives had supported appeasement of the Germans before the war. The same Tories were now clinging to power with warnings of socialist dictatorship. But, more to the point in the postwar climate, the Tories were preaching belt-tightening. Just when the people were looking for a break from the depressed economy — the rationing, the empty cupboards — they were being promised more of the same.

Unfortunately, when the votes were counted, both Jack's front-row position and his empathy didn't help his critical judgment. Unable to imagine a Labour victory, he filed a wrap-up election piece predicting a close Tory win. He wasn't alone; Churchill's overwhelming defeat was a shock to many.

While in England, Jack took advantage of

114

the opportunity to catch up with old friends. One of them, Alistair Forbes, registered this impression: "He struck me then that he was more intellectual than any other member of the family. He read more. He had a fantastically good instinct, once his attention was aroused to a problem, for getting the gist of it and coming to a mature judgment about it. He had a detachment which reminded me very much of Winston Churchill in the sense that his life had been protected by money."

Another friend, Hugh Fraser, who was running for Parliament himself at the time, saw him similarly. "He was always a great questioner. He always asked an enormous number of questions. He was very interested in things. For every one question I asked him he asked two at least." "Political to his fingertips" is how the British economist Barbara Ward recalled him. "He asked every sort of question of what were the pressures, what were the forces at work, who supported what." Such curiosity, such a need to inform himself and to sift carefully through what he was learning, would always form part of his m.o.

During this period, when he was pounding out stories for afternoon newspaper readers in Chicago, Kennedy also kept a personal diary. The entries in it further reveal him as unable to move past the idea of war's deadliness: "We have suffered the loss of nearly 8 hundred thousand young men — many of whom might become the leadership we will so desperately need."

What's more, he wrote presciently — somehow intuiting the existence of the atomic bomb, which wasn't yet publicly known — of what he saw in the future. "The clash may be finally and indefinitely postponed by the eventual discovery of a weapon so horrible that it will truthfully mean the abolishment of all the nations employing it. Thus science, which has contributed to much of the horror of war, will still be the means of bringing it to an end."

When it came to the ideological currents back home, he was critical of FDR. "Mr. Roosevelt has contributed greatly to the end of Capitalism in our own country, although he would probably argue the point at some point. He has done this, not through the laws which he sponsored or were passed during his Presidency, but rather through the emphasis he put on rights rather than responsibilities."

In Europe, Kennedy saw the brutality of the Russians to the vanquished Germans. "People did not realize what was going on in the concentration camps. In many ways, the 'SS' were as bad as the Russians." But he predicted the Red Army's treatment of defeated Berlin, especially its women, would leave a lasting mark.

As he was returning home from Europe — stopping briefly in London — he became alarmingly sick. His traveling companion at the time reported that it had "scared the hell out" of him, and that he'd never before seen anyone run such a high fever. It lasted for several days. When it was over, Jack claimed it had just been his malaria acting up.

Around Thanksgiving, his health improved, and he was back with his family at Hyannis Port. Rip Horton remembers watching him as he practiced with a tape recorder. "He made me speak into it and then played back the tape . . . and your voice always sounds awful to you. That was the first indication as to where his inclinations were then leading him."

Soon, though, Jack was being up front with his close friends about his intentions. "I've made up my mind," he told Chuck Spalding. "I'm going into politics."

"Geez, that's terrific," Spalding replied. "You can go all the way!"

Taken aback by such confidence from a close friend, Kennedy asked, "Really?"

"All the way!" Spalding recalls repeating.

Years later, Spalding explained that he'd believed Jack was one of those who'd come out of the war experience whole. "He was never pushed off this hard, sensible center of his being. I think he was beginning to get a kind of picture of himself. I think the picture of a public figure interested and capable in this area added to the dim outline of a successful politician."

Lem Billings, who by then was in the navy — he had used new contact lenses to get past the physical — took a similar view. "A lot of stories have been written and said about it. I think a lot of people say that if Joe hadn't died, Jack might never have gone into politics. I don't believe this. Nothing could have kept Jack out of politics. I think this is what he had in him, and it just would have come out, no matter what. Somewhere along the line, he would have been in politics. Knowing his abilities, interests, and background, I firmly believe he would have entered politics even had he had three older brothers like Joe."

When Jack asked Torby Macdonald what he thought of his running for Congress, his former college roommate — who'd grown up in a town near Boston — flatly stated that if his friend ran, he'd win.

Of all Jack's best pals, Red Fay was the sharpest in seeing Jack's inner directedness. When Jack told him of the pressure he was getting from his father — "I tell you, Dad is ready right now and can't understand why his fine son Jack isn't ready" — Fay understood that that wasn't actually the whole story. "Although Jack shammed indifference to the whole idea of a political career, there was an underlying determination to get started on what he considered a very serious obligation. I wasn't surprised early in 1946 when he made a very serious decision to run for Congress —

and when he asked me to come east to campaign for him, I came."

It was about this time that he met a new friend, Charlie Bartlett, down in Florida. "We were down there after the war, and, you know, gorgeous women were all getting divorces down there, and they were really good-looking girls. It was very upbeat, the whole thing, and I went to Palm Beach. My family lived in Hobe Sound. We drove down for the evening and went to this place called Taboo. And they had an orchestra and I was with a very, very pretty girl who was getting a divorce and it turned out she knew Jack and Jack came over and sat down and started telling me about his plans to go into politics. And I said, 'Well, I'm getting ready to go into the newspaper business.' And he said, 'Well, you know, I've been there now and I haven't been very deep but I have to tell you, you don't get anything done. You can't make changes. There's no impact. I'm going to go into politics and see if you can really do anything.'"

Bartlett, a sixth-generation Yalie, would be Jack's close friend from that day forward.

Jack knew the leap he was taking in running for Congress. "I had never lived very much in the district," he admitted years later. "My roots were there, my family roots were there. But I had lived in New York for ten years and on top of that I had gone to Harvard, not a particularly popular institution at that time in the 11th Congressional District. But I started early, in my opinion the most important key to political success, in December before the primary election next June."

Charlie Bartlett recalled the conversation they had. "He was very clear about his decision to go into Congress. Sometimes you read that he was a reluctant figure being dragooned into politics by his father. I really didn't get that impression at all. I gathered that it was a wholesome, full-blown wish on his own part."

Jack Kennedy's own thoughts support his friend's memory: "A reporter is reporting what happens, he's not making it happen, even the good reporters, the ones that are really fascinated by what happens and who find real stimulus by putting their noses into the center of the action, even they in a sense are in a secondary profession. It's reporting what happens, but it isn't participating."

By the time he made his decision, Jack, at the age of twenty-eight, possessed a level of intellectual preparation for public office uncommon even to seasoned career politicians. He had wrestled with the big-picture issues of war and peace in the 1930s, had survived the most extreme hazards of war, and been a firsthand observer of major international events. What he lacked was any practical grounding in the business of politics.

The fact that his father would take care of

what the political types call the "wholesale" — the media, the press relations — hardly let him off the hook. The relentless workaday demands of a campaign lay ahead. He, the candidate, had to be the one to master the "retail," which meant not just meeting voters one on one and winning them over, but inspiring them to join the effort. If you couldn't connect with voters, then your other advantages, in the end, counted for little.

With the help of a local PR firm, Jack would soon be making the rounds of community groups: VFW and American Legion posts, Lions and Rotary Club meetings, communion breakfasts and Holy Name societies. This was a new world to him. But it was a necessary part of achieving his ambition, and he did it all. Writing his stump speech himself, he drew on his recent travels as a reporter in Great Britain and Germany, but always made sure to emphasize his recent stopover in Ireland.

Simultaneously, Jack decided to teach himself about being Irish. The diary he'd been keeping in Europe now contained a number of scribbled book titles accompanied by their Dewey decimal numbers. He'd always liked to connect to knowledge through reading, and, on that score, nothing had changed. *Ireland and the President of the United States, Ireland in America, Ireland's Contribution to the Law,* and *Irish American History of the US* are some of the volumes he listed.

He was also soliciting the reactions of local political figures to his potential candidacy. But when he called on them, especially the Irish ones, he wasn't just making the mandatory courtesy visits, he was brushing up against the city's history. "For all Irish immigrants, the way in Boston was clearly charted," he dictated in a memo years later. "The doors of business were shut; the way to rise above being a laborer was politics."

His own path, he acknowledged, had been a privileged one. Being third-generation and not first makes a difference. "I had in politics, to begin with, the great advantage of having a well-known name and that served me in good stead. Beyond that I was a stranger to begin with and I still have a notebook which is filled page after page with the names of all the new people I met back there in that first campaign."

One of the new acquaintances was a fellow by the name of Dan O'Brien, who was skeptical about the young man's chances. After meeting him, Jack came away with these jotted-down impressions: "Says I'll be murdered — No personal experience — A personal district — Says I don't know 300 people personally. Says I should become Mike Neville's secretary. O'Brien says the attack on me will be — 1. Inexperience 2. Injury to me: me . . . father's reputation. He is the first man to bet me that I can't win! An honest Irishman but a mistaken one."

The candidate also recorded maxims that applied to the situation. Among them:

- In politics you don't have friends — you have confederates.
- One day they feed you honey — the next will find fish caught in your throat.
- You can buy brains but you can't buy — loyalty.
- The best politician is the man who does not think too much of the political consequence of his every act.

He also noted: "The one great failure of American government is the government of critics." Making the rounds and learning the ropes, he'd quickly recognized, as every politician must, the impossibility of pleasing everyone.

Now, for the first time in his life, Jack needed to make friends on a basis other than compatibility. Living on Beacon Hill, a young bachelor with no fixed address beyond rooms in the historic Bellevue Hotel, he lacked roots in the local community and needed to establish himself. The most important task was to enlist supporters who'd spent their lives in the district and would come on board, willing to stand up for him. While you could always hire a few professionals, the vast army needed for a win had to be made up of volunteers, those who helped him because they decided to.

The first hire was Billy Sutton, four years older than Jack and just discharged from the army. His description of the Jack of those days was a thin, bright-eyed figure with his hair cut close on the sides. Billy — whom I got to know well many years later — said that Jack had reminded him of the young Charles Lindbergh.

Before the war Billy had made himself useful in local politics as a result of his job checking gas meters, which naturally put him in touch with a wide variety of people. But he was the kind of guy who loved talking to anyone, and so, with Billy as his guide, Jack began trudging up and down the three-deckers of the old neighborhoods, introducing himself and asking for support. The person most surprised by this was his father. What Joseph Kennedy had yet to realize was the way the navy had changed his second son. The young man who returned from the Solomon Islands was not the one who'd left for there in early 1943, and a large part of the reason the experience so altered him was because it offered continual exposure to people unlike himself, from all over the country and from every walk of life.

The fact that he was a returning serviceman was a key factor from the start. Working-class fellows like Sutton — and, later, Dave Powers, who'd served with the Flying Tigers — were ready to accept a young rich guy who'd been awarded the Navy and Marine Corps Medal with a citation for "extremely heroic conduct." What convinced Powers was witnessing Jack's appearance before a group of Gold Star Mothers, those women who'd lost sons fighting in the war. "I think I know how you feel," he told them, "because my mother is a Gold Star Mother, too." When Powers heard Kennedy say that and saw the reaction, he signed on and never would stop working for his new boss.

What Jack Kennedy brought to the table, besides his sterling war record and those well-known Boston names — Kennedy and Fitzgerald — was his obvious affection for the old Irish world he now was entering. He loved hearing his grandfather's stories, from "Honey Fitz" himself, the city's long-ago mayor and congressman.

Not surprisingly, the daily slog of introducing himself to constituents was not quite compatible with a chronic back problem, not when it meant going up and down the stairs of multifamily houses day after day. Come early afternoon, Jack would take a nap, then continue the trudge of one-on-one campaigning on into the night. He did this for months, and not everyone liked to see him doing it. The local politicians viewed him for what he was, a carpetbagger.

His voting address, after all, was a hotel,

and he'd registered just in time to vote in the primary. Tom O'Neill, a local state assemblyman known as "Tip," wasn't impressed by the newcomer, war record or not. He was backing Mike Neville, the former Cambridge mayor, and the one whose turn it now was to hold the seat. "I couldn't believe this skinny, pasty-faced kid was a candidate for anything." He recalled the first time he met Kennedy outside the Bellevue Hotel: "He was twenty-eight but looked younger, and he still hadn't fully recovered from his war injuries. He also looked as if he had come down with malaria."

Tip's description tallies with that of other observers. To Billy Sutton, he "wasn't looking healthy then." To Mark Dalton, the young attorney who would become Kennedy's formal campaign manager, he resembled that same "skeleton" to which we've often heard him compared. His father, too, worried about his son's emaciation. "My father thought I was hopeless." Why? "At the time I weighed about 120 pounds."

Chuck Spalding suggested that Jack's precarious health, and his determination to surmount it at any cost, only added to the campaign's wild, even hectic, pace. "This impatience that he passed on to others . . . made everybody around him feel quicker." The trouble was, it didn't necessarily make for great organization.

One out-of-the-blue crisis almost derailed

Jack's first run for office before it even officially had started. It seems that while he was obsessively wearing himself out walking the neighborhoods, he'd somehow overlooked a giant detail. The one to discover it was his old navy pal Red Fay, who'd come east to help out, he said, "even though I was a Republican." Arriving in Cambridge, Fay found the headquarters a shambles of unpaid bills and invitations to speak, and was soon put in charge of trying to run the campaign on a more "businesslike basis."

One of the campaign workers casually asked Fay about the candidate's filing of his nomination papers. The deadline was that very afternoon, and yet no one had thought to do it. Not only that, it was now after five o'clock, and thus, past the deadline. So there they were, with Kennedy's petitions not in, and *the Boston Globe*'s late edition already reporting the fact. Yet, incredible as it seems, given today's 24/7 news cycle and minute-by-minute reaction speeds, no one was besieging the headquarters. Or even paying any attention.

"My God," Kennedy said when he heard the bad news. It was 6:30 in the evening. "A series of frantic phone calls were made," Fay reports. "Then, very quietly, the candidate and some loyal public retainers went down, opened up the proper office and filed the papers. Another couple of hours, and all the thousands of hours of work by the candidate and his supporters would have been completely wasted."

This is a loyalist's account of an after-hours escapade that had to have been blatantly illegal. But what's remarkable is that Jack himself went into the municipal building that night and did what had to be done, putting those petitions in the right pile as if they'd been there by the deadline.

Kennedy pulled off other escapades. Early in the race, a rival candidate, Joe Russo, had run this newspaper ad: "Congress Seat for Sale. No Experience Necessary. Applicant Must Live in New York or Florida. Only Millionaires Need Apply." The Kennedy campaign didn't get mad, it got even.

Locating another Joe Russo, they paid him a few bucks to file as a candidate. The effect would be to confuse voters and skim off some of the politician Joe Russo's votes. There was an Italian vote in the district and, this way, it would be divided.

But there were other sources of resentment. A popular newspaper column authored by a "Dante O'Shaughnessy" mocked Kennedy for being "oh, so British" and for having a valet who looked after him. Tip O'Neill recalled a far more daunting, more relevant advantage. Joe Kennedy had gotten *Reader's Digest* to publish a condensed version of the John Hersey *PT 109* piece that had run in *the New Yorker,* and now the campaign was mailing out 100,000 copies of it to voters. Tip couldn't even remember a candidate before Jack Kennedy who'd had the money to pay for first-class postage.

What you did was rely on campaign workers to deliver literature.

And, even more astoundingly, Joe Kennedy, who'd made money owning chains of movie houses, had gotten local theaters to show a special newsreel recounting the story of Jack's wartime heroism. No Boston pol, or voter, had ever before seen the like in a local congressional race. Or any race, for that matter.

An important — and brilliant — clincher came just days before the primary: Jack's father and mother hosted a tony afternoon reception, a formal tea party, at the Hotel Commander in Cambridge. Women from throughout the district were invited, and all were flattered and thrilled. They'd always read about such fancy society events in the papers, but neither they nor anyone they knew had ever been to one.

Kennedy was starting to create what Tip O'Neill called the "Kennedy Party," one separate from the regular Democratic organizations. He was making it happen by asking citizens who'd never been involved before to come on board. He, the millionaire's son, was seeking the help of regular folk, not just the predictable party faithful or the machine hacks. Anyone stopping by Kennedy's storefront headquarters would be asked to volunteer, and, in agreeing, they'd become, on the spot, "Kennedy" people. Thus, as word began to get around that someone's son or niece was "working for young Jack Kennedy," the popular appeal of the campaign grew, along with its strength.

Meanwhile, Jack himself continued acting in a way that was deeply impressive for someone of his wealth and name. He was out there going door to door on foot, and it was not simply a choice but rather a necessity. While his rivals could count on their associations with other politicians to further their candidacies, he was a newcomer who, despite his hard-core Boston bloodlines, didn't have those established connections. His only means of getting to know voters was to meet them himself.

With either Billy Sutton or Dave Powers by his side, he went everywhere. "He met city workers, he met letter carriers, cabbies, waitresses, and dock workers," Billy recalled. "He was probably the first of the pols around here to go into the firehouses, police stations, post offices, and saloons and poolrooms, as well as the homes, and it was probably the first Jack ever knew that the gas stove and the toilet could be in the same room." Having the gabby, comical Sutton — a gifted mimic of character high and low — with him provided great company.

He deliberately made the rounds of the

Cambridge city councilmen, putting up with their silent responses or sometimes outright abuse. He was showing that he had the guts to do it, gaining respect, if not for this election, for the next time. He was honoring the political rule of keeping his enemies in front of him, showing them he wasn't afraid and letting them know he had what it took to look them in the face.

At one candidates' event, he listened patiently to each of his rivals describe their difficult lives. When his turn arrived, he, son of one of the world's richest men, stood up and began, "I guess I'm the only one here who didn't come up the hard way."

He also did something else other candidates failed to think of, or were unable to imagine themselves doing, which was making a direct appeal to women. "Womanpower," he would tell Tip, "the untapped resource."

Red Fay reported that visiting junior colleges in the area with Jack back then was like traveling with the young, also very skinny Frank Sinatra. "They would scream and holler and touch him — absolutely, in 1946. I mean these girls were just crazy about him."

Finally, there was the undeniable stamina Kennedy poured into the race, working hard at it until the very last day. Years later he would say it was mostly a matter of getting started early. "My chief opponents . . . followed the old practice of not starting until two months before the election. By then I was way ahead of them. I believe most aspirants for public office start much too late. When you think of the money that Coca-Cola and Lucky Strike put into advertising day after day though they have well-known brand names, you can realize how difficult it is to become an identifiable political figure. The idea that people can get to know you well enough to support you in two months or three months is wholly wrong. Most of us do not follow politics and politicians. We become interested only around election time. . . . In my opinion the principle for winning a war fight or a Congressional fight is really the same as winning a presidential fight. And the most important ingredient is a willingness to submit yourself to long, long, long labor."

Ted Reardon, his older brother's close friend from Harvard, was running the get-out-the-vote effort. "We were constantly going over the voting lists to find where the Democrats were. We had four or five telephones going all the time, with volunteer girls calling up and getting out the vote. We used to stay until three or four in the morning."

Lem Billings, recalling the pace, said: "Remember, we were all amateurs and all very young. Everyone was either a young veteran or a young girl. We had people who'd lived in each district all their lives stationed at the polls. We tried to get as many volunteers with cars as we could, but we always had to hire an awful lot of taxis and these were all sent to addresses of Democrats who hadn't voted."

The big event each year in Charlestown, then a part of the 11th Congressional District, is the Bunker Hill Parade. The day before the primary, Jack marched in the parade. On this hot June day, the pressure and work of the campaign finally catching up with him, he collapsed before reaching the finish.

"I called his father," said the man whose house he was taken to. "I was instructed to wait until a doctor came. He turned very yellow and blue. He appeared to me as a man who probably had a heart attack. Later on I found out it was a condition which he picked up, probably malaria or yellow fever." In fact, it would take until the following year for Kennedy to find out the true, much more serious cause of his problem.

On the following day, Kennedy was up early and at the movies. It was a way for him to escape the early, misleading, mind-destroying tidbits of information about how the voting was going. That night, when the results were in, he'd beaten Neville by two to one. Joe Russo — the real one — finished fourth. The other Joe Russo, the one the Kennedy people had put up, managed to get nearly eight hundred votes. He finished fifth.

Jack Kennedy had started earliest and worked the hardest. He had done what was necessary, and more, and he had won. But what did he believe? And what were his loyalties? He had championed the concerns of his primarily working-class district: wages, unemployment benefits, the need for a national health care system. In deep ways, he was as Irish as his constituents. He'd run, after all, as a "fighting conservative," fearing in his heart the dark specter of Moscow, angered still by the ailing Roosevelt's giveaway at Yalta.

"What about Communism?" he asked a lawyer he knew who'd been supporting Mike Neville in the race. That fall he was already calling the Soviet Union, our wartime ally, a "slave state," clearly drawing a line between himself and his party's liberal wing.

This fighting conservative was already fighting a war that had not yet gotten its name.

CHAPTER FIVE
COLD WARRIOR

*While the hand of fate made Jack and me
political opponents, I always cherish the fact
that we were personal friends from the time
we came to the Congress together in 1947.*
— Richard M. Nixon, from a
letter written to Jacqueline Kennedy,
November 22, 1963

Jack Kennedy knew well before going to the
House of Representatives that he didn't intend
to stay there. He was headed for statewide
office, either the governorship or the U.S.
Senate. Even if he opted for the governorship first, it was only to be a stepping-stone.
His goal was the Senate, since what he really
wanted was to join the big national debates,
especially those on foreign policy. That was
where he intended to make his mark.

There were no near-term options for reaching his goal. If he ran against Senator Leverett
Saltonstall in two years — in '48 — he would
look impetuous. Besides, he'd formed an af-

The Daily News, *McKeesport*

The House class of 1946

fection for the older man. But if he waited to run against the other senator from the Commonwealth of Massachusetts, the august Henry Cabot Lodge, Jr., in 1952, it might be a suicide mission.

Lodge had sacrificed his first seat in the Senate to go off and fight in the war. Now, in '46, he'd won the second Massachusetts seat, with a smashing victory over Senator David I. Walsh, a four-term Democrat. So Jack would have to wait. Whatever and whenever he decided on for his next step he needed to prove himself with the job he'd won.

From the start, when he walked into his office on Capitol Hill, Jack Kennedy made it clear he was his own man. Arriving with a high profile, built first on his best-selling, prewar book and then on his news-making exploits in the South Pacific, he had no intention of compromising his hero's image by becoming just another Massachusetts Democrat. Out there in the Solomon Islands, he'd engineered the saving of ten men's lives; he was not about to sign on to someone else's crew. And that included the number two Democrat in the House, John McCormack, who, because he was the senior congressman from Massachusetts, expected a certain deference from his fellow Bay Staters.

He would not be getting it from young Kennedy. On the morning the about-to-be congressman was to take his oath, Billy Sutton met him at the Statler Hilton on Sixteenth Street, a few blocks north of the White House. Jack had just flown in from Palm Beach.

"You should be in a hurry," Sutton warned his boss, who showed up tanned and carrying his black cashmere overcoat. "You have a caucus meeting." In other words, McCormack was waiting for him up on Capitol Hill. "Well, I'd like a couple of eggs," Kennedy said, continuing to ignore the suggestion to get a move on. "How long would you say Mr. McCormack has been here? Don't you think Mr. McCormack wouldn't mind waiting another ten minutes?"

The Mucker wasn't about to let a new headmaster intimidate him. At that, he went into the hotel's drugstore lunch counter to join his new top aide, Ted Reardon, for breakfast.

Kennedy's little-concealed disdain for the John McCormacks of the world was not a trait he was ready to hide. He'd made it his business to win his seat free of the entangling alliances that tied up other new lawmakers before they could even get started. Establishing his independence was his purpose from the very first day. Since he didn't plan to spend the rest of his career as one of 435 members of the House of Representatives, he wasn't going to get hitched to McCormack, for the simple reason that he intended to pass him by.

Years later, when he was headed to the Senate, Jack Kennedy would advise his successor in Congress, Tip O'Neill, to "marry John McCormack." Such different behavior from his own, he said, was the better path for a man who by then had been Speaker of the Massachusetts legislature and who, he correctly assumed, would one day want to join the House leadership ladder.

The world Jack Kennedy found in Washington that winter of 1947 was a jamboree of Republican triumphalism. On both sides of the Capitol, committees were cooking up public hearings on the two hot-stove issues Republicans had championed in the previous election: the evils of Big Labor and the threat of Communism at home and abroad. Republicans had won both houses, the first time since before the Great Depression, with a simple slogan that was more a question than an answer, more a taunt than a promise: "Had Enough?"

Its meaning was clear. It summed up two decades of Democratic rule that had comprised an era of government activism or overreach, depending on the voter's degree of resentment. And during the '46 campaign it meant everything voters didn't like after V-J day, from rationing to the recent rash of labor strikes.

The new Republican majority came with a mission. Harry Truman could sit there in the White House and veto its bills, but he couldn't stop the new Eightieth Congress from investigating him, and that meant the whole twenty-year Democratic era. They were, in the words of one Republican congressman, going to "open every session with a prayer and end it with a probe." Almost forty investigative panels were setting up schedules to dig up corruption any way they could find it, with the entire Roosevelt-Truman record as their quarry.

Congress was looking for bad guys, especially those who were seen as soft on the Communist threat. Someone had to pay for the giveaway at Yalta, and FDR, who'd agreed to it, wasn't around to take the punishment.

Jack Kennedy had brought Billy Sutton to Washington as his press secretary and jack-of-all-trades — housemate included. Being from the Boston neighborhoods, he took a street-corner guy's view of things. So much was happening so fast that the spectacle on Capitol Hill seemed to him like a "Stop 'n' Shop, a supermarket of hearings."

The very day he arrived on Capitol Hill, Jack Kennedy met the fellow member of the House freshman class of 1946 whose destiny would wind up twinned with his own. Richard Nixon had just beaten a much-admired New Dealer and five-term Democratic incumbent in the battle for California's 12th District. It had been an upset victory tinged by telephoned whispers that Nixon's opponent was a "Communist."

Kennedy, however, was impressed by the drama of the triumph itself. "So you're the guy who beat Jerry Voorhis," Kennedy exclaimed on meeting Nixon at a National Press Club reception for freshman congressmen who'd fought in the war. "That's like beating John McCormack up in Massachusetts!"

At Harvard, Jack had gravitated to Torby Macdonald, hotshot of the freshman football team. Now it was the star of the House class of 1946 — this thirty-four-year-old Californian, like himself a navy man, who'd just pulled off the biggest political upset of the season.

"How's it feel?" Jack asked him. Here was the son of one of the richest men in the world showing Dick Nixon, the poor boy, true admiration. "I guess I'm elated," the Californian answered, plainly taken by the attention. In fact, Nixon's loyal presidential aide H. R. Haldeman told me decades later and just days before his own death that he'd always found Nixon's feelings toward Jack Kennedy "strange and inexplicable." It had been so from the start.

The two ex–naval officers from the South Pacific theater — Nixon had been a supply officer there — were both assigned to the Committee on Education and Labor. Now both were being thrown into the most intense battle of the season: the effort by the reenergized Republicans to rein in the power of organized labor. In those early months of 1947, it would offer Jack Kennedy his first chance for distinction.

Rather than join his fellow Democrats in simply opposing the measure, he decided to put forth his own "dissenting opinion." He had called Mark Dalton, the friend who'd managed his campaign, and asked him to join him in Washington. "John wanted to know what we — Billy Sutton was in the room — thought of the Hartley proposal and what he should do about it. We sat there and developed a position," recalled Dalton, who wound up manning the typewriter.

To Dalton, it was a billboard screaming the new congressman's ambitions. "People have always said to me, was John Kennedy running for the presidency from the start? Was he thinking of the future?" For Dalton, there was never any doubt — and certainly not from that moment forward.

But there was more still to learn about his boss, and it had to do with the way he kept his eye on the future competition. The morning Kennedy was scheduled to present his dissenting position to the Rules Committee, a congressman Dalton didn't recognize was offering the official Republican support of what would be the Taft-Hartley Act. "Listen to this fellow," Kennedy whispered as Dalton entered the cramped hearing room. "He's going places."

When the Republican member finished

speaking and took the seat next to them, Kennedy introduced him. "I'd like you to meet Richard Nixon of California." In the coming years Jack would be telling his family that Nixon was "brilliant," the smartest of all his colleagues.

Kennedy, of course, was also trying to establish himself. "There were very few Democrats who would speak as strongly as he did to labor," Dalton recalled. "The reaction was 'Kennedy is courageous,' just what Kennedy wanted it to be."

Thus, when he rose on the House floor to give what would be his maiden speech in Congress, he was taking on the power of organized labor as well as big business. "I told him that day that he reminded me so much of Jimmy Stewart in *Mr. Smith Goes to Washington*," Billy Sutton remembered.

Still, not everyone in the chamber was so thrilled. "You can imagine the reaction of the congressmen who had been there for years and had worked on this problem," said Dalton, "to be told that the new congressman from Massachusetts was filing a separate report."

A few days later, Kennedy and Dick Nixon got their first chance to match talents in an arena beyond Capitol Hill. A local group had asked a freshman member from western Pennsylvania, Frank Buchanan, to pick the two standouts in his class, one from each party, and invite them home for a debate. The topic would be the new labor reform bill, to be known as Taft-Hartley. The audience would be a mixture of business and labor people.

The pair was greeted at the train station early that evening and taken to the Penn McKeesport hotel. There in the ballroom, they put on vastly dissimilar performances. Nixon was the aggressor, punching away like a hungry middleweight. Playing to the Republicans in the mixed crowd, he pummeled Big Labor. Brutally, he listed all the troubles that had been dominating the postwar headlines: the automobile strike, the steel strike, the coal strike, the railroad strike. He had picked his side in the fight and was quite willing to taunt his enemies on the other.

The younger speaker, the one with the quaint New England accent and the slight limp, offered a more nuanced performance. Watching Nixon antagonize the labor people in the McKeesport crowd, Jack worked to soften the hostility of the business folks. There was much to say for the labor reforms the Republicans were pushing, he allowed, particularly its banning of "wildcat" strikes. His concern was that the legislation might go too far and lead to more trouble between management and labor, not less.

It was Jack's charm they witnessed that night. Nixon came into the room like a club fighter, eager to win the rivalry point by point.

A champion debater at Whittier College, he focused on his rival, challenging whatever he said. Kennedy, his focus on the audience, ignored his rival on the stage and concentrated on winning over the room. Knowing he had labor on his side — Nixon made sure of that — he wanted to end the evening with the business people convinced that he shared their concern for an end to the country's labor troubles.

What surprised those who greeted them and saw them off that night was the way these two partisans got along with each other personally. Before catching the *Capitol Limited* back to Washington, they grabbed hamburgers at the local Star Diner and talked over the new baseball season. Boarding at midnight, the two junior pols drew straws for the lower berth. Nixon won. Then, as the train rolled on toward Washington, they spent the early-morning hours discussing their true mutual interest, foreign policy, especially the rising standoff with the Soviets in Europe, which Bernard Baruch had just christened the "cold war."

Kennedy was drawn to those who shared his big-picture view of the world, and Nixon was one who did. Their responses to the threat posed by Communism's spread were similar, too. For both of them, it was a central issue of their generation.

In the morning-after press, it was Kennedy

who scored highest. The next morning's editions of the McKeesport *Daily News* ran a front-page photo of the smiling, handsome Kennedy, one that could easily have been of a popular local college grad. The shot of Nixon, on the other hand, caught him with his eyes darting sideways with a hunted look, his defiant chin displaying a beard well beyond the five o'clock mark. Even in black and white, the charisma gap was stark.

That March, President Truman called on Congress to stop the Red advance across Europe by approving U.S. military aid to help governments in Greece and Turkey resist Communist-backed insurgencies. Speaking to a joint session, he called this move crucial to American security. To those on the political left, the new "Truman Doctrine" was an unwelcome reversal from the pro-Russian policies of FDR. But for many of the young officers back from the war, the president was speaking the language they wanted to hear.

The day after Truman had addressed Congress, Russ Nixon — no relation to Richard — of the United Electrical, Radio, and Machine Workers of America, a union known for its sizable Communist contingent, told the Education and Labor Committee that labor unions had as much right to be led by Communists as by Democrats or Republicans. That was a far from popular view in the halls of Washington.

When his own turn arrived to quiz the witness, Congressman Jack Kennedy said he'd been "impressed by the dexterity" the witness had shown in fielding the earlier questions. Nixon, a Ph.D. in economics, had been Kennedy's Harvard instructor before joining the labor movement. Now the student to whom he'd given a B-minus his freshman year got to ask the questions.

Was Soviet Communism, he asked his former instructor, "a threat to the economic and political system of the United States?" No, Russ Nixon replied, the real threat to the country was its failure to meet the "basic economic problems of the people in a democratic way" as well as its failure to expand Americans' civil rights and in that way meet "the problems of the Negro people."

Kennedy then asked his instructor to defend what he said was the Communist Party's willingness to "resort to all sorts of artifices, evasion, subterfuges, only so as to get into the trade unions and remain in them and to carry on Communist work in them, at all costs."

Russ Nixon: I didn't teach you that at Harvard, did I?

Kennedy: No, you did not. I am reading from Lenin, in which is described the procedure which should be adopted to get into trade unions and how they conduct themselves once they are in.

His clever questioning of the left-leaning witness won Kennedy positive notice from the press gallery. "A freshman House member with the coral dust of Pacific Islands still clinging to his heels," UPI's George Reedy said in a radio broadcast, "stole the show from his older colleagues yesterday."

In May, Jack outdid that performance. He won a perjury citation against a Communist labor leader, Harold Christoffel, for his role in a wartime strike against a huge defense plant in Milwaukee.

He asked the witness why the union newspaper had strongly opposed war aid to Britain prior to the Nazi invasion of Russia, only to back it strongly thereafter. Why did it condemn "Roosevelt's War Program" when Hitler was in league with Stalin, then call for "All Aid to Britain, Soviet Union" in a banner headline once the Hitler-Stalin alliance was broken?

Kennedy had harder evidence that the labor leaders were under Communist Party discipline from Moscow. A former party member had testified that the 1941 Milwaukee strike was part of a "snowballing" of such work stoppage aimed at crippling the U.S. defense buildup. The labor leaders had been lying and

Kennedy had caught them.

"Would you call Russia a democracy?" Kennedy asked one. "I would not know. I do not think so," he replied. "I think I would like to inform you on what I believe to be the main difference between socialism in England and socialism in Russia," Kennedy said. "They have freedom of opposition which they do not have in Russia." When his witness said he didn't know if that was true or not, Jack went at him.

"Well, I do not think you are equipped to tell whether a member of your union is a Communist if you do not know any of the answers to any of the things that I have asked you."

Deeply impressed by his young colleague's work, the Republican chairman of the committee compared it to the opening shots at Lexington and Concord.

On June 5 — two years to the day after the Allies had met in Berlin, affirming the total defeat of Germany — Secretary of State George C. Marshall was Harvard's commencement speaker. He used the occasion to unveil a massive, complex plan for the economic reconstruction of war-torn Europe, funded by U.S. dollars. Though the Marshall Plan doesn't seem controversial today in the aftermath of its great success — *Time* called it "surely one of the most momentous commencement day speeches ever made" — it had its detractors.

One of them was Joseph Kennedy, Sr., who regarded the European Recovery Plan — the Marshall Plan's official name — as a terrible idea. A shrewder plan, he calculated, would be to let the Communists grab Europe, creating economic chaos that would lead to greater opportunities for businessmen like him down the road. His son disagreed. He believed that serious efforts to halt the Soviet advance in Europe were the only way to avoid repeating the mistake made at the Munich Conference of 1938, when Hitler was allowed free rein.

Had the Third Reich been confronted at a decisive moment, it was now believed, Germany might have retreated and never come to stage a deadly attack on Poland as it did the following year. The outcome of Munich, along with the thinking behind it, meant the Allies were thrown on the defensive. The World War II generation, having lived through the prewar appeasement and its consequences, had returned from the theaters of war in the South Pacific, Europe, and Africa determined to prevent a sequel to the tragedy that had interrupted and harrowed their lives — and erased so many more. This time, the dictator bent on encroachment and annexation must be stopped in his tracks.

To young men like Kennedy and Nixon, the Yalta Conference of February 1945, which had divided up postwar Europe, carried whiffs of another Munich. It represented a buckling under to a new enemy, but one even more subversive in its methods and more pervasive in its ambitions than the one who'd died in his Berlin bunker.

This firm resolve to defend Europe from Stalin was hardly a policy Jack's father, the ruthless builder of wealth, could embrace. Joe Kennedy had gone back to the isolationism he'd preached throughout the 1930s; his son, meanwhile, was moving in his own direction. "So many people said that the ambassador was pulling the strings for Jack, and he certainly was not," said Mary Davis, the congressman's secretary at the time. "Jack was his own man."

In fact, Jack Kennedy was starting to make it known, both privately and publicly, that he and his father disagreed on important issues.

"We were all at a cocktail party in the garden of Drew and Luvie Pearson," the senior Kennedy's friend Kay Halle recalled. "Suddenly, Joe said, 'Kay, I wish you would tell Jack that he's going to vote the wrong way.' I can't even remember what bill it was, but Joe said, 'I think Jack is making a terrible mistake.'

"And then I remember Jack turning to his father and saying, 'Now, look here, Dad, you have your political views and I have mine. I'm going to vote exactly the way I feel I must vote on this. I've great respect for you, but when it comes to voting, I'm voting my way.' Then Joe looked at me with that big Irish smile, and said, 'Well, Kay, that's why I settled a million dollars on each of them, so they could spit in my eye if they wished.'"

Jack's tough stand against the Soviets abroad and Communism at home made sense to his constituents up in Boston. Growing up, I saw this myself: Catholics as a group had it in our gut that Roosevelt had sold out the country's interests at Yalta. To us, the growing threat from Moscow increasingly resembled Hitler's prewar aggression. Supporters back home could see that Jack Kennedy, down in Washington, knew just how they felt, agreed with them, and was saying exactly what they were feeling.

Kennedy also knew he, the privileged son, was being watched back home for how he was handling the job. If he gave the cold shoulder to a single constituent, if a letter went unanswered, the word would get around. He'd be seen as having gotten too big for his britches. "He was very particular about people in his district and answering the mail," Billy Sutton recalled. "He didn't want anything to stay on your desk. If some poor soul or constituent needed help and he gave the assignment to you, you were liable to be riding home in the car and he'd say, 'Well, what about John White? What did you do for him?' And if you said, 'Well, I was going to do that tomorrow,' he'd almost tell you, you know, to get out of the car and go back to the office. He wanted you to do your job, and if you didn't, then you were in trouble."

Mary Davis understood the stakes. Her young boss wasn't down in Washington only to be a dutiful congressman. He wanted those constituents of his to help elect him senator. That meant at least doing no harm. "I would say that was always in the back of Jack's mind, and in the minds of the people who had supported him first for representative in the House. They always felt that this was a start and that he would go onward and upward."

There quickly came a time in that first year that Kennedy had to decide between going along and getting along: at issue was the man whose seat he had taken in Congress. Re-elected mayor in 1945, James Michael Curley had been convicted of mail fraud; he now sat, plotting, in Danbury federal prison. Curley's daughter was passing around a petition to the Massachusetts members of Congress asking for his release on health grounds. It was feared, the petition argued, that he would die if not released. A hundred thousand Massachusetts voters had signed a citizens' petition.

Kennedy friend Joe Healey was Jack's tutor at Harvard and continued to be a trusted advisor and occasional speechwriter. "I got a call from Washington. It was Congressman Kennedy, and he said he wanted to talk with me about a petition that had been brought to his office. The person who had brought the petition to his office was Mary Curley, the daughter of the former governor."

Healey was cautious in his advice. If Curley's illness was truly fatal, he said, the old pol should be given some last time with his family. If he wasn't as sick as he advertised, he shouldn't be treated any differently than anyone else convicted of his crimes. Kennedy agreed this was exactly the way to look at it. In fact, army physicians had examined him and found his health as good as any man of his age reasonably could expect to have. Kennedy said he could not, knowing that, in good conscience sign the document.

Hearing this, Healey pointed out it was going to be "a very politically unpopular thing to do." Kennedy's refusal to sign the Curley petition was of course infuriating to the local politicians back home. It turned out he was the only Massachusetts Democratic congressman to do so. "I guess I'm going to be a one-term congressman," he told one back-home advisor.

Mark Dalton, who worked for Kennedy unpaid and picked up his own expenses, was disgusted with the Curley ploy. "My strong reaction was that he was a young man starting his political career, just on the threshold of it, and I thought that the older people who were putting the pressure on him to sign this petition had a terrible nerve."

Jack had gone against his party and the state machine regarding something he knew in his bones was wrong. It was also an issue of pride; he didn't want to be a hack. Add in the matter of style: refusing to sign showed class. But standing against the pardon was both a political and moral risk that Kennedy would sweat for weeks to come. Joe Healey never forgot the episode.

Curley, he recalled, "lived for some ten years after this event, but as a congressman, I heard Jack Kennedy say that, if anything had happened to Mr. Curley during his stay in prison, it would have been the end of his political career." For his part, Jack would cite the Curley dilemma as a case study of how political fortunes turn on the unpredictable.

Years later, to put it in perspective, Tip O'Neill, once a Curley protégé, refused to defend him on moral grounds. In the midst of one of our long backroom conversations about the old days, he had put it bluntly and succinctly, how "Curly was crooked" even by the standard of those days. "Personally crooked?" I asked.

"Personally," he said with the firmest possible pronunciation.

But Jack Kennedy's independence on matters such as the Curley petition was unsettling to political observers. He had begun to build a reputation for standing alone, a two-edged sword. Edmund Muskie, who served as governor and later senator from Maine, recalled how Kennedy's behavior scared the clubhouse types. "I don't know whether the more foresighted of them saw in young Jack Kennedy a major political force or not, but they certainly recognized his political attractions and his political potential; and they were disturbed by his apparent determination to be independent of the 'regular' party organization."

Mark Dalton remembered another moment when Kennedy stood out. "I'm going to debate Norman Thomas at the Harvard Law School," said Jack one day, surprising Dalton, who had arrived at his friend's Boston apartment to find the congressman hard at work. So now his young friend was going to take on the quadrennial candidate of the Socialist Party. "There was Kennedy sitting on the sofa. There were two or three books open there and six or seven books on the floor opened. Each one had been written by Norman Thomas. The next day I got reports from several people, and everyone was agreed that John Kennedy had won the debate with Thomas."

Again, the old dichotomy. His colleagues saw the popular bachelor who lived the good life in Georgetown, the rich kid with such a great sense of humor. Few noticed the other Jack, the occasional Cold Warrior, the autodidact who crammed for off-campus debates, who quietly but steadily was preparing himself for something greater than labor law.

Like others, his secretary Mary Davis would come to learn that Jack Kennedy was not the fop he played so charmingly. For all the fun she saw him having, she could catch that spark of brilliance. "He didn't make that many speeches, and we didn't issue that many position papers when he was here in the House, but when he wanted to write a speech, *he did it*. I would say ninety-nine percent of that was done by JFK himself.

"I can remember the first time he ever called me in — I even forget what the speech was going to be on, but it was going to be a major speech, one of his first major speeches. And I thought, 'Oh, oh, this young, green congressman. What's he going to do?' No preparation. He called me in and he says, 'I think we'd better get to work on the speech.' And I said, 'Okay, fine.' And I thought he was going to stumble around, and he'll 'er, ah, um.'

"I was never so startled in my life. He sat back in his chair, and it just flowed right out. He had such a grasp of what he was saying, and was able to put it in such beautiful language. I thought, 'Wow. This guy has a brain.' I mean, you didn't get that impression when you first met him because he looked so young and casual and informal. But he knew what it was all about. He knew about everything."

Richard Nixon had a similar epiphany. Ted

Reardon recalled the time that Jack became deeply focused on an issue before the Education and Labor Committee, so much so that he went himself to the National Archives to look something up. "At the hearing, the thing I remember is when Jack started to talk, Dicky Boy sort of looked at him . . . with a look between awe and respect and fear."

Jack's greatest secret remained his bad health, the extent of which, until then, was unknown even to him. When Kennedy arrived in Washington that January, his problems had followed. "He was not feeling well," Mary Davis noticed. "I mean, he still had his jaundice, he still had his back problems."

"Emaciated!" is how his fellow congressman George Smathers of Florida remembers his frail classmate. The Florida Democrat, who had been assigned to the same hallway as Kennedy, vividly recalls that "every time there was a roll call, he'd have to come over on his crutches." Wanting to help, Smathers often would stop by Jack's office to give him a hand as his new friend made the painful journey across Independence Avenue to the Capitol to vote.

The various maladies from which he visibly suffered were being blamed on his war traumas, but that explanation, while infinitely useful spinwise, was only part of the story. For Jack the truth lay deeper, and he was about to discover it.

During the summer recess of 1947, a group of congressmen, Dick Nixon included, headed to Europe to study the impact of the Marshall Plan, which was now being implemented. For a *bon voyage* gesture — one that was, apparently, ignored — Kennedy had sent his married California colleague the names of a few women he might look up while in Paris. For himself, Kennedy also set off across the Atlantic, first to Ireland with his sister Kick, then to the Continent along with a Republican colleague to look into the Communist influence on European labor unions.

Arriving in London after falling ill on the first leg of his journey, he was rushed to the hospital, where he was diagnosed with Addison's disease, a serious disorder of the adrenal glands. Prior to Jack's release, the attending physician offered this grim prognosis to Jack's English traveling companion. "That American friend of yours, he hasn't got a year to live." Just as the *Queen Mary* docked in New York, a priest came aboard to administer to him the last rites.

He had lost his older brother in 1944. The husband of his beloved Kick had died the following year. Yet, on the return voyage home from England and near death, he showed himself as politically curious as ever. Much of his time was spent quizzing a fellow passenger on the new British health service created by the Labour Party.

Jack continued to keep tight the compartments of his life. Like the ship's captain he still was, he knew he couldn't sink if he kept each of them strongly secure from the other. In Georgetown, he basked in a princely life, attended by a housekeeper, Margaret Ambrose, and a valet, George Thomas, who delivered a home-cooked hot lunch to his Capitol office each day.

Meanwhile, Billy Sutton was with him 24/7, since Jack still couldn't stand to be alone. On those nights he didn't have a date for the movies, his "firecracker" provided entertainment and company. Mary Davis explained the dynamic between the two men this way: "He was someone he could completely relax with, who would be available, and who would be on call, who could do a thousand and one things for Jack, just being there, knowing that he had a friend close by."

Referring to the townhouse they shared on Thirty-first Street NW as akin to a "Hollywood Hotel," Billy cherished the memories of all the gorgeous women coming and going. "Thinking about girls is what kept Jack alive," he said.

Playing the field, rejecting any definite romantic attachments, gave him the freedom he craved. Refusing to give fealty to the Democratic leadership or to the liberal old guard gave him the independence he treasured.

Being able to enter each world without the baggage from the other gave him the breezy, debonair life he wanted. Anywhere he went he could simply be Jack Kennedy, the guy he wanted to be, the one he'd made himself.

"He did have a lot of close associations," Mary Davis recalled. But not "a lot of close personal friendships." Charlie Bartlett recalls the detached way his friend regarded political colleagues, no matter their status. "He used to enjoy kidding about the personalities on the scene, and there used to be a lot of jokes about different personalities from Sam Rayburn down, and even some sort of gossiping about the foibles of some of the senior statesmen in Congress." He liked to watch what they were up to, enjoyed charting their purposes and behavior — but at a distance.

George Smathers was the rare *social* friend Jack made in the House of Representatives. A marine in World War II, and son of a federal judge in Florida, he'd gotten to know Jack's father at the Hialeah Park Race Track in Miami. Smathers, not to put too fine a point on it, was a hack, knew it, and enjoyed it — and this gave him, for Jack, a special aura of honesty. Confiding that he voted whatever way would keep him in office, this made him, in a world of hypocrites, special indeed.

Kennedy told Charlie Bartlett he liked Smathers "because he doesn't give a damn." If he judged Dick Nixon to be the "smartest" guy on the Hill in those days, his pal George was the most fun to hang out with.

Smathers knew his role: he was Falstaff. Jack was still playing Hal, a prince whose fears, in those days, were not — or not yet — of coming kingship but of mortality. Smathers remembers his pal being "deeply preoccupied by death," talking endlessly on a Florida fishing trip about the best ways to die. He remembered Kennedy deciding it had to be drowning, "but only if you lost consciousness."

"Quick" — that was the key. "The point is, you've got to live each day like it's your last day on earth," he recalled Jack telling him. "That's what I'm doing." Ted Reardon recalled a similar conversation on the way home from Capitol Hill one late afternoon in Jack's convertible. "It was a bright, shining day. We had the top down. Out of the blue he said, 'What do you think is the best way of dying?'" A new friend, the newspaper columnist and Georgetown mandarin Joseph Alsop, recalled Jack's bluntness when it came to his short-range outlook. "Unless I'm very mistaken, he said that as a matter of fact, he had a kind of slow-acting — *very* slow-acting — leukemia and that he did not expect to live more than ten years or so, but there was no use thinking about it and he was going to do the best he could and enjoy himself as much as he could in the time that was given him."

Alsop could clearly see there was cause for

worry. "He used to turn green at intervals," he recalled. "He was about the color of pea soup."

As he had all his life, Jack found refuge from his health worries in the power of words and ideas. Reading remained his salvation, and not just of the newspapers that are the daily fare of most politicians. Billy Sutton recalls him staying up late at night with Arthur Schlesinger's *Age of Jackson*. Mark Dalton, perhaps the most thoughtful of the people around him back then, recalled a visit to Hyannis Port one weekend when Kennedy called him and another friend up to his bedroom.

He wanted to read them a passage by Churchill, possibly one from his magnificent study of the Duke of Marlborough, a heroic ancestor. "Did you ever read anything like that in all your life?" Kennedy demanded, thrilled again by his hero's work.

Dalton, obviously very fond of his friend in those days, believed he saw a side of Jack that rarely showed itself to others. "As I look back, the things that I liked most about John Kennedy were the small flashes of sentiment." He recalled a particular incident. "One morning I was at mass with him in the early congressional days down at the Cape, at St. Francis there. We were alone. We were about to leave the church, and John said, 'Will you wait a minute? I want to go in and light a candle for Joe.' And I was stunned at it. But it showed the deep attachment that he had for his brother Joe, and it also showed his religious nature. You know, there was a strong bond.

"Another day I can remember riding along with him in the car. He was driving. It was over by the Charles River here in Boston and he was humming a tune to himself, but he was way off. And I said to him, 'What are you thinking about?' And he said, 'I was thinking of Joe.'"

He would soon lose someone closer still. His sister Kathleen, widowed when her husband, Billy Hartington, was killed in 1945, now was being courted by another English aristocrat, Peter Fitzwilliam. In February 1948, Kick took the bold step of telling her mother about this new relationship. It was with yet another Protestant, this one married. Her mother threatened to disown her. But nothing could dissuade Kathleen. She had found true, passionate love and would not let go.

Now came tragedy. She and Fitzwilliam had left Paris on a chartered flight to Cannes. They had persisted in flying despite the bad weather, and then, in heavy rain, their plane crashed into the side of a mountain. Jack was listening to music on his Victrola when the first, preliminary call came.

When the next call confirmed the tragedy, he sat quietly listening to a recording of the Broadway musical *Finian's Rainbow*. He would never make it to the funeral of the person

164

he loved most. Setting out for the flight to Europe, he got only as far as New York. For whatever reason, he couldn't go on.

"He was in terrible pain," Lem Billings recalled of Jack. "He couldn't get through the days without thinking of her at the most inappropriate times. He'd be sitting at a congressional hearing and he'd find his mind drifting back uncontrollably to all the things he and Kathleen had done together and all the friends they had in common."

Chuck Spalding could see the specter the deaths of his friend's brother and sister had left in their wake. "He always heard the footsteps. Death was there. It had taken Joe and Kick and it was waiting for him."

Now he started to take risks. In September 1948 Kennedy decided to make a target of the powerful American Legion, declaring that this mainstream, middle-American organization of veterans hadn't had "a constructive thought since 1918." It was one of those marks of independence — his risk-taking again — that helped make him a hero to the young.

One of those who thrilled to Jack's taking on the Legion was Kenneth O'Donnell. A Harvard roommate of Bobby Kennedy and captain of the football team, he'd served in the Army Air Corps. When Jack "took on the American Legion," said O'Donnell, "that was big to the average veteran." Veterans,

O'Donnell believed, were looking for "a fresh face in politics."

Jack Kennedy fully intended to be that face. Dave Powers had put a Massachusetts map on the wall of Kennedy's Boston apartment, with colored pins indicating towns Jack had visited. "When we've got the map completely covered with pins," Jack told his aide, "that's when I'll announce that I'm going to run for statewide office."

By his second year in Congress, Jack Kennedy had committed to a cause: the Cold War. He'd already triggered a mild stir with his tough grilling of the left-leaning Russ Nixon and his indictment of Harold Christoffel. In 1948, when East Germany cut off West Berlin, Kennedy went there and saw for himself the heroic survival of its people, as well as the pro-American loyalty the situation was instilling.

As General Lucius Clay, commander of the American zone, put it, "the Russians, by their actions, have given us the political soul of Germany on a platter." The spirit of the West Berliners stayed with Jack for years to come.

Back home, the pursuit of the Communist threat continued to stir emotions. Dick Nixon had just led the successful exposure of Alger Hiss, America's top diplomat at the U.N. Conference in San Francisco. For denying that he had ever been a Communist, the well-connected Hiss now stood indicted for perjury. Jack, who saw Hiss as a "traitor," shared Nixon's indignation at the way Hiss had managed to install himself in critical government positions through the patronage of New Deal figures.

In September 1949 President Truman announced that the Soviets had exploded their first atom bomb, making it clear to the world that the United States no longer held a monopoly on the weapon that had ended World War II. Next came the declaration from China's Communist rebel leader Mao Tsetung that he had taken control of the entire Chinese mainland. America's WWII ally Chiang Kai-shek was trapped on the island of Formosa.

Kennedy was quick with his rebuke. "The responsibility for the failure of our foreign policy in the Far East rests squarely with the White House and the Department of State. So concerned were our diplomats with the imperfection of the democratic system of China after twenty years of war and the tales of corruption in high places that they lost sight of our tremendous stake in non-Communist China." He accused the Truman administration of "vacillation, uncertainty, and confusion."

To Kennedy, America's leaders were repeating the old prewar mistake of failing to confront aggression. Kennedy believed FDR had been as derelict in failing to stop Soviet ambitions in Asia as he had been in Europe. In a Salem, Massachusetts, speech, he described how "a sick Roosevelt with the advice of General Marshall and other chiefs of staff, gave the Kurile Islands as well as control of various strategic Chinese ports, such as Port Arthur and Darien, to the Soviet Union. This is the tragic story of China, whose freedom we once fought to preserve. What our young men have saved, the diplomats and our President have frittered away."

In January 1950 came another Cold War milestone. Alger Hiss, the accused Soviet spy, was convicted on two counts of lying under oath and sent to federal prison. That same month, desperate for material to use at a Lincoln Day talk to Republican women in Wheeling, West Virginia, Wisconsin's Senator Joseph McCarthy jumped on the anti-Communist bandwagon. Cribbing from a speech Nixon had just given on the Hiss conviction, McCarthy said there were 205 Communists in the State Department. His specificity hooded the recklessness of the accusation.

That June brought a real Communist menace. North Korea attacked American-backed South Korea. President Truman sent troops as part of a United Nations force. The next month came stunning news at home: Julius Rosenberg was arrested for stealing atomic secrets for the Soviets. Suddenly the country was under assault abroad *and* at home.

Kennedy strongly allied himself with the anti-Communist activism. While facing no political contest himself in 1950, he played a small role in helping Nixon win a Senate seat: he walked to Nixon's office and left a thousand-dollar check from his father. When he got the word, Nixon was overwhelmed that his Democratic colleague had crossed the political aisle like that. "Isn't this something!" he exclaimed to an aide.

Jack wanted what Nixon now had. Since they had come to the House together, he, Nixon, and George Smathers had enjoyed running banter on which of them would graduate first to the Senate. Smathers had gotten the jump early that year, beating a fellow Democrat in a Florida campaign notorious for its Red-baiting. Nixon now used similar tactics to beat the liberal New Dealer Helen Gahagan Douglas. Kennedy had to catch up.

"This rivalry developed and they were all shooting for the future," said Mark Dalton. Billy Sutton saw it in personal terms: "I think the thing that sent him to the Senate was George Smathers and Richard Nixon." He was clear about not intending to stay in the House. Jack told his new aide Larry O'Brien, whom he recruited to begin organizing Massachusetts for him politically, "I'm up or out." And he was ready to play rough. "I'm going to run!" he told Smathers. "I'm going to use the same kind of stuff."

CHAPTER SIX
BOBBY

All this business about Jack and Bobby being blood brothers has been exaggerated. They didn't really become close until 1952, and it was politics that brought them together.

— Eunice Kennedy Shriver

By 1951, Jack Kennedy's ambition was clear. He wanted very much to reach the Senate. Three times voted in, he'd proved himself an independent Democrat, an ardent anti-Communist, and he had been an efficient, if sometimes detached, steward of constituent services. Based upon his performance and popularity in such a heavily Democratic district, the House seat could have been his for life.

His chance at the Senate would arrive the following year when Henry Cabot Lodge, Jr., a Republican, came up for reelection. The only problem was that Governor Paul Dever, having already served two terms himself, was

170

Jack, Ethel, and Bobby, November 1952

also considering a job change. If Dever chose to take on Lodge and run for senator, Jack's only option would be to declare for the State House. Whichever happened, he'd definitely decided he wasn't going to stay put. Thus, in January 1951, he gave Tip O'Neill a heads-up.

"I've decided not to run for a fourth term in the House," he told him. "I don't yet know whether I'll run for the Senate or governor, but you can be sure of one thing: my seat will be open. I won't be making any announcements for at least another year, so don't tell a soul. But in case you have any interest in running, I wanted to give you a head start."

Getting ahead in politics generally requires solving a pair of equations, the first being the availability of an office that matches the politician's ambitions. The other is finding the right person to run the campaign. While waiting for Paul Dever to make his decision, Jack got a lead on meeting the second challenge.

Here's how it happened: In September, Kennedy set off on a seven-week fact-finding trip to the Far East. America was at war in Korea, Asia presented the premier foreign-policy front, and the issues presented by foreign policy continued to be his primary interest. The trip would have the added merit of establishing in voters' minds his firsthand experience. However, as the trip was being planned, a family issue arose, casting a slight shadow over it. The problem was pressure from his father to take along his younger brother Bobby. Jack's reaction was that his sibling, eight years his junior, would be nothing but a hindrance, a "pain in the ass."

While Jack had been a warm, loving brother to both Joe Jr. and Kathleen, still missing them terribly, he had yet to form close ties with the younger members of the family. At the time, Bobby struck him as a very different sort from himself, a far more churchy guy, a straight arrow who spent most of his time trying to impress their father with his dutifulness. But rather than Bobby's presence being an annoyance, the opposite turned out to be true. Spending their first ever quality time together, they managed to surprise each other.

As Jack traveled with his brother all the way from Israel to Japan — from the Mediterranean to the South China Sea, stopping in India and Indochina — what they found deepened his own long-standing fascination with foreign policy. But the circumstances they encountered also opened the eyes of both men to the sparks of postwar nationalism beginning to catch fire in each country they visited. While Jack admired the nobility of General Jean de Lattre de Tassigny, the French military commander he met in Hanoi, for instance, he sensed the war he was fighting was "foredoomed."

More important than any other knowledge Jack gained over the course of their journey was the strength of heart he discovered in Robert Fitzgerald Kennedy — and the extent of his brother's love for him. The evidence came during a moment of mortal peril when Jack, thousands of miles from home, suffered a frightening new episode of his Addison's disease. The younger brother more than rose to the occasion, showing his guts under pressure and also his resourcefulness. He got things done.

As Jack was flown from Tokyo to a U.S. military hospital in Okinawa, Bobby never left his side, keeping watch over him as his temperature rose to 106 degrees and he became first delirious, then comatose. It looked like he was dying, and for the second time he was given the last rites.

The upshot of this latest brush with death was a memory an older brother would be unlikely to forget. Where Jack had once seen only the puritan, he now recognized the protector.

Back home, Jack Kennedy once again focused on his quest to leave the U.S. House of Representatives behind. In his mind he was already out of there, and even began disparaging the 435 members as "worms." He'd had it with the House. He'd already begun spending weekends campaigning statewide, and the map hanging on the wall of his Bowdoin Street apartment was starting to be thickly covered in pins. Those were Dave Powers's markers indicating where a speech had been made or where his boss had shared a coffee with a significant political leader.

The time had come to face the big challenge. For him, running for governor in '52 would only be a connecting flight to the next destination. Chuck Spalding could see his friend's determination. Eventually, "if he was going to get anywhere, he'd always have to be able to beat somebody like Lodge . . . So, I think, he made the decision, 'I've been long enough in the House. It's time for me to move ahead. If I'm going to do it, I've got to take this much of a chance.'" Pitting himself against Henry Cabot Lodge — *now* and not later — had overwhelming appeal. Above all, it showed audacity, a quality that ranked high with Jack.

On December 2, 1951, Kennedy made the admission, rare for a politician, of personal ambition. He did it during an appearance — his first — on NBC's *Meet the Press.* The moderator had wasted no time zeroing in on the hot political rumor buzzing through the Bay State.

Lawrence
Spivak: When I was in Boston last week, I heard a good deal of talk about you. There were many who thought that you would be the Democratic nominee for the sen-

	atorship against Henry Cabot Lodge. Are you going to run?
Jack Kennedy:	Well, uh, I'd like to go to the Senate. I'm definitely interested in it. I think most of us in the House who came in after the war — some of them have already gone to the Senate, like George Smathers and Nixon and others, and I'm definitely interested in going to the Senate, and I'm seriously considering running.

But, to anyone paying attention, it was obvious it wasn't just the intramural rivalry of his '46 House classmates driving him. His thinking about matters beyond the scope of the typical House member, his grander notions, were in every way a part of who he was, of who he had become.

The mind of Jack Kennedy, in fact, was already busy with the big picture. He'd been traveling the world since his teens. He'd witnessed Britain and Europe up close in the late '30s, he'd fought in the war and come back to see the depressing events in postwar Europe and Asia. He'd honed a personal sense of what was wrong with U.S. influence abroad.

On his trip to the Far East, for instance, he'd had an eyewitness look at the predicament of France trying to hold on to its empire after

World War II, against the local resistance to colonial power. What he saw was the overriding strength of the Vietnamese people's desire for independence.

"You can never defeat the Communist movement in Indochina until you get the support of the natives," he explained in a speech on his return, "and you won't get the support of the natives as long as they feel that the French are fighting the Communists in order to hold their own power there. And I think we shouldn't give the military assistance until the French clearly make an agreement with the natives that at the end of a certain time when the Communists are defeated that the French will pull out and give this country the right of self-determination and the right to govern themselves."

He also articulated that Sunday morning a strong critique of the way America represented itself overseas. On that same *Meet the Press,* Spivak quoted back to Kennedy a remark he'd made about our diplomats being "unconscious of the fact that their role was not tennis and cocktails but the interpretation to the foreign country of the meaning of American life." Is this something, he wanted to know, Kennedy had seen for himself?

"I think something ought to be done about it. I think there are a lot of young men interested in going into the Foreign Service. I don't know where they get a lot of the ones I saw. I think we're not getting the representative, well-rounded type of young man to go to the Foreign Service that we should as a rule. . . . I was up at a college in Massachusetts two days ago, speaking, and I asked, out of five hundred students how many would be interested in going into the Foreign Service, and a surprisingly large number raised their hand. What I think is that they're not getting young men who are well-rounded, who are balanced, and who are what we like to think of as representative Americans."

This call to service for young Americans — especially as they might affect the developing world — marked the beginning of an idea that, a decade later, inspired the country. It was one of many emblematic ideas evolving in his mind even now.

That trip to the Far East had been a confidence builder. Upon his return, Jack had shared what he learned with the voters. It was a repeat of his performance in 1946 as he'd entered the political arena. Back then he'd talked mainly of his experiences in the Pacific Theater, along with the need to prevent another war like the one just ended.

Since then he'd grasped, both instinctively and intellectually, the central importance of nationalism in the new world order and how it would affect Great Power relationships, most crucially those between the United States and the emerging Communist monoliths of Russia and China. What he witnessed, and also deeply understood, was the way that people struggled to free themselves from foreign control. It was a fight that Kennedy, the Irishman and Mucker, could feel in his genes.

He was discovering his ability to absorb complexity. In understanding the dangers facing his country, he saw, too, the role he might play. He had a mission now. To survive the Cold War, his country must grasp its nature. If he could get to the Senate, he might change history.

Despite his resolve to move forward, come what may, Jack began 1952 still unsure which office he would now seek or who'd help him win it. He'd spent four years traveling the state, decorating the map with those pushpins, hitting small towns that statewide Democratic candidates rarely visited. But still he needed an organization that could deliver the vote. He needed *people*.

The very first recruit to the cause was Lawrence F. O'Brien, with whom Jack had earlier been friendly down in Washington and now got in touch with to see if he'd come on board. When Jack met him, O'Brien was on the staff of another Massachusetts congressman, Foster Furcolo. Before taking that job, he'd worked in his family's cafe and bar in Springfield. Well connected in Democratic politics in Springfield, he'd served as manager for three of Furcolo's campaigns.

One day on Capitol Hill, the two of them, Jack and Larry, had dinner, during the course of which O'Brien declared he'd had enough of Washington. Perhaps he'd also had enough of Furcolo. He was heading home.

At a later meeting in Boston, Kennedy asked him to help out with his own effort in the Springfield area, and O'Brien agreed. But it took a strong-arm play by his former boss to complete O'Brien's transition to Kennedy loyalist. O'Brien had agreed to set up a public meeting for Kennedy, only to have Jack get word from Furcolo that Springfield was *his* turf and he wanted it called off. Jack replied, too bad, he intended to go ahead as planned and Furcolo would just have to live with it.

Larry O'Brien was impressed. The son of Irish immigrants whose dad was a local Democratic leader, he saw Jack Kennedy as a new kind of Irish politician, virtually the antithesis of the typical Democratic pol from Boston. "Republicans were respectable. Republicans didn't get thrown in jail like Jim Curley," O'Brien would write, describing the divide between the two parties as it had long been. The thing was, Jack Kennedy was "respectable" in a whole new style. And what O'Brien, a seasoned strategist, saw was how Jack Kennedy could win votes, especially in the Boston suburbs, that the Democrats had been losing because of the dishonesty of scoundrels like Curley.

"But Jack Kennedy was different. If the Yankee politicians had their snob appeal, so did the Kennedys. Those suburban sons and daughters of immigrants might not say 'I'm a Democrat,' but I hoped they could be brought to say, 'I'm for Jack Kennedy.'"

To O'Brien, his new ally, Jack made the extent of his ambition clear. Pointing at the Massachusetts State House from the window of his Bowdoin Street apartment, he put it this way: "Larry, I don't look forward to sitting over there in the governor's office and dealing out sewer contracts."

In aiming high and refusing to be satisfied with even the governor's job — when what he wanted was to be a senator — Jack was showing how much his ambitions paralleled his father's. Joe Kennedy refused to settle for what his fellow Boston Irish regarded as good enough achievement, an upper-middle-class level of success. Joe wanted more — and allowed nothing to stand in his way. In his own words: "For the Kennedys, it's either the castle or the outhouse."

Besides O'Brien, the other key recruit joined the team as a result of Bobby Kennedy's intervention. In February 1952, Bobby got in touch with his college roommate Ken O'Donnell, suggesting he join the campaign effort. "He called me and said Jack was going to run, had not decided for what, but he was going to run."

Ken O'Donnell was a hybrid — a middle-class Irish guy who'd gone to Harvard, but whose dad had been the legendary football coach at Holy Cross. Raised in Worcester, he was both town and gown. In World War II, he'd served in the Army Air Corps based in Britain and flown more than thirty missions over Germany as a bombardier, often in the lead plane. During the Battle of the Bulge he was forced to crash-land between German and Allied lines. But his most harrowing exploit came when he'd had to climb down and kick loose a bomb stuck in the doors. He'd ended up hanging on to the plane for dear life — certainly a strong memory to carry into one's postwar career, and also a character-building one. His football career at Harvard only added to his appeal. On all counts, Ken O'Donnell was the kind of guy Jack Kennedy could admire and, eventually, trust.

At their first meeting to discuss the job, just five days after the call had come from Bobby, Jack was put off by O'Donnell's questioning of him. The problem was that Ken had asked him which office he actually wanted to run for, a reasonable enough question for a prospective campaign worker. Jack didn't like it. One reason was that he didn't know the answer. But Ken O'Donnell was just the kind of guy Jack needed to win, no matter his place on the ballot.

At home in Harvard Yard and on Soldiers Field, O'Donnell was equally at ease with those "lace-curtain" Irish who'd gained wealth and social self-esteem. Yet he knew, too, the working class with all its awe of pedigreed Yankees like Henry Cabot Lodge, Jr., and its entrenched resentment of the lace-curtain types. He knew the begrudgers, those Irish who made a specialty of hating those who either had a leg up on them or acted as if they did. Winning Ken O'Donnell's steadfast loyalty, which he soon did, was one of Jack Kennedy's crowning lifetime achievements.

Ken recognized Jack's voter appeal long before he went to work for him. "He started getting our attention because he made statements and did things that weren't the norm for politicians in Massachusetts. When he didn't sign Curley's pardon petition, it didn't mean much in terms of the position, but it meant something to my generation. We quietly watched . . . and here was a guy who bore some watching. Frankly, his money had something to do with it. He was wealthy, so he could be independent of the political machine. They can't crush him the way they can somebody else, because he has both the money to stand up to them and the guts to tell them to go to hell. He was one of us. He is a veteran. He has had enough. He can afford to take them on."

"Them" was personified by the name Henry Cabot Lodge. And, to illustrate exactly the weight that name once carried in the Commonwealth of Massachusetts, consider this famous bit of doggerel penned by a Holy Cross graduate:

In the land of the bean and the cod,
The Cabots speak only to the Lodges,
And the Lodges only to God.

The current Henry Cabot Lodge was the grandson of the first Henry Cabot Lodge, who'd beaten Jack Kennedy's grandfather John "Honey Fitz" Fitzgerald for the U.S. Senate. He was the Republican who'd successfully crushed Woodrow Wilson's struggle to establish the League of Nations following World War I.

In 1936 his grandson, at the age of thirty-four, assumed the ancestral Lodge seat. Then, in 1942, the younger Lodge joined the U.S. Army and served gallantly in North Africa while remaining a senator. His outfit won the distinction of being the first American unit in World War II to make ground contact with the German army. When President Roosevelt ordered that men serving in both the military and the Congress make a choice between the two roles, Lodge left the army in 1942. But after winning reelection that year, he chose to give up his seat to rejoin the army, the first senator to do so since the Civil War.

As a lieutenant colonel, Lodge distinguished himself in Europe by once single-handedly capturing a four-man German patrol. He was decorated with the French Légion d'Honneur and the Croix de Guerre. At the end of the war, he served as liaison officer and interpreter in the surrender negotiations with German forces. In 1946, he ran for the Senate again, now a handsome war hero come back to serve the people. As such, he drew extraordinary respect, especially among the Irish, who usually voted Democratic. He was viewed by them as a man of the people, a man's man, a strong-jawed Yankee who was a regular enough guy to come have a beer at the local bar. Though times were changing, such condescension still went over well. Lodge was the kind of high-standing Brahmin the Irish looked up to.

Ken O'Donnell understood that Senator Lodge was more than the well-born patrician, more than just his name or his family tree. He recognized the reality of Lodge's very genuine accomplishment, returning from the war and in '46 beating Senator David I. Walsh, a powerful Democratic fixture on the state's political scene for nearly half a century. "Lodge, killing off Walsh, became the giant of Massachusetts politics. He had a good organization, excellent staff, and he was honest. Lodge was everything people wanted in a politician."

By early 1952, Lodge was a major figure in national Republican politics. He would soon be an even greater pillar of the party. It was he who, sticking his neck out, asked General Dwight David Eisenhower, formerly supreme commander of the Allied Forces in Europe and now supreme commander of NATO, to run for president. When Ike rebuffed his proposal, Lodge went on *Meet the Press* and promoted the idea publicly. With the general's quiet support, he soon accepted the job of Eisenhower's campaign manager, entering him in the New Hampshire primary. When his candidate beat the Ohio senator known as "Mr. Republican," Robert A. Taft, in that momentous contest, Lodge had not only pulled off a considerable coup, but was now the closest advisor to a five-star hero headed for the White House.

Mark Dalton, a good friend to Jack whose speechwriting ability was his greatest asset, had been the official "campaign manager" for that first congressional run in 1946. More a pipe-smoking intellectual than a tough, savvy strategist, Dalton was once again nominally in charge of what was happening, but with no title and no real power. Unfortunately, he possessed none of the organization-building or tactical skills necessary to get up and running the sort of statewide campaign now called for. Besides that, he was absolutely incapable of mustering the strength to withstand the meddling of Jack's father, the nature of whose influence — he was paying the bills — could never for an instant *not* be dealt with. And this was a job that needed doing.

For all his wily self-made rich man's shrewdness, the estimable Joseph P. Kennedy lacked political sense. Good at making money, he had little or no gift for democracy. He thought you got your way in this world by cozying up to people at the top, and bossing everyone else. His notion of putting together an effective campaign team was to get a squad of old political hands together and then start barking orders. That was no playbook for winning elections, certainly not the one against Henry Cabot Lodge.

Therefore, the first thing O'Donnell — whose political grasp was instinctive — looked to accomplish once he signed on to Jack's effort was to get the old man's hands out of the pudding. And not just that, but from the instant he arrived on the scene, he recognized an even bigger issue, which was that nothing had been done, throughout those early months of 1952, to build a statewide organization that could ever hope to come together to unseat the formidable incumbent. What was deadly clear to O'Donnell was the extent to which the two problems were intertwined.

No one had the nerve to stand up to Joe Kennedy when it came to naming Kennedy "secretaries" across the state. O'Donnell recalled: "I said to Dalton, 'Look, we need to name a secretary or leader in each community to be a Kennedy man, and then that person can form committees and set up events, but we can't be sitting in this office.'" Soon, Ken would conclude that Dalton simply was "too nice to be in politics." But that wasn't the same as solving the problem.

Jack himself could not make up his mind. He wouldn't fire Dalton, but at the same time he wouldn't give him the authority to do the job, not even the title. If Dalton was too weak, and he, O'Donnell, too much the newcomer, then who was there around who'd be able to short-circuit Joe Kennedy's meddling, to talk back to him and keep him on the sidelines? Only one man seemed to fill the bill, O'Donnell concluded: his old roommate, Bobby.

Bobby, O'Donnell knew, understood how to gain his father's approval, for the simple reason that he'd spent his young life doing it. It was a task that Jack, who kept his distance from his father and was always wary of him, couldn't manage. By being the good son, Bobby had earned and could now cash in on his father's trust. If Jack was to win this election, the question of bringing in Bobby would have to be answered. And soon.

The date for Jack's big decision was April 6. That's because Governor Paul Dever had scheduled that date to announce which job he was running for. Would the governor think he might be able to beat Lodge, or would he decide to play it safe and seek a third term?

Joe Healey, Jack's Harvard tutor, went with Kennedy when he was summoned to the meeting with Dever, which took place at the grand old Ritz-Carlton across from the Boston Public Garden. "We arrived at the Ritz about three o'clock, went to a room, and waited. Governor Dever had a topcoat on, and he said — and I think these were his exact words — 'Jack, I'm a candidate for reelection.' And Jack said, 'Well, that's fine. I'm a candidate for the Senate.'"

There were many factors joining together to favor Jack Kennedy's Senate run in 1952.

A keen observer, Jack saw it was now the case that, whatever they'd felt previously, Irish voters could now express pride, and not resentment, when called upon to identify with their most socially and financially successful family. His own personal charm had a great deal to do with how the Kennedy name resounded. So did all the countless hours he'd put into meeting voters and making them feel that a connection had been made and that he was, really, one of them.

The Kennedy "teas" were a smart combination of old and new. A novel concept, they served to boost awareness of Jack's senatorial campaign, and at the same time create followers who would then, they hoped, turn into volunteers. The official hosts at the kickoff tea would be the former ambassador to the Court of St. James, the Honorable Joseph P. Kennedy, and his wife, Rose. After all, everyone knew the pair of them had spent time in London among the English. Why wouldn't they want to hold a "tea" to meet and greet the people of Massachusetts?

Thus, Kennedy's background, rather than his party, became the major element in his attractiveness to voters. What worked splendidly was the way the teas bridged the obvious gap. The invitees were excited and pleased to be there — working-class and middle-class women alike. It proved a brilliant strategy for claiming the majority of voters.

Across the state, Jack's attractive sisters Eunice, Pat, and Jean hit the hustings for him as they had in Cambridge six years earlier. Everywhere these events took place, Jack Kennedy came off as the kind of aristocratic Irishman that the public enjoying the cakes and cookies hadn't seen before — one of theirs, and yet the perfect challenger, well matched against the elegant Henry Cabot Lodge.

As David Powers would note, one basic truth about these receptions was that here was an invitation turning up in mailboxes amid envelopes normally filled only with bills. Finding themselves requested to come have tea with the Kennedys left many of the recipients astonished — and pleased. For the first tea held in his gritty hometown of Worcester, Ken O'Donnell made certain the invitations went out — specifically — to regular Catholics, rather than "lace-curtain" ones.

Here's his description of that afternoon: "It was a beautiful day. He was on crutches. He walked in and the room came to a halt. Everyone stared. He walked in and took over, and every one of those people just had hands on him, wanted to shake his hand and touch him. This little Italian lady was wearing a new dress and hat and gloves she paid $100 for and she could not get to him fast enough. They weren't the hoity-toity rich, they were the hardworking poor of Worcester, but today, this day, they all looked hoity-toity, all dressed to shake the hands of that young congressman and his family. The place was packed, lines out the door. You could not move. Packed. I knew then, *'We've got something going here. This guy, he's got it.'*

"He spoke, shook every single person's hand in the room. He was on crutches, and, by the end, it was clear his hand was swollen — and it was evident to me he was in pain, real pain. I remember being concerned about him. It was the first time I realized he had substantial health issues. I hate to say it, but I was concerned, also, from a political standpoint. I realized there was something more to his health problems and I was wondering what it was. I also was wondering whether you can elect a candidate who has to be on crutches all the time.

"He wasn't well known in Worcester. He hadn't spent a lot of time in Worcester, and hadn't gotten any good press in Worcester. It was something different. I wouldn't have gone, myself, and I didn't think my mother would go, but she was there. I was shocked to see her and all her friends. *Shocked.* I had never known them to bother with politicians. Then, I just *knew.*

"You're talking two or three thousand people on a Sunday who came out to meet him. They went through the line once and they'd go back again, then shake his hand again, then just stop and watch him, just watch him. They would not leave. Nobody would leave until he left, and even after he left they all just stood there in awe. It was just that I had never seen anything like it. I just felt this guy could go all the way."

In fact, the very visible strains of his physical infirmities caused Jack Kennedy — greeting voters as he stood there on crutches — to resemble distantly, and despite his wealth, a character like Dickens's Tiny Tim. His simple fortitude compelled people to root for him. When X-rays taken of Jack's spine in 1951 showed the collapse of support bones in his spinal column, it could hardly have been surprising to anyone who spent time with him, especially out on the road. Charlie Bartlett, who joined him on some of these trips, remembered Jack keeping a stiff upper lip through it all. "I must say, he always had a sort of stoic, sociable quality about it. He'd drive all over that damn state. With that back it must have hurt like hell, and he'd sit there with the coat collar up and drive through those cold Massachusetts evenings."

But even though Ken O'Donnell was now convinced Jack might actually have a very good shot at winning against the formidable Lodge, what was still needed was someone to run the show. "The whole operation had degenerated into a three-ring circus, with Joe Kennedy coming in once in a while disrupting things, Jack showing up only rarely, and nothing getting done the minute he left." Somebody had to play middleman.

"I knew the Kennedys well enough by then to know the only one who can talk to the Kennedys is a Kennedy. It took a Kennedy to take on a Kennedy. I knew Bobby was the only one with enough sense, who was tough enough and a regular enough guy to run the campaign. He'd be the only one able to turn to the father and say, 'No, Jack won't do it.'"

At this point Ken made his move. He phoned Bobby and laid it on the line, all but demanding he drop everything and get up to Massachusetts to run his brother's campaign. Otherwise, Jack was going to have his butt handed to him. Bobby hated what he was hearing, for the understandable reason that he wanted to build his own career as a Justice Department lawyer and thus his own life. But he could hear his friend's argument, knew it, probably, even before he heard it. Someone had to broker matters between his dad and Jack. He was the one — the only one — to do it, and do it right.

Now that Bobby seemingly was willing to leave his job and come run the campaign, there was the problem of selling Jack on the idea. O'Donnell recalled the scene in the car when he and his boss went head to head on it. The truth was, Jack didn't like hearing Ken had talked to Bobby without going through him first, but, at the same time, and despite his irritation, he saw the point.

First, Jack sounded off. He, above all, seemed stunned to learn that there'd been any lack of action on the part of his people. As O'Donnell remembers the tongue-lashing, Kennedy couldn't believe they hadn't begun naming local secretaries across the state. "As far as I'm concerned, this moment you can go ahead and begin. I'm not interested in the nuts and bolts of who's going to run what. That's the job of the organization and not the candidate."

But, after he'd finished giving O'Donnell a taste of his anger, he'd also obviously talked his way into a decision. Ken O'Donnell had won. "That was the day that Bobby decided he would move to Massachusetts. Bobby, as I recall, went back to get his own personal affairs in order, and then he came up."

Mark Dalton had seen it coming. Though he had his own law practice, he'd been volunteering time for Jack's political career, mainly writing speeches, ever since the victorious '46 race. He'd now given up his practice and come to work full-time for the congressman. It was a change in status, from friend and unofficial counselor to paid aide, and it would matter.

For him, the decisive incident occurred at a meeting at a social club in Fall River. As he made to leave, Kennedy had to pass the bar, where was parked a convivial trio "feeling no pain." The men garrulously corralled Kennedy. Dalton, ignoring the candidate's plight, had continued alone to the parking lot.

It was the wrong move. Jack wasn't happy. "He got in the car, turned around, and stuck his finger in my belly," Dalton recalled a half century later. "'Don't you ever let that happen to me again.'" Now he got the picture. "I was to take care of him with drunks. I was his caretaker, his bodyguard. That son of a bitch! Right in the belly! 'Don't you ever'!"

Jack's rough treatment of his old pal was a sign of something off-kilter in the relationship. For him, the problem with Dalton wasn't about getting waylaid by the Fall River drunks; rather, it was about the campaign,

195

his father, and the way things felt stalled. The final moment for Dalton came at a meeting where Joe Kennedy tore into him for leasing a new campaign headquarters without his permission. "He didn't like the building," O'Donnell remembered. "He thought we'd paid too much for it. He didn't like the owner. He thought the location was bad, and they had a great brawl about it."

When Jack refused to stand up for his campaign manager, Dalton had no choice except to quit. Bobby made the gesture of trying to soften the blow by asking him to stay on as speechwriter, but Dalton left the office that day with his belongings and never returned. "I decided that I could no longer play a role in the Kennedy campaign in view of the feeling which had developed. I wrote John a little note saying I was through and then I told him that I was through." Listening to him so many years later, it was obvious that Dalton never got over the way he'd been discarded.

Once Bobby arrived, he began working eighteen-hour days to get the campaign workers focused and up to full speed. "I didn't become involved in what words should go in a speech, what should be said on a poster or billboard, what should be done on television. I was so busy with my part of it that I didn't see any of that." Most important, when he moved in, their father moved out.

This was, just for the record, not Bobby Kennedy's first involvement in a Jack Kennedy campaign. He had a talent for organization. In the '46 race, as a twenty-year-old, he'd asked for the toughest area, East Cambridge, territory loyal to the former Cambridge mayor Mike Neville, Jack's strongest opponent, Tip O'Neill's candidate. But Bobby took it slowly, laying the groundwork, spending time playing softball with the kids of the neighborhood, killing the notion that the Kennedys thought themselves superior. His brother ended up doing better in that community than anyone had expected.

Bobby enjoyed one advantage over Jack, and it had to do with their attitude toward Joe. While his brother was stubborn in his dealings with their father, Bobby was respectful and needy for love. This created a smooth relationship, even if one layered with guile. He proved to be the essential cog in the Kennedy machine. No one else could have done what he was now doing. There he was, having left his job in Washington, working all out in the campaign, using his father's resources — money and public-relations clout — to produce the maximum impact where it counted, on the hearts and minds of the Massachusetts voters. Charlie Bartlett remembers listening to Bobby on the phone with the senior Kennedy. "Yes, Dad," Bobby kept repeating, "Yes, Dad." However, he wasn't taking orders; rather, he was pacifying. Where Jack always took their dad with a grain of salt and didn't mind letting him know it, the younger Kennedy boy never treated him as less than the paterfamilias.

It was now May and the election was six months away. Out in the field, Larry O'Brien was helping the cause by building the organization from the ground up, one Kennedy "secretary" at a time. What this meant, at a very basic, very significant level, was the creation of a totally different political network from that of the regular Massachusetts Democrats. "Our secretaries were making weekly reports to me, and they were growing more sophisticated from week to week. . . . For a long time neither Lodge nor the Democratic regulars realized what we were doing."

At their April 6 meeting at the Ritz-Carlton, Governor Dever had made it clear that Jack was going to have to build his own organization. Meaning, if he chose to go up against Lodge, it was his show, for he wouldn't be getting any help from Dever, who had his own race to run. But such a challenge also suited the Kennedy people. They wanted solid loyalty from their people, no confusion about which candidate mattered most.

For me, Ken O'Donnell personified the old brand of politics, which the Kennedys were customizing on a family basis. From the moment he signed on, he had one vocation:

helping and protecting John F. Kennedy. And right now, in the summer of 1952, his value lay in his ability to grasp and use the reality of post–World War II Massachusetts, the world he knew. As a man who'd lived between Worcester and Cambridge, between Holy Cross and Harvard, he had a natural understanding of those voters Jack Kennedy needed to pry away from Lodge. They were folks whose parents were loyal Democrats, while they, this new generation, reserved the right to cast their ballot candidate by candidate.

What Jack Kennedy was trying to do, helped by O'Donnell and others, wasn't going to be easy. They were trying to outflank Lodge, a moderate Republican, from the right and the left. In other words, Kennedy had to come off as both a tough Cold Warrior and a work-and-wages Democrat — which is precisely what he'd spent six years being. This allowed him to strike at his rival from the right for not being aggressive enough on foreign policy and from the left for not being sufficiently on the side of the average family struggling to make ends meet; that is, for not being a Democrat. It was a pincer move that was to work well again in a later Kennedy campaign. The strategy is to bash an opponent on both sides until you force him to go both ways to avoid the very charges you're making against him. The voter sees the targeted rival being pulled apart by his own hands.

Kennedy set his people digging for weak spots in Lodge's record. "Lodge was always on the popular side of every issue, which didn't necessarily make him an awfully good statesman, but might make him a satisfactory politician," Jack told Rip Horton. To prepare for the planned bombardment of Lodge, Ted Reardon, who'd been Jack's top aide on the Hill, began assembling an inventory of his voting on the issues. This carefully documented loose-leaf binder, each page covered in sheer plastic, was soon dubbed "Lodge's Dodges" — or, more irreverently, the "Bible" — and it provided the ammunition for the coming all-out assault.

Joe Healey, Kennedy's speechwriter, found himself impressed by Reardon's attention to Lodge's every word, tracking down every discrepancy. "The major credit belongs to Ted Reardon for certainly one of the most thorough jobs in this area I have ever seen."

From this point on, the campaign's operating structure quickly fell into line. Bobby, as the campaign manager, decided where the money went. This is always the supreme power that comes with that title. "Any decision you wanted, Bobby made," O'Donnell recalled. "If you were talking about spending two hundred bucks to do such and such, Bobby would say, yes, go ahead, and that was it."

The Kennedy Party, as it continued to grow,

was the perfect model of a volunteer operation. Those who came to work for Jack found themselves making a personal investment in the candidate's future, resulting in a campaign of relationship rather than transaction. In this sense, it wasn't about political payoffs, at least not in the business-as-usual way. Anyone who walked into a Kennedy headquarters was, right off the bat, given a task to do. His people knew the best method of earning and toughening loyalty was by quickly getting a newly interested citizen onto the team. Before you knew it, you were a "Kennedy person."

What happened, as in 1946, was that word would start to spread that a member of this family or that friend or neighbor was "working for Jack Kennedy." It made the campaign a kind of cement, ever expanding its hold. You pretty much *wanted* to take part. It was as simple as that for many people. And so the organization built on itself.

To enforce this, Bobby Kennedy repeatedly made it clear to one and all that there were to be *no* paid campaign workers. No exceptions. One local political veteran who'd supported Jack's campaign in '46 would learn the hard way that the campaign manager this time around wasn't about to be messed with. Here's Ken O'Donnell's account of what happened when that fellow failed to take the hint:

" 'How much money is the candidate going to give us to spend in our district?' this guy called out at a meeting. When Bob Kennedy ignored him and kept to the order of business, the man then stood up and cut Bobby off. 'Listen, kid, we've been around a long time, we know politics. You're wet behind the ears and you'd be better off in Washington than here, where you don't know what you are doing. You've got to pay these people; you want campaign people out working for you, you got to pay them, and you can afford it. The Kennedys are rich.' Bobby just stared at him. Then he got up, grabbed him by his collar, and showed him the door — and, as he was throwing him out in the street, he told him, 'Would you mind getting lost . . . and keeping yourself lost.'"

When the troublemaker appealed his case to Jack, Bobby didn't like it one bit. "Look, you get one guy like that crying, then you have to pay him and his volunteers to work. Then other people hear about it, and then they want to be paid to volunteer, and then we'll end up spending a million dollars in Boston alone. I'm not going to have him around. You asked me to run this campaign. I didn't want to, but now I'm here, so I will run it my way."

Jack was actually tougher than his younger brother. When Governor Dever began to worry that he was going to lose his race and saw Kennedy gaining strength, he offered to combine forces. Joseph Kennedy liked the idea; O'Brien and O'Donnell didn't. Jack agreed with his people, refusing to be Dever's life preserver. He gave Bobby the job of delivering the decision to his father and Dever both. "Don't give in to them, but don't get me involved with it," were the instructions. The older brother was becoming a hard-nosed, unsentimental politician. Bobby's role was to play the *part* of one.

From the beginning, the teas that started it all proved to be an excellent recruiting platform. As O'Donnell was to explain, "Nobody went to one who didn't fill out a card. We had them in every community, and . . . they allowed our organization to get going and to get our secretary in action." They became competitive events. "When Lowell had four thousand, Lawrence had to have five thousand. So the secretary had a great incentive."

Hugh Fraser, one of Jack's British friends visiting at the time, was impressed by the novelty of these occasions, referring to them as "shenanigans." "The 'tea party' technique amazed me," said Fraser, who'd never seen anything of its kind.

Anyone who organized a tea was required to provide a quota of signatures for Kennedy's nomination papers. Only 2,500 signatures statewide were required for a candidate in the Senate primary, but Dave Powers and Larry O'Brien had decided that they'd ask the regional organizers to produce a grand total of 250,000. The reason, according to

O'Donnell, was not just "psychological"; it was also a way to have a quarter-million voters not only committed but actively participating in the early stages, before the real fight started up in the general election campaign. Too, it was a gauge to help them figure how the organizers were performing and which ones were particularly effective.

The teas were aimed at winning the hearts of the working class, and also as a means of identifying and organizing the Democratic voter base. But equally crucial was the need to go after those Irish and other traditional Democratic voters who'd drifted away and might very likely stay drifted with the popular Ike as the Republican candidate.

It had been customary for statewide Democratic candidates in Massachusetts to expend their major effort in the larger cities, where most of their voters lived. In other words, they counted heavily on Boston. Jack Kennedy, instead, went out and methodically hit every neighborhood, including the largely Republican suburbs, ignoring the toll this relentless, unsparing, but extraordinarily effective effort to reach voters took on his physical well-being.

O'Donnell figured that Jack Kennedy could pull votes in small suburban communities where no other Democrat might. "We appreciated the fact that there were an awful lot of Democrats throughout the state, in those small towns, who'd moved out of Boston and out of the big cities into these small communities, had bought their own homes. They were Democrats, but ashamed of some of the antics that had been associated with the party." He saw these as potential Kennedy people.

Here again, Kennedy had gotten traction from his early start in places off the standard grid for Democrats. "We'd be in those homes — in the homes with seven or eight people, who'd remember having coffee with Jack Kennedy in 1947 or '48," said O'Donnell.

The Second World War had changed a great deal in American life. In the Northeast, as elsewhere, the Irish and other ethnic groups were seeing beyond the old boundaries, and didn't want to be the pawns of the big-city political bosses. They wanted the fresh air of the suburbs, the freedom of making up their own minds at election time. Many had gone to college under the GI Bill. They no longer felt confined by the politics of the old neighborhood. "Boston" meant a certain kind of old politics, and a sort they were only too happy to leave behind. This sense of the shifting times was definitely an idea the Kennedy campaign made skillful use of.

As election day approached, Tip O'Neill, facing no real opposition in the general election, got a call asking him to lend a hand. He was to be Jack's stand-in at an election-eve radio broadcast. Tip's script from Kennedy headquarters arrived just minutes before airtime. It "kicked the living hell out of Henry Cabot Lodge," O'Neill would recall, to his chagrin. Senator Lodge, who spoke next, was outraged by what he regarded as an ambush, and told O'Neill's wife, Millie, "The Kennedys would never give a speech like that for him. And I would never say the things about Jack Kennedy that he was saying about me."

Lodge had a far bigger problem. Throughout the course of the campaign he'd been greatly distracted by his efforts, begun the year before, to promote Eisenhower. This had earned him the bitter hostility of Republican voters steadfastly loyal to Ike's opponent for the nomination, Senator Robert Taft of Ohio, "Mr. Republican." Here Joe Kennedy saw his opportunity. He convinced the pro-Taft publisher of the New Bedford *Standard-Times* to reprint in full the glowing *Reader's Digest* article on his son's *PT 109* exploits, then to break ranks and endorse the Democratic candidate, young Jack Kennedy, outright. When Jack went on the attack, criticizing Lodge's absenteeism from the Senate, the newspaper dutifully repeated those charges in its editorials. Next, when Lodge countered by citing Kennedy's own poor voting record, the *Standard-Times* refused to publish the information.

To gain the endorsement of the equally conservative *Boston Post,* Joseph P. Kennedy got out his checkbook to write its pliable publisher a loan for $500,000. About this episode, Jack would later joke that for him to win his Senate seat his father had to "buy a fuckin' newspaper."

To pound home Lodge's weakness among Taft Republicans, Jack accused him of being a "100 percent" supporter of Truman's appeasing administration policy in China and the Far East.

But if Lodge was overly committed to Eisenhower's candidacy, Jack Kennedy was undercommitted to Adlai Stevenson's. He simply could not disguise his lack of faith in the Democratic presidential nominee, and, after having breakfast with him at the 1952 Democratic National Convention, Kennedy complained about his encounter to a friend, "Well, for Christ's sake. I don't know why I allowed myself to be railroaded into *that.* That was an absolutely catastrophic breakfast."

"What happened?" asked his listener.

"Well," Jack explained, "practically nothing happened. As I saw it, he was looking at me and he knew that I didn't really think he was the best candidate. He knew that I knew that he knew."

The one man who might possibly have saved Lodge's bid for reelection refused to help. When an S.O.S. came from Lodge's campaign asking Wisconsin Senator Joseph McCarthy to come to Boston and make a speech on behalf of the incumbent senator, McCarthy demurred. He told the conservative columnist William F. Buckley, Jr., in whose Connecticut home he was staying at the time, that Lodge had always opposed him. Young Jack Kennedy, on the other hand, he counted as a covert supporter. McCarthy even told Buckley he'd made the Lodge people a counteroffer he knew would surely be refused. "I told them I'd go up to Boston to speak if Cabot publicly asked me to. And he'll never do that; he'd lose the Harvard vote!"

Richard Nixon, meanwhile, had been put on the ballot as the Republican nominee for vice president, Ike's running mate. It was a skyrocketing leap for a congressman who'd gone to Washington the same year as Jack. The latter was gracious in a handwritten note. "Dear Dick: I was tremendously pleased that the convention selected you for V.P. I was always convinced that you would move ahead to the top — but I never thought it would come this quickly. You were the ideal selection and will bring to the ticket a great deal of strength. Please give my best to your wife and all kinds of good luck to you."

The Kennedy campaign, meanwhile, presented its own man as every inch an anti-Communist crusader as any Republican. When Adlai Stevenson made a campaign stop in Springfield, Massachusetts, Sargent Shriver — who was an employee of Joe's in Chicago and would marry Eunice Kennedy the following year — sent him a very pointed note. "Up there, this anti-Communist business is a good thing to emphasize."

Sarge Shriver also let it be known, in a briefing paper, exactly what the Kennedy people wanted the Democratic presidential candidate to say about the local boy when speaking on his behalf. Stevenson should say it was Kennedy, not his Republican colleague from California, Richard M. Nixon, who'd been the first to expose Communists in organized labor. He "was the man . . . that got Christoffel . . . not Nixon."

The pitch was legitimate. Earlier in the year, Jack had attended an anniversary dinner of the Spee, his Harvard club. There, one of the speakers told the gathering how proud he was that their college had never produced "a Joseph McCarthy *or* an Alger Hiss." Kennedy jumped from his chair. "How dare you couple the name of a great American patriot with that of a traitor!" he exclaimed, and left the dinner early.

The Kennedy family's close association with Joe McCarthy wasn't an asset everywhere in the Commonwealth. In fact, it hurt him badly with one particular community. Jewish voters had reason enough to question the younger Kennedy's attitudes, given his father's record of unveiled anti-Semitic comments and sentiment. Now the senior Kennedy once more expressed himself outrageously and stirred up the problem anew. When a campaign aide passed around a proposed statement attacking McCarthyism, Joe Kennedy went wild. "You and your . . . sheeny friends . . . are trying to ruin my son's career." Although Jack tried to assure the campaign worker, who was not himself Jewish, about his father, the episode became notorious.

Senator Lodge saw an opening. His campaign began distributing literature spotlighting a report by Herbert von Dirksen, who'd been the last German ambassador to Great Britain before World War II. In it the author recounted Joseph Kennedy's support for Hitler's prewar actions against the Jews. Lodge then recruited Congressman Jacob Javits of New York, a Jewish Republican, to come and speak to a large Jewish gathering in Mattapan. In his talk, Javits stressed repeatedly that Jack was "the son of his father." As Tip O'Neill remembered the event, "He didn't have to be any more explicit."

But Javits, one of the smartest national legislators of his era, also had an indictment of Jack personally. Publicly critical of President Truman's spending policies, Kennedy had voted for a House amendment to cut back foreign aid. While the measure dealt with the overall Middle East spending package, the reduction affected Israel, too. Despite Kennedy's out-front backing for the creation of the Jewish state and his recent visit to the country, Javits's attack stung. As O'Neill told

the story, it took Majority Leader John Mc-
Cormack himself to damp down the fire by
spinning it that Kennedy had voted a "token"
reduction of U.S. aid to Israel in order to
save it from a larger cut. It was a simple case
of a respected politician — McCormack was
known as "the Rabbi" for his strong support
of Jewish concerns — looking out for a fellow
Democrat.

The father's reputation, nastily earned as
it was, would always be a problem for Jack.
As Ken O'Donnell himself noted, "You can't
stop a whispering campaign if it's true." If
Jack could never adequately defend his father's attitudes, he certainly didn't share
them. He knew that Jewish fears were legitimate. "They have problems you don't know
anything about," he'd remind O'Donnell.

His health, too, continued to be an issue he
could never ignore. In October he made the
mistake of sliding down a fireman's pole in
Everett, Massachusetts, an impulsive act that
worsened the state of his already weakened
back. "He was in intense pain towards the end
of the campaign," his aide John Galvin recalled. "I'm convinced that there were times
when he was walking around almost unconscious."

Despite such all too real medical handicaps,
which couldn't be disguised, the boyish Jack
continued to win fans. That summer of 1952,
three hundred Capitol Hill news correspon-

dents had voted Congressman Kennedy of Massachusetts the "handsomest" member of the House. In order to capitalize on this perception, Jack proceeded to sign up for a special course offered by the CBS network on how to use the new medium of television to best advantage; it was a savvy move, since, by then, about half the households in the country owned a set. This habit of self-improvement was a pattern he continued, going on to take other courses in subjects ranging from speed-reading to public speaking.

On November 3 — the eve of Election Day — General Eisenhower, the Republican candidate for president, ended his national campaign in Boston. Ahead in the polls, he was completing his march to the American presidency bearing tribute to the man who'd led him to the fight, the noble Henry Cabot Lodge.

" 'It looks like Eisenhower's going to win easily,' " Torby Macdonald recalled telling Jack as the ballots were being counted the next night, " 'but I don't think that necessarily means it's going to affect you in Massachusetts.' He said, 'Why not?' I said, 'Well, I think you represent the best of the new generation, really, the newly arrived people. And Lodge represents the best of the old-line Yankees. I think there are more of the newly arrived people than there are of the old-line Yankees.' "

Macdonald never forgot what came next. "Then, out of the clear blue sky, he asked me a question. 'I wonder what sort of job Ike will give Cabot?' I just thought to myself that if I were in Jack's position, listening to these returns . . . Where do you get that kind of serenity?

"By twelve o'clock that night, there was a definite conclusion that Eisenhower had carried the state by 200,000 votes. John Barry, a well-known writer for the *Globe,* went on TV and said authoritatively: 'On the basis of the returns now received by the *Boston Globe,* it is definite that Governor Dever has been defeated for Governor of Massachusetts, that Congressman Kennedy has been defeated, and Senator Lodge has been reelected to the United States Senate.'"

"Well, all hell broke loose," O'Donnell recalled the moment. "The congressman called Bobby, furious — and Bobby cut him off and said, 'Look, on the basis of our numbers and our chart and the basis of what we have and our computations, we are winning the race. And if the trend continues with little drop-off, we will defeat Lodge. The television and newspaper predictions are wrong.'"

O'Donnell, O'Brien, and Bobby remained optimistic. Based on their calculations, the Kennedy vote was doing what it had to even as the candidate kept calling the headquarters and arguing.

"Finally, he got so frustrated he came down around midnight or so," O'Donnell said, "and began to run the slide rule himself. He went town by town, and we walked him through it. But it became confusing to him, and he just kept telling us that the reports we were getting on the television and those we gave to him simply did not square at all."

Governor Dever then telephoned and told Kennedy that, on the basis of the returns, they were both defeated and should concede together. O'Donnell recalled the dramatic response. "The congressman, who by now had learned our system — in fact, had made some improvements to it, typically, and knew it better than we did — said to the governor . . . that on the basis of our computations we were *not* defeated — and that, in fact, on the basis of our figures he was about to win by a narrow margin."

At this point, there remained a general sense Kennedy had lost. Looking beyond their headquarters, they could see what appeared to be the electoral reality. Outside there were rowdies — "Irish bums," O'Donnell called them, local fellows with various bones to pick — shouting drunkenly, "Jack Kennedy, you're a loser and a faker! You're in the shithouse with your old man!" Mainly, they were giving it to Bobby, who'd been the tough guy in the campaign.

By then, according to O'Donnell, "it was

just us sitting around drinking coffee. Even most of the girls had left. It was a very disheartening moment.

"At about three or probably closer to four in the morning, only the major cities were still out . . . Worcester . . . Springfield . . . and I remember Bobby and the congressman began to give me some grief, because I'd dismissed the hand-picked Kennedy secretary the congressman had selected in Worcester — he was a faker and I'd replaced him with someone I knew and trusted. Now Bobby was saying to me, 'Everything rides on Worcester and your judgment. If we lose, it's your fault.'

"Well, it was beautiful: he hadn't completed the sentence, literally not gotten the words out of his mouth, when I got a call from our man in Worcester saying we'd carried it by five thousand votes. And that, we all knew, was the final clincher. The congressman and Bobby looked at me in astonishment. Then the congressman said to me, 'You're either the brightest or the luckiest SOB on the planet!' "

After the votes were tallied in the big cities, with Worcester and Springfield now in the Kennedy column, the candidate continued strongly, surpassing other Democrats. "Even in these little towns, we were running four, five, or six percentage points ahead of any Democrat and ahead of Dever. The margin of victory can really be found in all those small communities where he'd spent all that time and done all that work in for the past six, seven years. It was now paying off. Every weekend he could, he'd been out there meeting people, having coffee with them, handshaking — and it was now paying off as it was intended to." The Kennedy Party strategy had worked.

The proud incumbent, there in his headquarters across the street, refused to accept defeat. "We could see him sitting there in his suit coat, looking very calm, watching the returns. What's he waiting for? Why won't he concede? What does he know that we don't? The senator-elect kept asking me, 'Are you sure?' Yes, we were sure, but we were worried. At one point, he even joked, 'Is this what victory looks like?' We were sitting at the card table — the congressman, Dave, Bobby, Larry, myself, and just a few of the girls. The fair-weather types had all gone home.

"Finally, about six or six thirty, Lodge conceded. He walked across, looking dapper, and the congressman, now the senator-elect, said what a bunch of bums we all looked like. 'Put a tie on, for God's sake,' he told Bobby. Lodge came over and shook the newly elected senator's hand. He seemed very disconnected, as if he still could not comprehend that this young fellow had somehow bucked the tidal wave called Eisenhower.

"We ended up winning by seventy thousand votes in a very tight contest; I mean, we knew we were winning, but we also recognized it was very tight. The governor had lost by four-teen thousand votes at this time."

Lyndon Johnson telephoned immediately after the results were in, causing Jack to re-mark, "That guy must never sleep." O'Brien, though, saw the cunning: "Johnson wasn't wasting any time in courting Kennedy's sup-port." The Senate's democratic leader had just been defeated and Johnson was gunning for the job.

The next night there was a celebration, and all the Democratic hacks and coat holders and meal tickets shamelessly showed up, driving O'Donnell and O'Brien crazy. Unfazed by the strange faces in the room, the victor per-formed in classic fashion. "The senator-elect got up on a table and sang a song in that fa-mous Kennedy off-tune manner. It was pretty awful. Then it was he and Bobby singing to-gether, in a duet. It was just awful, too."

The Eisenhower-Nixon ticket carried the country by 7 million votes. In Massachusetts, Adlai Stevenson suffered a crushing defeat. Jack Kennedy, meanwhile, had carried the state against Ike's number one man.

He'd taken on the best and beaten the best. He walked out of the race with a solid organi-zation. He had shown his ability to cut people loose — Mark Dalton, after all, had been a close, deeply devoted champion — who failed to meet his needs. All the while, he let his younger brother take the heat for such acts and thus gain the reputation for being the ruthless one. Bobby, Kenny O'Donnell, and Larry O'Brien were now a rare combination of ice-cold efficiency and die-hard loyalty. The skipper had a new crew, a great one. They'd been blooded by a tough battle fought against the odds and won.

Jack and Bobby — and Kenny, too — would be together for the duration, and they would stand together in the worst crisis of the Cold War, when the stakes were much higher than a Senate seat.

CHAPTER SEVEN
MAGIC

She could be amusing in a direct, caustic way; and she understood the art of getting on with men completely . . . never asked an awkward question.
— David Cecil, writing about
Lady Melbourne in *Young Melbourne*

In Washington, Tip O'Neill was moving into his new office in the House of Representatives. By coincidence, his predecessor was packing up right across the hall. As he stepped into Jack Kennedy's outer office, Tip could hear him engaged in a heated backroom argument with his secretary, Mary Davis.

"Mary, now don't be silly. You're coming to the Senate with me."

"No, Senator, I'm not. I'm going to be working for Congressman Lester Holtzman of New York."

"Now, Mary, you know you're coming with me."

"I am not, Senator, and that's all there is to it."

O'Neill could hear the dispute going back and forth. Finally, he heard Mary say, "And the reason I'm not going with you is that Congressman Holtzman has offered me six thousand dollars."

"Tip, can you believe this?" Jack said when he walked out and saw O'Neill.

"I'm paying her four thousand dollars, and I've just offered her forty-eight hundred. That's a twenty percent raise. But this guy wants to give her six grand the first day he's here. There's not a broad in the world worth six thousand a year."

Mary Davis had similar memories of the standoff. When Kennedy won the Senate race, she accepted the mission of building a clerical staff. To this end, she recruited a team of secretaries to assist her with managing the mail and other constituent work.

"They were all experienced, knew exactly how to do things, what to do, where to go, and they really could have been an invaluable asset to the functioning of his Senate office. But he called me one day from Palm Beach and said that he'd been discussing the situation with his father, who wanted to know: Did you find out exactly who they are, what they are, what the salaries are going to be?' "

Joe Kennedy, still watching the purse strings, wasn't above keeping his eye even on the funds the Senate provides its members for hiring staff. "I told him," Davis said, "what

I thought the salaries should be, in line with the money we were being allocated. I thought he was going to go through the ceiling!"

She was surprised because she'd set the pay levels for the skilled staff members she'd picked based on the standard allocations from the Senate. But while this might seem routine practice, and wholly acceptable, her focus on the reality of the office's likely day-to-day needs was, in fact, shortsighted. Her eye to office management and not political strategy, she was failing to consider the larger picture. It simply wouldn't have occurred to her that the Kennedys, father and son both, intended to start right away building a wider constituency, one that would extend far beyond the Commonwealth of Massachusetts.

The money, therefore, had to stretch further.

For this reason, Jack rejected both the top-drawer hires and the top-of-the-line pay scale. According to Davis: "He said, 'Well, I don't think we're going to be able to work that out.' And I said, 'Well, why not?' He said, 'Well, number one, I have to have a Polish girl on the staff, I have to have an Italian on the staff, I have to have an Irish girl on the staff, I have to have, you know, these different ethnic groups.' And I said, 'That's ridiculous! You know, a staff member is a staff member.' He said, 'No, *you* don't understand. I've got to have these ethnic groups.' "

Rejecting the pay levels she'd determined appropriate for the newcomers, Kennedy figured sixty dollars a week about right as an upper limit. He believed Mary herself was asking for too high a weekly check.

Hearing this, she was having none of it. "Sixty dollars a week! You've got to be joking. Nobody I've lined up would be willing to accept a job at that salary. I have to have competent, capable staff who can back me up. If I don't, I won't have a life to call my own."

She remembered only too clearly what came next: "His famous reply to me was, 'Mary, you can get candy dippers in Charlestown for fifty dollars a week.' And I said, 'Yes, and you'd have candy dippers on your senatorial staff who wouldn't know beans. If that's what you want, I'm not taking charge of it.'

"He didn't believe me. And that's when I said, 'Uh-unh. Not me.'"

So Tip O'Neill's memory was on the button. She'd continued to stand up to Kennedy despite numerous attempts on his part to win her over. He'd simply pushed her past the breaking point, and his cajoling was to no avail. After six years of working for him, Davis knew the man too well. The issue, for her, anyway, wasn't the money in and of itself. It was a question of whether Jack Kennedy, born to great wealth, was going to give her, Mary Davis, what she knew the U.S. Senate had decided was owed to anyone taking the supervisor job Jack was offering her.

In the end, he didn't budge.

What can be seen here is how the financier Joseph Kennedy exerted enduring control over anything in his son's life having to do with money. Well able to maintain his independence on the matters that counted most with him — policy, politics, his personal associations — Jack was faced with the fact that his father still could tell him what to do if there were dollar signs involved.

There was another rule in play here: when you worked for the Kennedys, you quickly learned that a staffer is a staffer. You needed to understand the limits of the relationship, and also the borders. Mark Dalton had learned that the hard way. As he would tell me, all those years of dedicated volunteering for Jack were forgotten the day he went on the Kennedy family payroll. Before him, the beloved Billy Sutton — the onetime press secretary, entertainer, and live-in buddy — had suffered the same fate. It seemed that he'd asked his salary to be upped from sixty-five dollars a week, a request Jack didn't take well.

Larry O'Brien, shrewder politically than the others, understood the problem and avoided it. "If you work for a politician, he tells you what to do, but if you maintain your independence, you can now and then tell him what to do." Seeing the lay of the land, he decided to return to Springfield after helping Jack win the Senate race.

O'Brien had the situation nailed. He'd worked hard to achieve a balance of mutual respect in his relationship with Jack, and he intended not to let it get *out* of balance. Even as his loyalty grew, so did his awareness of the senator-elect's nature. The man so steadfast in his friendships, carrying along pals from prep school, college, the navy, and his social world, looked upon staff as employees. He had his needs; they had their tasks. Each was obliged to understand his place as well as his task, to honor the bounds of his role and its tenure. The Kennedys believed that anyone could be replaced. So it was, even with a one-time boon companion like Billy Sutton.

Cut loose from the role he'd so cherished and filled so well, Billy still, years later, loved revisiting spots where once he'd hung out with Jack: the diner downstairs from 122 Bowdoin, Jack's apartment, the federal buildings where Jack's offices had been, and political hangouts such as the Parker House hotel. He was like a toy soldier waiting for its young owner to come back.

There's a measure of defense to Kennedy's cutthroat approach to personnel. In Washington, a city packed with people who kiss up and kick down, Jack never kissed up. Although it may not perfectly justify the harshness of his discarding people like Dalton and Davis and Sutton, each of whom had been powerfully loyal to him for a decent number of years, it does put it in the context of the place and its morality. Isn't the definition of a just man one who treats all the same? Jack Kennedy was equally his own man in both directions, caring no more for the feelings of those of higher authority than he was of those who served — or ceased to serve — at his pleasure.

His cheapness, though imposed by his father, came at some cost. George Smathers caught sight of the chaos left in Mary Davis's wake: "I'd go down to his office and it would always seem as in so much pandemonium, such a disarray . . . Everyone in his back office was very friendly, but it didn't seem to me as though there was any organization to it, and I used to tell him so." Jack couldn't believe he was hearing this from a colleague whose own operation was hardly a model of professionalism.

Smathers, to his credit, actually saw past the seeming daily disorder to what lay behind. "His mind was on bigger things. I never did feel that he was a well-organized man either in his personal life or in just the mundane matters of running an office. If the work got done, that was all that really concerned him."

His victory over Henry Cabot Lodge had placed him on a career pedestal sufficient for most men. Yet in Jack's own mind he was merely at the foot of the mountain he now contemplated climbing. To reach the top he would need to further share his vision and also himself, to let a lot more people know who Jack Kennedy was. Even more important, he'd have to successfully signal the country he was ready to lead it.

It was simply a matter of random placement, but Jack Kennedy's new Capitol Hill office was directly across the hall from that of the new vice president. Richard Nixon was in Room 362, Kennedy in 361. Already, both their futures, at least on the surface, seemed mapped out.

The inhabitant of 362, many figured already, was tagged to be his party's nominee for president once the incoming Ike finished his two terms. Opposite him, the senator assigned to 361 was marked to spend — and end — his political career as a New England Democratic moderate, a rich man's son with a celebrated war record who'd shown himself to be a tough Cold Warrior. Being a Roman Catholic, the limitations to Senator Kennedy's political future were clear to any observer. Hadn't the country been electing Protestants to the White House since the first peal of the Liberty Bell?

Even before Kennedy moved into Room 361, he was interviewing people to sit at its desks. One of the hopefuls was a twenty-four-year-old lawyer from Nebraska. Ted Sorensen had grown up a world apart from the Ivy League, from Cape Cod, from the Stork

Club, and from the U.S. Navy. He came from Scandinavian and Jewish parents, had been a conscientious objector and a dedicated supporter of Adlai Stevenson. What grabbed Jack about him, perhaps, was a reference he presented that praised his "ability to write in clear and understandable language" and, more important, called him "a sincere liberal, but not the kind that always carries a chip on his shoulder." Jack liked him already.

The result was a five-minute meeting in the hallway outside the office of the Massachusetts senator. Of the encounter, Sorensen would write, "In that brief exchange, I was struck by this unpretentious, even ordinary man with his extraordinary background, a wealthy family, a Harvard education, and a heroic war record. He did not try to impress me with his importance; he just seemed like a good guy."

Sorensen was surprised even to have been summoned for an interview. He'd sent in his application despite hearing that Jack hired only staffers his father himself might choose. Meaning Irish Catholics, and with few exceptions to this rule. Yet it took only five minutes for Kennedy to make the decision to hire the young stranger. It was another example, one of the most important in its consequence, of Jack *not* being his father's son.

Ted Reardon, tapped to run the Kennedy senate office just as he had the House operation, understood what was happening. Jack was starting to reach beyond his old regulars and past the Massachusetts Irish. He was upgrading his team. He wasn't picking new pals; he had different criteria now. "Jack had the ability to have guys around him whom, personally, he didn't give a damn about as a buddy . . . but he was able to get what he needed from them."

Ted Sorensen was the ideal Kennedy staffer. Not only would he go on to help draft some of Kennedy's most glorious words, ones that stirred the world and resonated down through the decades, but he knew his role. In time it became hard for either man to say who had written what. Ted offered many of the lyrics, but it was always Jack's music. If they were never social intimates, theirs was a collaboration of the heart. Indispensable as he was, Ted Sorensen would write extraordinary prose under the spell of Jack Kennedy.

However, there were issues Sorensen wanted to resolve before coming on board. Although anti-Communist, he was also anti-McCarthy, and so requested a second interview with the senator-elect. It was then he voiced to him his concerns that "he was soft on Senator Joe McCarthy and his witch-hunting tactics. JFK must have thought I was a bit odd, as well as headstrong and presumptuous, a new job applicant asking questions about his political positions. But he did not resent it, calmly explaining that McCarthy was a friend of his father and family, as well as enormously popular among the Irish Catholics of Massachusetts."

Kennedy went on to tell Sorensen he didn't "agree with McCarthy's tactics or find merit in all his accusations." Hearing it all, Sorensen accepted. Now, for the first time, Jack had someone at hand whom neither his father — nor his late brother — would have hired. For Jack Kennedy, Ted Sorensen would be his "intellectual blood bank," providing him the Churchill-like phrase-making we now associate with him. "I never had anyone who could write for me until Ted came along," Kennedy would later tell Tip O'Neill. There was cruelty in the comment, and it bothered O'Neill. Before Sorensen arrived, Jack had gotten speechwriting help from his former Harvard tutor, Joe Healey, who was also a good friend of O'Neill's.

As for Sorensen, he understood the boundaries. "I never wanted to be JFK's drinking buddy; I wanted to be his trusted advisor." It was enough for him — or, at least, he protested as much to the end — to be "totally involved in the substantive side of his life, and totally uninvolved in the social and personal side."

Clearly, Jack had found a devoted ally, someone who could see through to the idealist in the politician. Sorensen knew whom he was serving. "He was much the same man in private as he was in public. It was no act — the secret of his magic appeal was that he had no magic at all. Few could realize, then or now, that beneath the glitter of his life and office, beneath the cool exterior of the ambitious politician, was a good and decent man with a conscience that told him what was right and a heart that cared about the well-being of those around him."

Yet it didn't take Sorensen long to realize he and Jack came from very different worlds. "During my first year in JFK's Senate office, when dropping me off after work to catch my bus home, he confessed that he had never ridden one in his life."

They spent an enormous amount of time together, working, thinking, and planning. Not long before his death, Sorensen wrote this: "I do not remember everything about him, because I never knew everything about him. No one did. Different parts of his life, work, and thoughts were seen by many people — but no one saw it all."

In the beginning she was Jackie Bouvier. The year was 1951. To hear the name now conjures up that early time and a young, fresh beauty untouched by fame and position.

But what was it about this young woman? Looks, certainly. Jackie was stunning, with large eyes so far apart it took two eyes to see them. Her beauty was original. She was elegant, self-contained, aristocratic. To Jack she was the only woman he "could" have married, he once confided to Red Fay.

Charlie Bartlett had been one of Jack's best friends ever since they met and began hanging out together in Palm Beach in 1945. Now living in Washington, where he was working for the *Chattanooga Times,* he remained a careful observer of his pal. "The thing to remember, and that really made him special in my book, was a mind that went right to the problem. I mean, he must have inherited it from his old man. When you discussed anything with Jack, politics mainly, he'd go right to the bottom. He had a wonderful way of separating all the crap from the key issue. . . . It made him great fun to discuss things with.

"He always had a pretty clear picture of the motives of the people he was with, and he was good on that. I don't know how to say it, but Jack wasn't, sort of, in love with humanity. He was cool. His attention moved quickly. That mind would start going, and he did get bored awfully easily. This was part of his being spoiled, and I found it sometimes annoying. I mean, if you wanted to get into a long story, why, you were apt to not have Jack with you at the end of it."

When the moment came for settling on a partner, Jacqueline Bouvier managed to grab his attention and hold it. She possessed both the personality and the pedigree. She also lacked what Jack himself lacked: a childhood cushioned by a warm upbringing. She, too, had been raised by a cold, willful mother and had a father — the handsome but philandering, alcoholic stockbroker known as "Black Jack" Bouvier — who did exactly as he pleased. Whether she told him about her childhood, or he intuited it once they'd met, it could have made her intriguing. Jack was most of all driven by curiosity.

Asked once to describe Jackie in a word, he chose *fey*. Her otherworldly qualities made her unlike all the other women he'd known and dated. She was detached, elusive, like him.

Jackie, who'd spent her first two years of college at Vassar, followed by a junior year in France, was finishing her college degree at George Washington University. She felt about France the way Jack did about Great Britain. Like Jack, she'd sought escape and refuge in books when she was young, especially as she sought shelter from her parents' stormy marriage. Her father, John Vernou Bouvier III, was as unreliable as he was attractive, and her parents' 1928 marriage lasted just a dozen years. Jacqueline Lee — Lee was her mother's maiden name — was the firstborn child, in 1929; her sister, Caroline Lee, known as Lee, came four years later. Jack Bouvier was sixteen years older than Jackie's mother, Janet.

Jack Kennedy, twelve years Jackie's senior, noticed that their age difference seemed to appeal to her.

Jackie's part-time job at the *Washington Times-Herald* as an "Inquiring Camera Girl" resembled the one Inga Arvad once had held, while requiring far less writing. All Jackie had to come up with were brief captions for the snapshots she took of whoever was being featured that day.

The encounter that set off the romance between Jack Kennedy and Jacqueline Bouvier occurred one evening at Charlie Bartlett's house. "I leaned across the asparagus and asked for a date," Jack would recall in a much-quoted line. A Georgetown dinner party was a perfect setting for what began — at least, in the eyes of others — as a fairy-tale union, and became an almost mythical one.

Even at the outset, though, the courtship was uneven; nothing out of the ordinary there. Jack would ask her out for a date, then disappear. Yet he always returned. Following his election to the Senate, he proposed in '53, and she accepted. The chemistry between them, however you try to analyze it, was undeniable, and they knew it.

While he was wooing her, Jack presented Jackie with copies of his two favorite books, John Buchan's autobiography, *Pilgrim's Way,* and Lord David Cecil's *Young Melbourne.* These men each expressed, in their different ways, ideals of honor, sacrifice, and political nobility that continued to inspire him. When she learned his favorite poem was Alan Seeger's "I Have a Rendezvous with Death," she memorized it. In the years to come, he would often have her recite it for him.

"Jack appreciated her. He really brightened when she appeared," Chuck Spalding recalled. "You could see it in his eyes. He'd follow her around the room watching to see what she'd do next. Jackie interested him, which wasn't true of many women."

Jackie's temperament, though, was very far from the rambunctiousness of the large and competitive Kennedy brood. "Jackie was certainly very bored by politics and very bored by the very aggressive camaraderie of the Kennedy family, which was absolutely foreign to her nature," Alistair Forbes said. "Fortunately, I think, she also spotted that it was really foreign to Jack's nature." She saw him as being more sensitive and "much less extroverted than they all were."

Jackie offered the handsome and popular young senator a social status he didn't quite have on his own. For all their recently amassed wealth, his family was still nouveau riche and thus lacked entrée to certain clubs, certain circles. Jack knew it, didn't like it, but made the best of it. His friends, mostly, were like him — the sons of the successful — but others, met at Choate and Harvard and in

Palm Beach, were from old money or old bloodlines. Charlie Bartlett, himself an old-line Yalie, could see the effect the Bouvier name had on his friend.

Bartlett, however, liked to speculate, in later years, on what Jack's life would have been like had he chosen another sort of wife. "There was this beautiful girl up in Boston. Her name was K. K. Hannon. Her father was a policeman. She was gorgeous. If Jack had married her, she could have dealt with him, I think. She was Irish and tough and damned good-looking. But, no, he had to marry up."

Jackie, whose father's infidelities had helped destroy his marriage, recognized she was marrying a husband of similar habits. "Well, she knew what she was getting into when she married him," Bartlett said. "She was in love with Jack, and he had this terrible habit of going out with these other girls." As Bartlett figured it, his friend's intended bride simply made a vow that she'd "take it all on, and she did."

Jack's concern was more on the politics of his decision. "I gave everything a good deal of thought," he announced in a letter to Red Fay out in San Francisco. "So I am getting married this fall. This means the end of a promising political career, as it has been based up to now almost completely on the old sex appeal. Let me know the general reaction to this in the Bay area."

In fact, with an eye to the likely fallout from the coming change in his marital status, he managed to keep secret his engagement until after *the Saturday Evening Post* had run a long-planned feature headlined "Jack Kennedy: The Senate's Gay Young Bachelor." Later, without telling his fiancée, he invited a *Life* photographer along on a sailing trip that she'd supposed would be time alone for them.

To reap the political benefit of their boss's engagement, O'Donnell, together with O'Brien, began to plan a large event for all the "Kennedy Secretaries" from the previous year. To get the reluctant Jack to agree, they told him, "They haven't seen you since the election and they all want to give you a gift and so forth," O'Donnell recalled his pitch to the bridegroom. It was a classic, canny Kennedy event, a party to honor the engaged couple for which the guests paid admission and were more invested in their hero for having done so. "For the time and the place, it wasn't cheap. But the faithful were willing to shell out ten dollars for a chance to see the senator they'd helped elect and to meet his beautiful fiancée. They felt included, even 'related.'"

O'Donnell described the celebration he staged: "They paid for their meal, paid for their drinks, and they gave the senator and Jackie a gift. One of the few organizations in the history of mankind that were paying him instead of him paying them, but we knew he wouldn't pay for it, so we had to, or he wouldn't come — since he didn't want to, anyway. Though, once they were there, he had a great time."

The wedding party convened the weekend of September 12, 1953, in Newport, Rhode Island, where Jackie's remarried mother, now Mrs. Hugh Auchincloss, lived at Hammersmith Farm. The groomsmen included Lem from Choate, Torby from Harvard, and Red Fay from the navy, plus Chuck Spalding, Charlie Bartlett, and George Smathers. The ceremony was held at St. Mary's, a nineteenth-century church in the Gothic style. Society pages around the country pronounced it the "wedding of the year."

When Fay showed up, the ever-competitive Jack asked him as soon as the two men were alone what he thought of Jackie. "I said, 'God, she's a fantastic-looking woman.' And then I added, 'If you ever get a little hard of hearing, you're going to have a little trouble picking up all the transmission.' " Jack laughed, loving his navy pal's reaction to the classic Jackie whisper.

Jack was about to embark on a new life, yet there remained evidence that he himself, the onetime Mucker ringleader, had changed little over all those years. Fay noticed the way he enjoyed the bit of culture clash that occurred between a few of his cronies and the Newporters. "Almost across the street from Hammersmith Farm were the green fairways of the Newport Country Club," he said, "where I'd often played during the war. The gentry of Newport had opened up their club for men in uniform, but with the end of the war the doors had shut tight again."

Somehow, Fay and Kennedy's aide John Galvin — "looking more Irish than Paddy's Pig" — got themselves onto the course to play a round. At this point Fay hadn't realized that the relaxed wartime regulations were no longer in force. The club had returned to its firm rule that all nonmembers must be accompanied by a club member. "I hope you two enjoyed your game of golf," Jack teased them, "because as a result of it there was almost a total breakdown of relations between the mother of the bride and her dashing prospective son-in-law. I'm afraid that they feel that their worst fears are being realized. The invasion by the Irish Catholic hordes into one of the last strongholds of America's socially elite is being led by two chunky red-haired friends of the groom."

Still, the temporary vibe of spontaneous, unpredictable fun was welcomed by at least a few Newporters. Fay recalls a comment made by the lifeguard at a nearby beach where the Kennedy guests were swimming and playing touch football. "I want to tell you," the young man said, "this is the first time this place has had any life in it since I've been here."

The wedding weekend was not proceeding without discord. Jack had asked Red to be the master of ceremonies at the bachelor dinner. Eventually, this favoritism seemed to cause resentment among his fellow ushers, especially as the evening wore on and more alcohol was imbibed. "Torby Macdonald stood up at the other end of the table, took his water glass, and hurled it the length of the table; and it hit me on the chest. Then it fell to the table and shattered. Since I'd had a few drinks, the natural response was to start down the table after him. Luckily for me — because I'm sure Torby would have taken me apart — Jim Reed and the president, then senator, grabbed me and the thing was averted."

Also in attendance at the wedding and the dinner were Ken O'Donnell and Larry O'Brien. As the former describes it, "There were only a few political people invited, and we stayed together and talked politics. I met some of the gentlemen for the first time, like Spalding. I'd known Lem through Bobby. I met Smathers for the first time. And Charlie Bartlett. But we didn't talk to them much. The Boston political guys sat with the other Boston political guys and drank with the Boston political guys, and we mostly talked politics and what the future might be for the senator."

Lem Billings, Jack's oldest friend, felt the need to have a personal heart-to-heart with the bride. "She was terribly young, and I thought it would be best if she were prepared for any problems. So I told her that night that I thought she ought to realize Jack was thirty-six years old, had been around an awful lot, had known many, many girls — it sounds like an awfully disloyal friend saying these things — and that she was going to have to be very understanding at the beginning. I said he had never really settled down with one girl before, and that a man of thirty-six is very difficult to live with. She was quite understanding about it and seemed to accept everything I said."

Rather amazingly, Lem then reported this exchange to Jack. "Of course, later I told him everything I'd said to her — and he was pleased because he felt it would make her better understand him."

Chuck Spalding had his own telling memory of the weekend. To him, it was as if his friend were actually two people at his own wedding — one being the groom, and the other a grand observer of the entire event, watching it as if from afar, the way an outsider might see it. To Spalding, this other Jack was totally detached from what was happening, this lifetime pairing of him with another.

On the wedding weekend, one thing is sure, which is that the newlywed Jack Kennedy was clearly thinking beyond the imaginings of the ordinary groom. Sailing in the waters off Hammersmith Farm, he gazed at his wife's

241

family's cove on Narragansett Bay and said to Bartlett, "This would be a helluva place to sail in the presidential yacht."

By the time the honeymooning couple arrived in San Francisco — they'd gone first to Acapulco and then on to San Ysidro Ranch in the hills above Santa Barbara — the reality of the union between the thirty-six-year-old Jack Kennedy and twenty-four-year-old Jackie Bouvier was asserting itself. Here's Red Fay's account of hosting the two near the end of their wedding journey: "When Jack and Jacqueline came to the West Coast on their honeymoon, the pressures of public life too often intruded on the kind of honeymoon any young bride anticipates. For example, on their last day on the West Coast, Jack and I went to a pro football game. I'm sure this didn't seem a particularly unusual arrangement for Jack."

Jack Kennedy continually craved such fresh company. He liked the rush of excitement that came with it. Perhaps that enjoyment was rooted in those times in his youth when he'd been confined to bed. Bored easily by sameness, he preferred to keep moving, wanted the movie to stay exciting, liked people to be forever fascinating — and he wanted never to be alone, or too long with the same person.

The trouble was, as at least one friend saw it, those around him let him get away with it. In Charlie Bartlett's words, "they spoiled

him. . . . They spoiled the hell out of Jack.
. . . I wish they hadn't, actually." People came
to understand that, attractive as he was, Jack
could be coldly self-indulgent. Yet his company was magnetic and his joy in life was irresistible.

Jack and Jackie were, both of them, like
characters out of Fitzgerald, two people with
old-world aspirations, but like most Americans, self-inventing. Lem Billings, I think,
had it right when he said: "He saw her as a
kindred spirit . . . he understood the two of
them were alike. They had both taken circumstances that weren't the best in the world
when they were younger and . . . learned to
make themselves up as they went along. Even
the names, Jack and Jackie: two halves of a
single whole. They were both actors, and I
think they appreciated each other's performances. It was unbelievable to watch them
work a party. Both of them had the ability to
make you feel that there was no place on earth
you'd rather be than sitting there in intimate
conversation with them."

Chapter Eight
Survival

The world breaks everyone and afterward many are strong at the broken places.
> — Ernest Hemingway

Jack Kennedy had faced death often in his life. He'd spent much of his teenage years with doctors examining him, saying what an "interesting" case he presented. Leukemia, even, was mentioned. He never did manage to escape the knot he felt in his stomach, a chronic reminder of the frequent invalidism he'd lived with in youth and which now followed him into adulthood. When the Japanese destroyer cut through *PT 109,* barely missing him, the pounding he took said, *This is what it feels like to die.* Once home, the surgery performed on his back left him with a pain he was forced to live with. In London, there was the diagnosis of Addison's.

In 1954, Jack had a choice to make. He could play it one way, living a diminished life that would lead, very likely, to worse. Or he could risk it all — just as he'd done when he left Plum Pudding Island and swam out into that channel in hope of rescue. He was thirty-seven years old and staring at a future that promised a different sort of torture than he might have suffered at the hands of the Japanese. His steadily worsening back promised a return to the sickbed he'd endured as a boy. This time, however, his dreamed-of future would no longer be looming before him, but, rather, drifting forever into the past.

He would, of course, throw everything he had on the table. Rather than accept a lessened existence, he chose to bet his life on the operating room.

The year began with him executing a masterstroke. As a freshman congressman, he'd shown his independence by withholding his signature from the sleazy Curley petition. Now, in his second year in the Senate, Kennedy made an even bolder move, separating himself from the ranks of his fellow New Englanders. He voted for the creation of the St. Lawrence Seaway, connecting the Atlantic Ocean with the Great Lakes. This meant backing a public works project that could mean the loss of Boston Harbor's importance as a major shipping port.

That 1954 January vote made him an unpopular figure in Massachusetts. It wasn't hard to understand why. The carving out of

Dumbarton Oaks **20**

21

McCarthy & Cohn

22

Ted Reardon

a direct route from the Atlantic to the Great Lakes could be seen in New England only in terms of its economic threat to the region. The Northeast was already in decline, and those factories engaged in shoemaking and in textiles, especially, were moving to the nonunionized, cheap-labor South. If ships could find their way to the Midwest without docking at Boston Harbor, huge numbers of jobs would be lost. The men and families who relied on those jobs — the townies of Charlestown and other harbor areas — wondered aloud why their young Irish representative in Washington wasn't now safeguarding them.

"The story circulated around the state," said Ken O'Donnell, who was friendly with many longshoremen, "that the Seaway was being built to take care of his father's Merchandise Mart . . . that he was caught at last, paying off Joe Kennedy for all the money he spent on the election."

In 1945 Joseph P. Kennedy had purchased the Merchandise Mart, the giant Chicago landmark and, at the time, the largest building in the world. Who stood to gain more from the opening of a direct shipping lane to the Atlantic than the man reaping the profits from this giant center for retailers and wholesalers situated there near Lake Michigan?

Tip O'Neill saw a grander political motive in Kennedy's vote. He spotted it as the first clear signal that Jack Kennedy's horizons stretched well beyond the job he now held. "I knew Jack was serious about running for president back in 1954, when he mentioned that he intended to vote for the St. Lawrence Seaway project. The whole Northeast delegation was opposed to that bill, because once you opened the Seaway, you killed the port of Boston, which was the closest port to Europe. The Boston papers were against it, and so were the merchant marines and the longshoremen. But Jack wanted to show that he wasn't parochial, and that he had a truly national perspective. Although he acknowledged that the Seaway would hurt Boston, he supported it because the project would benefit the country as a whole."

The burst of vitriol directed at him spurred his historical curiosity. "After he had been in the Senate for less than a year," Sorensen would write in his late-in-life memoirs, "JFK called me into his office and said he wanted my help researching and writing a magazine article on the history of senatorial courage."

Kennedy had come upon accounts of the heat John Quincy Adams — later the country's sixth president — had taken not quite a century and a half earlier for a transgression similar to his own. As a Massachusetts senator, Adams had voted against the economic interests of New England when he supported President Jefferson's embargo on Great Britain because of its attacks on American ships. As a result, he lost his Senate seat. Eighteen years later, though, Adams entered the White House.

Kennedy was another New Englander with wide ambitions. Still a Cold Warrior, he maintained his belief that the global struggle against Communism must remain his country's prime concern. "If we do not stand firm amid the conflicting tides of neutralism, resignation, isolation, and indifference, then all will be lost, and one by one the free countries of the earth will fall until finally the direct assault will begin on the great citadel — the United States," he would declare in a 1956 commencement speech at Boston College. He had only contempt for those men and women — and this included fellow Democrats — who refused to regard the fight against Communism as the essential struggle of the times.

Yet he worried how the struggle was being waged. A stark example was the desperate French fight in Indochina. Weakened by its humiliation in World War II, France was fighting to regain its international stature, to hold on to its colonial empire. Its conflict with the popular Vietnamese leader, Ho Chi Minh, had become a grinding war of attrition. Many on the American right, Vice President Richard Nixon included, wanted to go to the aid of the French. Communism, they felt, must be resisted on every square inch of global real estate.

When the North Vietnamese forces, the Viet

Minh, surrounded the French army at Dien Bien Phu in '54, Nixon grew more hawkish still, telling news editors he supported sending "American boys" to replace them. He then backed a secret plan, code-named "Operation Vulture," to drop atom bombs on the Viet Minh. He, other Republicans, and some Democrats like Jack Kennedy had blamed President Truman for "losing" China by not giving sufficient aid to the anti-Communist Chiang Kai-shek. The Eisenhower administration could not afford to lose Indochina.

Despite his own anti-Communism, Jack Kennedy resisted falling into line. For the first time, he broke with the Eurocentric view of the Cold War. He also challenged the Republicans' position that the United States could defend itself worldwide on the basis of its nuclear supremacy alone. We could not intimidate an adversary such as Ho Chi Minh with the threat of dropping a hydrogen bomb in the jungles of Indochina. It would not be credible.

The argument he was using was the same one he'd employed to justify Britain's failure to confront Hitler at Munich: the *capability* to fight such a war was not in place. "To pour money, material and men into the jungles of Indo-China without at least a remote prospect of victory would be dangerously futile and self-destructive. I am, frankly, of the belief that no amount of military assistance in

Indo-China can conquer an enemy that is everywhere and at the same time nowhere, 'an enemy of the people' which has the sympathy and covert support of the people."

Equally important to him was the reality he'd seen for himself during his trip to Indochina three years earlier. And that reality was the power of nationalism. On this issue Jack Kennedy found common ground with the newly elected Republican senator from Arizona, Barry Goldwater, who demanded, as the price for American aid, that the French promise Indochina its independence.

But it was closer to home that Cold War issues were causing Senator Kennedy the greatest challenges. Since January 1950, Joseph R. McCarthy, the Republican junior senator from Wisconsin, had made himself into a force to be reckoned with. His relentless effort to unearth Communists within the government and the American establishment made "McCarthyism" the one-size-fits-all label pinned to the national Red hunt. With bullying zeal, McCarthy and his Senate subcommittee unjustly tarnished and in some cases ruined reputations.

McCarthy was fueled by the temper of the times. In August 1945, the people of America had looked out upon a world dominated by the United States as by no other country in history. Within a year, the geopolitical shifts were so alarming that Winston Churchill spoke of an Iron Curtain being drawn down between free Western Europe and an Eastern Europe falling increasingly under the control of Moscow. Within two years, the victory in Europe had largely been undone. Czechoslovakia and Poland, the countries that had been the casus belli of World War II, were now under Soviet domination.

Other news from around the globe added to the sense of disillusion and insecurity across America. In 1949, the same year Mao Tse-tung claimed all of mainland China, the Soviets exploded their first atom bomb, an event that occurred shockingly in advance of American predictions — or expectations.

In 1950 came the conviction of the top American diplomat Alger Hiss, who'd presided at the United Nations Conference in San Francisco, which Jack Kennedy covered for Hearst, for his role in a Soviet espionage plot. The fear of Communism on the advance would spike violently with the coming of the Korean War. In July of that year, a thirty-two-year-old New Yorker, Julius Rosenberg, was arrested for helping to pass atomic secrets to Moscow; a month later, his wife, Ethel, was taken into custody.

This was the national mood when Joseph McCarthy entered stage right. He'd begun his crusade in January of 1950 in a speech to a Republican women's group in Wheeling, West Virginia. There he borrowed phrases from a speech Richard Nixon had just given on the Hiss conviction. McCarthy upped the ante by declaring that Hiss was only the iceberg's tip, that the State Department actually, if unknowingly, harbored large numbers of dedicated Communists — and all committed to the sabotage of American interests in favor of those of the Soviet Union. Unchecked, he would ride high on the brazenness of such charges, reaching his zenith of popularity in January 1954. At that juncture, 50 percent of the American people held a favorable opinion of the Wisconsin senator, just 29 percent an unfavorable one.

But his downhill slide was about to begin, precipitated by CBS's Edward R. Murrow, a broadcaster who'd made his reputation reporting from London during the Blitz and who was revered for his integrity. In March 1954, Murrow aired a special entitled *Point of Order!* in which he attacked McCarthy, and dared him to present an on-air rebuttal. McCarthy's response offers a classic example of how he strung together events to craft his outrageous indictments.

"My good friends," he said, "if there were no Communists in our government, would we have consented to and connived to turn over all of our Chinese friends to the Russians? If there were no Communists in our government, why did we delay for eighteen months, delay our research on the hydrogen bomb, even though our intelligence agencies were reporting day after day that the Russians were feverishly pushing their development of the H-Bomb? Our nation may well die because of that eighteen months' deliberate delay. And I ask you, who caused it? Was it loyal Americans? Or was it traitors in our government?"

There you have it, an absurd but compelling case against those in high places. It was the old charge of rot at the top. If the Chinese Communists took over China, it was the doing of Commies in our own government. If the Russians had sprinted forward and now had flaunted their H-bomb, it was because we'd slowed down to let them catch us. In short, if anything bad happened, the reason is we were stabbed in the back.

McCarthy loved charging respected figures with bad faith, thus lending a catchy populism to his accusations of treason. In his view, it was the country's best and brightest who were selling us out. "The reason why we find ourselves in a position of impotency is not because the enemy has sent men to invade our shores, but rather because of the traitorous actions of those who have had all the benefits that the wealthiest nation on earth has had to offer — the finest homes, the finest college educations, and the finest jobs in government we can give."

To validate this belief system, he fixed in his sights on such lofty officials as President

Truman himself, Secretary of State Dean Acheson, and his predecessor, George Marshall, who'd been army chief of staff in World War II. He attacked them all, famously calling Marshall the perpetrator of "a conspiracy so immense and an infamy so black as to dwarf any previous venture in the history of man."

Of course, no demagogue ever has a lifetime career, and Joe McCarthy's own downfall was determined when he decided to focus his crusade on the presence of hidden Communists in the U.S. Army. The target he selected for attack was an army major, Dr. Irving Peress, a dentist who'd been a member of the American Labor Party, believed to be a Communist Party front. When Peress's commanding officer at Camp Kilmer in New Jersey, Brigadier General Ralph Zwicker — a Silver and Bronze Star recipient who'd been a hero of the Battle of the Bulge — appeared before his committee, the senator taunted him, saying he was "not fit to wear that uniform."

That encounter showed the extent to which McCarthy was beginning to spiral out of control. His absolute fall from grace came a month later in a moment of television history. The newly launched American Broadcasting Corporation, ABC, covered gavel to gavel the thirty-six days of hearings convened. The April 1954 broadcasts of the Army-McCarthy proceedings gave the audience sitting at home the chance to examine McCarthy's own conduct as well as the wild charges he brought against army personnel.

Thus, with the entire country watching — on some days, as many as 20 million people — he self-destructed, with the help of a righteous attorney, Joseph Nye Welch, the army's chief counsel, who objected to the senator's innuendo-filled attack on one of his staff lawyers for a past membership in a left-wing legal group. Voicing his distaste, he accused McCarthy of "reckless cruelty" and then asked whether he had "no decency." It was a stunningly unexpected comeback, and one that marked McCarthy as a pure bully. For the first time, many Americans focused on Joe McCarthy's tactics and didn't like the looks of them.

Not everyone turned on McCarthy. More than a third of the country remained loyal to him after the five weeks of legal spectacle. His fellow Irish-Americans were especially defiant, seeing him as a lonely challenger to the country's political, diplomatic, and academic elites.

Within days of the Army-McCarthy hearings, Senator Ralph Flanders of Vermont, a Republican, introduced a resolution to censure his colleague and remove him from the chairmanship of his committees. It read, in part, "Were the Wisconsin senator in the pay of the Communists, he could not have done a better job for them." Now that public opinion had turned on him, the Democrats were free to cast Joe McCarthy as their ultimate arch-villain.

Jack Kennedy had a McCarthy problem and he knew it. Joining his fellow Democrats, who were now calling for McCarthy's head on a pike, put him in a serious dilemma. For one thing, up until this moment he'd successfully managed to say nothing on the subject of Joe McCarthy's harsh tactics. It was a silence he would, in the years to come, always have to answer for. Outside the Senate, moreover, he was actually known to be quite friendly with the man. The pair of them had hung around together during Jack's early congressional days, and McCarthy, handsome in a Black Irish way, had been out on dates with Jack's sisters. A close friend of Bobby's wife, Ethel, McCarthy was a kind of unofficial uncle to their two young children, especially the eldest, Kathleen. Because of his friendship with the Kennedys, McCarthy had refrained from endorsing his fellow Senate Republican Henry Cabot Lodge in the race he lost to Jack. The December before, Jack had been a guest at McCarthy's wedding, as had many of the Kennedy family.

Another problem for Jack was Bobby's closeness to the senator. For half the previous year, he'd been a McCarthy staffer. Their father, a financial supporter of the Republican senator as well as a friend, had helped pave the way for the job. However, Bobby had quit, smarting under the fact that he was outranked by the senator's chief counsel, Roy Cohn, a fellow whom he despised. But his departure didn't last long. The next January he switched sides, hired now by the investigating committee's Democratic minority as its chief counsel.

When the time came for the Democrats to move against McCarthy, it would fall to the twenty-eight-year-old Bobby, despite his continued personal loyalty, to write the draft of the Democratic members' report on the senator's out-of-control conduct. While it targeted Cohn's behavior, it placed responsibilities on the committee's chairman. "Senator McCarthy and Mr. Cohn merit severe criticism," and "the Senator cannot escape responsibility for the misconduct of Cohn. Nor can he excuse the irresponsibility attaching to many of his charges. The Senate should take action to correct this situation."

Still, it was one thing to staff the committee report, as Bobby, acting in his official capacity, had done. It would be a very different matter to vote for the historic censure of a colleague — a man who was also a friend — as Jack would now be asked to do.

There *had* actually been rumblings against McCarthy in the Senate for several years at this point, including a declaration made by his own party members that denounced smear tactics — in effect, McCarthyism — without mentioning the names of any specific lawmaker. In response, McCarthy contemptuously dubbed Senator Margaret Chase Smith of Maine, who originated the declaration, along with the six fellow Republicans who joined her, "Snow White and Her Six Dwarfs." With the Army-McCarthy hearings having weakened McCarthy and made him at last vulnerable, Senator Flanders's intention was now to deliver the coup de grâce.

Yet, even given the rising swell of condemnation, Jack Kennedy remained resistant when it came to voting to censure a man whose wedding he'd attended, for whom his brother had worked, and to whom his father had provided sizable contributions. Had Jack joined the vote against McCarthy, it would have meant a dramatic, even traitorous break with his father and brother, who'd devoted themselves so totally to his career and were not ready to abandon a fellow anti-Communist and close friend.

How was he going to handle it? Personal connections aside, there were other factors affecting his ultimate decision when it came to the McCarthy censure vote. An important one, of course, was how it played back home. The same people of Massachusetts who'd supported Jack on the basis of the old loyalties were largely — and vehemently — in McCarthy's corner. These men and women saw the battle as one pitting the Ivy League establishment against the working-class Irishman. For such Americans, here was a contest between those who seemed far too dainty, if not neutral, on exposing Communists in government and regular people who were willing to play rough.

It was bad enough Jack had gone to Harvard, but here he would be taking sides against one of his own — a fellow who happened to be the best-known Irishman in the country. It would be an act of betrayal, nothing less. Whatever Joe McCarthy's faults, most Irish-Americans viewed his motives as right, while those of his enemies were, at best, suspect.

In Jack Kennedy's own office, the enormous tribal significance of the McCarthy issue was brought home by Ken O'Donnell, whose brother Warren was then a student at Holy Cross. After Warren had delivered a strong classroom attack on McCarthy and his methods, his older brother recalled, "He was told to sit down, and the rejoinder from the priest, quite coldly, was: 'I guess I shouldn't expect anything less from someone whose brother went to Harvard and is friends with Jack Kennedy.'"

O'Donnell, who was running the Kennedy office in Boston, keeping watch on the constituents and their concerns, insisted that Jack's voting against McCarthy would be "political suicide." He never changed his mind.

"The feeling was *that* strong. If he'd voted for censure, there's no question it would have ended the career of Jack Kennedy in Massachusetts."

He believed that the only course was for Jack "to avoid the vote. McCarthy was deteriorating to nothing more than the subject of barroom brawls. In time, he would fade. These haters always do, and, if you argued against him, you were a Communist. My view was that we needed to stand back and allow him to self-destruct."

The passions of that historic moment created strange alliances. O'Donnell could never forget what he'd seen one night at a favorite political hangout. "I was in the Bellevue bar, having a drink, and we were watching the hearings. Bobby Kennedy had this altercation with Roy Cohn right on television. Remember, it was a group there, watching, of Boston Irish politicians, some truck drivers, and hardworking guys, most tinged with anti-Semitism. So Cohn wasn't the type of fellow you'd think they'd like. Yet every single person in that bar cheered and yelled and hoped he'd belt Bobby one."

Jack *got* this. Despite his seeming golden-boy status, he felt the lure of the underdog throughout his life; once a Mucker, always a Mucker. For this reason, he *got* Richard Nixon, his early congressional buddy, in ways that others in his circle never did. A part of him, the stubborn part — the part still dominant — cheered just about anyone liberals loved to hate.

Two years earlier he'd walked out of that Spee event after another attendee had dared compare McCarthy with Alger Hiss. Jack, after all, had run for Congress as a "fighting conservative." His identity as a Cold Warrior was well known. Besides the all-politics-is-local aspect, there was the issue of Communism itself and what it actually meant in the context of American life and American security. There were those who took its threat seriously and those who pooh-poohed it, with Jack squarely in the vigilant camp, a position he'd arrived at long before.

He'd criticized FDR's compromises at Yalta, and blamed Truman for the losses in Asia. "I'm very happy to tell them I'm not a liberal," he'd declared in a *Saturday Evening Post* interview the year before.

Even years later, when he'd begun to identify himself as a "liberal," he would confess to having little sympathy for the people McCarthy had persecuted. "I had not known the sort of people who were called before the McCarthy committee. I agree that many of them were seriously manhandled, but they represented a different world to me. What I mean is, I did not identify with them, and so I did not get as worked up as other liberals did."

The decision would come down to the

coldest calculation. Sorensen, in his memoir, summed up the situation: "JFK knew that if he voted with his fellow Democrats and anti-McCarthy Republicans on a motion to censure McCarthy, he would be defying many in his home state and family, but if he voted against such a motion, he would be denounced by the leading members of his party, by the leading liberals and intellectuals in the country and his alma mater, by the leaders of the Senate, and by the major national newspapers."

That spring of 1954, as he looked to both past and future — his entangling ties to McCarthy and what they would cost him later — Jack Kennedy found himself staring into the face of mortal danger. In April, the back pain from which he'd long suffered turned unbearable. X-rays taken showed that the fifth lumbar vertebra had collapsed, a result believed by some to be a result of steroids prescribed over the years for his Addison's disease. According to the historian Robert Dallek, he couldn't even bend down to pull a sock onto his left foot; only by walking sideways could he get up and down stairs.

Yet Kennedy managed to keep any awareness of these ever-encroaching medical setbacks from the public. Snapshots taken that May show Jack, Jackie, and Bobby Kennedy enjoying the Washington spring, playing touch football in the park behind Dumbarton

Oaks. Wearing a T-shirt, Jack looks sunny and healthy. Jacqueline, still in her preregal stage, appears joyously youthful and untroubled.

The photographs reveal nothing of either's pain. You can see in these pictures neither the dire reality of Jack's health nor the sadness his infidelities were already causing the twenty-four-year-old he'd married just the autumn before. "I've often wondered if I'd do it again," Charlie Bartlett would say of the two he'd brought together after seeing the one hurt the other so. "I don't understand Jack's promiscuity at all." Yet all that's apparent in the images of those halcyon days are the skills the pair shared in their concealment.

As bad as his condition was, however, it was about to get worse. By August his weight had dropped from 180 pounds to 140. So bad was the back pain that Jack needed to remain on the Senate floor between votes rather than attempt the commute from his office across Constitution Avenue. As the days passed, with little to stimulate him except agony, he arrived at a point of existential decision: the choice was between living a life of increasingly limited mobility — ending up in a wheelchair was inevitable — or else taking an enormous risk by submitting to spinal surgery.

In describing to Larry O'Brien the operation he chose now to endure, he minced no words. "This is the one that kills you or cures you."

To John Galvin, he explained that he was going to New York, to the Hospital for Special Surgery there, because his Boston doctors had advised against the procedure. "They said the best thing to do would be to stay with the crutches and live, rather than take the chance on the operation and die. He told me then, 'I'd rather die than be on crutches the rest of my life.'"

What intensified the danger was his Addison's disease. It meant his body could not produce the adrenaline needed to deal with the shock of surgery. The steroids he was taking complicated matters still further by reducing his ability to stave off infection. Jack knew that he faced the possibility of dying on the operating table. None of this was foreign territory to him.

With this high-risk surgery now on his calendar, Kennedy had to take on two political crises. One was the McCarthy censure, the other even nastier.

The midterm elections were coming in November, and Jack's Massachusetts colleague Foster Furcolo was running for the Senate. Jack didn't like the man's ambitions, which happened to be the same as his own. In fact, he didn't like the man, marking him as an "empty suit," a politician with no other reason to seek public office than the status it accorded the winner. It didn't help that Furcolo, whose base was Springfield, hadn't endorsed Jack in '52.

The antagonism between them was at once tribal and personal. Ever since Larry O'Brien, once a Furcolo staffer, had joined up with Jack in 1950, there'd been bad blood. Six years apart in age, the two legislators were both Harvard grads, both focused on getting ahead politically. Beyond that, they were simply rivals for the same turf: one Italian, the other Irish. As far as Jack was concerned, the Commonwealth wasn't big enough for both of them.

In the summer of 1954, their simmering feud came to a boil. Furcolo was the Democratic candidate for Senate, the same job Jack already had — if Furcolo won, it would make him the junior senator — and he looked to Jack for his backing. But there was no way Jack wanted Furcolo to become his political equal either in Washington or in Massachusetts. Complicating matters even more, Jack felt affection for the incumbent Furcolo wanted to run against, the Republican Leverett Saltonstall, a Brahmin of the same stripe as the man Jack had vanquished, Henry Cabot Lodge. As the Commonwealth's pair of senators, Jack and "Salty" had built a good working relationship.

"This was the circumstance for Kennedy's oft-quoted remark that 'sometimes party asks too much,'" Ted Sorensen recalled. In fact,

Jack engaged him in a secret plan to undercut Furcolo's chances. "When I had been with him barely eighteen months," the aide recalled, "JFK took me to Boston, where he decided to oppose quietly the Democratic Party's nominee for the Senate against Leverett Saltonstall, JFK's Republican Senate colleague, in the 1954 election." It was another caper, like sneaking into the Massachusetts State House after hours to file his '46 nominating petitions. It was willful deception. Kennedy needed to make it *look* like he was being the loyal party man all while his bright young brain truster would be using his skills as a researcher-writer to provide ammo for the enemy.

Lending Sorensen to Saltonstall was only part of the plan. Late that summer, Kennedy met with Ken O'Donnell and Larry O'Brien at the Ritz-Carlton Hotel and instructed them to get on board to assist the Democratic candidate Robert Murphy, who was running for governor. The scheme called for Jack to endorse Murphy for governor and Furcolo for the Senate on the same live TV program. This being the era before videotape, Furcolo would have Jack's backing but would be unable to keep showing it in TV ads.

Kennedy's mistake was his failure to keep his dislike for Furcolo as secret as he kept his plotting. When the night of the live appearance arrived, Furcolo got a prebroadcast copy of Kennedy's intended remarks and blew up.

"Furcolo told him he wouldn't go on the show unless he received a more forthright and direct endorsement," O'Donnell recalled. "The senator then gave him that famous line, 'You've got a hell of a nerve, Foster. You're lucky you're here.' The senator next, quite coldly, went on to remind Furcolo of the time he had refused to endorse him. The exchange was quite heated." The actual telecast, however, went off smoothly enough. As they were leaving, Furcolo even wished Jack well with his coming surgery — "The main thing is, take care of your back" — a gesture of goodwill that Jack saw as entirely insincere.

Then hell broke loose. Even if the papers failed to notice that Senator Kennedy neglected to offer a personal endorsement of Furcolo, one radio station — albeit with a bit of help — got it cold. "I was riding into town that next morning," said O'Donnell, "and I heard on the radio that Senator Kennedy's not naming Foster Furcolo had been a direct affront. That he'd done it on purpose and, in fact, was not endorsing Foster Furcolo. The report quoted Frank Morrissey."

Morrissey was Joe Kennedy's man, the one he'd assigned to hang around his son's political operation and report back anything his boss wanted to know. Here's O'Donnell's account of that morning-after: "I called Frank and asked him to come over immediately.

When he got there, I put it right to him and asked, 'What happened here?' He told me he thought it was off the record. I just stared at him. Couldn't believe it. All our preparation out of the window. I remember my exact words. I walked over and opened the window and said, 'Frank, jump.' He looked around and then looked like he would cry."

O'Donnell, who recalled the scene in all its drama years later, had no trouble recognizing the very real damage. Every politician in the state now knew what Jack Kennedy thought of Furcolo and how he'd undercut him in their one and only joint television appearance. "We'd been building up a solid residue of party regulars, and now they pointed to this and said, 'We were right about him in '52. He and his people are a bunch of Harvard bastards who take care of themselves. They don't care about the party. Kennedy does not want Furcolo in there because he'll compete with him. Kennedy doesn't *want* two Democratic senators.'"

A tribal war now loomed. Italians in Massachusetts had been voting for Irish candidates for generations. Now one of their own, Furcolo, was seen getting the bum's rush by a prince of the Irish side. Needing both groups in order to win statewide, certainly to win big, the Kennedys recognized the cost of the screwup as well as anyone. Here, though, Jack had made himself vulnerable by allowing his feelings to get in the way of his political calculation.

On October 10, Jack checked into the Hospital for Special Surgery. The operation was postponed three times, finally taking place eleven days later, on the twenty-first. Only then, before he was taken into the operating room, did he finally address the Furcolo problem. O'Donnell recalls the effort it took. "I kept pushing and, through some process of negotiation and with Bobby's help, we finally extracted a statement from him. It was unsatisfactory, but covered the problem. What we did was disavow Morrissey."

At the same time, O'Donnell knew it wouldn't fly. He would call the snubbing of Furcolo, who lost that November, "the only wrong political move Jack Kennedy ever made."

The back operation did not go well. After more than three hours in the surgeons' hands, Kennedy was left with a metal plate inserted in his spine. At that point he developed a urinary tract infection that failed to respond to antibiotics, sending him into a coma. The news spread around the political world that the handsome Massachusetts senator's life was in jeopardy.

"The odds made by the political wise guys were that he wouldn't live," Ken O'Donnell recalled, "and that if he did live he'd be a cripple. It became 'he might not make it.'"

Evelyn Lincoln, the secretary in his Senate office, got the terrible news that "the doctors didn't expect him to live until morning." The Kennedy death watch even was reported on television. For the third time in his life, Jack was given the last rites of his church. Jacqueline Kennedy, never one to practice her religion openly, went down on her knees to pray. Richard Nixon, being driven home that night, was heard to moan: "That poor young man is going to die. Oh, God, don't let him die." His Secret Service agent never forgot it.

Rallying in the night, against the odds, Jack pulled through. "The doctors don't understand where he gets his strength," the hospital told Lincoln when she called to ask about the patient the following morning. But the ordeal left a darkness in Kennedy.

"The tenor of his voice was tinged with pain," Ken O'Donnell said. "You could detect it in his voice even over the telephone. It was the first time in my experience with him — and I'd say, in his life — when he was, in fact, disinterested completely in politics. John Kennedy was at the lowest point of anytime I'd known him in his career, physically, mentally, and politically. He was at the bottom. It seemed over."

Back in Washington, the two Teds, Reardon and Sorensen, had been left in charge. The trouble was, Jack had given Sorensen, his young legislative assistant, no guidance on what he wanted to do about the upcoming vote to censure Joseph McCarthy. Sorensen, for his part, never called his boss's hospital room to ask how he wanted to be counted on the issue. Perhaps, it was simply preferable not to ask. He said he "feared the wrath of the senator's brother and father more than the senator's" if he declared Jack in favor of the McCarthy censure. In the end, Sorensen concluded, "I . . . suspected — correctly — that there was no point in my trying to reach him on an issue he wanted to duck."

On December 2, 1954, the Senate at last brought down the curtain on the peculiar political spectacle starring Senator Joseph McCarthy. Except for the absent Kennedy, every Democrat, joined by half the Republicans, voted for the condemnation. The controversial senator would live just two and half years longer, dying of acute hepatitis brought on by alcoholism. By that time, his anti-Communist crusade and his political significance both were long over.

The man in the New York hospital bed had missed the vote.

Kennedy tried to make light of it. "You know, when I get downstairs, I know exactly what's going to happen," he told Chuck Spalding upon leaving the hospital a few days before Christmas. "Those reporters are going to lean over me with great concern, and every one of those guys is going to say, 'Now, Senator, what about McCarthy?' Do you know what I'm going to do? I'm going to reach for my back and I'm going to yell 'Oow!' and then I'm going to pull the sheet over my head and hope we can get out of there."

Jack left it to Bobby to carry the family's continuing respect for their fallen Irish-American ally. In January, while Jack was recuperating in Palm Beach, his younger brother was honored at a Junior Chamber of Commerce dinner as one of the country's "Ten Outstanding Young Men." When the evening's speaker, Edward R. Murrow, rose to address those in attendance, Bobby walked out of the room, a silent protest against a man who'd played a significant role in bringing down McCarthy. When the senator died in 1956, Bobby Kennedy flew to Appleton, Wisconsin, for the funeral and stayed with the mourners' procession all the way to the gravesite.

Now Jack Kennedy had survived another brush with death. He was helped through the crisis by the one strong emotional reality of his life: old friendships. One name high on the list was Red Fay. "In January 1955, Bobby called to ask if I could come to Florida. The family was worried about Jack, and didn't know whether he was going to live. The doctor felt that he was losing interest, and a visit from someone closely associated with happier times might help him regain his usual optimism and enjoyment of life. I flew to Palm Beach and spent ten days with him."

It was an opportunity for someone who cared about him to realize what Jack was up against. Fay watched as his recuperating friend gave himself a shot as part of the treatment for his back. " 'Jack,' I said, 'the way you take that jab, it looks like it doesn't even hurt.' Before I had time to dodge, he reached over and jabbed the same needle into my leg. I screamed with the pain."

Down in Palm Beach, with time on his hands, surrounded by Jackie and family members, he took up oil painting and spent hours playing Monopoly. His convalescence lasted for almost six months and was interrupted only by a trip back to New York for a second surgery. While in Florida he grew close to his new brother-in-law, the young Hollywood star Peter Lawford, who'd married Patricia Kennedy the year before. "I think we hit it off because he loved my business. He loved anything to do with the arts and motion pictures. It never ceased to amaze me."

The British-born Lawford, who'd been in films since he was a young boy, observed Jack with an actor's keen eye. He got as good a look at him as anybody. "I don't think anybody ever made up John Kennedy's mind for him. I don't think anybody swayed him, including his father. I think he took what he wanted and then sifted it, you know, evaluated it. Then he did what he wanted to do with it." Lawford was amazed at Kennedy's self-discipline and his will to make the most of every day, the preciousness of time to him. "He was really ill with that back, but he fought his way through that, and, as you know, wrote the book while he was lying on his back."

The book was *Profiles in Courage*. It was Kennedy's tribute to eight U.S. senators who during their legislative careers had taken positions highly unpopular with their constituents. Though Kennedy dug up the stories and sketched out his intentions, Ted Sorensen did most of the actual writing. So it's fair to call the project a collaboration. The bookish child had been father to the man. "He was enormously well read in American history and literature," Hugh Fraser, the British politician and longtime friend, recalled. "I mean, to me, staggeringly so." Charlie Bartlett saw the book as an obvious undertaking for Jack. "I think the whole concept of the really gutsy decisions made by men with seats in the Senate fascinated him. So when he had this time, I suppose it was natural for him to turn to it." Bartlett, like all the others gathered around Jack in Palm Beach, would watch him, still unable to rise from bed, writing upside down on a board suspended above him.

In his memoirs, Sorensen explained that they worked on the book by letter and telephone. The reason was, he was in Washington helping hold down the fort in Kennedy's office while his boss was on his back down in Florida. The way Sorensen explained the enterprise, Kennedy played an especially serious role composing the first and last chapters and that he, the aide, wrote the first draft of the rest.

The theme and the bulk of the content were pure Jack. As smart as Sorensen was, and even given his familiarity with politics — his Republican father had been the attorney general of Nebraska — he was nonetheless a twenty-seven-year-old. He'd arrived in Washington only four years earlier, armed with a law degree but no on-the-ground political experience. He would admit that he was nowhere as well read as Kennedy in American history.

The voice of John F. Kennedy seems to me to be noticeably audible in *Profiles in Courage*. For example, in the opening passages, you read, "Where else, in a non-totalitarian society, but in the political profession is the individual expected to sacrifice all — including his own career — for the national good?" It's a quip that, I think, captures Jack Kennedy's own ironic style. Another sentence, I believe, derives from his ability to see things from the inside out as well as the outside in: the prospect of forced retirement from "the most exclusive club in the world, the possibilities of giving up the interesting work, the fascinating trappings and the impressive prerogatives of Congressional office, can cause even the most courageous politician a serious loss of sleep."

Here's a story that comes clearly from the insider Jack: "One senator, since retired, said that he voted with the special interests on every issue, hoping that by election time all of them added together would constitute nearly a majority that would remember him favorably, while the other members of the public would never know about — much less remember — his vote against their welfare." That senator was George Smathers, his pal who'd once said he didn't "give a damn." That business about the senator being "retired" was a cover.

David Ormsby-Gore, now a member of Parliament, stayed in touch with his friend as he recovered. "He must have been getting near the end of the book — but one of the lessons he had drawn from examining these moments in American history was that there were very much two sides to each problem. Now, this didn't prevent him being capable of taking decisions, and knowing that somebody had to make decisions, but it did always prevent him saying, 'I know that I have got nothing but right on my side, and the other side is entirely wrong,' and he never would adopt that attitude.

"He said that one of the rather sad things about life, particularly if you were a politician,

278

was that you discovered that the other side really had a good case. He was most unpartisan in that way. . . . He wondered whether he was really cut out to be a politician because he was often so impressed by the other side's arguments when he really examined them in detail. Where he thought that there was a valid case against his position, he was always rather impressed by the arguments advanced."

At the end of May, with the help of physical therapy, a corset, and a rocking chair, Jack was set to proceed gingerly with a career that had hung, along with his life, in the balance. Pale and limping, he returned to Capitol Hill more sensitive than usual to imagery. When a Senate page, Martin Dowd, saw the long-absent senator approaching on crutches and opened the Senate chamber door for him, Kennedy tore into him. "Shut that door!" Kennedy yelled to the crushed seventeen-year-old. Unwilling to drop the matter, he confronted Dowd a moment later. "Don't you touch that door until I tell you to!"

Sorensen could sense how his boss had grown tougher, not just on others but himself. The political columnist and Kennedy friend Joseph Alsop also recognized the transformation: "Something very important happened inside him, I think, when he had that illness, because he came out of it a very much more serious fellow than he was prior to it. He had gone through the valley of the shadow of

279

death, and he had displayed immense courage, which he'd always had."

That June, Kennedy gave a party in Hyannis, inviting to Cape Cod not just his own supporters, but also a sizable group of Democrats who'd never been active for him. Ken O'Donnell helped pull it together. "Larry and I got a call saying he was coming back to Massachusetts and the first thing he wanted to do was have a political reunion of the Kennedy secretaries." Clearly, the purpose of the event was to prove to the faithful how healthy he was. It was to show others, coming out of morbid curiosity, that he remained formidable.

"The thing I remember most about the event was that he was physically able to move around. There were no crutches. They had softball games and so forth, and it was an excellent outing. A very successful political event — an all-day affair." O'Donnell could see Jack's appeal to the rank-and-file types hadn't faded. "What struck me the most and to me was critical was that he still held the same old attraction for people. All our people loved him, but you knew there was no question about that. If he'd returned flat on his back or in a wheelchair, our people would have been there. But I was watching the others. The reaction from the professional politicians that were there: *they* loved him. Loved him, despite themselves."

If Kennedy was going to go further in

politics, he needed to bring all the factions of Massachusetts together. He needed to win over those who practiced politics day in and day out. "It was important for our political futures and for the senator's that if we were going to take the next step, we had to know them on an intimate personal basis. We realized how important it was that they shouldn't feel we were snobs, that we didn't look down on the 'regulars.'"

It was obvious that Kennedy's renewed vigor had stirred a healthy fear among the Massachusetts Democratic stalwarts. Abandoning him might well mean abandoning the winning side. No political regular likes being tied to a loser, and while a young senator sidelined for six months with medical problems might have the voters' sympathy for a time, what good was he? Besides, Jack Kennedy had end-run them over the years, and many had been waiting for him to get his comeuppance. His sunny reappearance at that June picnic was therefore vital to his prospects.

"Out of that affair," O'Donnell said, summing up the situation, "I think, at least in our minds, we accepted that, for Senator Kennedy, the bottom point had been reached. Now there was a solid foundation from which to build forward."

Moving into the future, the Kennedy Party needed to reach out to the wider Democratic organization and win it to the cause. It was no longer enough to woo and charm. To win the big prizes Jack now needed to master the rougher side of politics. To intimidate those he could not seduce, he'd have to play the game harder than his rivals.

CHAPTER NINE
DEBUT

Politics is essentially a learning profession.
— Arthur M. Schlesinger

When 1956 began, Jack Kennedy was far from a household name. By year's end, he'd managed to step into the ring as the most exciting Democratic challenger for the American presidency. He'd gotten there by sheer audacity.

President Eisenhower, having enjoyed a successful first term, was continuing to reap the prestige earned by his wartime victory. Despite the fact he'd suffered a heart attack the previous year, he was still expected to seek and win reelection. Offering himself to the task of opposing him was Governor Adlai Stevenson. The real question was who would be the Illinois Democrat's running mate.

That was the brass ring on which Jack Kennedy, now thirty-nine, began to focus. He'd gotten the heads-up from Theodore H. White, then reporting for *Collier's* magazine, that he was on Adlai's shortlist. Though pos-

Filing petition for senate reeletion, 1958 **23**

Adlai Stevenson **24**

sibly no more than a signal to Catholic voters in Massachusetts that Stevenson understood their importance, the result was to get Kennedy thinking.

Why *not* make a move in '56?

But if he were to do so, Jack saw how critical it was for him to arrive at the national convention and give the right impression. As an attractive war-hero-turned-thoughtful-politico, he could easily come across as the perfect complement to Adlai: youthful, active, eastern, Catholic, well-rounded. The prospective negatives of his candidacy — his religion and his relative conservatism — could even be regarded as ticket balancers.

Such boldness is in itself a selling point. But before he could turn his attention to this exciting notion of competing on the national stage, Jack Kennedy first had to face up to serious trouble back home. The problem was a central-Massachusetts farmer whose nickname derived from his cash crop: William "Onions" Burke, chairman of the Massachusetts Democratic Party.

Onions was a John McCormack guy, and an especially tribal Irishman. He hated the academic elite, Ivy Leaguers, and liberals. He couldn't stand Adlai Stevenson. His idea of a Democratic leader was McCormack, a devoutly Catholic congressman from South Boston, who'd come to Washington in 1928 and risen to House majority leader. So Onions was a problem. For Jack to woo Stevenson, he needed to convince him he could deliver New England. Initially, he and Onions agreed to split the Massachusetts delegates going to the national convention. Burke then pulled a double cross, and organized a quiet write-in campaign for McCormack in the April primary that ended up beating Stevenson, whose name was on the ballot. McCormack won big: 26,128 votes to 19,024. It made Kennedy look like a political eunuch, a pretty boy who couldn't control his people.

If Jack Kennedy couldn't deliver his state in the primary, how could he be counted on at the convention? And if he couldn't deliver votes, why should Stevenson even consider him as a running mate? Onions had put Jack, who now wanted badly to be on the Stevenson ticket, in an embarrassing situation.

Onions now added insult to the injury. "Anybody who's for Stevenson," he declared to the press, "ought to be down at Princeton listening to Alger Hiss." The accused Soviet agent had just been released from federal prison. Invited to speak at his alma mater, he'd been celebrated as a returning hero. Translation: being for Adlai was the same as being for Alger. Joe McCarthy couldn't have phrased it better.

Burke's slur was unmistakable, intentional, and uttered with impunity, by a guy who figured he could get away with it. He'd put Kennedy in a position where he had no choice but to destroy the man who'd said what he had.

Kennedy knew he couldn't let the charge go unchallenged. Until now, he'd been content using the political process simply as a mechanism for winning office. He'd avoided involvement in local politics. That had been his father's early advice, and it still was. According to Bobby, his father had been telling his children that local Massachusetts politics was an endless morass. "You're either going to get into the problems of Algeria or you're going to get into the problems of Worcester."

But, for Jack, Onions's attack made his choice clear. Now he had to get down and dirty. He'd used the Massachusetts Democratic Party to win elections to office, but he'd never actually joined it, much less tried to lead it. He would now either prove himself a leader or be forever at the mercy of the *locals*. And that would be a problem, because, unlike him, they weren't big thinkers. Nor did they regard themselves, of course, as national statesmen. Neither were they as liberal as the national party. The reputation that Massachusetts would gain for liberalism, never fully on the mark, was not the case even then. In 1956, it was Joe McCarthy country.

To get rid of Chairman Burke and the threat he presented, Kennedy needed to switch to a new brand of politics. He had to shift back from the wholesale politics of speeches and position-taking to the retail politics of the clubhouse. And he had to be tough. He needed to beat Burke in the back room, where the television cameras weren't watching.

To this end, he ordered his staff to run a personal check on every member of the state Democratic committee. "Find out everything about them. Who do we know who knows them? What time do they get home from work at night? I'm going to ring their doorbells and talk to each one of them personally." Armed with this intelligence, Kennedy began to travel the state, visiting a sizable percentage of the eighty committeemen.

The election for state chairman that year was held at the Bradford Hotel in downtown Boston. Larry O'Brien recalled the Kennedy hardball: "We argued that Onions shouldn't be allowed to attend the meeting since he wasn't a *member* of the committee. To back up our ruling, we had two tough Boston cops guarding the door, one of whom had reputedly killed a man in a barroom fight. Burke arrived with some tough guys of his own. Just as the meeting was about to begin, he and his men charged out of the elevator and broke past our guards. One of the leaders was 'Knocko' McCormack, the majority leader's two-fisted three-hundred-pound younger brother. As shouting and shoving spread across the meeting room, I called the Boston police commissioner. He arrived minutes later.

"'I'm O'Brien,' I told him. 'You've got to get those troublemakers out of here.'

"'One more word out of you, O'Brien,' the commissioner replied, 'and I'll lock you up.' I hadn't known the commissioner was a McCormack man. The whole thing was a scene out of *The Last Hurrah*. The two candidates for state chairman almost settled matters by a fistfight. There was shouting and confusion, and as the roll call began, one member who'd gotten drunk attempted to vote twice."

The guy Kennedy had chosen as his candidate, Pat Lynch, wound up winning two to one. "He and his millions don't know what honor and decency is," Burke complained. Kennedy had risen to the occasion, done exactly what was necessary, changing his tactics to suit the situation, ambushing his complacent rival on his home turf. On the afternoon of victory, he made sure the press understood that the day marked a "new era" in Massachusetts politics.

The fact is, Jack Kennedy had no intention of staying involved in townie politics. He knew it was like quicksand: you got into the fray, picked sides, made enemies, and could never free yourself from it. He now needed to reengage himself in national politics.

As a Roman Catholic, Jack Kennedy would have been, until this moment, an unlikely candidate for national office. World War II had changed things, however, and it was obvious that now there were ways to position oneself favorably as an Irish Catholic, to take advantage of the changes. He needed to make the case that the number of Catholics Stevenson had lost in '52 could be lured back to the fold with the right running mate. Catholics liked Ike, who'd vanquished Hitler, and were turned off by the divorced Adlai, who couldn't escape the contemptuous label "egghead," attached to him not just for his shiny high forehead but also because of his intellectualism.

Kennedy gave the job of proving the case for putting him on the ticket to Ted Sorensen. It was the same sort of tricky assignment he'd handed his legislative assistant two years earlier when he'd sent him up to Boston to work on the sly for Saltonstall against Furcolo. Again, Sorensen proved equal to the task, knocking out a seventeen-page memo showing the power of the Catholic vote in fourteen key states. It demonstrated how Catholics' defection in '52 had cost the Democrats the election. It showed, too, that they had split their tickets in the election, voting for Democrats for the House and Senate, but Ike for president.

However, Kennedy also understood that such a sales pitch coming from him would be seen exactly for what it was. It might even trigger a backlash. To camouflage the effort, he had the Sorensen memo distributed by

Connecticut's John Bailey, the state Democratic Party chairman, a close Kennedy ally. In any case, the "Bailey Memorandum," as it was marketed, went out to fifty top Democrats thought to have Stevenson's ear. A few days later, it showed its power. Stevenson's campaign manager, Jim Finnegan, asked for a dozen copies of "that survey" that was going around. "You know, about the Catholic vote," the Philadelphian said.

Jack went to Chicago prepared for lightning to strike. He phoned Tip O'Neill and asked him to let Bobby take his place as a Massachusetts delegate. He said his brother was the smartest politician he knew and he wanted him there on the convention floor in case the odds broke in his favor.

He, nonetheless, remained cool about his prospects. On the way home from the Hill with Ted Reardon that summer, he sounded easygoing about the whole thing. "After all this, I may actually be disappointed if I don't get the nomination. Yes, and that disappointment will be deep enough to last from the day they ballot on the vice presidency until I leave for Europe two days later." He was thinking about his coming end-of-summer cruise along the south coast of France with Torby Macdonald, George Smathers, and his youngest brother, Ted.

It was at this moment that Jack Kennedy got one of those big breaks that made so many other ones possible. After Governor Edmund Muskie of Maine, another rising young Democratic figure, turned down the opportunity, Kennedy won a big role on the first night of the national convention in Chicago. He, a freshman senator, was asked to narrate a documentary film on the Democratic Party.

It would turn out to be the highlight of the convention's opening. Hearing his distinctive New England accent echoing across the floor of Chicago's International Amphitheatre and broadcast over the country's television and radio stations, Americans discovered a new voice. *The Pursuit of Happiness,* created by Dore Schary, a Hollywood producer who'd made his name at RKO and MGM, was projected onto huge screens in the convention hall. It made Jack Kennedy the Democrats' star of the night.

The applause in the hall, swelled by his friends, was prolonged when Jack was introduced from the floor. Edmund Reggie, a Catholic delegate from Louisiana, was astonished by this young promising Democrat. "I didn't even know Senator Kennedy existed. The Louisiana delegates sat across the aisle from the Massachusetts delegation. And the first time I ever remember seeing him is in a film that he narrated."

Nothing that Jack Kennedy had done before, not the offices he'd won, the books he'd written, even the heroics in WWII, would propel him so mightily as what had just happened. Everything before was now prelude.

The sensation created by Jack's role in the convention film had an immediate effect. Stevenson picked him to be his chief nominator, Kennedy having gotten the word from Adlai himself on Wednesday morning. It came with the assurance that he was still in contention for the vice presidency.

Kennedy and Sorensen then went to work, laboring together on the speech until six o'clock in the morning. Criticized by *the New York Times* for relying too heavily on a "cliché dictionary," the speech, nonetheless, was a genuine rouser. In it Kennedy warned that the Democratic ticket would be facing fierce opposition in the fall from "two tough candidates, one who takes the high road and one who takes the low road."

The knock on Vice President Richard Nixon thrilled its intended audience. The liberals loved it, and continued throughout the campaign to repeat the line. In fact, it became a refrain, resonating throughout the months of the contest. Kennedy had understood exactly what he was saying and precisely whom he wanted to hear him. He was playing to the Nixon haters. It was a theme to which Stevenson, once nominated, would return. He wanted his fellow Democrats to keep in mind that Ike had been the first sitting president to have a heart attack. What would happen, he implied, if he died and Dick Nixon became president?

At eleven o'clock on Thursday, the convention's fourth night, Adlai Stevenson made a surprise announcement: instead of picking his running mate himself, he would let the delegates do it. Seven of the country's thirty-four presidents, he reminded them, had risen to office because of an incumbent's death. Bluntly implying it could happen again — "The nation's attention has become focused as never before on the . . . vice presidency" — Stevenson told the hundreds of assembled Democrats he wanted the decision made by the party rather than by a single man.

When the convention opened, Senator Estes Kefauver of Tennessee had been the front-runner. The field now included Senators Lyndon Johnson of Texas, Hubert Humphrey of Minnesota, and Albert Gore, Sr., of Tennessee, Mayor Robert Wagner of New York, and John F. Kennedy of Massachusetts.

Fourteen years older than Jack Kennedy, Kefauver had gained national attention for chairing a 1950 Senate committee investigating organized crime; in the '52 election he'd sought the Democrats' nomination for president but lost, in the end, to Stevenson. Trying again, this time he'd won a number of early primaries before falling to Stevenson in later big-state contests. He and the other contenders for vice president, including Kennedy, now entered upon what would be a twenty-four-hour effort to secure the honor of being Adlai's running mate.

"Call Dad and tell him I'm going for it," Jack instructed Bobby.

Reached in the South of France with the news, Joseph P. Kennedy was livid. Bellowing what an "idiot" his son was, he could be heard all the way across the room. Jack was ruining his career with this move. "Whew!" Bobby said, after the connection was broken. "Is he mad!"

To place his name in nomination, Jack picked Governor Abraham Ribicoff of Connecticut. This choice of a Jewish politician, the son of immigrants who'd begun his political career in the Connecticut state legislature back in the late '30s, was a shrewd one. Equally savvy was the next phone call he made. At one in the morning, he reached George Smathers, asking him to give the seconding speech. When the Floridian asked what a Southern conservative might say that could help, Kennedy assured him it was a no-sweat assignment. "Just talk about the war stuff," he said.

Kennedy now had to figure out how to beat the seasoned pros lined up against him. He already had a base of support in the Massachusetts delegation, and in the early days of the convention, he'd realized, during various sessions, that he'd emerged as leader of the

New England region. He now had just hours to extend his support beyond it.

As his taxi headed toward the convention hall that Friday dawn, a sleepless Kennedy was clenching his fist, whispering again and again to himself: "Go! Go! Go!" Charlie Bartlett attributed it to his friend's innate love of competition. "The way Stevenson laid that challenge on the floor was what really challenged him. At that point he decided this was going to move. And, of course, everybody was all around *ready* to move. I remember the whole family was milling around, ready to go. As soon as the competition arose, he lost his reluctance. He really went for it."

For the rest of the morning, Kennedy would personally do much of the hour-to-hour campaigning. He discovered he had surprising strength in the South. Part of this was the result of antipathy toward Kefauver due to his record of civil rights support. But there was also clearly goodwill toward Kennedy himself, as a result of his war heroism and his reputation as a moderate. Many Southern delegates saw him as standing apart from the liberal pack.

Of course, he also had to face prejudice. "If we have to have a Catholic," Speaker of the House Sam Rayburn told Stevenson, "I hope we don't have to take that little pissant Kennedy." But some Catholics were themselves a problem. James Farley, the old New Deal warhorse who'd helped make FDR and then broken with him when he ran for his unprecedented third term in 1940, gave Stevenson his opinion: "America is not ready for a Catholic yet."

Kennedy also took a hit from the party's liberal wing, who knew he wasn't really one of them, who'd never forgotten, let alone forgiven, his failure to cast a censure vote against Joe McCarthy. To woo the keepers of the New Deal flame whom he'd spent his early congressional years bashing over Yalta and the loss of China — those same liberals with whom he said he did "not feel comfortable" — he now needed to do some genuflecting.

When he managed to set up a meeting with Eleanor Roosevelt in Chicago, the former first lady and Democratic grande dame didn't make it easy. She'd let it be known how "troubled" she was by "Senator K's evasive attitude on McCarthy." Her opinion wasn't changed by their get-together. Elaborately orchestrated, it turned out to be a disaster, with the rapport between them nonexistent. When Mrs. Roosevelt raised the McCarthy issue, Jack replied that it was "so long ago" it didn't help. He also quibbled that the time to censure the Wisconsin senator had been when he returned to the Senate for his second term in 1953.

FDR's widow was having none of it. In full dudgeon, she berated Jack in front of everyone present, including other politicians who came and went throughout the discussion. Mrs. Roosevelt correctly saw herself as not just Franklin Roosevelt's partner within the Democratic Party but his political heir. She regarded Kennedy's approach to her as less than sincere, which it was.

Balancing his failure to win over Mrs. Roosevelt, there now came good news. They began to get promises of support from delegates far and wide. Two or three in Nevada, one in Wyoming, one in Utah, and so forth, people who were for Jack Kennedy personally, but represented no large group of votes or delegates. They'd knock on the door of the hotel suite and say, "My name is Mary Jones. I've seen the senator on television and I think he is wonderful." Or, "I'm from Oregon, and I want to vote for him."

Winning the support of big-state delegations was a more serious challenge. Charlie Bartlett described the process of Jack going to the Democratic bosses of the country — all complete strangers to him — and asking for their backing. It was an intimidating group that included the major honchos of the New York machine. But he was breaking new ground.

"After Stevenson had thrown down the challenge, it was all beginning to accelerate, and he was obviously quite excited. I said, 'Look, there's Carmine DeSapio. You ought to go and see what you can do about him. He might be able to help you.' I wish I had a movie of that scene. There he was — this rather slight figure, and DeSapio was a rather big fellow — and the reporters were all around DeSapio, completely ignoring Kennedy. But he went up and shyly said, 'Excuse me, Mr. DeSapio, but my name is John Kennedy from Massachusetts, and I wondered if I could have a few words with you?' That was the beginning. As I remember, he got a pretty good chunk of the New York vote." It was like his old door-to-door campaigning in the Boston neighborhoods.

When the public balloting began, Kennedy mustered surprising strength, with the Southern bloc contributing to his numbers. "Texas proudly casts its fifty-six votes for the fighting sailor who wears the scars of battle," Senate Majority Leader Lyndon Johnson hollered when his state's delegation was recognized. The first ballot count was John F. Kennedy, 304 delegates; Estes Kefauver, 483; Albert Gore, 178. A total of 686 was needed for the required two-thirds majority.

With the second balloting, momentum further shifted to Kennedy. Once again, he was drawing more support than expected from the Southern states. "I'm going to sing 'Dixie' for the rest of my life," Jack promised aloud as the states reported their counts to the podium. With 646 delegates, victory seemed assured.

Kennedy and Kefauver were now the two

main contenders. The other candidates were flagging. The next ballot would be the decider.

Ted Sorensen was watching the broadcast from campaign headquarters at the Stockyards Inn, as was his boss. "The second ballot was already under way, and a Kennedy trend had set in. The South was anxious to stop Kefauver, and Kennedy was picking up most of the Gore and Southern favorite-son votes. He was also getting the Wagner votes. Kefauver was gaining more slowly, but hardly a handful of delegates had left him. Bob Kennedy and his lieutenants were all over the floor shouting to delegations to come with Kennedy. Our television set showed wild confusion on the convention floor and a climbing Kennedy total. But the senator was as calm as ever. He bathed, then again reclined on the bed. The race was now neck and neck, and Kennedy knew that no lead was enough if it could not produce a majority."

The religious issue was about to intervene. The governor of Oklahoma stayed with the also-ran Gore, his candidacy now dead in the water, rather than back a Catholic. "He's not our kind of folks," he told a Kennedy pleader. With South Carolina, Illinois, and Alabama all seeking recognition to shift their delegates to Kennedy, the convention chairman, Sam Rayburn, instead recognized Oklahoma, which switched its Gore votes to Kefauver.

Rayburn then called on Senator Gore, who now threw his own dwindling number of delegates to his fellow Tennessean.

Kennedy, who'd been in the lead, could see that the trend had shifted. "Let's go!" Kennedy said to Sorensen. Once inside the Amphitheatre, he began pushing his way through the crowded floor up to the podium. While some convention officials tried to stop him, urging him to wait for the balloting to be completed, Jack walked onto the rostrum, smiling. Speaking impromptu, he congratulated Kefauver, saluted Adlai Stevenson for allowing the delegates to choose his running mate, and called for making the nomination of Kefauver unanimous.

That moment up on the stage, before the national television cameras, was Jack Kennedy's unforgettable debut as a national leader.

In a matter of hours Jack had learned a slew of lessons. He'd discovered the need for state-of-the-art communications on the convention floor; the need for an ongoing, accurate delegate count; for a perfect grasp of the minutiae of convention rules. Friendships were important, too. Celebrated senators mattered less. Estes Kefauver had beaten Jack because he knew delegates personally; after all, it had been his second time around and what he himself had learned in '52 he'd put into action now. Wearing his trademark coonskin cap — a reference to his pioneer ancestors — Kefauver was a familiar figure who had shaken a lot of hands in a great many small towns. Unlike him, Jack Kennedy lacked the experience of traveling the length and breadth of the country itself and connecting with voters face-to-face.

These lessons, absorbed and put to use later, were nothing in contrast with his triumph. He had taken a near-miss for the vice-presidential nomination and converted it, at the moment he raced to the podium, into a career-changing event. He had gone to Chicago one of several Democrats looking to the White House, and now was a subject of national fascination. In an inspired gesture of magnanimity, he had, in effect, won the first national primary of 1960.

In the short run, of course, all he counted was the loss itself. Just an hour ago, his vote total was rising, seeming to clinch the deal. Now he was absorbing the defeat. As Jackie and his aides gathered around him in their hotel suite, he refused to be cheered by those who said the close defeat was the best possible outcome, that he'd made a name for himself without having to endure the thrashing in November everyone expected for the Stevenson ticket.

"He hated to lose anything, and glared at us when we tried to console him by telling him he was the luckiest man in the world," says

Ken O'Donnell. The defeat brought Kennedy to a sober reckoning. He now believed that whatever lip service they paid to tolerance, the main party leaders, such as Rayburn, would simply not let him — young, independent, and Catholic — become their nominee. The 1956 experience also marked Kennedy's metamorphosis from dilettante to professional. "I've learned that you don't get far in politics until you become a total politician," he told his crew. "That means you've got to deal with the party leaders as well as with the voters."

Until that week in Chicago, the Kennedy people had been parochial in their experience and their outlook. But what had just happened to Jack — this incredible almost getting the vice-presidential nomination — was no real guide to what they'd have to do now. He, Jack Kennedy, needed to get out in the country, among the future delegates on their home ground, doing what Kefauver had done, but better.

"It was too damned close not to be disappointed," Kennedy would say years later. "Kefauver deserved it. I always thought that, with his victories in the primaries. Because I had done much better than I thought I would, I was not desolate. I was awfully tired. We had worked awfully hard, and we had come damn close."

Jackie Kennedy would recall how hard her

husband had driven himself in his chase for votes: "Five days in Chicago, never went to bed."

What mattered was that John F. Kennedy now owned an edge on which he'd had no claim before. Change was stirring out in that vast territory beyond Capitol Hill. Those who'd watched on television had seen a dazzling sight. In a sea of gray faces, the camera had lingered on the handsome countenance of Jack Kennedy. It had spotted, too, his radiant spouse: anyone with Jacqueline Kennedy by his side could hardly be counted among life's losers. Moreover, by making himself so visible, even in defeat, Jack Kennedy had gained the advantage that would carry him to victory four years later — those millions of Catholics who'd seen him felt pride, then were disappointed, and now were on his side, ready for the next chance.

Yet Jack Kennedy was not, we now know, the perfect vessel for the hopes of America's Roman Catholics. Though he and his gorgeous wife seemed in public a stunning portrait of the adoring, supportive couple, the reality behind the picture was far from perfection. As planned, once the convention ended, Jack left Chicago for a sailing trip in the Mediterranean with Torby, Smathers, and his brother Teddy tagging along. Just as he'd hung out with a buddy during his honeymoon, he was defecting again at another less

304

than ideal moment. Left behind was his wife, eight months pregnant with their first child.

During his absence, Jackie found herself faced with dangerous complications of the pregnancy, necessitating a Caesarean. But it was too late. On August 23, less than a week after the convention ended, Jackie delivered a stillborn daughter she had wanted to name Arabella. She suffered this tragedy without the presence of her vacationing husband. He wasn't even close by.

Jack had hurt his wife deeply. While he had always refused to accept his father's politics, or his selfish view of the world, when it came to his marriage he was Joe Kennedy's true son. Jackie was able to see the effect her husband had on other women, and it wasn't easy. Yet she'd given him the nickname "Magic" for his ability to walk into a room and seduce all present. Charlie Bartlett could see the effect on her of his pal's behavior in those early years of marriage. "She wasn't the carefree, happy Jackie Bouvier anymore." But Jack's behavior now traveled beyond casual infidelity. He wasn't there when she needed him. He'd shown off his wife at the convention for political gain, then left her to suffer her tragedy alone.

It was Bobby, usually politically astute, who made the decision not to alert his brother about what had happened. His reasoning seemed based on the belief that Jack's returning from a pleasure trip to console his grieving wife would be the wrong sort of reunion. It was a bad call, and the newspapers got the story. George Smathers made it his business to persuade Kennedy to return home pronto, telling him that his marriage was at stake and, along with it, his ambitions for high office.

That fall Jack Kennedy traveled the country for Adlai Stevenson. He owed him, after all. What Stevenson was giving him now was actually better than the vice-presidential nod; it was the perfect trial run. It set Jack loose on the political circuit as a Stevenson man. To the Democratic Party, still dominated by its liberal faction, this was an incalculable benefit. After August 1956 Jack knew what he possessed, and what he needed to change. He was a smart and engaging outsider, a moderate in a party still run by its liberal establishment.

To win the next prize he sought, he'd have to become part of it. He would do what was necessary.

CHAPTER TEN
CHARM

A little touch of Harry in the night.
— William Shakespeare, *Henry V*

What we are born with are our gifts. What
we learn are our prizes. Jack Kennedy came
into the world with good looks and wealth,
and the social confidence that accompanies
them. He possessed an instinctive trait for
getting to the heart of a matter that enabled
him to direct himself to the essence of a challenge. He possessed also an ability — rare and
somewhat unsettling — to separate himself
from the emotions of those around him. He
was uncannily astute, moreover, when it came
to seeing the motives of those he encountered.
That he could know what moved others but
not be moved himself brought hurt to those
close to him, but it was for Kennedy himself
a source of strength and provided for him an
almost scary independence.

All these gifts would have been his had he
never embarked on a career in professional

Senate Rackets Committee, 1959 **25**

26

Ben Bradlee

27

Ted Sorensen

politics. His prizes were what he picked up along the way. He now understood better than he might have before how the candidate who starts early gives himself the advantage. He saw how much simple personal contact mattered when you wanted something from people. He'd recognized the truth of that during his first race, back in '46, when he was out at dawn, campaigning at the Charlestown docks, and then staying with it until late in the evening when he sat with constituents in their living rooms. To accomplish his goal, he'd practically killed himself — and it had worked.

He'd learned, too, in that first, winning effort, that the ambitious politician such as himself needs to create his own organization; he cannot expect existing political factions to whisk him forward. And he quickly realized that the key to forging loyalty within his organization was the invitation itself. The mere act of asking someone to become a Kennedy person was the step that mattered. Nothing builds fealty like getting people out there working for you. With time, discipline, experience, and trust, Jack Kennedy had forged a strong team, one that had been blooded in battle and now was ready for a fresh attack on an even greater trophy.

At the 1956 convention, Kennedy had begun to set the course for the next four years. Above all, he had made his presence known. But the strong backing for Kefauver, known as both a heavy drinker and difficult maverick, had been a clear sign that liberals didn't see Jack as one of their own — which, of course, he wasn't. The truth is, even Stevenson himself had reservations about the Tennessean who'd been twice his rival before he was his running mate. "Kefauver has never done anything to me," he told his friend the historian Arthur Schlesinger. "I just instinctively don't like that fellow."

The pivotal revelation in Chicago for Kennedy and his budding strategists was the emerging power of the primaries. A big change had occurred in the way Americans choose presidents. Consider the difference in how Adlai Stevenson had won his party's nomination in 1952 and how he gained it again in '56. In January of '52, he'd been summoned to meet with President Truman. In that meeting, Truman had offered him the presidential nomination, as if it were a Kansas City patronage job. Stevenson, to the dismay of his host, turned it down. He said he wanted to run for reelection as governor of Illinois.

In March, Truman met with him a second time and offered the nomination again. Stevenson once more held back. Only at the convention itself, staged in Chicago, did Adlai finally bow to the "Draft Stevenson" pressure and agree to be the party's candidate against Dwight Eisenhower.

What's particularly interesting, given what came later, is that, during all those months Truman and the party were urging Stevenson to run, Senator Kefauver was out there doing his own thing, running and winning primaries, including the New Hampshire contest in which he famously upset the incumbent, Truman. So, in 1952, what mattered was not victory in the primaries, but the blessing of the president, along with the excitement Stevenson was able to stir on the convention floor by the rousing speech he gave, which started a stampede for his nomination.

Four years later, the nomination went to the same man — but by a very different route. As he had before, Kefauver again won New Hampshire, this time swamping Stevenson. He went on to secure the primaries in Minnesota and Wisconsin. But then Stevenson turned the tide, winning in Oregon, Florida, and California, where he'd retained his popularity among the Democratic faithful. By the end, he won more primary votes, overall, than Kefauver.

So, if Jack Kennedy was to win the presidential nomination in 1960, there was only one route for him. He needed to go out in the country and build the basis for winning primaries. Here he faced a set of personal challenges. One concern was his health. His Addison's disease required that he pace himself and, as needed, take time off to rest. In addition, he would have to contend with the perennial twin curses of his bad back and weak stomach. "I know I'll never be more than eighty to eighty-five percent healthy," he told Red Fay, "but as long as I know that, I'm all right."

Beyond that were more basic challenges. How could he possibly run for president of the United States? Charlie Bartlett had challenged him. After all, he didn't know the country. For all his intellectual curiosity, Jack had spent very little time in the real United States, if by that we mean the way regular Americans know it. Until he entered politics, Jack's America had been Hyannis Port, Palm Beach, and the Stork Club. The product of elite prep schools and Harvard, he'd spent summers in Europe, touring with his chums and staying with his family in the South of France. During his father's tenure in London, he was the ambassador's son, a privileged American youth among the titled.

To win nationally, Kennedy would have to get out there and stay — from now until 1960. The goal would be to build a whole national organization, just as he'd constructed a local one in the 11th Congressional District in 1946, and then across the Commonwealth of Massachusetts in the lead-up to the Lodge race in '52. He'd be required to "retail" himself the way he'd done in both those earlier races. Certainly, the countrywide scale of the enterprise was daunting, and he could hardly piggyback on any existing organization. This meant a whole new Kennedy Party from coast to coast.

Only by getting out there before everyone else could he build the sort of support he'd be able to use to dominate the Democratic big shots, especially the governors, who, he'd learned, control the bulk of the delegates. But before he could give them the Onions Burke treatment, he needed to secure his own clout.

At first, it was just him and Ted Sorensen. The two of them would head out together across the country to introduce Jack to the local political people, the ones who'd likely be chosen as delegates to the next national convention. "For Christmas that year, 1956," Sorensen recalled, "I gave him a blank map of the United States, with each state shaded or colored . . . according to a code indicating what percentage of that state's 1956 convention delegation had supported him for vice president. He pored over that little map often in the next few years, and it became a guide to our early strategy and travel priorities in his quest for the presidency."

The hosts welcoming them out there in America's cities and towns responded well to the attention of the glamorous Massachusetts senator. "The smaller states," Sorensen remembered, "were flattered by this attention; the large states were pleased to have him

speak at their annual fund-raising dinners."
Wherever he traveled, he was a hit, and for
Sorensen, it was the hair-raising adventure of
a lifetime: "To reach small towns not served
by major airlines, private planes were an un-
avoidable part of political campaigning. Most
politicians can tell stories of scary plane travels. Prior to my journeys with JFK, at least
two sitting senators had been killed in small
plane crashes."

He found his boss to be great company. It
almost always was just the two of them, with
the budding candidate giving the speeches,
shaking hands, getting to know people, while
his aide took down the names and details.
"It was more than a list of names and addresses. I attempted to add to the file notes
on which people were most influential in each
state, their attitudes toward JFK, and the issues that mattered most to them. I also made
certain that they received Christmas cards,
personal notes, some even phone calls, from
JFK, gradually building a 'Christmas card
list' of thirty thousand influential Democrats
across the country." With a goal of meeting
every potential delegate, it meant dealing with
a lot of politicians.

In those days the word *politician,* used today
almost exclusively for candidates and office-
holders, applied to those fellows behind the
scenes as well. They were the ones calling the
shots, picking the future mayors and gover-

nors. In the late 1950s and early '60s, many of those less visible pols — the party chairmen, the big-city bosses, the ward captains — were Irish Catholics. Actually, almost all of them were. "When we said good-bye to almost every Irish-American mayor, party leader, or legislator we met around the country," Sorensen recalled, "JFK would turn to me and say — depending on whether our host had been warmhearted or cold, compassionate or conservative — 'Now, that's our type of Irish.'"

With some of this crowd, their mission would prove a hard sell. The city bosses from New York, Philadelphia, Cleveland, and Chicago were the people Kennedy most needed to win over. Having them on board would lay the foundation for winning over big-state governors such as David Lawrence of Pennsylvania and Pat Brown of California. Such men were skittish about Kennedy, perhaps even resentful. Why back another Al Smith, the Irish-Catholic New York governor who'd lost to Herbert Hoover in the presidential race of 1928? Based on Smith's performance, Kennedy could run and wind up bringing scores of other Democrats down with him, embarrassing Catholics like them in the process. Some begrudged the fact of Kennedy's effort itself. If he could take it on, it undercut their own egos. Why weren't they themselves running for president?

The key players the traveling duo of Kennedy and Sorensen hooked up with might include a congressman, an influential delegate, a governor, or sometimes just an old friend or relative. It was an education in national politics for both of them. "Those early trips were a way to test the presidential waters for 1960, to make friends and contacts while ascertaining whether a young, inexperienced Catholic senator would have any serious chance as a presidential candidate," Sorensen said. "We discovered that there was no true national party, only a coalition of forty-eight — later fifty — state parties. JFK set out to win them over, state by state, building grass-roots support, starting in smaller states, and encircling the big cities until we were ready to tackle them."

They also operated with a low enough profile to avoid any backlash. Many of their stops were in remote corners of the west and Midwest where, as Sorensen put it, his man's "candidacy could make solid gains without alerting the national party and press barons to mount a 'Stop Kennedy' movement." By late in 1959, Kennedy had personally contacted half the delegates who would be headed to the 1960 Democratic Convention.

Larry O'Brien was separately traveling the country for Kennedy. His accounts of that period show what a pioneer effort the mere idea of such canvassing was at the time. "My main job, in those early months, was to go on the road, to travel around America to build a campaign organization, as seven years earlier I'd traveled through Massachusetts in search of Kennedy secretaries. I would pay special attention to the potential primary states, since we knew that Kennedy would have to score well in the Democratic primaries to have any chance for the nomination."

Indiana was a typical destination, a central state where O'Brien spent days chatting up mayors, sheriffs, state legislators, and union officials. "I introduced myself as a representative of Senator Kennedy, a potential candidate for President in 1960. I soon realized I was a long way from Massachusetts, that most often Jack Kennedy was just a name, an image on a television screen. People were polite, sometimes interested, but there was no great groundswell for him. I found some support, a sheriff here, a mayor there, but more important, I found concern about Kennedy's religion."

O'Brien's account of a trip through California revealed the problem Kennedy would have with fellow Catholics. "I paid a courtesy call on Governor Pat Brown in Sacramento, who was himself considered a dark-horse possibility for the presidential nomination or, more likely, the vice-presidential nomination. He was in a difficult position. Stevenson had a great deal of support in California, and I assumed the Stevenson people were hinting that Brown might be Stevenson's running mate if he could deliver his state to their man. Brown certainly knew that, as a Catholic, he wasn't going to be on the ticket with Kennedy. We had a pleasant talk, but we both were playing our own little games."

After this, he met with Jesse Unruh, the astute Democratic leader of the California State Assembly. Unruh announced his support for Kennedy right away and stuck with him even when it got tough. "Jesse," O'Brien would tell him, "Senator Kennedy has every politician's name written in one of three books, and yours is written in Book One, in gold letters."

In this way, O'Brien worked his way across the country, finding both resistance and acceptance, but also people who were waiting to commit. What he didn't come across was the enemy doing the same thing that he and his candidate were doing: getting out there and meeting people one on one. "As I moved from state to state making friends, nailing down support, I kept waiting for the opposition to show up, but it never did. . . . It always amazed me how other politicians underestimated Kennedy. Johnson and Symington weren't taking him any more seriously in 1959 than Henry Cabot Lodge had in 1952. His opponents never discovered how tough, gutty, and ring-wise he was — until it was too late.

"We were lucky in 1959, because if his opponents for the nomination had started earlier and worked harder, they could well have blocked Kennedy's nomination," O'Brien recalled. "Instead, they sat tight, the Washington columnists kept writing about what a political genius Lyndon Johnson was, and we kept locking up delegates."

Because he had neither the party liberals nor the congressional leaders behind him, Jack was creating his own national political organization. Charlie Bartlett was amazed at his old friend's commitment. "I don't think anybody realizes, really, how much of a job that was. I mean, those weeks that he put in . . . and going into these towns where he really didn't know many people and there was no great Kennedy organization. He was traveling most of the time alone or with Ted Sorensen. It wasn't very lavish. But he traveled a long road. This was, of course, part of his strength."

Kennedy's feeling that his fate lay with a presidential run strengthened his resolve not to take a veep nomination. "He was urged to accept the vice presidential nomination to avoid a dangerous controversy," Sorensen recalled, "to which he replied, 'Oh I see, Catholics to the back of the bus.'" Kennedy still felt the sting of whatever anti-Catholic attitudes he'd come across over the years, even if they'd never been directed at him personally.

The four-year marathon taxed Kennedy to

his limits. "As hard as it is on the speechwriter, a presidential campaign is even tougher on the candidate," Sorensen said. "It is impossible for him to remember the names of all the people whose hands he shakes, to remember the time of day, the day of the week, and the town in which he is speaking; to remember his own previously stated positions on issues, much less those of his opponent. All day, the press is outside his door and window, the rooms are full of sweat and smoke, his hand is bruised, scratched, full of calluses. In JFK's case, one callus burst with blood. Everyone you meet wants something from you, your time, your endorsement, your support for some local project or measure; and then you move on to three more stops in three more states before you fall into bed."

Kennedy's physical condition had improved somewhat since the surgeries of 1954 and early '55, but his suffering continued. The pain in his back, attributed to loss of bone mass, was being alleviated with numbing injections. In September of '57, an abscess was removed from his back at New York Hospital, where he remained a patient for three weeks. Not long after that, a bout of flu sent him back into a hospital bed.

For everything that ailed him he was taking a daily smorgasbord of prescription medications, hardly the usual diet for a man of forty. Yet they all proved nothing more than stopgaps when it came to putting an end to his on-going health troubles. The cortisone he took for the Addison's, however, had the positive side effect of filling out his face, and he didn't mind that at all. As perilous as his health remained, he looked better than he ever had.

Ted Sorensen could do little to alleviate the strains of the road on Kennedy. "In the late 1950's when we traveled the country together, I would ask each hotel to provide him with a hard mattress or bed board. When that failed, sometimes we moved his mattress onto the floor of his hotel room." It was a replay of what had taken place in 1943 as young Lieutenant Kennedy was seen placing a piece of plywood under his mattress when he was training for PT-boat duty. "In retrospect, it is amazing that, in all those years, he never complained about his ailments," Sorensen recalled. "Occasionally, he winced when his back was stiff or pained as he eased himself into or out of the bathtub.

"On the political circuit I assumed that his practice of eating in the hotel room before a Democratic party luncheon was intended to avoid the bad food and constant interruptions that characterized his time at the head table. But now I realize after reading an analysis of his medical file, that his many stomach, intestinal, and digestive problems required a more selective diet." Jack, it turns out, was a man typical of his World War II generation. He didn't complain.

As Sorensen noted, he'd committed himself to a year-upon-year commitment "best suited to fanatics, egomaniacs, and superbly fit athletes." Jack Kennedy, well-rounded, pleasure-loving, was none of these.

As a candidate, Kennedy quickly had begun to give off the glow of celebrity. No politician had ever gotten the kind of star treatment he was accorded. It had begun at the Democratic Convention in Chicago: his debut in the public eye there threw the spotlight on him and his wife as well. In April 1957, he'd been awarded the Pulitzer Prize for Biography for *Profiles in Courage,* the book he'd dedicated to Jackie. Their first child, Caroline Bouvier Kennedy, was born in November 1957.

Whenever Senator Kennedy showed up at a local Democratic dinner in some small city where there were more hands to shake, it was if a Hollywood star had come to town. It was still the age of the glossy magazines, many of them pictorials. *Look, Life, the Saturday Evening Post,* all weeklies back then, did spreads on Jack and Jackie, as did *McCall's* and *Redbook.*

"Senator Kennedy, do you have an *in* with *Life?*" a high school newspaper writer once asked the roving candidate. "No," he shot back, "I just have a beautiful wife." There was a professional's assessment if ever there was one. But the fuss didn't stop with the romantic-couple angle. The TV series *Navy Log* did an episode on *PT 109*. The Knights of Columbus magazine *Columbia* offered a salute to a brother knight. And at the end of 1957, in the issue of December 2, he was *Time* magazine's cover boy, painted looking thoughtful by Henry Koerner, whose unmistakable celebrity portraits were often featured there.

This ongoing stream of media attention continued into the 1960 primaries. "You could go to the A&P store," his rival Hubert Humphrey would later say, revealing his exasperation, "you could go to any grocery store. You'd pick up a women's magazine — there would be a wonderful article. He had the publicity. He had the attraction. He had the *it*."

The Jack and Jacqueline Kennedy Show had a powerful effect even on people who normally paid little attention to politics but now could not take their eyes away. Eventually, the "it" to which Humphrey referred would achieve a name: *charisma,* not a word much in popular use until the Kennedys made it so.

While the stillbirth in 1956 and Jack's absence from the country at the time caused Jackie much pain, she and her husband had made their peace with it. Celebrating their new small family, they moved into a town house in Georgetown. Again, all the public saw were the pictures. Photos of infant Caroline with her splendid-looking parents captivated the American public.

Nonetheless, the audience with which Jack most needed to make inroads wasn't falling for it. Not yet, anyway. The liberals, given life by Franklin Roosevelt and still in love with Adlai Stevenson, were looking for gravitas. Here, again, Jack Kennedy went to work, with the help of his most trusted and productive lieutenant. For several years now, Ted Sorensen had been turning out all kinds of articles under Kennedy's name. They appeared in such journals as the *General Electric Defense Quarterly,* the *Bulletin of the Atomic Scientists,* and the *National Parent-Teacher.* Their purpose, Sorensen conceded, was "to promote Senator John F. Kennedy as a man of intensive progressive thought, balancing the flood of superficial articles about his looks and his romance with Jackie."

There remained the challenge of winning over the Stevenson people. "I'm not a liberal at all," *the Saturday Evening Post* had quoted him just after his election to the senate. "I never joined Americans for Democratic Action or the American Veterans Committee. I'm not comfortable with those people."

Still, his pursuit of the intellectuals who persisted in carrying a torch for Adlai was soon to begin in full earnest. The winning of the Pulitzer for *Profiles,* in fact, had been no happy accident. Rather, it was the result of energetic lobbying by Jack's dad. Through the good offices of Arthur Krock, a *New York Times* columnist and Kennedy friend, Joe was able to approach the members of the Pulitzer screening board, one by one. Even Rose Kennedy, for a change, was clued in. "Careful spadework," she said, was the key. Joe learned "who was on the committee and how to reach such and such a person through such and such a friend."

In this way, Kennedy senior and the influential Krock were able to get the job done. Rose, not always happy with her husband's backroom activities, loved this bit of work. "Things don't happen," she said with untroubled pride, "they are *made* to happen." That May, no doubt in recognition of the Pulitzer honor, Jack was named to chair the panel to select the five greatest senators in history, their portraits to be hung in the Capitol's Senate Reception Room. The quintet chosen were Henry Clay of Kentucky, John C. Calhoun of South Carolina, Daniel Webster of Massachusetts, Robert Taft of Ohio, and Robert La Follette, Sr., of Wisconsin.

The fact that Kennedy now was being taken seriously as a historian exerted its appeal over the Stevenson crowd, as it was meant to. Meanwhile, Kennedy won another distinction, one that would carry him nearer to the goal of influencing international affairs that had motivated him since first entering politics. He found himself appointed to the Senate Committee on Foreign Relations. Now came his first curtsy to the Democratic Left, which needed to be a clear sign that he'd departed from his rigid orthodoxies of the early postwar years, a semaphore signaling that he shared the liberals' more sophisticated attitudes.

On the Senate floor in July 1957, Kennedy called boldly for revision of the Eisenhower administration's Eurocentric foreign policy. America, he said, should end its automatic alliance with its colonialist World War II allies and recognize instead the rising aspirations of the developing world. "The most powerful single force in the world today is neither Communism nor capitalism, neither the H-bomb nor the guided missile," he began. "It is man's eternal desire to be free and independent." His criticism was aimed at French colonial rule in Algeria. Kennedy explained that France's 1954 defeat at Dien Bien Phu had not resulted from a shortage of military power. France would have lost the war in Indochina, he argued, even if it "could afford to increase substantially the manpower already poured into the area."

The speech, certainly prophetic for U.S. policy, stirred up the pot, just as he intended. "His words annoyed the French, embarrassed the American administration, and almost certainly would not satisfy Algerian nationalist leaders," the London *Observer* tartly noted at the time. "But they did one thing: they introduced Kennedy the statesman." This is precisely what he intended. Lou Harris, Kennedy's new pollster, was to confess that the "Algeria speech" had, in fact, been customized to appeal to the wing of the party whose backing his client needed. It was meant to show the liberals just how far Joe Kennedy's boy had come. The irony, Harris noted, like everyone else who knew Jack, was that his boss probably read more and was a good deal more informed than those on the Democratic Left into whose political bed he was trying to climb.

Kennedy had been careful to embed his argument in sound Cold War thinking; that is, that the fight in North Africa was weakening the far more important contest with the Soviet Union. "The war in Algeria, engaging more than 400,000 French soldiers, has stripped the continental forces of NATO to the bone," he declared. "It has undermined our relations with Tunisia and Morocco." And, more directly against U.S. interests: "It has endangered the continuation of some of our most strategic airbases, and threatened our geographical advantages over the Communist orbit." Kennedy was still anti-Communist, but now he was connecting this great cause with America's revolutionary roots. "The great enemy of that tremendous force of freedom is called, for want of a more precise term, imperialism — and today that means Soviet imperialism and, whether we like it or not, and though they are not to be equated, Western imperialism."

Kennedy was remembering the compelling force of nationalism he'd seen firsthand on that trip to Indochina in 1951. He was being true to what he'd discovered himself.

The Algeria speech offered political benefit with little if any cost. It appealed to the Northern liberals, but not at the expense of the Democratic South. Algerian independence had no chance of angering those Southerners who had rallied to him in Chicago the previous summer.

Kennedy was still trying to have it both ways: he wanted to be the liberals' candidate while not giving up those he'd won over in '56. Even as he seduced the Democratic Left with urbane commentary on colonialism, he wanted to protect the popularity with Southerners that he'd demonstrated during his vice-presidential tug-of-war with Estes Kefauver. Whatever maneuvers he was slyly executing in order to win over the liberals, he wanted, at the same time, to keep himself positioned as the best hope of moderate and conservative Democrats. And this group included those Southerners still holding fast to segregation.

Such folks liked the fact he was a "moderate," and he wanted to keep it that way. In the same year he gave the Algeria speech, Kennedy voted for the amendment to the 1957 Civil Rights Act that allowed jury trials for local officials charged in civil rights cases. While passage of this amendment was viewed as critical to avoiding a filibuster, it was also seen as a way for all-white Southern juries to continue, routinely, to acquit defendants in such cases. Kennedy's position on the jury-trial question earned him a rebuke from the NAACP, but maintained the warm regard of his colleagues below the Mason-Dixon line.

The man himself was more complicated. Kennedy had an instinctive contempt toward discrimination. Speaking at the Somerset Club, a private men's club in Boston, he suffered an introduction by a member who jokingly insinuated that the Democrats were the party of "the help." After hearing this, Jack remarked to his friend Alistair Forbes: "Well, I wondered why more people weren't blushing with shame. But can you believe that such people can still be around?"

Forbes recalled, "He was a man wholly devoid of rancor, and his personality was completely well integrated so that he had no worries of any kind at all. He could see everything with a sort of detached view.

"And yet he was aware of the interplay of snobbish forces in his life. In England he could see which English people basically didn't like Americans, and he knew people who didn't like Irish people. He was always amused and interested by this sort of sin, but absolutely unaffected by it because he was his own man and happy with his money in the bank — and damn good-looking."

George Smathers agreed. He said his friend was "always greatly interested in civil rights." Then he amended that: "Put it this way — not civil rights legislation so much, but civil rights because he was against discrimination. I think he felt that, as an Irishman, somewhere along the line he had been discriminated against. I don't know, but I did get the feeling that he felt that other Irishmen had felt the sting of prejudice."

At the same time, Kennedy operated at a distinct remove from certain realities, even as he crisscrossed the country broadening his reach. Forbes, for one, was struck by his lack of awareness about black America. "I remember very late, sometime in the fifties, he'd only just heard the phrase 'Uncle Tom' and was like a man who'd just made this extraordinary discovery. 'Do you know that Clayton Powell's got this marvelous expression?' he asked me." Powell, it seems, had been talking to Jack about a black colleague in Chicago, saying, "The trouble with him is he's an Uncle Tom." Learning this new expression from Harlem's congressman delighted him.

Politically, he knew that if he wanted to make his way into liberal hearts and minds, he had to forge ties with those who cared about such issues as civil rights. He wanted very much to have the support of men such as Arthur Schlesinger, one of the co-founders of Americans for Democratic Action and a longtime Stevenson stalwart. Here's an entry in Schlesinger's journal from 1959. It displays just what kind of effort Jack Kennedy was mounting to win over a man whose support was critical.

July 19 — Jack Kennedy called up around noon and asked us to come to dinner at Hyannis Port this evening. Marian could not go, so I went alone. The Kennedy place was less grand than I had imagined. I expected miles of ocean frontage with no alien houses in view; but it is a cluster of Kennedy houses, all large and comfortable but not palatial, in the midst of a settled community. Jackie Kennedy was the only other person present, and we all drank and talked about from 8 to 12:30. I only brought two cigars, one of which Jack took, having typically no cigars in the house. Jackie wanted for a moment to go and see *A Nun's Story,* which being screened in a projection room in one of the other houses; but, though somewhat encouraged by Jack to go, finally stayed the evening out with us. She was lovely but seemed excessively flighty on politics, asking with wide-eyed naivete questions like: "Jack, why don't you just tell them that you

won't go into any of those old primaries?"
Jack was in a benign frame of mind and did
not blink; but clearly such remarks could, in
another context, be irritating. This is all the
more so since Jackie, on other subjects, is
intelligent and articulate. She was reading
Proust when I arrived; she talked very well
about Nicolas Nabokov, Joe Alsop, and
other personalities, and one feels that out of
some perversity she pretends an ignorance
about politics larger even than life.

As for Jack, he gave his usual sense of
seeming candor. I write "seeming" without
meaning to imply doubts; so far as I could
tell, he was exceedingly open; and this was,
indeed, the freest, as well as the longest, talk
I have ever had with him. As usual, he was
impersonal in his remarks, quite prepared
to see the views and interests of others. He
showed more animation and humor than
usual and, indeed, was rather funny in some
of his assessments of people and situations.
He seems fairly optimistic about his presidential chances. He thinks that Humphrey
can't win, that Johnson will take care of
Symington, and that he will go into Los Angeles with a large delegate lead. He seems
to regard Stevenson as the next most likely
person to get the nomination.

Then an uncomfortable subject was broached.
"We had considerable talk about McCarthy.

Kennedy said he felt that it would be a good idea to admit frankly that he had been wrong in not taking a more forthright position. I said that he was paying the price of having written a book called *Profiles in Courage*. He replied ruefully, 'Yes, but I didn't have a chapter in it about myself.' "

The conversation that night in July of 1959 is telling in so many ways. The invitation itself was a fine gesture, with the arranging of an intimate evening around one person, a figure Jack saw as powerfully influential. Well aware of the liberal rancor over his failure to oppose McCarthy, he now was working at being convincingly conciliatory. Schlesinger observed his efforts: "I think he genuinely thinks he was wrong about it; but says he was constrained for a long time because Bobby had joined the committee staff — over Jack's opposition, he says. He also said that his father and Joe were great friends, and that his father would defend Joe as a person to this day."

During the course of the evening, Jack showed contempt for President Eisenhower, saying he refused to hang around with his old comrades in arms from the war. "All his golfing pals are rich men he has met since 1945." He also went after Ike's willingness to drop Nixon from the ticket in '56. "He won't stand by anybody. He is terribly cold and terribly vain. In fact, he's a shit."

But he was less candid on other matters.

When Schlesinger pushed him on his Addison's disease, he said the problem with his adrenal glands was caused by his wartime malaria, it had cleared up, and he was okay. "No one who has Addison's disease ought to run for President; but I do not have it and have never had it." He then claimed he was no longer taking cortisone, that, in fact, he took nothing. It was a pattern of denial that he would continue as he now campaigned for the backing of a group — the liberals — whose approval he'd never sought in the past.

Over the period from '57 to '59, Kennedy also had to build bridges with another key power in the Democratic Party: labor. Kennedy had started his Capitol Hill career on the Education and Labor Committee and made a name for himself by being tough on suspected Communist sympathizers among the union leaders. Now Bobby and he were targeting the corrupt ones.

The Senate Select Committee on Improper Activities in Labor and Management, to be famously known as the "Senate Rackets Committee," was formed in January 1957. Senator John McClellan initiated the temporary panel to investigate the rivalry between Dave Beck and Jimmy Hoffa for the presidency of the International Brotherhood of Teamsters. Both men were accused of bribery and, in Hoffa's case, fraud. McClellan brought Bobby Kennedy with him from the Government Operations Committee. He named him chief counsel and investigator. Bobby, in turn, named Ken O'Donnell, his administrative assistant, as his top aide.

Jack worried what this would do to him politically. Bobby's new job now associated his brother with the Republicans and pro-management Democrats who dominated the committee. Any attacks on organized labor by Bobby Kennedy, a bulldog in pursuit of his goals, would be seen by labor and its political friends as an attack by Jack.

Bobby understood this. "If the investigation flops . . . it will hurt Jack in 1958 and in 1960, too. . . . A lot of people think he's the Kennedy running the investigation, not me. As far as the public is concerned, one Kennedy is the same as another Kennedy."

That mention of 1958 alluded to Jack's reelection campaign. Seeing his weak opposition, Senator Kennedy begged Republican pals back home in the Commonwealth to put up a stronger candidate so he could at least prove *something*. What he ended up demonstrating was his overwhelming support among Massachusetts voters as he defeated the martyred Vincent J. Celeste, representing the Republicans, 1,362,926 to 488,318. The result of this rout was that Joe Kennedy at last saw great worth in Ken O'Donnell and Larry O'Brien. Not only had they delivered the goods; they'd done so without taking up much of Jack's precious time. The efficiency of their performance had the effect of ensuring less interference from Joe, who now trusted the pair of them, in the big contest to come.

The Rackets Committee managed to strip Dave Beck of his title as president of the Teamsters Union and also to expose, by use of wiretaps, a plot set up by Hoffa and organized crime figures to establish phony locals to vote him in as president. This was new ground Bobby Kennedy was plowing. Over at the Federal Bureau of Investigation, Director J. Edgar Hoover still refused even to recognize the existence of the Mafia.

That November a meeting of organized crime figures in Apalachin, New York, was discovered by local police. But when Bobby Kennedy asked the FBI for records on the bosses, he discovered it had none. So he opened up his own hearings. The star witness was Salvatore "Sam" Giancana, heir to Al Capone. Kennedy interrogated him about his operations, which included hanging his victims on meat hooks and stuffing them into trunks of cars.

Robert Kennedy: Would you tell us anything about any of your operations, or will you just giggle every time I ask you a question?

Sam Giancana:	I decline to answer because I honestly believe my answer may tend to incriminate me.
Kennedy:	I thought only little girls giggled, Mr. Giancana.

Bobby Kennedy was both fearless and relentless. On the wall of his office, buried in the basement of the Senate Office Building, was a quotation from Winston Churchill: "We shall not flag or fail. We shall never surrender." It didn't win him any friends in the labor world, or in those political fiefdoms where union leaders freely operated. A number of big-city mayors felt the heat and didn't like it, didn't like the paths Bobby Kennedy was heading down.

Meanwhile, Jack Kennedy's performance on the Rackets Committee impressed one of Bobby's assistants. Pierre Salinger, a reporter for the Saturday Evening Post who Bobby hired as an investigator, saw Senator Kennedy zero in on whatever relevant issue was at hand: "John F. Kennedy had clearly done his homework. . . . In what is essentially a nebulous area, he was very incisive in his questioning. He was able, with a question or two, to do what it seemed to me to take hours to get to from other people on the committee." He was careful not to lump the clean labor executives in with the bad. "Senator Kennedy made a special effort not to join the Republicans and conservative Democrats on the committee when it came to dealing with honest union leaders like Walter Reuther of the United Auto Workers."

Yet even the UAW was held to account. In Ken O'Donnell's words, Jack "was not only good in terms of defending the union, but several times, armed by Bobby, he went right after the union and was probably tougher on them than some of the Republicans. He criticized them for the use of violence against their own men and against the company. He was tough, but tough in an appropriate way. The intellectual ability of Senator Kennedy and Bob Kennedy was established with the UAW. Reuther and the UAW saw the Kennedy brothers as not only honest, keeping their word, but also that they were both smart as hell. It wasn't an image that the union had held of either brother up until that point."

The Democratic governor of Maine, Edmund Muskie, who would enter the Senate himself in 1959, said the hearings made Kennedy a heavyweight there. It was the facing down of the criminals that impressed them. "I think that his performance in the Senate added tremendously to his stature, and to the respect which all his Senate colleagues, even those with a different political philosophy, had for him. I know that it was performances like this that enlisted the support of people like Dick Russell and other giants of the Senate. They *did* respect him. It wasn't just because they liked him, because they were attracted by his charm, because he had a way with words. They respected his guts . . . respected him as a man."

But Kennedy cited the struggle for labor reform as further proof that "the Presidency is the source of action . . . There is much less than meets the eye in the Senate." Yet his service on the Rackets Committee gave Jack another memorable victory. He'd made himself a *reputation,* as had his brother. Both were seen now as tough, independent reformers, racket busters. The image remains suspended in the mind, in black and white, of the two of them staring insolently at the crude thug there in the witness seat. We see Bob, the hot-blooded Irish cop, asking questions close into the microphone; Jack, the cool brother, tapping his fingernails on his teeth, that old habit that betrayed his cunning.

Jack Kennedy made few new personal friends from the time he entered politics. But that was about to change. On a warm winter Sunday early in 1959, Ben Bradlee, a correspondent for *Newsweek,* and his second wife, Tony, were wheeling a baby carriage along N Street in Georgetown. In it was their baby boy, Dino. Another couple, Jack and Jackie Kennedy, were also enjoying the winter sunshine, with two-year-old Caroline. The couples, similar in background, quickly became friends.

Bradlee had been a young naval officer in World War II, and his experience had included being at the helm of his destroyer as it navigated Japanese waters. The bond with Kennedy was secured further by their prep school and Harvard backgrounds. Bradlee would say that he was, in fact, higher up in the social "stud book" than Jack Kennedy, having descended from an old New England family around a lot longer than the immigrant Kennedys. Ben was the sort of guy — smart, handsome, ironic, and seemingly fearless — that Jack liked on sight. A working journalist, Bradlee now counted as a close friend a man bent on achieving the presidency. "Nothing in my education or experience had led me to conceive of the possibility that someone I really knew would hold that exalted job."

Bradlee soon saw clearly the obstacles ahead for his new pal, what he called "the mines" he'd have to navigate: "His age — at forty-three, he'd be the youngest man ever elected president, and the first one born in the twentieth century. His religion — too much of America believed that a Catholic president would have to take orders from the pope in Rome. His health — he'd been given the last rites several times. His father — Joseph P. Kennedy's reputation was secure as a womanizing robber baron, who'd been anti-war and seen as pro-German while he was ambassador to Britain during World War II, and pro-McCarthy during the fifties."

When Bradlee asked Jack if it didn't seem "strange" to him to be running for president, Kennedy offered even his friend a stock reply: "Yes, until I stop and look around at the other people who are running for the job. And then I think I'm just as qualified as they are." When he asked if he thought he could pull it off, Kennedy's answer was even more studied: "Yes. If I don't make a single mistake, and if I don't get maneuvered into a position where there's no way out."

It was, in fact, a troubled time, as the 1950s were coming to a close. The country that had proudly, gloriously led the forces that vanquished the Axis dictators now had a growing set of worries when it looked beyond its borders in almost any direction. From the earliest moments of his run for the presidency, the country that Jack Kennedy was hoping to convince he could lead was beset by an unsettling feeling. Americans sensed they were losing pace in the Cold War, and weren't sure how this had happened. The Soviets were moving worldwide; we were fading as a global power, not dramatically, but undeniably.

In October 1957, the country even became wary, suddenly, about the grandfatherly leadership of Dwight Eisenhower. The launching of the Soviet space satellite *Sputnik* sent an ugly shiver down the spines of complacent citizens long convinced of their country's enduring edge against the "Soviet menace." We'd been told by Wernher von Braun and Walt Disney — in 1955 more than 40 million of us had watched on TV the gung-ho film *Man in Space,* which they'd made together — that the United States would be the first to launch a satellite into orbit. Now the Russians had done it. Our leaders had committed the worst sin a politician can — as Churchill once noted: to promise success and then fail.

The second tangible sign of losing pace came on New Year's Eve 1958. That evening the Cuban president, Fulgencia Batista, a dictator who'd been up until that moment agreeably rotten, sneaked out of Havana at midnight and headed into exile. His departure allowed the bearded leader Fidel Castro, a young lawyer-turned-guerrilla clad in fatigues, to come down out of the Sierra Maestra and assume power. When Castro, who'd sold himself as a democratic reformer, announced his allegiance to Marxist-Leninism, the Soviet Union had an ally ninety miles from our coast.

There was also intangible evidence of America's failure to keep pace against the encroaching Soviet menace. As we fought the battle of the global game board, there came a creeping sense ours was not the winning side.

Kennedy had run on the spirit of the returning vet in '46, then, in 1952, had catapulted himself past the Yankee order in Massachusetts, thanks both to the creative way he again worked his own tribe and also to its own rising self-estimation.

Now, with Ike aging and the decade slowing, the candidate saw how his fellow Americans were reacting against the dullness, feeling a restless urge to *do something*. Even in their prosperity, they knew the times weren't living up to their aspirations, felt the pang of their unchallenged spirits. Jack Kennedy, having been out there in a way no one else was, sensed the mood of the country in a way uniquely his own, and now staked his claim on the task of getting us moving again.

CHAPTER ELEVEN
HARDBALL

See DiSalle and make sure he is going to meet his commitment.
> — The candidate's instructions,
> October 28, 1959

At the 1956 Democratic Convention, Jack Kennedy had allowed himself to be at the mercy of the delegates. From now on, *he* was going to call the shots. He would be the one making other politicians do his bidding. He would do, on a national scale, what he'd accomplished at home, when grabbing control of the Massachusetts Democratic Party committee. This would mean wooing those he could, playing hardball with the ones he couldn't.

In early November 1958, Kennedy won reelection to the U.S. Senate for his second term by a margin of three to one. Later that month Jack stopped by Tip O'Neill's office, wanting to talk to Tip's top guy, Tommy Mullen, about how the vote had gone in their district,

New Hampshire Primary

28

West Virginia Debate

29

the one Jack himself had once represented. Tip remembered, "Together, the two of them, Mullen and Kennedy, went over the district precinct by precinct — where the Irish lived, where the Jews lived, and so on, with every ethnic group. Jack wanted to know how each one had voted because he intended to use that information on the national scene for the 1960 presidential election. I'd never seen anybody study the voting patterns of ethnic and religious groups in a systematic way before, and I don't think that most people realized then, or appreciate now, that Jack Kennedy was a very sophisticated student of politics."

Looking around, Kennedy wasn't impressed by the field he would face. "There's nothing there in 1960," he told a doubting Charlie Bartlett, who argued he should wait at least eight years. "This is really the time," Jack insisted. The Rackets Committee had made him a celebrated figure. Bobby, too. "For the couple of years there, all you heard was the name Kennedy," Ken O'Donnell recalled. Jack's tough, evenhanded treatment of both labor and management had shown "a different kind of Democratic politician." He gave the impression of being independent, fearless.

At the same time, the Kennedy brothers were creating a reputation for themselves as dangerous enemies, even when it came to fellow Democrats. Thanks to them, George Chacharis, a onetime millworker who was the mayor of Gary, Indiana, went to prison for conspiracy and tax evasion. Pierre Salinger recalls that Jack preferred killing a politician to wounding one. " 'A wounded tiger,' he always said, 'was more dangerous than either a living or a dead one.' "

It was Salinger's first exposure to Jack Kennedy's ruthlessness. Up until then, Jack had appeared, on the surface, the one with the easygoing nature. Salinger was fascinated. He was learning what Ken O'Donnell and others had before him. Bobby was the one who'd gained the reputation for ruthlessness, but Jack could be pitiless.

Two important strategy meetings, looking to the immediate future, were staged six months apart in 1959. The first, with everyone flying to the Kennedy family house in Palm Beach, was held in April. It was here Jack revealed himself as a man fully in charge of his troops and the operation upon which they were embarking.

"At Palm Beach, the senator was in full command," Ted Sorensen recounted. "He was still his chief campaign manager and strategy advisor. He knew each stage, the problems it presented, the names of those to contact — not only governors and senators but their administrative assistants as well, not only politicians but publishers and private citizens. He kept in touch with the Kennedy men in every state, acquired field workers for the primary states, made all the crucial decisions, and was the final depository of all reports and rumors concerning the attitudes of key figures."

Sorensen knew, by now, his boss's special way of dealing with "rumors." "Whenever word reached him of a politician who was being privately and persistently antagonistic, the senator would often ask a third party to see the offender — not because he hoped for the latter's support, but because 'I want him to know that I know what he's saying.'"

Ted Sorensen, now a veteran well acquainted with Jack's thinking and his wishes, briefed the others in Palm Beach on the campaign to date. O'Donnell recalled, "Sorensen dominated much of this meeting — with the exception of the senator, of course. He'd done a great deal of research on each primary and the pros/cons for and against, so he talked and we listened. Then Senator Kennedy and his father would respond accordingly. Bobby, Larry, and I had little to contribute. We listened carefully.

"The main thrust of the first conversation was that the senator planned to set up some sort of organization in Washington, D.C., reasonably rapidly," O'Donnell continued. "This was the first and critical step towards putting together professional organizations. Steve Smith, husband of Jack's sister Jean, was going to come down from New York, open and run the office in Washington, to begin organizing the campaign. Sorensen had been the record-keeper on where the candidate stood with regional party leaders. As Steve took over and became more and more familiar, he increasingly took over that role from Sorensen. He oversaw the filing system that recorded how Jack stood with the delegates and politicians across the country.

"If the senator met a delegate and the delegate said that he'd support Kennedy if he ran for president . . . then either Dave Powers or Ted would make such a notation on the card and give it a number. The numbering system began with a ten. If a delegate was a ten, that meant he was a totally committed Kennedy man." The card was then "returned to the main file in the Washington campaign office and then the senator would write the person a thank-you letter."

According to O'Donnell, "There was still an element of hush-hush: Steve Smith's headquarters bore no mention of the Kennedy campaign. They couldn't have asked for a more anonymous office without lying: the sign read simply, 'Stephen E. Smith.'" The Kennedy campaign was still, at this point, purposely under the radar.

In addition, the Kennedy team at Palm Beach had moved on to the wider issues facing the candidate throughout the country. Sorensen took notes of the questions posed. It came down to what had been learned in

1956: Who calls the shots when picking delegates, and how do we influence them? This inevitably led to the question of which state primaries the candidate would have to enter.

It was not clear if winning primaries, even a great many of them, would be enough to secure the nomination. As recently as 1952, Kefauver had won practically all of them; still, the convention had "drafted" Stevenson. The goal now was to win as many primaries as possible, meanwhile convincing the big-state governors to climb aboard the bandwagon. It was still a common practice for governors to run in their own state primaries, then arrive at the convention to broker their delegates in backroom deals.

To win, Kennedy would have to do it the hard way, dominating enough primaries that as the convention approached, those governors would go to him. Only that way could he gain the momentum he needed. Jack, after all, wasn't a party favorite with either the liberal or Washington establishments. If the old Roosevelt crowd prevailed, it could well be Adlai Stevenson again. If Lyndon Johnson proved able to leverage his sizable Capitol Hill clout, the nomination might be his.

"By taking the case directly to the people, as he intended, he felt he'd be able to pick up a great many delegates," O'Donnell said. "I think, very early, he took the position that the leaders and professionals will, in the end, follow their delegations. He believed he could succeed in building a fire under these leaders by appealing directly to the voters and to the delegates."

The governors most on his mind were a trio composed of David Lawrence of Pennsylvania, Pat Brown of California, and Mike DiSalle of Ohio. These men, so the idea went, "would begin to get nervous and, though their inclination might — or not — be for John Kennedy, in the end they would follow their delegates."

Kennedy knew he faced a problem with all his fellow Catholics. He needed to overcome their ingrained belief that one of them could not be elected president. To do that, he'd have to convince the governors to support him in the face of what many of them believed to be their own self-interest, fearing as they did that a Catholic on their state ballot would hurt the chances of their other candidates. Yet there was also something deeper at work. Any Catholic governor was at the top of the heap, as far as Catholic perception was concerned; he'd risen as high as he could up until that moment. Maintaining that ceiling on his possibilities meant he could congratulate himself on reaching the pinnacle he'd attained.

The cold fact was that these governors feared a backlash among their states' voters. Bishop Wright, a politically savvy Catholic leader from Worcester, Massachusetts, and longtime family friend of the O'Donnells, had become the bishop of the Diocese of Pittsburgh. He warned O'Donnell that "he didn't believe Governor Lawrence would support Senator Kennedy. The bishop indicated that friends had talked to him and that the governor was still exactly in the same spot he'd been in 1956, still horribly fearful of the problem a Catholic candidate would present to the Democratic ticket nationally. The governor also believed that under no circumstances would people in the state of Pennsylvania support a Catholic at the top of the ticket." His nervousness was understandable, given that he was the first Catholic to hold his position.

Governor Pat Brown of California, also Catholic, was resisting Kennedy's approaches. His aide Fred Dutton admitted later that he'd been urging his boss to hold off backing the Massachusetts candidate. "The truth of the matter is that Brown, privately, was very strong for Kennedy at that stage. It was me arguing that it made sense in terms of California politics — and everything else — that the governor stay uncommitted. This was something between just Brown and me, but Kennedy was completely aware of it. He had it right down to the gnat's eyebrow."

Brown had a high regard for Kennedy. "There was no bullshit to the man," the former governor told me long into his retirement. He'd seen how Kennedy had come west well prepared. "His complete familiarity with California politics was incredible," Dutton recalled. "I would guess he knew more about California politicians than any of the chief California Democratic politicians of the period." But it wasn't all soft sell. "O'Donnell and O'Brien were out several times," said Dutton, "and made strong private approaches to various individuals — *threatening,* in fact, is the only accurate word."

With O'Donnell and Bobby still on the Rackets Committee through the first half of 1959, the campaign progressed at a gradual pace. In the period between Palm Beach and the second strategy meeting in October, the senator continued to travel the country seeking out delegates. O'Brien and O'Donnell, at the behest of Bobby, began accompanying him on these trips, allowing Sorensen to remain in Washington, "working on issues and speeches."

When Bobby left the committee in July in order to write his own book, *The Enemy Within* — billed as a "crusading lawyer's personal story of a dramatic struggle with the ruthless enemies of clean unions and honest management" — he also took a hiatus from the campaign. O'Donnell noted with regret the difference his absence made.

The Kennedy campaign's second crucial meeting that year was convened at Bobby's Hyannis Port house in October. Again, Jack conducted it, once more demonstrating his leadership strengths, but also the in-depth knowledge he'd gained. This time the group included influential Democrats in need of continual reassurance that they were backing the right candidate. Among them were Governor Abraham Ribicoff of Connecticut and that state's party boss, John Bailey. When they left, each man present had designated responsibilities for which he'd volunteered.

For example, Larry O'Brien would handle California, Maryland, and Indiana, and Hy Raskin, a Chicago lawyer and onetime Stevenson loyalist, took Oregon. There were no salaries; just their expenses were paid by the campaign. And now, with his book finished, Bobby was free to assume the reins of the entire effort. They needed him "to take control and get it all organized in order to be effective," said O'Donnell.

Currently looming was the decision whether to run in Ohio or Wisconsin. Since both primaries were held at the same time, a choice had to be made. If Kennedy tried to campaign in both, he'd be spreading himself too thin. It was decided that a win in Wisconsin, where a poll by Lou Harris showed him ahead, made the most sense. It would prove he could win in a Midwestern farm state against a regional rival, Senator Hubert Humphrey of neighboring Minnesota.

Here, the great potential advantage was

identical to the disadvantage: his rival's geographic edge. Humphrey had for years been a popular figure in Wisconsin. Beating him in his own territory would send a very definite signal. Here's how O'Donnell recapped Kennedy's thinking: "He said, 'I'd be running against Hubert, who practically lives in Wisconsin. Minnesota and Wisconsin have about the same economic problems, Hubert obviously being on the right side. While I — a city boy from Boston — am not going to be on the right side of some Wisconsin problems.'"

Thus, with Wisconsin obviously such a challenge, it made victory there all the more significant. "He felt it would be a great gamble and, if he lost, it would knock him out of the ballpark, totally." There was just one real danger the candidates saw to the enterprise: a battle with the Protestant Humphrey could draw unfavorable attention to Kennedy's Catholicism and thus hurt him in primaries coming after.

But if Kennedy forfeited Wisconsin to Humphrey, focusing instead on Ohio, it would be a mistake, imagewise. Forgoing Wisconsin, with its largely rural population, would leave Kennedy seeming too much the candidate destined to take only the ethnic, big-city states.

Once the decision was made to campaign in Wisconsin, then the task was to figure out how to claim Ohio through other means.

What happened next is an example of just how tough a politician Jack Kennedy had become. He and Bobby were about to give Governor Mike DiSalle of Ohio a variation on the Onions Burke routine.

DiSalle was presumed to favor Senator Stuart Symington of Missouri, who was Harry Truman's candidate to head the Democratic ticket. With DiSalle still owing a debt to Truman — he'd given him a sizable job in his administration, director of the Office of Price Stabilization, during the Korean War — the Kennedy people figured he was spoken for. That is, if the Ohio governor ran as a "favorite son" in the state's primary, he'd then be expected to hand over his delegates to Symington at the convention.

But what if the Kennedy people didn't intend to leave that option open to him? Soon, Kennedy warned DiSalle, "Mike, it's time to shit or get off the pot. You're either going to come out for me or we are going to run a delegation against you in Ohio and we'll beat you." And the truth was, Jack Kennedy was popular enough in Ohio to pull it off.

So, even if he wasn't actively campaigning there, Ohio was still hugely critical for him, especially now that he'd been acting tough and holding a club over the head of the governor. At a press event organized by Ben Bradlee, one *Newsweek* reporter challenged Kennedy by asking him what his plans were for showing the skeptics he wasn't "just another pretty boy from Boston and Harvard." According to Bradlee, Jack didn't hesitate before replying: "Well, for openers, I'm going to fucking well take Ohio."

Before getting rough with DiSalle, the Kennedys needed to mend fences with labor. Kennedy declared that the United Auto Workers convention in Atlantic City would be his next destination to, as O'Donnell put it, "stop some of this drift" toward Humphrey and Stevenson, both reliable cultivators of organized labor.

At the UAW event, Kennedy further closed the distance between himself and Humphrey. The Minnesotan delivered a rousing speech that was received with great enthusiasm. Still, according to reports, the "wild and frenzied" reception given Jack Kennedy by the convention-goers surpassed it. And that wasn't all. He'd won the support of the UAW leader, a highly regarded liberal. "The fact that Walter Reuther would walk away and say nice things about Jack Kennedy, which he did forcefully from that moment on," said Ken O'Donnell, "that was a significant breakthrough for us."

In a colorful episode, O'Donnell arranged a discreet meeting between Kennedy and Richard Gosser, "very much the old-school labor union type of fellow and not of the new-breed Reuther type." Accompanying Gosser were his handlers, who "looked like wrestlers and like they might break a few legs when called upon. The senator shot me a look."

Gosser confided to Jack that "the rank-and-file members of his locals were all without exception for John Kennedy" and that "all the resources that he could bring to bear in Ohio would be put at Senator Kennedy's behest."

O'Donnell recalled that Gosser "got very emotional, and while he was talking, his false teeth kept popping out. So, in between sentences, he'd reach up and shove them back in, with some force. The senator winced the first time, as it looked rather painful. Then, as Gosser kept doing it with every sentence, the senator would look over at me with that quizzical expression that said, 'What have you gotten me into here?'" As comic as it was, it was a politically important meeting. Jack Kennedy was making allies he never could have imagined.

In all his years in politics to date, Jack Kennedy, the opposite of a joiner, had maintained his independence, and cherished it. He took special pride in not being part of the coalition of liberals and labor leaders dominating the Democratic scene of the 1950s. Yet, as he now moved to identify himself with them — he had begun calling himself a liberal — he was determined to preserve his separateness in private. "I always had a feeling that he regarded them as something apart from his philosophy," Charlie Bartlett said. "I think he saw the liberals as the sort of people who ran like a pack." Ben Bradlee concurred, with even greater bluntness: "He hated the liberals."

Despite the fact that Vice President Richard Nixon was heavily favored to be his party's candidate for the White House this time around — it was his turn — and despite Kennedy's shots at him on the stump, friends of Jack knew he was anything but a Nixon hater. Whatever he might say out on the campaign trail, when at home he refused to join in when Nixon was being ridiculed. Ben Bradlee recalled how this annoyed Jack's "card-carrying anti-Nixon friends."

For example, one evening Jacqueline Kennedy had invited their old neighbors Joan and Arthur Gardner to dinner. There'd be just the two couples and Rose Kennedy, who was stopping by on her way to Palm Beach. Mrs. Gardner made a crack about the "dreadful" Richard Nixon, fully expecting her host to chime in with his agreement. He didn't. "You have no idea what he's been through," Kennedy defended him. "Dick Nixon is the victim of the worst press that ever hit a politician in this country. What they did to him in the Helen Gahagan Douglas race was disgusting."

Kennedy would take pains, even, to avoid hurting Nixon's feelings. Arriving at a 1959 social event at which Nixon had reason to expect him, Kennedy changed his mind at the last second and decided it would be impolitic to be seen attending. Later, he stopped by the vice president's office, with the apologetic explanation that he "did make it out there but at the last minute a crisis arose." He'd had to avoid someone who was leaving just as he was arriving, he said, a person whom he'd rather didn't know about his friendship with Dick. "Nixon is a nice fellow in private, and a very able man," he would tell a British reporter around this time. "I worked with him on the Hill for a long time, but it seems he has a split personality and he is very bad in public, and nobody likes him."

Charlie Bartlett had a memory of an especially telling moment. He and his wife, Martha, spent New Year's Eve 1959 with the Kennedys. Something his old friend said that night caused him to write a note to himself the following morning. "Had dinner with Jack and Jackie — talked about presidential campaign a lot — Jack says if the Democrats don't nominate him he's going to vote for Nixon." Bartlett told me that he figured moments like that are what get pals of famous people to write memoirs. He never did.

On January 2, 1960, John F. Kennedy stood in the Senate Caucus Room, one floor up from his office, and announced his candidacy. "The presidency is the most powerful office in the Free World," he declared. "Through its leadership can come a more vital life for our people. In it are centered the hopes of the globe around us for freedom and a more secure life. For it is in the Executive Branch that the most crucial decisions of this century must be made in the next four years — how to end or alter the burdensome arms race, where Soviet gains already threaten our very existence . . ." He was offering himself as a latter-day Churchill, warning his people that the enemy was arming while America was asleep. It was an homage to his hero and, at the same time, a son's declaration of independence from his father's support for Neville Chamberlain and appeasement.

It was also a challenge to would-be rivals. He spoke of his relentless cross-country campaigning "the past forty months." He'd been out with the people since September 1956. Where were they? "I believe that any Democratic aspirant to this important nomination should be willing to submit to the voters his views, record, and competence in a series of primary contests." He was daring Lyndon Johnson, master of the Senate, to come out and joust in the open fields. Better yet, he was using his weakness — his lack of a power base like Stevenson's in the loyal Roosevelt cotillion or Johnson's among the Senate barons — to suggest they do what he *had* to do: build a national organization from scratch.

But he kept coy about where he intended to make his fight. He would enter the New Hampshire primary, but keep his other options open. "I shall announce my plans with respect to the other primaries as their filing dates approach." He was keeping other information hooded, too: a biography stapled to the prepared speech lightly wallpapered over significant facts.

The official handout opened with a description of his father having "served under Franklin Roosevelt," a bland portrait of that terribly bitter relationship. It described the candidate as having been "educated in the public schools of Brookline, Massachusetts," an obvious effort to democratize his elite upbringing. The document further said he'd attended the London School of Economics "in 35–36." This was an obvious effort both to claim distinction and hood the serious illness that sent him back home from the LSE within days of his arrival, not to mention his registration at Princeton that same fall and the subsequent relapse that cost him the academic year. Illness, such a powerful part of Jack Kennedy's biography, was clearly not something to be admitted in this version. Finally, the sheet highlighted the candidate's *"WAR RECORD,"* something his opponents in the upcoming primaries, most particularly Hubert Humphrey, didn't possess.

The campaign was on! The season had

arisen for selling strengths and diverting attention from weaknesses. Jack Kennedy was now running to be the champion of the party that had twice run Adlai Stevenson, a party still liberal at its heart, working-class in its gut. Traveling to Boston that evening, he summoned Arthur Schlesinger and John Kenneth Galbraith, two keepers of the liberal keys and Stevenson regulars, to dine with him at the grand old Locke-Ober restaurant.

"At dinner he was, as usual, spirited and charming, but he also conveyed an intangible feeling of depression," Schlesinger jotted in his journal later that night. "I had the sense that he feels himself increasingly hemmed in as a result of a circumstance over which he has no control — his religion; and he inevitably tends toward gloom and irritation when he considers how this circumstance may deny him what he thinks his talents and efforts have earned.

"I asked him what he considered the main sources of his own appeal. He said obviously there were no great differences between himself and Humphrey on issues, that it came down to a question of personality and image. 'Hubert is too hot for the present mood of the people. He gets people too excited, too worked up. What they want today is a more boring, monotonous personality, like me.' Jack plainly has no doubt about his capacity to beat Nixon and can hardly wait to take him on."

When it came to pulling out ahead of the Democratic pack, Kennedy wanted to take as many big states as he could in his fight for the nomination. He also needed to decide where to put the biggest effort, where to devote the better part of what he had: his polling, his time, his money, his family, his father. Mike DiSalle, the Ohio governor, was still holding out on him. Privately supportive, he was still withholding his public endorsement. Though he had promised to come out for Kennedy, when Christmas 1959 came and went he was still wiggling. He now explained to Kennedy that, as a Catholic, his backing would not be as beneficial to him and recommended he find some non-Catholics in Ohio to back him. Kennedy got the message: DiSalle was trying to welsh on the deal.

At a Christmas meeting among Jack, Bobby, Joe Sr., and Ken O'Donnell, the decision was made to send Bobby out to Columbus to get Mike DiSalle on board once and for all. O'Donnell remembers Jack's teasing his brother: "You're mean and tough, and can say miserable things to Mike that I cannot. And if you get too obnoxious, then I'll disown and disavow what you said and just tell DiSalle, 'He's a young kid and doesn't know any better.'" Bobby, not amused, replied, "Thanks a lot."

Early that January, Bobby Kennedy, accompanied by John Bailey, met with DiSalle.

Afterward, the indignant governor called O'Donnell and Senator Kennedy to complain. "He was furious," said O'Donnell. "He told me that Bobby was the 'most obnoxious kid he'd ever met,' that Bobby practically had called him a liar and said 'We can't trust you. You will do what you're told.'

"In essence, Bobby'd done exactly what he'd been told to, of course. And then Bailey called me privately, saying he'd been horrified at the conversation. Bobby was awfully tough, completely unreasonable, rude and obnoxious, and totally demanded that DiSalle come out for his brother immediately. And if he did not, well . . . he threatened him." To Bailey, it had sounded just like the kind of pressure mobsters applied.

According to a *Newsweek* feature, the taking of Ohio made for "a pretty dramatic story," one that pitted DiSalle's desires against the Kennedy Party's own, as well as its "six months of careful effort." Bobby had secured the endorsement and more. Jack, making good on his determination to claim Ohio's delegates at the convention, had fashioned for himself a reputation.

Not only were such rivals as Lyndon Johnson, himself no slouch at brutal manipulation, put on notice by the Kennedy brothers' maneuver, but so were the country's political bosses, such as Carmine DeSapio of New York and Richard Daley of Chicago. They saw how

Mike DiSalle was now running, committed to delivering his state's delegates to John F. Kennedy at the national convention, and they were impressed.

In March, Kennedy won the New Hampshire primary with 85 percent of the vote. It was a big, if expected, victory. The Wisconsin primary, held the first week in April, was a contest between Jack's national celebrity and Hubert Humphrey, the boy next door. Democratic voters in both his own state and the one to their east were looking to him to represent their own brand of Midwestern liberalism on the national scene. He was also enormously strong on farm issues, an area where his eastern rival was something of a city slicker.

Stumping around this alien landscape brought the fighter in Jack into sharp relief. "You think I'm out here to get votes?" he said, sitting in a Wisconsin diner one morning early in the campaign. "Well, I am, but not just for their vote. I'm trying to get the votes of a lot of people who are sitting right now in warm, comfortable homes all over the country, having a big breakfast of bacon and eggs, hoping that young Jack will fall right on his face in the snow. Bastards."

Hubert Humphrey was, within his own realm, a uniquely well-respected Democratic figure, having stood up to anti-Semitism when he was Minneapolis mayor in the late 1940s. He'd also called upon his fellow party members to commit themselves to taking on the issue of civil rights at the 1948 convention. It was the speech he gave supporting this conviction that led to the Dixiecrat walkout there and to the third-party nomination of the segregationist candidate Strom Thurmond of South Carolina.

Because Wisconsin's economy mirrored that of Minnesota, and because its Catholic population was low, the primary could be seen as Humphrey's to lose. Facing these facts, the Kennedy people started early and hit hard. At the beginning of January, Bobby dispatched Kenny O'Donnell there to live full-time in the lead-up to the primary. "He knew we had to run the same type of campaign we'd run in Massachusetts — therefore we needed to have someone full-time from the Kennedy organization giving actual day-to-day direction," O'Donnell said. Soon Bobby and Teddy Kennedy — whose first child, Kara, was born in February — followed O'Donnell, living with their wives and families at the Hotel Wisconsin in Milwaukee for seven weeks. Bobby, by this time, was the father of seven.

Pat Lucey, a former Wisconsin assemblyman who'd go on to the governorship, was an early supporter of Kennedy in the state. Watching the candidate, Lucey was impressed with his well-disciplined retail politics. As Lucey describes it, Senator Kennedy's day began early and kept to a "grueling" pattern. "He was campaigning at six o'clock in the morning and probably at a shopping center at ten o'clock that night. Finally, he started running out of steam and thought he'd made enough of the right impression to let up a little bit." The purpose had been achieved. The image of Jack Kennedy standing in freezing dawn weather at the factory gates was now fixed in the mind of the voter. For Pat Lucey, the result could be summed up as the "effective presentation of a celebrity."

Humphrey, for his part, tried to portray the smart Kennedy operation as a negative. "Beware of these orderly campaigns," he declared. "They are ordered, bought, and paid for. We are not selling corn flakes or some Hollywood production." To imply further shallowness, Humphrey took aim at what he saw as his opponent's superficial appeal. "You have to learn to have the emotions of a human being when you are charged with the responsibilities of leadership." And then, if that wasn't enough: Jack Kennedy had "little emotional commitment to liberals," he took pains to remind his listeners. There was truth to this, of course. Kennedy's newfound liberalism had been neatly packaged since the 1956 Democratic Convention.

But Kennedy enjoyed a state-of-the-art edge. Using Lou Harris's polling data on local attitudes and concerns, Jack knew what people had on their minds, which arguments would win their interest. It was a breakthrough technique, and one that would change modern campaigning in the years to come.

By this point Jack was becoming keenly attuned to the image he projected. Having encouraged Charlie Bartlett to fly to Wisconsin to watch the reaction he drew from the crowds, he quickly revealed this self-awareness, even if he wasn't about to make any adjustment to fit in with the local scene. When they'd finished dinner after his arrival, Bartlett was startled to hear the candidate ask: "Shall I wear this blue overcoat?" He was indicating his usual coat. "Or shall I wear this?" Now he was holding up a sporty brown herringbone. "Why not wear that one?" Bartlett suggested, pointing to the second. "It looks like Wisconsin." This brought a swift retort: "Are you trying to change my personality?"

Bartlett also put effort into trying to convince him to wear a hat. "It was as cold as the devil up in Wisconsin. I bought him one of those fur hats with the flaps on it and tried to get him to wear that. But he wouldn't." In Bartlett's phrase, as time went on, it was his old friend who "killed the hat."

With loudspeakers throughout the state blaring the Oscar-winning song "High Hopes," sung by Frank Sinatra — its lyrics now specially tailored for Kennedy's candidacy — the presidential hopeful put on a dazzling show in Wisconsin, especially in its ethnic communities. He made a lasting impression when he appeared at a Polish event in Milwaukee, mainly because Jackie took the stage briefly and addressed the gathering in their native language. "I have great respect for the Polish people. Besides, my sister is married to a Pole," she told them. Then she said, pronouncing the words carefully and correctly, "Poland will live forever." Her listeners went wild.

A moment later, her husband caught the attention of Red Fay, asking over the tumult with a pleased grin: "How would you like to try and follow that?" Yet Jackie wasn't her husband's sole secret weapon in Wisconsin. Working for him there was a fellow who stayed under the radar and away from crowds. Paul Corbin was a campaign operative with a flair for dirty tricks. Later to be legendary in some political circles, Corbin began a close and lasting friendship with Bobby Kennedy during that push to win the 1960 Wisconsin primary. Probably his most famous stunt at the time had him distributing anti-Catholic material — ostensibly written by fearful Protestants — throughout largely Roman Catholic neighborhoods. Nothing incites voters to support their own kind like hard evidence they're under assault from others.

For their own campaign song, the Humphrey people had chosen the tune of "Davy Crockett," the jaunty theme of a hit Disney

TV show. The problem was that their man was no more "king of the wild frontier" than he could claim to have "killed himself a b'ar when he was only three." It was Jack Kennedy, who'd proven his grit and courage in his youth, who was plausibly heralding a new frontier.

While Kennedy believed his hard work would pay off, he also knew he had to win. "You have to keep coming up sevens," he said, admitting, implicitly at least, that the outcome of the Wisconsin primary remained a crap shoot. However, on April 5, the balloting day, he admitted to Ben Bradlee the confidence he felt. "On the day Wisconsin voters went to the polls, he flew to some town in northern Michigan in the *Caroline* for a midday political rally before coming back for the returns, and I went with him. During the flight, I asked him for his prediction in each of the ten Wisconsin election districts. He wouldn't tell me, but agreed to write them down and put them in a sealed envelope, if I'd do the same. We did, and Kennedy put them casually in a drawer on the plane, and switched the subject. Two or three days later, I was back on assignment on the Kennedy family plane and remembered the envelope. He pulled it out and showed me the predictions. I'd put down 'Kennedy 7, Humphrey 3,' out of an abundance of caution; I really thought it would be eight to two. Kennedy himself had put down, 'JFK 9, HHH 1.'"

Despite a surprise attack from liberals trying to make last-minute political capital of the thousand-dollar contribution he'd delivered from his father to Nixon in 1950 — an episode Kennedy aides were under instructions to deny — the Massachusetts senator had scored a big victory. The final count was 478,901 votes for John F. Kennedy to Hubert Humphrey's 372,034.

But the results, the way they were presented, were inconclusive for two reasons. First, the press covered the Wisconsin Democratic vote in terms of congressional districts, of which there were ten: Kennedy took six, Humphrey four. Calling it that way made it appear a far narrower victory than a comparison of total votes for each candidate. This is because three of Humphrey's four victorious congressional districts lay along his home state's border and could have been expected to go his way. Kennedy's friend Lem Billings had run the campaign in one of those districts and would later comment on the outcome there, saying, "In all fairness to myself, Humphrey was a very beloved figure in that district."

Another reality helping, spinwise, to offset Humphrey's loss was his victory in the congressional district that included Madison, the state capital, where the University of Wisconsin campus was also located. It was the single district Humphrey carried that was *not* on the

Minnesota border, and for that reason it was judged to be a clear and unexpected upset of Jack Kennedy. Madison was the center of liberalism in the state, and even though Kennedy lost the district only narrowly, it looked bad. Why couldn't Jack persuade the liberals he so needed to win the nomination that he should be their candidate?

The election-night coverage harped on the religion issue. Kennedy had won in six of the state's ten congressional districts, the commentators decreed, mainly because Wisconsin's Republican Catholics, rallying to their own, had crossed over to vote for him on the Democratic ballot.

"Kennedy is, of course, Roman Catholic, Humphrey a Congregationalist, and Nixon a Quaker," Walter Cronkite reminded listeners. "And some observers think that the election has resolved into a religious struggle." Sitting on a couch and smoking a small cigar, Kennedy watched Cronkite make this assessment with simmering rage, furious at seeing his victory recast along the very lines that represented a truth about himself that he could never change.

"One of the most elaborate and intense campaigns in the state's history will end up achieving nothing," another broadcaster intoned. After all the trudging through the snow, the hand-shaking, and the speechmaking, Jack was being denied the proper credit for snatching Wisconsin out of Humphrey's grasp. Now the only choice was heading to heavily Protestant West Virginia, where the Democratic primary was scheduled for one month and five days later.

Adversity had again presented Jack Kennedy with a truth and a test. Wisconsin reminded the country of the hazard posed by his religion. He had predicted this himself at the April strategy meeting the previous year. Now the press was rehashing the same old story. Kennedy resented it, and to his sister Eunice, he spelled out the consequences of Wisconsin: "It means that we've got to go to West Virginia in the morning and do it all over again. And then we've got to go on to Maryland and Indiana and Oregon and win all of them." He had to keep coming up sevens.

In deciding to throw his hat in the West Virginia primary, Jack Kennedy again had to overrule his father. Ben Bradlee recalled the two of them knocking heads over it. "When the question of West Virginia came up for discussion, Joe Kennedy argued strenuously against JFK's entering, saying, 'It's a nothing state and they'll kill him over the Catholic thing.' A few minutes later JFK spoke out. 'Well,' he said, 'we've heard from the ambassador, and we're all very grateful, Dad. But I've got to run in West Virginia.'"

Lem Billings saw it as his old school friend's drive, his compulsion to rise to the occasion.

"He knew that if he dropped West Virginia, particularly for a Catholic reason, it would be interpreted as meaning that a Catholic could never be president of the United States."

Upon entering West Virginia, Kennedy must have felt his initial determination had bordered on bravado. The focus on his Catholicism was having an effect. Lou Harris's numbers, which had been giving Kennedy a 70–30 lead in West Virginia, now showed Humphrey ahead 60–40. Pierre Salinger knew exactly what the turnabout boiled down to. "The reversal was, of course, produced by the addition of a single word to his poll. Harris had neglected to tell the people in West Virginia in his first one that John F. Kennedy was a Catholic. So we were right up against it there. But if we lost in West Virginia, we were gone."

It suddenly didn't look good. The unthinkable — an anti-Kennedy turnaround, a building backlash — might well be looming ahead. In Washington, the oddsmakers — including the self-interested Nixon, whose own future was tied to whomever the Democrats finally nominated — were betting that Jack couldn't pull it off. Now it appeared that the nomination would have to be brokered, after all, at the convention in Los Angeles, a scenario that squared with Lyndon Johnson's own game plan. The Senate leader imagined getting together with the delegates and wooing them in the same tried-and-true manner he used on senators before a key vote. He'd work the states one at a time, using his allies from the Hill as local kingmakers. Then, when the time came to pick the party's nominee, the convention would choose a candidate who could actually win in November — not a Catholic, not a young backbencher who'd yet to do much of anything where it counted: on Capitol Hill.

Around this time, Lyndon Johnson called on Tip O'Neill in his office. The Senate leader said he understood O'Neill's first loyalty was to his Massachusetts colleague, but that "the boy" was obviously going to falter after not getting the nomination on the first ballot. He lobbied O'Neill for his commitment on the second.

In West Virginia, Humphrey pressed the advantage he'd gained in Wisconsin. With the strains of "Give Me That Old Time Religion" coming from his campaign bus, he tried to play the faith advantage over Kennedy to the hilt. There was nothing subtle about it. Its verses had featured prominently — and ominously — in the film *Inherit the Wind,* a stirring drama based on the 1925 "Scopes Monkey Trial." In the movie, released that year, the song comes to stand for the beliefs of the rural Christian fundamentalists opposed to any teaching of evolution, and in West Virginia its message was clear: Humphrey understood who the voters were, and Roman Catholic wasn't part of the description.

Cannily — and what choice did he have? — Kennedy himself began citing his Catholicism at every opportunity, but often in the same context as his navy service. If his critics wanted to make his religion, rather than his political experience, the issue, he was willing to play their game. It was the game of politics at its most masterful. His brother Bobby would call this ploy "hanging a lantern on your problem." Lem Billings recalled how, of necessity, the strategy had shifted. While in Wisconsin Jack had "pretty well avoided the religious question," in West Virginia he "jumped into it with both feet. He pounded home day after day about religion." There it became the issue, out in the open.

Kennedy showcased his service record in World War II to extinguish voters' fears about possible conflicted loyalties; his allegiance was to the United States, it always had been and always would be. Why else had he risked his life in the Pacific? "Nobody asked me if I was a Catholic when I joined the United States Navy. Nobody asked my brother if he was a Catholic or Protestant before he climbed into an American bomber plane to fly his last mission."

William Battle, who'd served in the PT boats with Kennedy, introduced him to a much-respected Episcopal bishop, Robert E.

Lee Strider, with strong political influence in the Charleston area. "Young man, I should tell you right off the bat the only time I have ever voted Republican was when Al Smith ran for the Democratic nomination," was the churchman's opener to Kennedy, as Battle recalled. "And it was because of the Catholic issue. The way he handled it."

Battle remembered the look Jack shot him, basically "What the hell did you bring me up here for?" And then Strider smiled. "That's the way he handled it," the bishop told his visitor. "Smith would not discuss it. You've handled your religion entirely differently. I'm satisfied, and I'd be delighted to work with you." The next morning local papers throughout the coalfields region ran stories headlined: "Bishop Strider Supports Kennedy!"

Ken O'Donnell noted the way Kennedy was affected by what he saw in West Virginia. "Here right in our midst was a great mass of people totally ignored, yet they didn't complain as he talked to them. They didn't like it; they weren't lazy, they were just people who'd been in poverty so long they didn't know a way out." Pierre Salinger saw the same thing. "I believe West Virginia brought a real transformation of John F. Kennedy as a person. He came into contact, really for the first time, with poverty. He saw what had happened as a result of the technological changes in coal mining. He saw hundreds of people sitting around the city with nothing to do. It affected him very deeply. It really, in my opinion, changed his whole outlook on life."

What now made a difference to the campaign's fortunes in West Virginia was the inherited prestige of Franklin Delano Roosevelt, Jr. The president's son and namesake was brought in to strike at the Minnesotan's soft underbelly, his failure to fight in World War II. From here on in, the gloves were off. The conclusion of that conflict was just fifteen years in the past, and memories of its horrors and its casualties, along with its many great acts of heroism, hadn't faded. Ben Bradlee knew how Jack always wanted to know where a fellow of his generation had been in the "wor-ah." It was a key for him, a key to sizing up other men.

Humphrey was vulnerable, and the wartime president's son spread the news. Humphrey twice had attempted to enlist only to be rejected for medical reasons. But to guarantee that no voter remained unaware of who'd served and who hadn't, the Kennedys undertook a comprehensive education program. Souvenir *PT 109* insignia emblems of Jack Kennedy's wartime heroism were put on sale at the affordable price of a dollar. A letter from FDR Jr. endorsing the young candidate, was mailed to West Virginia voters. It was postmarked Hyde Park, New York, unmistakably signaling its connection to America's greatest Democrat.

Out on the campaign trail, Kennedy made it clear to the curious crowds that came to hear him that here was a chance for little West Virginia to choose the country's top leader. "The basic strategy was a psychological one," Pierre Salinger recalled. "That is, let West Virginia play a role in selecting the next president of the United States. If Hubert Humphrey wins the West Virginia primary, he will never receive the nomination of the Democratic Party. Therefore, you are throwing your vote away. If John F. Kennedy wins the West Virginia primary, you will have selected the next president of the United States."

Salinger confessed the campaign's subtext. The state had a lot to gain from electing a president. "West Virginia, the fiftieth state in the union in defense contracts, wanted to be with a winner who would remember it. John F. Kennedy sold West Virginia on the fact that if he became president he would never forget West Virginia."

Money also played a crucial role. The county political people expected to be paid for their election efforts, and the Kennedys would do what was expected. West Virginia was a state, after all, where the facts of political life weren't overseen by reformers. The decisive swing came on election eve, when the largest amounts yet of Kennedy cash started falling into outstretched hands. Humphrey could do little but complain. "I'm being ganged up on by wealth. I can't afford to run around this state with a little black bag and a checkbook."

Salinger didn't argue with the assessment. "We were running the campaign there as if you were running a campaign to elect a ward leader in New York or Chicago. We whipped this campaign down to the sheriffs, the district attorneys, and the councilmen because this is the way you win elections in West Virginia."

The Nixon backer Charles McWhorter, a native of the state, saw it as a daunting preview of the general election. "They went through West Virginia like a tornado, putting money — big bucks! — into sheriffs' races. You were either for Kennedy or you weren't. The Kennedy people just wanted the gold ring. They were ruthless in that objective. That scared the shit out of me."

In the last days, Kennedy was campaigning so hard that he lost his voice. Trying to rest it, he scribbled a note to Charlie Bartlett just as the final showdown at the polls was about to occur. What he wrote said it all: "I'd give my right testicle to win this one."

But, as he had told Ben Bradlee, he would not be maneuvered into a corner. He would not let the entire campaign hang on winning one difficult primary. His mind was racing ahead to whatever the West Virginia results might require. He warned his old college friend, and now U.S. congressman, Torby Macdonald, who was running the Kennedy campaign in Maryland, that he might need him more than ever. The primary there was to take place that Friday.

"If Jack were beaten in West Virginia," Macdonald said, "then this would be a bail-out operation, in which he'd win so overwhelmingly in Maryland that everyone would forget about West Virginia. It may have been wishful thinking, but that was the point — and that's why I worked as hard as I did in Maryland."

Just as Jack Kennedy had refused to sit on that little island in the Solomons, awaiting a rescuer for him and his men, just as he'd swum again and again out into the water looking for help, just as he'd sent Barney Ross when he couldn't do it, now he was sending an S.O.S. to his buddy Torby. When it came to survival, he was not a pessimist, but he was seized by the fear that West Virginia had slipped from his hands.

He made sure to fly back to Washington, D.C., as the actual election was getting under way. He'd look even more a loser should the results go against him and he was there, hanging around in West Virginia, on primary night.

To pass the time while the votes came in, the Kennedys, joined by the Bradlees, went out to dinner. Getting away from the action and the teasing hints from the early returns is standard political practice. For his sanity, a candidate needs to remove himself, however momentarily, from the minute-to-minute rumblings and false reports bringing alternating euphoria and gloom. It's also a pleasure to find yourself alone with good friends after weeks of craziness with strangers.

Bradlee remembers: "The Kennedys asked us to sweat the vote out with them at dinner, but dinner was over long before any remotely meaningful results were in. After a quick call to brother Bobby at the Kanawha Hotel in Charleston, we all got into their car and drove to the Trans-Lux theater to see *Suddenly Last Summer*. Bad omen. It was a film with a surprise ending, whose publicity included a warning that no one would be admitted after the show started."

They ended up at a film showing around the corner from the White House. To Bradlee it seemed like porn. "Not the hard-core stuff of later years, but a nasty little thing called *Private Property,* starring Kate Manx as a horny housewife." Bradlee said he and Kennedy "wondered aloud if the movie was on the Catholic index of forbidden films" — it was — and "whether or not there were any votes in it either way for Kennedy in allegedly anti-Catholic West Virginia if it were known he was in attendance."

"Kennedy's concentration was absolutely zero," Bradlee recalled. "He left every twenty minutes to call Bobby in West Virginia. Each time he returned, he'd whisper 'Nothing definite yet,' slouch back into his seat and flick his teeth with the fingernail of the middle finger on his right hand, until he left to call again."

Word suddenly came that Kennedy had won. The foursome headed to National Airport and boarded the *Caroline* for the short hop to the state that had just defied all the doomsayers, all the experts, all the Democrats backing the wrong horse.

The moment of Kennedy's victory speech, O'Donnell recalled, was both ecstatic and poignant. "He gave the usual speech — about the hard work, and about what wonderful people they all were, and that he would keep his word to them. . . . And if he won the presidency he intended to come back to West Virginia and keep his word. That all the things he'd seen there that disturbed him so much, as president of the United States he'd do something about. That hadn't just been campaign talk. It was a commitment. And then he moved in and worked the room and shook everyone's hand."

What a night! "The place was jammed and it was around two a.m., and he came over and thanked us," O'Donnell continued. "He pulled me aside and shook his head and said, 'What the hell happened? We won!' I just laughed and shook my head, looked at Bobby, who was exhausted. He nodded." For his part,

Salinger could see a weight had lifted: "He was elated. He knew he'd been nominated."

Ben Bradlee, though, was stunned to see how little attention the exhilarated victor showed his wife that night. "Kennedy ignored Jackie, and she seemed miserable at being left out of things. She was then far from the national figure she later became in her own right. She . . . stood on a stairway, totally ignored, as JFK made his victory statement on television. Later, when Kennedy was enjoying his greatest moment of triumph to date, with everyone in the hall shouting and yelling, Jackie quietly disappeared and went out to the car and sat by herself, until he was ready to fly back to Washington."

The candidate was alone in his triumph.

CHAPTER TWELVE
CHARISMA

How does Jack get them girls to squeal that way?

— Senator Herman Talmadge
of Georgia

Jack Kennedy's singular personal appeal was recognized by Ken O'Donnell for the first time at the Worcester tea in 1952. He noticed how women simply stared at the candidate. The effect Kennedy had on people, most noticeably women, is visible today in films from the Wisconsin primary. You see high-school-age girls racing down the sidewalk merely to capture a glimpse of him. As the campaign entered the general election phase in 1960, and the crowds around Kennedy grew deeper, these young women — "jumpers" they were called — would leap into the air to see over the heads of those in front of them.

It takes more than sex appeal, however, to win the American presidency. To gain the Democratic nomination, those victories in

Wisconsin and West Virginia were necessary, but not sufficient. Jack still needed to conquer the resistance of pivotal governors, many of whom were Catholic like himself. It was not about whom they liked, or with whom they felt comfortable; the decisive question was whether they could be pushed to do what they didn't want to do: commit, put their own political careers on the line for a guy who might well be stopped short of the nomination, halted for the sin of having the same religion as their own. These men had their own ambitions, too. They wanted the leverage, the clout that comes to a governor who arrives at a national convention with a bevy of delegates under his control.

But Jack Kennedy wanted those delegates under his control. He wanted the nomination locked up before he reached Los Angeles for the basic, understandable reason that he'd seen what could happen in the middle of a Democratic Convention roll call. People who don't want you to win can stop you in your tracks, just at the very moment when you and your people think you've got it in the bag. Just four years before, he'd seen it unfold like that in Chicago.

So, to prevent it from happening again, he was taking certain steps, of a sort familiar to the Onions Burkes of this world.

It had started with Ohio. Bobby's strong-arm treatment of Mike DiSalle had ensured that the Ohio governor was headed to L.A. on the Kennedy bandwagon. Next had been Maryland, whose primary came the Friday after West Virginia's. Bobby, now an expert at strong-arm tactics, had taken care of the dirty work there, from the moment the campaign learned that Governor J. Millard Tawes planned on running unopposed on the primary ballot as a "favorite son." He wanted to arrive in California with the state's delegates under his personal control. The Kennedy brothers, however, thought otherwise. Just as he had in Ohio with DiSalle, Bobby went to meet with Governor Tawes personally. Here's Ken O'Donnell's account:

"We talked to the governor and suggested that the governor might want to talk to Bobby Kennedy alone, that he'd acquaint him with what our desires and our intentions were, and that he'd relay back to the senator what Governor Tawes's intentions and desires were. We ushered the governor into a bedroom and Bobby went in and the governor was not happy, looking over his shoulder for some assistance. But there was none forthcoming. We closed the door."

Once the door opened again, Tawes had agreed to what the Kennedy forces wanted: an open run for the primary in Maryland.

The Kennedy treatment of Governor Pat Brown of California was cordial, if only in comparison. Brown, after much prodding from Jack himself, O'Donnell, and O'Brien, worked out a deal. It was simple enough: he'd run on the ballot unopposed in his home state and then hand over his delegates at the convention if Kennedy continued to sweep the primaries and lead in the Gallup poll. Even with this agreement between Brown and Jack, Bobby continued to put pressure on the California governor. Although Senator Kennedy had agreed not to run in the California primary as long as Pat Brown was the only candidate on the ballot, Bobby filed a last-minute delegation. It was an insurance policy against the possibility of Hubert Humphrey attempting a comeback in delegate-rich California, where loyalties to the old liberal crowd ran high. Bobby agreed to withdraw the Kennedy slate of delegates only after Humphrey gave his personal guarantee he wouldn't try to sneak in at the wire.

Fred Dutton, who was Pat Brown's top political guy, thought this final move showed moxie on the Kennedy side. "It was a pretty good example of the sort of hard-boiled game that the Kennedy group was playing. They were just protecting themselves, they said."

Even after the California primary, the Kennedy campaign wouldn't let up. According to Dutton, "The Kennedys, as soon as the primary was over with, ran a very aggressive war of nerves to try to get Brown to come out for them and to pull over as many California delegates as they could. Bobby was in the state a half-dozen times; Larry O'Brien came out and met with me. They had every right to be worried, since a strong pro-Stevenson contingent made it increasingly difficult for Pat Brown to support Kennedy if he was going to protect his own skin in local politics. Liberals loyal to Adlai were beginning to make an eleventh-hour run for their twice-nominated hero. He'd taken on the challenge of Ike, went the argument. Didn't he deserve the chance to beat the now far more beatable Nixon?"

Bobby again refused to allow any possibility of this romance with the past taking hold. He was keeping his fingers around Brown's throat. "He was calling up and was impatient, a little petulant, and not at all understanding of why Brown couldn't make up his mind." Dutton figured he either didn't understand Brown's political problems or, if he did, he wasn't going to show he did. Bobby Kennedy was not the sort to see it from the other guy's point of view. Besides, his job was not to be convinced. "I'm not running a popularity contest," he told *Time*'s Hugh Sidey. "It doesn't matter if they like me or not. If people are not getting off their behinds and working enough, how do you say that nicely? Every time you make a decision in this business, you make somebody mad."

Next in line was Pennsylvania. Jack Kennedy knew that Governor David Lawrence feared a backlash if he supported him. Having been the first of his religion to rise to this position there, he was uneasy about endorsing a fellow Catholic. To win Lawrence over, Jack needed an inside man. He found him in U.S. congressman William Green, who chaired the Democratic Party in Philadelphia. Green was a consummate big-city political boss. Two years earlier he had used his clout to get Lawrence the nomination for governor. After West Virginia, he was convinced his fellow Irish-Catholic had proven himself the strongest candidate. He believed no other Democrat would stand a chance of beating Richard Nixon. With the bulk of Pennsylvania's delegates in his control, he began putting pressure on Lawrence to drop his loyalty to Stevenson and lead the delegation to Kennedy.

Despite Green's backing, the governor remained stubborn. Lawrence remained neutral even after Kennedy's impressive victory in the Pennsylvania primary as a write-in on the ballot. Time was starting to run short, and the deal needed to be closed. Thus, at the invitation of Governor Lawrence, Kennedy spoke at a luncheon in Pittsburgh that included the county leaders in the western part of the state. Lawrence himself introduced Kennedy, but wasn't very warm. Implying in his remarks that Kennedy's write-in triumph still wasn't the last word, the governor seemed to have asked Jack to Pittsburgh to audition for a job he'd already won.

Understanding that he'd been set up, Kennedy strode to the stage. "I could tell, as Governor Lawrence was speaking, that the senator was very angry," O'Donnell recalled. "He got up and laid it out cold and hard to them, that these political leaders better think what was going to happen to the Democratic Party if the candidate who'd won all the primaries and amassed all the delegates could be denied the nomination simply for being an Irish Catholic. He told them they'd better think long and hard about what might be left of the Democratic Party should they follow this course.

"Then he ended with a tough — and I mean *tough* — attack on Lawrence, kicking him good and hard where it hurts the most. All the color drained from Governor Lawrence's face. He was stunned. There was a muttering in the room and a nodding of heads in agreement, along with chilly looks directed at Lawrence . . . who got up suddenly, almost knocked his chair over, and rushed out the door, claiming he had a meeting to go to. He didn't even say good-bye to the senator, just fled the room. The rest of the people at the meeting got up and cheered and swarmed the senator."

New York was a different story. There Kennedy had all the Irish bosses working for him. As Daniel Patrick Moynihan, former aide to Governor Harriman, described the situation: "It was still the last moment in history where Irish political leaders had that much power." Rip Horton, Kennedy's Choate classmate and Princeton roommate, was a New York volunteer who saw Kennedy's religion pay dividends in the cities. "This organization, this Kennedy-for-President movement, encompassed everywhere: Albany, Syracuse, Rochester, and Buffalo. So the politicians were responding to the electorate," seeing he might be a help to local candidates in their elections. His momentum was starting to be infectious.

Preparing for a possible power play at the convention, the Kennedy campaign began shuttling through the Midwest attempting to tie down delegates. Adlai Stevenson, presidential nominee of 1952 and 1956, was not ready to accept a changing of the guard in the Democratic Party. Moving into May, Kennedy still had received no support other than neutrality from Stevenson. "God, why won't he be satisfied with secretary of state?" he demanded of a Stevenson loyalist.

On the eve of the convention, Jack asked Adlai, one last time, to back him. Again, the answer was no. When Kennedy made it clear he had the votes for the nomination, Stevenson still refused. Now came the threat: "If you don't give me your support, I'll have to shit all over you. I don't want to do that, but I can and I will if I have to." Nothing worked. The old campaigner wasn't ready to give up his one last chance for glory. Eleanor Roosevelt would arrive in Los Angeles still bearing the torch for Adlai, but it was a flame that burned, just as brightly, against this younger favorite. The year before, Jack had sent a young ally, Lester Hyman, to secretly test her attitude toward him. Asked her opinion of a potential Kennedy presidency, and not knowing Hyman's loyalties, Mrs. Roosevelt let loose with a broadside. "We wouldn't want the Pope in the White House, would we?" Hyman, who is Jewish, told me he almost fell off his chair.

To Kennedy, the more formidable presence at the convention would be Lyndon Johnson. Kennedy kept his opinion of the Senate majority leader well guarded. To Ben Bradlee, he would refer to Johnson as a "riverboat gambler," although leaving the impression that that wasn't necessarily a bad thing.

Jack Kennedy had demonstrated over the years two vital capabilities that would now come into play. First, he was, generally, able to view situations without having his vision distorted by anger or any other emotion. Second, he could see through to the essence of a problem. Like Harry Hopkins, the FDR advisor Churchill once dubbed "Lord Root of the Matter," Jack Kennedy was focused, shrewd, and incisive when it came to his basic interests.

And what he now knew, perfectly clearly, about Lyndon Johnson was that he'd beaten him. He understood that when Johnson went over his list of supporters at the Democratic Convention in Los Angeles, the proud man would have only senators, and that was if they were lucky enough to be there themselves. Jack, on the other hand, had delegates. After four years crossing and recrossing the country, he not only had them but knew a good number personally.

Johnson's only hope lay in lassoing together a large enough herd of western delegates to add to his base in the South. Ted Kennedy, working for his brother in the mountain states, was able to shatter that strategy. And, with the help of Stewart Udall, a Tucson lawyer, he got half the Arizona delegation to declare early for his brother. It was a shocker right there in LBJ's southwestern backyard, and the press play it got contributed significantly to the waning of the Texan's chances.

Nonetheless, Kennedy flew to the Los Angeles convention still concerned with LBJ's plans as well as Adlai's. Tony Bradlee was on the same plane and had been given a list of questions by her husband to ask him. "He was having throat problems, and to save his voice, he took the list and wrote in his answers. The first question was 'What about Lyndon Johnson for vice president?' His tantalizing answer was 'He'll never take it.'"

Jack Kennedy arrived in California far better prepared than he'd been four years earlier in Chicago. This time around he had the organization ready and backing him up as he entered the convention hall, and all the technology he'd been missing before, such as the walkie-talkies that would keep his operatives in continual contact. The country had been divided into "six regions, and every region was manned and they had a telephone and they were in touch with the Kennedy Shack which served as the command post. Pierre Salinger published a daily convention journal designed to look like an impartial newspaper." All their efforts to build a "Kennedy Party," starting back in early '46 for that first congressional race, were now paying off. This time Bobby was masterminding its tactics, while, above him, Jack, the consummate political professional, was in command.

In the beginning, Kennedy looked a shoo-in. But then, Lyndon Johnson threw down the wild card of Kennedy's health. "It was the goddamndest thing," he said with mournful relish, "here was this young whippersnapper . . . malaria-ridden, yallah . . . sickly, sickly." The wily Texan was well aware that the young front-runner rolling up his delegate total in the Los Angeles Memorial Sports Arena was suffering from health problems far worse than malaria, and, riverboat gambler that he was, he had no desire to keep that knowledge to himself.

For Jack Kennedy, who'd come so far, truth posed the greatest threat to him. By hook or crook, LBJ had learned the name of Jack's most dreaded weakness. His staff, led by John Connally, were now ready to deploy what they knew: namely that, living as he did with Addison's disease, the Massachusetts senator was perpetually at risk for new infections while also dependent on cortisone injections to keep him functioning. When Connally daringly called a press conference to lob this grenade, the Kennedys were enraged. Pierre Salinger had only one word for the maneuver: *despicable*.

As it had been in the past — in the Wisconsin primary, for example, when the issue was the thousand-dollar check hand-carried by Jack to Dick Nixon — the response was all-out self-protection. To scotch the accusation of ill health, Kennedy's physician, Dr. Janet Travell, was thrown into action, on the principle that what they couldn't defend, they would deny.

The release of a complete medical workup on the candidate would have handed Kennedy's rivals, including Richard Nixon, enough to bury him. Given the closeness of the election, his Addison's disease would undoubtedly have proven decisive. What if the public had learned of his regular intake of steroids, the degeneration in his bones that it caused, the corset he wore for his congenital back problem, his lifetime of stomach illness? What if they knew his constant tanning was to cover up the sickness that gave his skin a yellowish tint? What if the voters knew Kennedy and his people were engaged in a massive cover-up? Would they have responded as well as they did to his great call to arms?

Lyndon Johnson now took unerring aim at another of Kennedy's vulnerabilities, this one a matter of public record: namely, his father's backing of appeasement. "I wasn't any Chamberlain-umbrella policy man . . . I never thought Hitler was right," the majority leader reminded his listeners.

Kennedy kept his cool — and his cunning. And so, when Johnson challenged him to speak with him before the combined Texas and Massachusetts delegations, he accepted. "We seized on the opportunity to push it into a debate situation," recalled Pierre Salinger. Kenny and Bobby, however, were worried not just about what theatrics Johnson might pull, but about the possibility of an embarrassing brawl between the two delegations. "There were a few rough Irishmen in the Massachusetts delegation, as well as Kennedy men who wouldn't mind hitting a few Texans after some of the slurs they'd made against Kennedy, Catholics, and especially the Irish," said O'Donnell. "So our concern, Bobby's and mine, was that here we'd be on nationwide television and the potential for the best ruckus show of the year was there. We could be guaranteed that if it were to happen the Republicans would play it over and over again."

"I was really digging at Johnson pretty hard," Salinger remembered. He was angry, still, at the attacks on his candidate's health — accurate as they were. He'd chosen to fight back by accusing Johnson of lacking guts, claiming he was afraid of Kennedy, and so forth. Then he got a phone call. "I heard the voice on the other end of the line say, 'Young man, this is Phil Graham.' I'd never met Phil Graham before in my life." Of course, he knew who the *Washington Post* publisher was.

"And he said, 'I just want to say one thing to you. Don't tear something apart in such a way that you can never put it back together again.' I said, 'Okay,' and hung up the phone. Of course, it immediately dawned on me what he was trying to say to me. It was that there was a chance of a Kennedy-Johnson ticket." Graham, it turns out, was pushing Johnson to accept the vice presidency if Kennedy offered it, and was pushing the idea of the ticket to LBJ as being for the good of the country.

With Lyndon Johnson's arrows having failed to hit their mark, the next rival Jack needed to render impotent was Adlai Stevenson. He'd retained scattered loyalists, but his support since '56 had rusted, even on his home turf,

Illinois. Despite some packing of the galleries, there was no demand for Adlai on the convention floor or in the deal-making back rooms.

Still Stevenson's supporters persisted, keeping up the drumbeat, hoping the scene they were creating on the television screen would stir the delegates. Senator Eugene McCarthy of Minnesota gave the convention perhaps its most memorable oratory. "Do not turn away from this man. Do not reject this man. . . . Do not reject this man who has made us proud to be Democrats. Do not leave this prophet without honor in his own party."

But nothing happened. The Kennedy "operation was slick, well financed, and ruthless in its treatment of Lyndon Johnson's Southerners and the uncredentialed mob that was trying to stampede the convention for Stevenson," noted John Ehrlichman, then a young campaign worker for Richard Nixon secretly scouting the opposition.

Beating Vice President Nixon was not going to be easy. Jack was going to need support in the once-reliable Democratic South. His decision to offer the job of running mate to Lyndon Johnson was a model of cold-blooded politics. The fact was, no one else brought to the table what LBJ did, which was Texas and much of the South. The big surprise was that he might accept the prize if offered. But such was the case. And one person who found himself a go-between, helping to seal the deal, was Tip O'Neill.

Johnson's mentor was Sam Rayburn — a fellow Texan and the powerful Speaker of the House — who made it his business to contact Tip, saying, "If Kennedy wants Johnson for vice president, then he has nothing else he can do but to be on the ticket." Instructing O'Neill to find Kennedy and tell him what he'd just said, he even passed on the phone number for Jack to call.

Tip located Jack that night at a legendary Hollywood hangout, Chasen's. When the two met on the sidewalk outside the restaurant, O'Neill gave Jack the phone number and told him what Rayburn had said: Lyndon would accept if offered. "Of course I want Lyndon," Kennedy replied. He said to tell Rayburn he'd be making the call that night.

The full story of what lay behind John F. Kennedy's selection of Lyndon Baines Johnson remains murky to this day. When Salinger asked his boss for "some background" on the making of the decision, Jack was unforthcoming. "He said, 'Well, I'd just as soon not tell you. I don't think anybody will ever really know how this all really came about.'" Bobby, opposing the choice, had urged him to withdraw Johnson's name. Jack himself appears to have wavered.

What remains impressive is his ability to absorb the attack he took from Johnson and his people and keep his political bearings. "It was a case of grasping the nettle," Schlesinger wrote in his journal for July 15, 1960, "and it was another evidence of the impressively cold and tough way Jack is going about his affairs." Indeed, in putting the Johnson assault in its place, Jack was simply sorting matters into compartments, as he often did. Fending off a last-ditch challenge to his nomination was one matter. Finding someone to help him in November was totally another. Whether Johnson had played tough to try to secure the presidential nomination for himself was no deterrent to his running as Jack's vice president. Not in Jack's eyes. Not now. Rather, it was an indicator of how tough Johnson was prepared to fight by his side.

Charlie Bartlett could sense Jack was brooding about the necessity of picking Johnson, just as he'd brooded four years earlier over the need to back the less than fresh Pat Lynch as his Massachusetts party chief in 1956. But he also remembers Joe Kennedy standing there in his smoking jacket and slippers saying, "Don't worry, Jack, in two weeks, they'll be saying it's the smartest thing you ever did." For once, the father's political judgment was on the money.

With the issue of his vice-presidential choice resolved, and the waves of history lapping at his feet, now came Kennedy's speech accepting the nomination.

What most people recall is the debut of his presidential signature. "Today some would say that those struggles are all over — that all the horizons have been explored — that all the battles have been won — that there is no longer an American frontier . . . But I tell you the New Frontier is here, whether we seek it or not. Beyond that frontier are uncharted areas of science and space, unsolved problems of peace and war, unconquered pockets of ignorance and prejudice, unanswered questions of poverty and surplus.

"For the harsh facts of the matter are that we stand on this frontier at a turning point in history. We must prove all over again whether this nation — or any nation so conceived — can long endure; whether our society — with its freedom of choice, its breadth of opportunity, its range of alternatives — can compete with the single-minded advance of the Communist system."

Kennedy was really harking back to the same question that presented itself just before World War II, the one that had gripped him and driven his interest in foreign policy. It had not lost its relevance, for what he was asking was, could the democracies match the dictatorships when it came to responding to a dire threat? While we see the allusion to Lincoln in the wording, the question itself is pure twentieth century — only it was now Khrushchev, not Hitler, in opposition to us.

But it wasn't just America's Democrats who had their attention focused on the convention concluding in Los Angeles. The about-to-be Republican candidate, Richard Nixon, was watching television that night, viewing it carefully with the eye of a professional, and deciding, when all the shouting was over, that he was encouraged by what he'd seen.

Theodore White, then doing the reporting for his landmark book *The Making of the President, 1960,* described the response of the Republican cohort this way: "They sat rapt, then content, then pleased. The rapid delivery, the literary language, the obvious exhaustion of the Democratic candidate . . . all combined to invite in them a sense of combative good feeling." Nixon told those with him that he thought Kennedy had turned in a poor performance, his speech above people's heads and delivered too rapidly. He could take this man, his longtime colleague, now a known quantity, on TV — or so he felt.

So Nixon, made confident by what he'd seen, and trusting his judgment, was in a mood receptive to the idea of televised debate. Kennedy, when the moment came, jumped at the opportunity. "I took the telegram to him," Pierre Salinger said. The networks were proposing a candidates' debate, and, in the Kennedy camp, the decision to agree was quickly made. "The feeling was that we had absolutely nothing to lose by a debate with Nixon. If we accepted right away, we'd put Nixon in a position where he *had* to accept."

No one, least of all Jack, could have predicted the vice president's psychology or realized that Jack's performance at the convention had allayed Dick Nixon's worries about going head to head with him in front of the cameras. But by saying yes to a debate, what Nixon was handing his opponent was, in fact, a platform of such value that not even the senior Kennedy's wealth could have purchased it. Here was an opportunity for Jack to face the American people and claim for himself a measure of the recognition already Nixon's. Eight years in the vice presidency had given his rival a mammoth edge. TV would now hand it to the challenger.

The Kennedy themes, devised to differentiate his candidacy from Nixon's, all looked to the future. While the one man was so closely associated with both the long-standing positives and the more recent negatives of the Eisenhower era, the other could recast the country's complacency as a trap. Elect him, Jack Kennedy promised, and he'd arouse citizens to a new urgency, a new determination to face up to the challenges ahead. The United States was slowing down; everyone knew that. But he, John F. Kennedy, would get it moving again. He'd take on the Soviet threat, close the "missile gap," and bring the enemy to the bargaining table. He would arm America, not to fight, but to parlay. In short, he'd do what Winston Churchill might have done to prevent World War II, had his own countrymen listened to him back in the 1930s.

Meanwhile, Kennedy had a vibrant domestic agenda as well. He vowed to be a Democratic activist in the tradition of Franklin Roosevelt, bringing medical care to the elderly, federal aid to education, and strong enforcement of civil rights.

When the two came together face-to-face, the strategy was for Nixon to be squeezed, maneuvered into appearing both weak on defense and inactive on the home front. The tactic had worked against Henry Cabot Lodge in 1952, and, since you repeat what works, Kennedy intended to deny Nixon any chance to benefit as a moderate-sounding Republican. Not hard enough on defense, not soft enough on taking care of people: Kennedy would keep up the punches and send his rival into a defensive crouch, trying to match point for point every charge made against the Eisenhower record.

However, before he could go head to head with Nixon, Kennedy first needed to deal once again with the religion issue, which, despite his facing it head-on in West Virginia, had never really gone away. The need to do so once again came in early September, as he was whistle-stopping his way down the Pacific coast from Portland to Los Angeles. Suddenly, at one stop, he was peppered with questions about a meeting of 150 ministers just held at Washington's Mayflower Hotel. The purpose of the gathering, called Citizens for Religious Freedom, had been to band Protestant clergymen together to work against the election of a Roman Catholic president.

The meeting's organizer, Norman Vincent Peale, the longtime pastor of New York's Marble Collegiate Church and author of the best-selling *The Power of Positive Thinking,* also hosted his own radio program, *The Art of Living.* Thus, he was a popular and influential figure, now committed to using his clout against Jack Kennedy. "Our freedom, our religious freedom," he proclaimed, "is at stake if we elect a member of the Roman Catholic order as president of the United States." He worried that the pope was poised to assert his authority over any Catholic aspirant to the White House. His mission was convincing his fellow Americans of that risk.

As the waiting reporters clamored for a statement, Kennedy's initial response was curt: "I wouldn't attempt to reply to Dr. Peale or to anyone who questions my loyalty to the United States." Later, though, he'd remark to Ted Sorensen — after hearing Peale had claimed "the election of a Catholic president would change America" — "I would like to think he was complimenting me, but I'm not sure he was."

Yet, as he traveled on, it was becoming increasingly apparent that his responses to date still weren't enough to put the issue to rest. He decided to accept an invitation to speak to the Protestant ministers of Houston. When he stood there in front of them, he intended to address thoughtfully what he'd actually come to view as legitimate questions about his loyalty. The effect of it, he hoped, would be enough to arouse the loyalty of all Americans, not only Catholics, who'd felt the sting of prejudice. Though it's true he was sending mixed signals, telling Protestants not to vote their religion at the same time he was courting the Catholic vote, still, the eloquence he brought to bear upon bigotry cut deep and created a watershed moment in American politics.

The math, in fact, was straightforward enough. Kennedy understood the electoral power his religion actually gave him. While just one voter in four was Catholic, these citizens had sizable leverage in the states with the most electoral votes. So he needed, first off, to minimize the anti-Catholic vote by hanging the "bias" tag on any Protestant vote against him. Jews and other minorities would then get the picture, he hoped, and rally to the cause.

He also had to keep it light; he couldn't allow himself, ever, to get publicly defensive. When Harry Truman, campaigning for Kennedy and sounding only like himself, let loose at Nixon-loving Southerners, telling them they could "go to hell," the profanity earned him a pious rebuke from the Republican candidate himself. Kennedy, though, dispatched a clever telegram to the highly partisan, and also Nixon-hating, former chief executive. "Dear Mr. President," he wrote, "I have noted with interest your suggestion as to where those who vote for my opponent should go. While I understand and sympathize with your deep motivation, I think it is important that our side try to refrain from raising the religious issue."

En route to address the Greater Houston Ministerial Association, he made a stop in El Paso. *Look* magazine's Bill Attwood, who was friendly with Jack, saw him there and has recounted a telling exchange. "It was night and we were late, and a crowd of 7,000 people had been waiting at the airport for hours. They wanted to yell and cheer, and they wanted him to wave his arms and smile and say something about the Texas sky and stars. But he just strode out of the plane and jabbed his forefinger at them and talked about getting America moving again. And then he turned and climbed into a car and drove away.

"A few days later . . . I told him the crowd had felt let down and suggested that the next time he should at least wave his arms the way other politicians did and give people a chance to get the cheers out of their throats. Kennedy shook his head and borrowed my notebook and pencil — he was saving his voice for the day's speeches — and wrote, 'I always swore one thing I'd never do is' and he drew a picture of a man with his arms in the air." There were limits to what he would do to win votes.

But someone else was impressed — and extremely so — that night at the El Paso airport. According to Ken O'Donnell, Sam Rayburn, the legendary "Mr. Democrat," told him "ten times after we got to the hotel he had never seen such a crowd in El Paso and certainly not at that hour of the night. He didn't quite understand it, saying 'This young fellow has something special. I just didn't realize until now.'"

While the Kennedy advisors all agreed that a speech on his religion was necessary, they were equally against their candidate's accepting the Houston invitation. Jack Kennedy himself was the sole voice in favor. "In the end, he alone made the decision to go," O'Donnell recalled. "It came about casually; he was in shaving . . . and came out of the bathroom and said, 'Notify them we're going to do it. I'll give the speech. This is as good a time as any. We might as well get it on the record early; they're going to be asking this throughout the rest of the campaign. So, I'm going to do it.'"

In the hours leading up to the speech, Kennedy continued to wonder aloud if he'd made the right decision. Then, just before leaving his hotel room in his black pinstriped suit, a nonpolitical issue arose. "Look!" he told the ever-present Ken O'Donnell, pointing at his shoes. "They're brown!"

Finally, Dave Powers, the staff guy in charge of wardrobe, was located. His response brought common sense to bear: "I think, Senator, you'll be behind a podium and nobody will notice it on television. . . . I think this once you'll be okay."

"Really, Dave," Kennedy replied, "so you don't think anyone will notice that I have brown shoes with a crisp black suit?"

"Nah, nobody will notice. I mean, come on, Senator, most people in America only have one set of shoes — and, Senator, those shoes! Those shoes are brown! You know what you did tonight, Senator! You know what you did! You sewed up the brown shoe vote." At this, even Jack began to see the humor.

Kennedy walked into the meeting room alone. To make sure the audience viewing clips at home got the message, the advance man, Robert S. Strauss, had picked the "meanest, nastiest-looking" ministers to put in the front row. Assuming the role of defendant in the argument, Jack offered respect to these serious citizens with doubts about his loyalties. The invited ministers had a perfect right to question him, he said. But once having satisfied themselves as to his sincerity, they also had a responsibility to move on to other issues.

Kennedy's opening presentation in Houston was, perhaps, the finest of the campaign. "So, it is apparently necessary for me to state once again not what kind of church I believe in, for that should be important only to me, but what kind of America I believe in. I believe in an America where the separation of church and state is absolute, where no Catholic prelate would tell the president — should he be a Catholic — how to act, and no Protestant minister would tell his parishioners for whom to vote."

O'Donnell described Senator Kennedy's performance there as "dancing on a needle." On the one hand, he had "to satisfy this audience with regard to a Catholic in the presidency; and yet at the same time he had to be careful not to jeopardize his position with the Catholics across the country, the Catholic Church, or the Catholic priests." If he "came across as too conciliatory to these people, some of whom were outright bigots, it would destroy his candidacy and his position."

Not only did Kennedy speak eloquently; he presented himself with careful dignity, at the same time displaying an elegant pugnacity when roused. This was especially true in the long question-and-answer period that followed his speech. One focus of attention was Kennedy's rejection of a 1947 invitation to address a dinner in Philadelphia to raise funds for a Chapel of the Chaplains. It had been intended as an interfaith house of worship honoring the four chaplains who went down with the *Dorchester* in World War II. Kennedy had, at first, accepted the invitation, only to later turn it down. He'd done so at the request of the local archbishop, Dennis Cardinal Dougherty.

Kennedy's answer was that he had lacked the credentials to attend the dinner "as a spokesman for the Catholic church." When pushed further on the question again, he'd finally had enough. "Is this the best that can be done after fourteen years? Is this the *only* incident that can be charged?" But in the end, he'd been respectful, made all his points, stood his ground, and came away looking like a winner.

There are many ways of preparing for a life on the political stage. To the usual list — remembering the names of people you meet once, smiling at proven enemies — Jack Kennedy now added making noises like a seal. Given to bouts of self-improvement — his famous speed-reading is an example — he had been concerned about the timbre of his voice, how he sounded to listeners when he spoke in public. His performance at the Los Angeles convention had not been that strong and he knew it. The loud daily barking, then, was an exercise assigned to him by the vocal coach David McClosky, one that Jack chose to practice in the bathtub. Unexpectedly hearing him emit these very peculiar sounds caused even the most loyal of his aides to wonder if there wasn't, perhaps, a new health problem.

Jack's ongoing transformation had other aspects, with one significant physical change being inadvertent, a side effect of the medication he was taking for his Addison's. More than saving his life, the cortisone he'd been taking had transformed his face, fleshing out his features. Billy Sutton, who'd lived with him during those early years in Washington, would remark that he'd never looked better than he did in those months of running for president against Richard Nixon.

But cosmetic advantages didn't guarantee elections. True enough, Dick Nixon had looked old even when he was young — he was, in fact, just four years the senior of his Democratic rival — but he'd also spent two terms as vice president in the shadow of the prize they both were after. He was no one Jack could take for granted.

Throughout that fall, Dave Powers, Kennedy's campaign "body man," used the specter of Nixon to motivate his boss each morning. He once told me that he'd walk into Jack's room, in whatever town they happened to be in, pull open the curtains, and begin, tunelessly, to serenade the candidate: "I wonder where Dick Nixon is this time of day. I wonder how many factories he's been to, how many events he's had already."

The coming debates were, of course, of far greater importance than a typical day on the campaign trail, and Jack Kennedy knew it. Hadn't Nixon won his original seat in Congress by stomping on a first-rate New Dealer, Jerry Voorhis? It had been a no-holds-barred assault when he'd run against Congresswoman Helen Gahagan Douglas, defeating her in the even nastier 1950 Senate race, in which her lone success was in hanging on him a lasting nickname, "Tricky Dick."

But as much as Jack had to be wary of Nixon, there was also the fact that they'd be facing each other in front of a huge audience, bigger than any in history. That year, 1960, wasn't the first one in which television coverage had to be taken into account by presidential campaigns. It was, however, the first one in which *nearly every voter* had a television.

There were to be four debates, the first scheduled for September 26 in Chicago.

"Kennedy took the thing much more seriously than Nixon," recalled Don Hewitt, the CBS producer assigned to direct the candidates' first encounter. The Democrat had asked Hewitt to meet with him a week early in a hangar at Chicago's Midway Airport. "Where do I stand?" Jack kept asking, eager

417

to get an idea of what the setup would be in the WBBM studio. On the afternoon of the debate, wearing a terry-cloth robe, Kennedy lay in bed in his hotel room, clutching a fistful of cards in his hand, each with a probable question and its staff-prepared answer. Drilling him was Ted Sorensen and his other legislative assistant, Mike Feldman. After each card had been dealt with, Kennedy would throw it on the floor. Additionally, there was the "Nixopedia," which Feldman had prepared — in a binder like the once-invaluable "Lodge's Dodges" — to track and detail Nixon's positions.

The pollster Lou Harris recalled Kennedy standing on his Ambassador East Hotel balcony with the sun on his face. "He was nervous, and would hit his fist. There he was, walking back and forth, hitting his fist." To pass the time, Kennedy kept asking his pollster how he went about the business of calculating public opinion.

Also there with Kennedy was a veteran of the new camera-driven politics. Bill Wilson had been a young television producer when hired by Adlai Stevenson's campaign in 1956. His role was to help the TV-shy candidate perform as best he could in the new medium, since, for all his eloquence as a platform orator, Stevenson was a primitive as far as TV was concerned. When the set in his hotel room went on the blink, for example, he telephoned Wilson to come fix it. He saw no difference between a television advisor and a TV repairman. Nonetheless, Stevenson had kept Wilson through the primaries and into the general election, although never quite sure what the point was. Such basic resistance was not the case, though, with Wilson's new employer, who understood very well the importance of the tiny screen that sat there in voters' homes.

As the two participants arrived at the studio, there was a moment of mutual appraisal that gave a harbinger of what was to come: Jack looked like a million bucks and Nixon knew it; Nixon looked terrible and Kennedy knew it. In the tapes from their prebroadcast rehearsal, you can see Nixon's confidence shatter the instant Jack walked onto the set.

"He and I were standing there talking when Jack Kennedy arrived," Hewitt recalled. Tanned, tall, lean, in a dark, well-tailored suit, the Democratic candidate positively gleamed. Photographers, seizing their chance, abandoned Nixon and fluttered about their new prey like hornets. The senator bore no resemblance to the emaciated, jaundiced, wounded figure he'd been. "He looked like a young Adonis," Hewitt said simply.

Bill Wilson recalled his candidate's strategy: "The design was that we attack Nixon and everything he was saying. He had to get the floor. He had to be the one that had the control and had the sense of command on the stage, which he did. I told him the things that counted in terms of his body language and when you look at the camera, you're only talking to one person. When you're doing a debate or sitting, you're talking to one person and that's the lens."

Once the two men were on the stage together, going through the rehearsal, the psychological battle was on. Asked to pose with his rival, Kennedy appeared barely to notice him. They could have been total strangers for all the interest Jack Kennedy showed in the colleague with whom he'd enjoyed cordial terms since 1947. Nixon, for his part, seemed intimidated. From the moment Kennedy strode in, hijacking the attention of the photographers, he was not the same man. Visibly deflated by his rival's matinee-idol aura and seeming nervelessness, Nixon slouched in his chair, his head turned away, as if in retreat.

Pierre Salinger recalled Nixon's pale, unhealthy appearance. The vice president had injured his leg in August, with a subsequent knee infection forcing him off the campaign trail and into Walter Reed Hospital. He did not yet seem entirely recovered from the ordeal. "Nixon looked awful off camera. He really did. Kennedy went back to his dressing room and remarked how awful he looked." It seemed to Salinger that Nixon's ghastly appearance boosted Kennedy's confidence. "I think he thought that Nixon was afraid."

"Do you want some makeup?" Hewitt asked Kennedy. Hearing the Democrat's "no," Richard Nixon also declined it, ignoring the fact that his opponent had just spent days campaigning in the California sun and that he, himself, hadn't fully regained his health. Kennedy's people were taking no chances. "I was in the greenroom," recalled Wilson, "and they were playing with him, asking him all kinds of questions. Bobby was there. Anyway, I said okay, we've got to close it down, he needs about ten minutes before he goes on to get quiet and I've got to put some makeup on him.

"Ted Rogers, who was Nixon's guy, said, 'When's your guy going to get makeup on?' And I said, 'Well, after your guy's going to get it.' Rogers was wary. If the other guy didn't ask for it, his guy wasn't going to. 'Nixon's not going to get his makeup,' he said, 'until John Kennedy does.' And I said, 'Well, it looks like it's a Mexican standoff.' "

Both candidates now retired to their separate rooms. Wilson understood the dangers of going on without makeup, even for the already telegenic Kennedy. "So I went back and I said, 'You know, we've got to do makeup. You've got a great tan; you look fine.' But the lights in 1960 in studios were just broad and heavy, not like anything you see in studios today. They were just hot as hell. And if you put a little bit of makeup all over the face, it closed the pores. They wouldn't sweat."

Finally, Wilson quietly ran out to get makeup, and when he returned, cleared the room of the others. "And the last thing Bob Kennedy said after I said everybody's got to get out, was 'Kick him in the balls, Jack.' It was a beautiful moment, because that was the whole strategy."

The Kennedy guys had one more trick up their sleeve. Nixon was nervously waiting for the clock to tick down to the debate's starting time. The countdown commenced over the loudspeaker. "Five minutes to airtime." Nixon was staring at the studio door. Now there were only three minutes left. As Wilson described it, "Nixon was still watching the door, as tense a man as I had ever seen. By then, I was sure that no one had summoned Kennedy, and I was about to dash after him, when the door swung open. Kennedy walked in and took his place, barely glancing at Nixon. Kennedy had played the clock perfectly. He had thrown his opponent off stride. He'd set him up for the kill."

In fact, Nixon may have arrived already off his stride, for reasons other than his impaired health. His running mate, Henry Cabot Lodge — Jack's old opponent, who should have known better — had warned him to try to "erase the assassin image." In other words, Nixon was not to be his hardfisted self, but rather more of a gentleman, a Nixon who'd be unrecognizable, say, to those citizens of California who'd seen him in action against Voorhis and Helen Douglas. "Kick him in the balls" would have been more useful counsel to him as well.

"The candidates need no introduction," the moderator, Howard K. Smith, announced to 70 million watching Americans. Richard Nixon, for his part, looked ill at ease, unshaven, middle-aged. Jack Kennedy, by contrast, seemed poised, with his legs crossed and his hands folded on his lap. Nixon sat in his chair awkwardly, his legs side by side, his hands dangling from the chair arms. He was wearing a gray suit that didn't flatter him in the harsh light, and soon he would be perspiring profusely.

By agreement, the focus of this first encounter was domestic policy. Believing the size of the audiences would grow with each debate, the Nixon people had insisted on saving foreign policy until last. In his opening statement, Kennedy showed he was intent on playing the game strictly by his rules, but hardly by Nixon's plan. "Mr. Smith, Mr. Nixon," he began, slyly equating the status of a two-term vice president and a television newscaster. "In the election of 1860, Abraham Lincoln said the question is whether this nation could exist half slave and half free. In the election of 1960, and with the world around us, the question is whether the world will exist half slave and half free, whether it will move in the direction of freedom, in the direction of the road that we are taking, or whether it will move in the direction of slavery."

Kennedy then pushed the detonator. "We discuss tonight domestic issues, but I would not want . . . any implication to be given that this does not involve directly our struggle with Mr. Khrushchev for survival." What he was doing was introducing precisely the topic Nixon had thought was postponed.

The United States needed to be strong economically, Kennedy declared, not just to maintain the American standard of living but because economic strength buttressed our fight against the Communists. "If we do well here, if we meet our obligations, if we are moving ahead, I think freedom will be secure around the world. If we fail, then freedom fails. Are we doing so much as we can do?" he asked an anxious country. "I do not think we're doing enough."

Kennedy's words struck home for his largest audience ever. In eight minutes he'd shown himself as infinitely more appealing than the fellow who'd been vice president of the United States for eight years. There wasn't a word of his opening presentation anyone could have argued with, not a sentiment his fellow citizens couldn't share. No, the country was not meeting its potential. No, we were not the same nation of doers who'd, heroically and with such sacrifice, ended World War II. Yes, we could do better. And, yes, with the right leadership, it was in our power to "get the country moving again."

After observing this tour de force, Nixon took his turn with the look of a man dragged from a five-dollar-a-night hotel room and thrust before the unforgiving glare of a police lineup, a man charged with a crime of which he knew, if not he himself, his political cohorts were guilty. Afraid to project the "assassin image," he was stymied. "Mr. Smith, Senator Kennedy, there is no question but that we cannot discuss our internal affairs in the United States without recognizing that they have a tremendous bearing on our international position. There is no question that this nation cannot stand still, because we are in a deadly competition, a competition not only with the men in the Kremlin but the men in Peking." Then, finally: "I subscribe completely to the spirit that Senator Kennedy has expressed tonight, the spirit that the United States should move ahead."

Incredibly, Nixon was agreeing with his challenger. Yes, domestic policies affect the country's foreign situation. Yes, we cannot afford to "stand still." Yes, Kennedy has the right "spirit" to lead. His only concern was that Kennedy's statistics made the situation appear bleaker than it was.

He gave a similar response on Kennedy's call for medical care for the aged: "Here again may I indicate that Senator Kennedy and I are not in disagreement as to the aim. We both want to help old people." Minutes later: "Let us understand throughout this campaign that his motives and mine are sincere." And, after a small reminder that he knew "what it means to be poor," he offered yet another genuflection to Kennedy's goodwill. "I know Senator Kennedy feels as deeply about these problems as I do, but our disagreement is not about the goals for America but only about the means to reach those goals."

Only? The race for the presidency is "only" about "means"? With staggering humility, Nixon was telling the largest American political audience ever assembled that his rival was not only a man of unquestioned sincerity but one of unassailable motive. It was merely a matter of method that separated the two applicants for the world's most towering position. To avoid coming off as his nastier self, Dick Nixon was presenting himself as Jack Kennedy's admiring, if somewhat more prudent, older brother.

Throughout, he kept his attention fixed exclusively on Kennedy. Just as he had at McKeesport, Pennsylvania, thirteen years earlier, Nixon was ignoring the audience. He seemed to crave his opponent's approval, even to the point of rebuking his own administration. "Good as the record is," he averred, "may I emphasize it isn't enough. A record is never something to stand on. It's something to build on."

As the sitting vice president of the United States dealt with each of his opponent's points, he tried desperately to elevate himself to an Ike-like pedestal, one from which Kennedy was just as determined to knock him. Asked about Nixon's campaign charges that he was "naïve and sometimes immature," Kennedy explained how the two men had come to Congress together in 1946 and how both served on the Education and Labor Committee. "I've been there now for fourteen years, the same period of time that he has, so our experience in government is comparable." He went on to quote the unassailably noble and beloved sixteenth president: "Abraham Lincoln came to the presidency in 1860 after a rather little-known session in the House of Representatives and after being defeated for the Senate . . . and was a distinguished president. There is no certain road to the presidency. There are no guarantees that if you take one road or another that you will be a successful president."

But more than either contestant's words, it was their images, projected on millions of black-and-white Admiral and General Electric televisions, that affected the American judgment. Each time Kennedy spoke, Nixon's eyes darted toward him uneasily, the same look that Kennedy's aide Ted Reardon had spotted more than a decade before at a House committee meeting. When Nixon was on, Kennedy sat, sometimes professorially taking notes, at other moments wearing a sardonic expression as he concentrated on his rival's answers. Sargent Shriver later noted that it was his brother-in-law's facial language, more than anything he said, that in the end decided the results. By raising an eyebrow at Nixon, Jack had shown he had the confidence to lead the country.

In the hours that followed, the challenger was convinced he had won. "Right after the debate, he called me up at the hotel," Lou Harris recalled. "'I know I can take 'im. I know I can take 'im!'" Kennedy had exulted. He was not alone in the assessment. A despondent Henry Cabot Lodge, who had given Nixon the misguided advice to go easy on his rival, watched the last minutes of the debate with dismay. "That son of a bitch just lost the election." On the other side of the case, those hearing the debate on radio — a much smaller audience — were more favorable to the Republican. Lyndon Johnson, listening in his car, was one of them. He thought Nixon was the winner.

But it was a debacle for the vice president. After weeks of parity in the polls, one candidate now moved into a clear lead. A Gallup survey taken in the days following the first debate found Nixon with 46 percent approval and Kennedy pulling ahead to 49 percent. Who had "won" the debate? Forty-three percent said Kennedy; 29 percent called it even. Just 23 percent gave it to Nixon. Kennedy's captivating but also commanding performance in the first debate now made him the country's number one box office attraction.

Nursing his wounds, Nixon sought a weapon with which to make his fighting comeback. He found one in a current Cold War issue, counting on it to be the club with which he might beat his rival. Since the Communist takeover of China in 1949, the two offshore islands of Quemoy and Matsu had been occupied by the forces of Chiang Kai-shek's government on Formosa. The Chinese Communists had been shelling Quemoy and Matsu, demanding their evacuation. In an interview with NBC's David Brinkley, Kennedy had questioned the U.S. policy of helping Chiang's forces defend them, saying they weren't essential to the defense of Formosa.

If his opponent was willing to back down in the face of Communist aggression, as Nixon saw it, he was going to call him on it. How could any American leader allow the other side to annex even a small chunk of global territory and not see it as an invitation to further aggression? He was ready to attack.

Nixon's people, meanwhile, recognized they had other fronts to deal with as well. How their candidate looked mattered as much, obviously, as anything he said. This time Nixon was prepared to wear makeup. There'd be no macho hesitancy as before. He had his own dark suit to wear, and he'd been downing several milk shakes a day to give him the bulk he'd lost in those weeks in the hospital. But none of this would matter, his aides realized, if he showed the same sweaty look he had in that first, disastrous encounter with Kennedy in Chicago.

On the evening of October 7, Bill Wilson arrived with the Kennedy brothers at NBC's Washington bureau for the second debate. They walked into the studio to realize that someone had set the temperature practically to freezing. It felt like a meat locker. "What the hell is this?" Jack asked. After complaining loudly to no avail, Bobby darted in anger to the control room. Bill Wilson remembers racing down to the basement of the building, looking for the air-conditioning unit. "There was a guy standing there that Ted Rogers had put there, and he said don't let anybody change this. I said, 'Get out of my way or I'm going to call the police.' He immediately left and I changed the air-conditioning back. Ted wanted to keep his job because of the fuck-up in the first debate."

That night, Nixon showed that he'd been preparing himself not simply to look better than in the first encounter with Kennedy but to fight better as well. There was no more of agreeing in principle. He knew he needed to draw a line. "I should point out here that Senator Kennedy has attacked our foreign policy. He said that it's a policy that has led to defeat and retreat, and I'd like to know, where have we been defeated and where have we retreated? In the Truman administration, six hundred million people went behind the Iron Curtain, including the satellite countries of Eastern Europe and Communist China. In this administration we've stopped them at Quemoy and Matsu. We've stopped them in Indochina. We've stopped them in Lebanon. We've stopped them in other parts of the world."

Nixon's reference to Quemoy and Matsu was impossible to ignore. Kennedy's response was tortured. "We have never said flatly that we will defend Quemoy and Matsu if it's attacked. We say we will defend it if it's a part of a general attack on Formosa, but it's extremely difficult to make that judgment." Then he started to backpedal. "I would not suggest the withdrawal at the point of the Communist gun; it is a decision finally that the Nationalists should make, and I believe that we should consult with them and attempt to work out a plan by which the line is drawn at the island of Formosa."

Kennedy was now in Nixon's Cold Warrior target zone. Fighting Communism, Nixon charged, wasn't about being wishy-washy. "The question is not these two little pieces of real estate — they are unimportant. It isn't the few people who live on them — they are not too important. It's the principle involved. These two islands are in the area of freedom. We should not force our Nationalist allies to get off them and give them to the Communists. If we do that, we start a chain reaction. In my opinion, this is the same kind of woolly thinking that led to disaster for America in Korea. I am against it. I would not tolerate it as president of the United States, and I will hope that Senator Kennedy will change his mind if he should be elected."

For the first time, Nixon had scored a hit. He'd wounded Kennedy where the Democratic candidate himself knew his own party was vulnerable. The point of contention, after all, was one at which Kennedy himself had taken aim back in the "Who lost China?" period. He knew firsthand the potential firepower of the issue: if the Democrats found themselves positioned again as the party of "appeasement" in Asia, they were finished. In the days ahead, Nixon continued to hit Kennedy for a craven willingness to cede territory to the enemy. "I think it is shocking for a candidate for the presidency of the United States," he said in speech after speech, "to say that he is willing to hand over a part of the Free World to the Communist world."

432

However, what Nixon portrayed as strength, Kennedy saw as brinkmanship. Why would we risk war with the Chinese Communists over such a slight point as this? It made no sense. What it seemed to be about was Nixon wanting to fight the Communists on their own terrain and at significant peril of it going global. "Mr. Nixon is not interested in policies of caution in world affairs," he told a partisan audience at the Waldorf-Astoria. "He boasts that he is a 'risk-taker' abroad and a conservative at home. But I am neither. And the American people had caught a sufficient glimpse of the kind of risks he would take when he said in 1954, 'We must take the risk now of putting our boys in Indochina on the side of the French if needed to avoid further Communist expansion there.' That is a foolhardy and reckless decision. How much wiser it would be to follow the president's original recommendation — to persuade the Chinese Nationalists to evacuate all military personnel and any civilians who wish to go — now, when we would not be seeming to yield under Communist pressure, before real pressure is put on again."

There were now two hurdles facing Jack Kennedy as he headed into the third debate, on October 13. One was that he continued to be pegged as the squeamish candidate, ready to pull back from Quemoy and Matsu, while Nixon remained the vigilant champion, loudly prepared to hold the line. Helping to prepare him that day, Arthur Schlesinger observed his jitters. "I had the impression that he was a little nervous about the Q-M issue."

The other problem was the new debate format, which separated the candidates physically, the Democrat in a studio in New York and his Republican opponent 2,500 miles away in Los Angeles. With an entire country between them, Kennedy's ability to intimidate his rival, so crucial a factor in their first encounter, would be gone.

NBC's Frank McGee posed the first question, asking Kennedy about his charge that Nixon was being "trigger-happy" in regard to Quemoy and Matsu. If that was so, would Kennedy be willing to take military action to defend Berlin? Ignoring the Asia reference, Kennedy limited his answer only to a commitment regarding Berlin. But when Nixon took his turn, he swiftly moved the issue back to the now notorious offshore Chinese islands. "As a matter of fact, the statement that Senator Kennedy made was, to the effect that there were trigger-happy Republicans, that my stand on Quemoy and Matsu was an indication of trigger-happy Republicans. I resent that comment."

On the attack now, Nixon challenged Kennedy to come up with the name of a Republican president who'd led the country into war. "I would remind Senator Kennedy of the past fifty years. I would ask him to name one Republican president who led this country into war. There were three Democratic presidents who led us into war."

Boldly, Nixon cited the pre–World War II legacy of Munich, comparing Kennedy's position on Quemoy and Matsu to the appeasement policy toward Hitler's Germany that his father had supported as ambassador to Britain. "This is the story of dealing with dictators. This is something that Senator Kennedy and all Americans must know. We tried this with Hitler. It didn't work. He wanted, first, we know, Austria, and then he went on to the Sudetenland, and then Danzig, and each time it was that this is all he wanted." Before a national television audience of millions, Richard Nixon was calling Jack an appeaser. He was reminding him of his father's disgrace.

"Now what do the Chinese Communists want?" he asked, building dramatically to his climax. "They don't want just Quemoy and Matsu. They don't just want Formosa. They want the world."

With the third debate over, Kennedy took off for Michigan. He was scheduled to spend the night in Ann Arbor and then begin a whistle-stop train tour of the state the next day. Arriving late at the University of Michigan campus, he found nearly ten thousand students waiting for him. Speaking in front of the Michigan Union building, he suddenly, out of nowhere, made a proposition. "How many of you who are going to be doctors are willing to spend your days in Ghana? Technicians and engineers? How many of you are willing to work in the Foreign Service and spend your lives traveling around the world? On your willingness to do that — not merely to serve one year or two years in the service — but on your willingness to contribute part of your life to this country, I think will depend the answer whether our society can compete."

The speech lasted barely three minutes. He told Dave Powers he'd "hit a winning number" with it. He'd said it all before, pretty much, in that 1951 appearance on *Meet the Press* after he'd come back from the Far East. He'd talked then about sending off smart and idealistic young Americans to represent their country around the world. This time, however, he was speaking as a candidate for president. This time he was talking about something he would *create*. He was talking about the Peace Corps.

There on the steps of the Michigan Union, at two in the morning, he'd imagined out loud the genesis of a phenomenon that would change American lives. An idea that had not before existed in the minds of his countrymen now did: that of non-military service on foreign soil. Harris Wofford, a campaign aide and early civil rights activist, along with other Kennedy staffers, felt he'd been so angered by Nixon's taunt about the Democratic habit of starting wars that he determined to push in a totally different direction. In the closing weeks of the campaign, Jack began to pair the call for nuclear disarmament that he'd been making with his vision of a "peace corps of talented young men and women, willing and able to serve their country."

As for Quemoy and Matsu, Kennedy wanted it dropped, and to this end, he sought out Secretary of State Christian Herter, a former Massachusetts governor, to help broker a deal. The idea was that he, the Democratic candidate, as a point of national solidarity, felt it unwise to give the impression America was divided on the China issue. Kennedy's people told Herter their candidate was even prepared to change his position in order not to appear out of step with administration policy.

Hearing this, Nixon, surprisingly, agreed to a moratorium on discussions of the disputed Chinese islands. Whatever the vice president's posturing, as far as Kennedy himself was concerned, if there was ever to be a Cold War showdown, such an escalation made sense only when the value of the ground being fought over was indisputable.

And he knew of a hot spot near home, approximately ninety miles off the southern tip of Florida. On the night before the second debate with Nixon, Jack gave a major speech in Cincinnati attacking what he called "the most glaring failure of American foreign policy today . . . a disaster that threatens the security of the whole Western Hemisphere . . . a Communist menace that has been permitted to arise under our very noses." In short, he blamed the Republicans for losing Cuba, just as he and others had once blamed the Truman administration for the loss of China. He reminded his audience that two recent American ambassadors to Cuba — Arthur Gardner and Earl Smith — had warned about the danger of Fidel Castro and his brother Raul.

Castro, he said, "with guidance, support, and arms from Moscow and Peiping, has made anti-Americanism a sign of loyalty and anti-Communism a punishable crime, confiscated over a billion dollars' worth of American property, threatened the existence of our naval base at Guantánamo, and rattled Red rockets at the United States, which can hardly close its eyes to a potential enemy missile or submarine base only ninety miles from our shores."

He ended the speech by directly addressing the people of Cuba. "Be of stout heart. Be not dismayed. The road ahead will not be easy. The perils and hardships will be many. But here in America we pledge ourselves to raise high the light of freedom — until it burns brightly from the Arctic to Cape Horn — and one day that light will shine again."

Nixon felt the pressure. How could he be

sounding alarms about Chinese islands and not defend one just a short boat ride away? He began to push the administration to take action against Castro. His greatest hope was that it would expedite the attack of armed anti-Castro Cubans on the island, a clandestine CIA-backed operation already under way for several months. But the most he could accomplish, to show his muscle, was the Eisenhower administration's declaration of a trade embargo perfectly timed for the eve of the last debate.

Quick to respond, Kennedy termed the embargo an "empty gesture . . . which will have so little impact on Castro as to be almost meaningless." All it would do, he said, was speed up Cuban reliance on trade with the Communist countries. Without clearing it with Kennedy, speechwriter Richard Goodwin put out a statement raising the ante. "We must attempt to strengthen the non-Batista democratic anti-Castro forces in exile and in Cuba itself, who offer eventual hope of overthrowing Castro. Thus far, these fighters for freedom have had virtually no support from our government."

Kennedy was calling for an armed assault on Cuba by anti-Castro forces backed by the United States. It was an extraordinary proposal to make in the middle of a campaign, and it enraged Richard Nixon. That's because he was aware of top secret American plans to do exactly what Kennedy was proposing. He suspected that Kennedy was as well. Dean Acheson, who'd served as Truman's secretary of state, later warned that Kennedy had gone too far. "He was likely to get himself hooked into positions which would be difficult afterwards."

As he prepared to meet Kennedy for their fourth debate, Nixon continued fuming over that "fighters for freedom" statement. To follow such a recommendation, he declared disingenuously, would cause key Latin American countries to denounce not only the United States, but the U.N., too. What's more, such aggression would serve as "an open invitation for Mr. Khrushchev to come in, to come into Latin America and to engage us in what would be a civil war and possibly even worse than that."

To find new ground during their last televised meeting, Kennedy zeroed in on another area of dissatisfaction with Republican governance. And that was Americans' growing sense they were falling behind the Soviets in space and strategic weaponry. At the same time, the economy was slowing. From 5.9 percent in August, the nation's jobless rate rose to 6.4 percent in October. Between the conventions and Election Day, 330,000 people were thrown out of work. Not many of those hundreds of thousands of workers could ignore that their pink slips had been handed to them while Ike sat in the Oval Office, with Dick Nixon as his second in command.

On October 19, a group of African-Americans politely asked for service at the Magnolia Room in Rich's, the grand Atlanta department store. The lunch counters at drugstores and other downtown businesses were strictly whites-only. Coretta King described how it was in those days: "There was hardly a place outside our own neighborhoods where a Negro could even get a soda except by going to the side door and having it handed out." Among those arrested and charged with trespassing at Rich's that great day was the Reverend Martin Luther King, Jr. While the other sit-in demonstrators soon were released, a judge denied King bail, sentencing the civil rights leader to six months at hard labor in Reidsville State Prison. The defendant, he said, had violated probation on an earlier charge of driving in Georgia with an Alabama license.

Coretta, pregnant at the time, was naturally horrified — and very frightened — when she learned her husband had been roughly awakened at night, placed in handcuffs and leg chains, hurried into a car, and driven two hundred miles into rural Georgia. She shared her worry with a longtime friend, Harris Wofford. After discussing the situation with his fellow Kennedy aide Louis Martin, Wofford persuaded Sargent Shriver to take the case for action to the candidate, seizing a moment when Ken O'Donnell and the other political aides were out of the room.

"Why don't you telephone Mrs. King and give her your sympathy," Shriver suggested to Jack. "Negroes don't expect everything will change tomorrow no matter who's elected, but they do want to know whether you care. If you telephone Mrs. King, they'll know that you understand and will help. You will reach their hearts and give support to a pregnant woman who is afraid her husband will be killed."

"That's a good idea," Kennedy said. "Why not? Do you have her number? Get her on the phone." Mrs. King would later recount to Wofford what Jack had said. "I want to express my concern about your husband. I know this must be very hard on you. I understand you are expecting a baby, and I just wanted you to know that I was thinking about you and Dr. King. If there is anything I can do to help, please feel free to call me."

Afterward, the press quickly learned from Mrs. King about John Kennedy's having reached out to her. "It certainly made me feel good that he called me personally and let me know how he felt. I had the feeling that if he was that much concerned, he would do what he could so that Dr. King was let out of jail. I have heard nothing from the vice president or anyone on his staff. Mr. Nixon has been very quiet."

Beyond the hearing of any reporters, however, Kennedy worried out loud that even his little gesture had been too much. When asked about the call to Mrs. King, he appeared irritated at the leak. The campaign manager, Robert Kennedy, was downright furious. "Do you know that three Southern governors told us that if Jack supported Jimmy Hoffa, Nikita Khrushchev, or Martin Luther King, they would throw their states to Nixon? Do you know that this election may be razor close and you have probably lost it for us!" he scolded Wofford and Shriver.

But Bobby soon transferred his anger to the "son of a bitch" judge who'd thrown the book at King. He called Governor Ernest Vandiver of Georgia, and then, taking his advice, called the judge himself, who ordered King released on bail.

Louis Martin, an African-American, was elated when his friend Bobby Kennedy phoned in the early-morning hours with news of his successful mission. "You are now an honorary brother," he said.

Meanwhile, Kennedy's opponent had remained silent on King's predicament. The baseball hero Jackie Robinson tried and failed to get him to say something. "He thinks calling Martin would be grandstanding," Robinson said mournfully. "Nixon doesn't understand."

For this he would pay dearly. Martin Luther King, Sr., like his son a prominent Atlanta minister, now decided to endorse Kennedy publicly despite the religious difference between them. "I had expected to vote against Senator Kennedy because of his religion," the elder King somberly told his flock in the Ebenezer Baptist Church during the exultant welcome-home service held for his rescued son. "But now he can be my president, Catholic or whatever he is. It took courage to call my daughter-in-law at a time like this. He had a moral courage to stand up for what he knows is right. I've got my votes, and I've got a suitcase, and I'm going to take them up there and dump them in his lap."

Up at Kennedy headquarters in Washington, Wofford and Louis Martin were about to make history. Collecting all the appreciative and admiring comments pouring in from black leaders and others praising the Kennedys' efforts on behalf of the Kings, they found a pair of Philadelphia ministers willing to sponsor publication of a pamphlet, "The Case of Martin Luther King," which laid out the story of the Kennedy-King episode in bold language.

"No-Comment Nixon versus a Candidate with a Heart: Senator Kennedy," one caption read. "I earnestly and sincerely feel that it is time for all of us to take off our Nixon buttons," the Reverend Ralph Abernathy, a King ally, was quoted in the document. "Since Mr. Nixon has been silent through all this, I am going to return his silence when I go into the voting booth."

The pamphlet, two million copies of which were printed on light blue paper and delivered to black churches the Sunday before the election, would be dubbed "the blue bomb." Though it never stirred even the mildest alarm among conservative white voters, who'd remain loyal to the national Democratic ticket, it moved black America overnight to the Democratic side of the ballot, from the party of Lincoln to that of the Kennedys. Martin Luther King, Jr., summing up the episode's meaning, was eloquent: "There are moments when the politically expedient can be morally wise."

On November 2, Kennedy gave a major address at the Cow Palace in San Francisco. He spoke on two topics: the importance of nuclear disarmament and his plans for the Peace Corps. That afternoon, sitting in the bathtub at the Palace Hotel, he talked to Red Fay about how the campaign was going. "Last week, Dick Nixon hit the panic button and started Ike speaking. He spoke in Philadelphia on Friday night and is going to make about four or five speeches between now and the election. With every word he utters, I can feel the votes leaving me. It's like standing on a mound of sand with the tide running out. I tell you he's knocking our block off. If the election was tomorrow I'd win easily, but six days from now it's up for grabs." Then, suddenly, he changed the subject and began to tell his old friend, who'd been to war with him, what he intended to talk about that night: his great plans for this new corps of Americans working for peace throughout the world.

But the tide was clearly turning. Ike was out there drawing enormous crowds, and Nixon was playing rough. "You know, it's not *Jack's* money they're going to be spending!" The debates were yesterday's news, and voters were fickle.

To a Nixon accusation that he was a "barefaced liar," Kennedy retorted: "Having seen him in close-up — and makeup — for our television debates, I would never accuse Mr. Nixon of being barefaced." Away from the microphones and reporters' notebooks, he could be vicious. "He's a filthy, lying son of a bitch and a dangerous man," his aide Richard Goodwin heard him say once. To Red Fay, he articulated his dislike: "Nixon wanted the presidency so bad that there were no depths he wouldn't sink to, to try to achieve his goal. How would you like to have that guy deciding this country's problems when it became an issue of what was best for the country or what was best for Dick?"

Fay called it a "180-degree reversal from what it was back in the Congressional years when Jack Kennedy wrote me on November 14, 1950, about how glad he was to see Nixon win big in his Senate race." Kennedy also was worried about last-minute dirt, waiting for Nixon's people to hit him with evidence of his "girling," as he referred to it. He never did. Perhaps the voters would not have believed it if he had. How could they? One Nixon aide, watching news footage of Jack and Jackie in the final hours of the campaign, suddenly was struck by the power of the beautiful couple's allure. *Good God,* he remembered thinking to himself, *how do you run against that?*

Yet, all the time, the momentum of the 1960 campaign, the reality of the here and now, was shifting about him. He sensed he was losing California and wanted desperately some more days of campaigning, especially in the farm-rich Central Valley. But the schedule had been set. Promises had been made to the bosses of New York. The men who'd helped him win the nomination were now calling in their chits. They wanted him *there.*

It's hard to know how a campaign is going from the stump, Ken O'Donnell knew. Being in the bubble skews your perception. Unlike Jack, Bobby was at headquarters, getting phone calls and detecting very strongly that the question of religion was now back with a vengeance. "They're much more concerned back at the headquarters because they're seeing it. We've been to the Philadelphias and the Chicagos, Oklahoma — with big crowds across California, Arizona, New Mexico, Texas. Wild crowds. So we don't see it."

O'Donnell said that he, along with the rest of the staff, now feared that the "silent bigot" would emerge as the decider, the voter who'd never voice his anti-Catholicism but would cast his or her ballot accordingly.

New York on the final weekend proved disastrous. Kennedy was increasingly convinced that he had blown his chance at the presidency by not going back to California. His time would be split between pleasing the city's powerful bosses and its equally important liberal groups. To get where he was, he'd needed both. Now, facing Election Day, he especially needed the bosses. It was like a comedy in which the hero's on a date with two different people, simultaneously zipping back and forth to keep both appeased. Jack was forced to move from one hotel, the Carlyle, to another, the Biltmore, for breakfast, then back to the Carlyle for still another breakfast.

The exhausted candidate's simmering frustration finally rose to a dangerous boil when he was expected to ride in a New York City parade organized by the local Democratic strongman Carmine DeSapio. It was pouring rain, and as he was driven back to Manhattan from an appearance on Long Island, Jack finally had had enough. His breaking point reached, he kicked everyone out of the car, insisting that his driver abandon the motorcade and return to his Upper East Side hotel. En route, however, the driver took some wrong turns. "I was beginning to panic now," O'Donnell recalled. "I was soaking wet, angry. Our motorcade had also gotten lost — and I'd lost the senator."

When he reached the Carlyle, the drenched Kennedy was forced to wait for his suitcase, which had been mistakenly taken to the Biltmore. Disgusted, he commandeered O'Donnell's bedroom and once again threw everyone out. Lyndon Johnson, unaware of the meltdown, wanted to greet his running mate. Said O'Donnell, "Well, the next thing I see is Lyndon being literally thrown out of the room by a rather irate young Irishman from Massachusetts." The shock was enough to make Johnson worry about the political bed he'd made.

Next, Kennedy demanded that O'Donnell set about canceling the parade DeSapio had planned. "I don't give a shit if they have five million people out there. Cancel it. Either you tell them, or I will. If you don't have the balls to tell them, I'll tell them. Send them in," he instructed O'Donnell.

"Look, Senator, this is my fault. I'll tell them. But you're not going to lose." O'Donnell couldn't change his boss's mood. Jack's reply: "Just cancel the fucking thing."

On November 8, as Americans went to the polls to vote for their thirty-fifth president, early returns showed a big Kennedy victory. Connecticut's results came in quickly and strongly. Philadelphia gave Jack a plurality of 330,000 votes. Then, the news began to shift. "It started out like gangbusters," Pierre Salinger recalled. "It started out like we were going to win by a landslide. In fact, the computer said we were. Then, everything started to go bad all over the place. By midnight it was a real dog race." The religious issue was doing its damage.

The news from Ohio was devastating. Kennedy, watching TV at Bobby's Hyannis Port house with the others, rolled up his sleeve to show how much his hand had swollen. "Ohio did that to me. They did it there." But as upsetting as it was, it was also unexpected. "All those people now say they knew we would lose Ohio," said O'Donnell. "Well, if they did, they kept it to themselves until election night, when returns showed we lost it. Ohio was one that came as a shock to all of us."

Nixon was picking up Midwestern states in landslide fashion: Iowa, Indiana, even Wisconsin, where Kennedy had campaigned so hard that recent winter. As election night turned to morning, Jack saw the heartland turning against his candidacy. They were rejecting him. "I'm angry," the author Teddy White heard him say.

Though Kennedy would later insist the words he'd spoken were "I'm hungry," the situation suggests that the word White recorded might be taken as the more reliable. Nebraska was another wipeout. "Nebraska has the largest Republican majority of all fifty states," Rip Horton, who'd run the campaign there for his old Choate classmate, recalled. "His religion was definitely a handicap out there. They used to have meetings in churches. They'd advertise these meetings, various denominations, telling people to come to a mass meeting on why they shouldn't vote for a Catholic for president."

Yet even with these losses, Kennedy was managing to stay in front. "If the present trend continues," Richard Nixon told a loyal crowd waiting in the Ambassador Hotel in Los Angeles, "Senator Kennedy will be the next president of the United States." As supporters shouted out for him not to concede, Nixon doggedly kept on. "Certainly, if the trend continues and he does become our next president, he will have my wholehearted support."

"Does this mean you're president, Bunny?" Jackie Kennedy asked her husband. "Why don't you give up?" someone else in the room exhorted the face on the television screen. "Why should he?" Kennedy jumped in. "I

451

wouldn't in his place."

Jack was done for the evening. "What am I going to tell the press?" Pierre Salinger asked. "Tell them I went to bed," came the answer. "Wake me up if anything happens." With that, he walked out into the Cape Cod night, headed for his own house. When he awoke, he was the next president.

Ted Sorensen beat Salinger to him with the news. That morning they watched intently as Herb Klein, Nixon's press secretary, read the telegram Nixon had sent from California, before flying at dawn back to Washington. "I want to repeat through this wire the congratulations and best wishes I extended to you on television last night. I know that you will have the united support of all Americans as you lead the nation in the cause of peace and freedom during the next four years."

Nixon wasn't playing by the rules and Jack resented it. It had been a close election, yet here was his opponent denying him the courtesy of a televised concession. It was part of the ritual, and yet he'd ducked out at the climax, leaving his press secretary to do the job. He, Jack Kennedy, would never have behaved in such an unsportsmanlike manner. Once he'd known he'd lost the vice-presidential race in 1956, he'd *raced* to the podium.

As he greeted and thanked his top political aides O'Donnell and O'Brien, he now struck them both as a different man. The battle had been hard fought and won.

When the Secret Service detail arrived at Hyannis Port at 5:45 a.m., the agents knew the names, faces, and roles of each of Kennedy's people. Seeing Ken O'Donnell at the Kennedy compound that Wednesday afternoon, the chief of the Secret Service unit approached him as he got out of his car. "Mr. O'Donnell, the president has informed the Secret Service that we will now be reporting to you and that you are now our boss, in charge of the Secret Service for the length of the president's term of office. What would you like us to do right now?" It was the first indication that Kennedy intended him to come to Washington.

President-elect Kennedy's plans did not include appointing a chief of staff. He, Jack Kennedy, was going to be at the center. Everyone else, including O'Donnell, now a special assistant, and Sorensen, special counsel, would be arrayed around him, each spoke of the wheel competing for his attention. Jack would design a White House operation to match his compartmentalized personality. No one would control him. He would, in that fashion he loved, *have things under control.*

Still, before he could relax in his triumph and enjoy his cresting euphoria, Kennedy needed to secure the victory against any doubters. The problem was that the historically close tally had left questions about certain state results. Those in dispute were in Illinois — especially Cook County, where Chicago is located — and in Lyndon Johnson's Texas. It remained unclear in the first days after the election whether Richard Nixon intended to demand recounts or otherwise challenge the results. In order for John Kennedy to be able to move forward as chief executive, an extraordinary measure was required: someone must indicate, clearly and convincingly, that he had, without question, won the election. The person who needed to do so was Dick Nixon.

It fell to Joseph P. Kennedy, a master at the deal and knowing whom to call, to figure out the way. A longtime friend of Herbert Hoover, he was able to pick up the phone and quickly reach the eighty-six-year-old former president. The message he delivered to Hoover was a straightforward one: it was in the country's interest for the newly elected president and the defeated Nixon to get together. Hoover listened and understood. He'd once lost a presidential election himself, and survived. Plus, over the years Nixon had come to regard him as a political father figure. For both these reasons, Nixon would listen to him and respect his counsel.

The Saturday after the election, the excitement and fatigue of the campaign had faded from the fallen candidate. Defeat, both dull and cruel, had taken hold. The loyal Herb

Klein could see it plainly. "Nixon was, in my opinion, more unresponsive than at any time I had known him. He was completely depressed and had finally realized, four days later, that he'd lost the election."

Nixon and his retreating corps of advisors were assembled that night in Key Biscayne, Florida. It was there he took the call from Hoover and heard the big-picture case for getting together with Kennedy. "I think we are in enough trouble in the world today that some indications of national unity are not only desirable but essential."

But, as always in such moments, there were dimensions that existed beyond the easy explanations. After talking to Hoover, Nixon's glum mood suddenly lifted. "It was the difference between night and day," Klein said. While Nixon was on another phone calling President Eisenhower for guidance, Klein took a call from Kennedy, who hadn't wanted to wait for Nixon to ring him. The upshot was the two men agreed to meet the following Monday in Key Biscayne.

The meeting accomplished just what the Kennedys intended: providing a photo op to showcase the image of loser meeting winner. "Ladies and gentlemen," Jack Kennedy told the press, "I just wanted to say that the vice president and I had a very cordial meeting. I was delighted to have a chance to see him again. We came to the Congress the same day fourteen years ago, and both served on the Labor Committee of the House of Representatives. So I was anxious to come here today and resume our relationship, which had been somewhat interrupted by the campaign." Had the two discussed the campaign during their hour-long meeting? "I asked him how he took Ohio, but he did not tell me," Kennedy joked. "He is saving it for 1964."

The vote count would turn out to be incredibly tight — Kennedy: 34,226,731; Nixon: 34,108,157. But now the results had been validated by the face-to-face meeting on Nixon's own turf.

Jack Kennedy's ultimate trophy had been won by virtue of the truth he'd grasped about his country, one that Richard Nixon had failed to see. "He had done it by driving home the simple message of unease," *Time* reported, addressing "the things left undone in the world, where a slip could be disastrous." The historian Arthur Schlesinger enlarged on the same point in his diary. "He wisely decided to concentrate on a single theme and to hammer that theme home until everyone in America understood it — understood his sense of the decline of our national power and influence and his determination to arrest and reverse this course. He did this with such brilliant success that, even in a time of prosperity and apparent peace, and even as a Catholic, he

456

was able to command a majority of the votes."

Victory confirmed, Jack could focus anew on those ideals of peace and heroic leadership that had inspired him since youth. The new president had a favorite quote from Lincoln that he liked to carry with him on a scrap of paper. He'd used it in speeches, but now it spoke to him personally. "I know there is a God, and I know He hates injustice. I see the storm coming and I know His hand is in it. But if He has a place and a part for me, I believe that I am ready."

CHAPTER THIRTEEN
LANDING

He who learns must suffer, and, even in our sleep, pain that cannot forget falls drop by drop upon the heart, and in our own despair, against our will, comes wisdom to us by the awful grace of God.

— Aeschylus

John F. Kennedy, the youngest man ever elected to the White House, understood how incredibly close the race had been. He also recognized the meaning of his slender margin, a victory that was far from a mandate. Both he and his rival had sought to show the strength and the will with which they would confront the Soviets. Now that he'd triumphed, little, really, had changed. Except that now the task was at hand.

A critical first endeavor involved the reassurance of two important government officials: both J. Edgar Hoover and Allen Dulles — the FBI and CIA directors, respectively — had to be told their jobs were safe. To have done

Inauguration

31

Meeting with Khrushchev

32

otherwise would have unsettled the country. Therefore, urgent phone calls were placed to each man in the earliest hours of the interregnum. For JFK, retaining Hoover offered the premium of putting a lid on, among other prospects, the troublesome "Inga Binga" material in his files.

President-elect Kennedy put a pair of Republicans in top cabinet posts, naming Douglas Dillon, who'd been Eisenhower's undersecretary of state, to run the Treasury Department and placing the Ford Motor Company president, Robert McNamara, at Defense. The clubby Dillon, with his old-money connections, appealed to Kennedy the man. McNamara, showing no lack of toughness, made a point, when they discussed the job, of asking Jack whether he'd written *Profiles in Courage* himself. An air corps lieutenant colonel by the end of World War II, McNamara had a Harvard MBA and at Ford had been one of the famous "Whiz Kids," a group of ten returning veterans who came in and revitalized the company.

Looking to the liberal faction, which he needed both to acknowledge and include, the president tapped Adlai Stevenson to be his United Nations ambassador, Walter Heller as chief economic advisor, and Arthur Schlesinger as all-around Renaissance man.

Now, as always, concessions needed to be made to the senior Kennedy. It was, after all, the tribute Joe's money and support deserved. Since his sons' futures were of the utmost importance to him, posts for both younger Kennedy brothers were part of the bargain: Bobby would be attorney general, Ted would get Jack's senate seat once he turned the required age of thirty.

Jack laughed with Ben Bradlee at the absurdity of the youngest president ever elected picking his brother, eight years younger than he, as attorney general. When Bradlee asked him how he planned to deliver the news to the press, his probable course of action had a familiar ring. Kennedy said, "I think I'll open the front door of the Georgetown house some morning around two a.m., look up and down the street, and if there's no one there, I'll whisper, 'It's Bobby.'" There was no getting around the appointment for what it was: sheer, unadulterated nepotism.

"I think he hadn't really thought about how to run the government until he got elected," Ken O'Donnell said. "He was a very single-minded person. Politically, each battle he fought one at a time. There were very few things that were clear when he was elected."

Kennedy's "spokes of the wheel" approach had been championed by the presidential scholar Richard Neustadt, but such an organizational principle, in fact, followed his natural inclination. Unlike the former army officer Eisenhower, who appointed a strong chief of staff to run his agenda and team, Kennedy refused to have anyone between him and his advisors. Shrewdly, he set up two doors to the Oval Office, one manned by O'Donnell, the other by his secretary, Evelyn Lincoln. This system worked well: cabinet members had to fight their way past O'Donnell, while pals could whiz past Lincoln.

There was little camaraderie among Jack's chosen men, and several ongoing rivalries. O'Donnell resented the partnership Sorensen assumed with Jack. Ben Bradlee, the Washington sophisticate, failed to see the appeal of Lem or Red. Bobby, meanwhile, resented how much his brother reached out to Torby. As couples, the Bradlees and the Bartletts hardly ever saw each other for the simple reason that as couple-to-couple friends to Jack and Jackie, to invite them at the same time would create a redundancy. Thus, they were asked over on different nights. Together, of course, all of them had a purpose, to keep Jack company, to ensure that he was never alone, never bored, never stuck.

Harris Wofford, Kennedy's civil rights advisor, described insightfully how he and the others fit in. "The president-elect was a complex political leader in a complex situation. He was not anyone's man — not Stevenson's or Bowles's, and not Mayor Daley's or John Bailey's, not the Civil Rights Section's, and not the Southern senators'; not his father's and not Bobby's. He had one foot in the Cold War and one foot in a new world he saw coming; one hand in the old politics he'd begun to master, one in the new politics that his campaign had invoked."

Kennedy picked Clark Clifford, who'd been President Truman's counselor, to be his liaison with the outgoing Eisenhower staff. An astute observer of men and power, Clifford recognized early on John Kennedy's ability to detach himself *from himself.* You'd see him sitting at meetings, Clifford once told me, and you could almost imagine JFK's spirit assuming a form of its own and rising up, the better to look down on the group and assess its various members' motives and agendas. It was the same uncanny detachment Chuck Spalding had seen in Jack on his wedding day.

Not all the people in the U.S. government, even at the top, owe their positions to the president. This remains one of the challenges of being chief executive in the American system. The reality of that limited control over people dawns eventually, if not right away. There's also the need to lay down clear presidential orders.

Take the time JFK and his aides gathered around a swimming pool in Palm Beach, with dark-suited agents wearing sunglasses crouched protectively around them. JFK told O'Donnell, the White House official he'd personally posted to oversee the Secret Service, to have the agents back off. He wanted them to change to sports shirts and lose the fighting stance. "Nobody's going to shoot me, so tell them to sit down and relax a bit."

More than one Kennedy friend commented how happy he seemed in those days, making decisions while enjoying the Florida weather and waiting for Inauguration Day. Feeling buoyed up as he did — so thrilled and excited about his new circumstances, and proud to have pulled off what he had — he determined to stay fit as president. Said Charlie Bartlett: "I remember he told me, 'From now on I'm really going to take care of myself.'" Bartlett also heard him make a different sort of commitment to the future. It had to do with his marriage. "'I'm going to keep the White House white.' He said it right out there on that terrace."

Kennedy and Ted Sorensen had been devoting a good deal of that Palm Beach time to writing Jack's inaugural address. Composed in the tropical air, it was delivered on January 20, 1961, when the Washington temperature hovered in the low twenties and eight inches of snow had fallen that morning.

Given the ongoing challenge of the United States–USSR relationship and its immense significance in the election, that theme would command the heart of the speech. Its focus was on strength — not as a prelude to war, but as an instrument for peace. "Man holds in his mortal hands the power to abolish all forms of human poverty and all forms of human life."

The Churchillian notion of peace through strength had echoed throughout Jack's adult life. "We dare not tempt them with weakness. For only when our arms are sufficient beyond doubt can we be certain beyond doubt that they will never be employed." America would arm not to fight, but to parlay its power into protection. "Finally, to those nations who would make themselves our adversaries, we offer not a pledge but a request: that both sides begin anew the quest for peace, before the dark powers of destruction unleashed by science engulf all humanity in planned or accidental self-destruction."

Those decisive phrases have not lost their resonance. "Let both sides, for the first time, formulate serious and precise proposals for the inspection and control of arms — and bring the absolute power to destroy other nations under the absolute control of all nations. Let both sides seek to invoke the wonders of science instead of its terrors. Together let us explore the stars, conquer the deserts, eradicate disease, tap the ocean depths, and encourage the arts and commerce."

The one domestic policy reference would be Kennedy's commitment to "human rights" at home as well as abroad. At the end came the words that passed into the world's consciousness: "And so, my fellow Americans, ask not what your country can do for you — ask what you can do for your country."

To some who'd once been at Choate and paid attention in chapel to the words of Headmaster St. John, a lightbulb flickered. The irony is that Jack Kennedy, the Mucker now grown up, was appropriating the very rallying cry from which he'd felt so alienated as a rebellious student.

The act of asking, in fact, marked the passage of John Kennedy through his public life. Most politicians make promises. They tell people what they will do for them, dangling the prospect of jobs, or government spending, with elections and "pork" irrevocably intertwined. That approach was certainly politics-as-usual for Lyndon Johnson, who always sought ways to find a person's "button" — that thing he wanted, or feared — that would put him in his power. Kennedy was never like that. From the very start, he called on people to come out, to join, to be active, to be part of something larger than themselves. At the beginning, when Jack was little known, it had been a necessity, but it evolved into a grander vision, one that changed lives exactly as George St. John once had preached.

In Moscow, the Soviet leader, Nikita Khrushchev, had been sounding a different call to arms, in his case a boastful one. The progress of the international Communist cause, he'd told his countrymen on January 6,

466

had "greatly exceeded the boldest and most optimistic predictions and expectations." Encouraging "wars of liberation" such as the one under way in South Vietnam, he then emphasized the crucial position of Berlin in the struggle being waged against Marxism's enemies. "The positions of the USA, Britain, and France have proved to be especially vulnerable in West Berlin. These powers . . . cannot fail to realize that sooner or later the occupation regime in that city must be ended. It is necessary to go ahead with bringing the aggressive-minded imperialists to their sense, and compelling them to reckon with the real situation. And would they balk, then we will take resolute measures. We will sign a peace treaty with the German Democratic Republic."

Once he'd heard those declarations, Jack Kennedy's sense of purpose — mission, really — was focused on their possible consequences. Did Khrushchev actually intend to sign a treaty with East Germany that would throw the USA, Britain, and France out of West Berlin, where they'd governed as allies since 1945? According to Arthur Schlesinger, Kennedy couldn't stop reading and re-reading those words. Did they mean war? And would the United States be forced to escalate to nuclear war if the Soviets made good on their threat? Could an American president let the Communists grab West Berlin, the very symbol of Cold War defiance?

This is the specter Jack Kennedy was forced to contemplate in those early days of his presidency: the real chance that he alone would have to choose between nuclear war over Berlin or a historic capitulation to a European aggressor, a second "Munich." Somehow he was able to greatly enjoy these early weeks after the inauguration. Living, as he did, in compartments, he didn't let the worry show. He found comfort where he had since youth, in the close company of old friends.

During those early weeks after they'd moved into 1600 Pennsylvania Avenue, the Bartletts came to visit and the First Couple took them on a stroll down the streets surrounding the White House. Escaping through the guard gates was a way of testing his freedom. That night both Jack and Jackie spoke of their commitment to saving the buildings surrounding Lafayette Park, just across Pennsylvania Avenue. The Eisenhower administration had considered leveling the historic townhouses to put up government office buildings. They also mentioned their desire to restore the White House itself. When they found their way up to the ornate Indian Treaty Room in the Old Executive Building, Kennedy practiced using the microphone used by Ike during press conferences. Charlie sat in the back, listening to how the new president sounded from there. The brand-new president was having fun in his discovered world and sharing it with a beloved pal. He wasn't letting his hidden dread affect the occasion. As Chuck Spalding once told me, even amid crisis, "Jack's attitude made you feel like you were at a *fair* or something."

Lem Billings arrived on Friday and stayed a week. He was the Kennedys' first house-guest and their most frequent. Soon he'd have his own room, and would show up unannounced and stay as long as he liked. He was never issued a White House pass, but the Secret Service agents all knew him. He joined the couple, too, on weekends at Glen Ora, their retreat in the Virginia horse country. Often, Jackie was the one inviting him. She wanted Jack to have someone to hang out with when she was out riding. The presence of Jack's old Choate roommate ensured there'd always be company to lighten the mood.

Lem never took for granted Jack's friendship, cherished it, and was always there for him. "Jack was the closest person to me in the world for thirty years," he said, and no one doubted it. Still, even he found it difficult to explain Jack's enduring loyalty. "I've often wondered why, you know, all through the years, we continued to be such close friends, because I never kept up on politics and all the things that interested him. What he really wanted to do, on weekends, was to get away from anything that had to do with the White House."

In fact, escaping the White House even on weeknights appealed greatly to its new occupant. One time he had Red Fay buy tickets ahead of time for *Spartacus,* allowing them to slip into the nearby movie theater unnoticed once the lights were down. Fay never forgot an incident that occurred a few nights later, walking across Lafayette Park. A fellow standing in the shadows caught the attention of the Secret Service agents, who checked him out by shining their flashlights at him. "What would you do now if that man over there pulled a gun?" Kennedy suddenly asked his buddy from the PT boat days. "What would you do to help your old pal?"

As they walked on, they began talking about assassination, the word itself rather antiquated, given that there'd been none since McKinley. "You know, this really isn't my job, to worry about my life," Kennedy said. "That's the job of the Secret Service. If I worry about that, I'm not going to be able to do my own job. So I have just really removed that from my mind. That's theirs to take care of. That's one of the unpleasant parts about the job, but that's part of the job."

Fay had moved from California to work at the Navy Department. Once he was on the federal payroll, Jack teased him. "Listen, Redhead, he'd say, I didn't put you over there to be the brightest man that ever held the job of Undersecretary." He said that he wanted him there for his honest judgment about what he saw. But, clearly, the president wanted Fay's company as well. Jack had arranged for another PT buddy, Jim Reed, to be made assistant secretary of the treasury, and for Rip Horton to go to the Army Department. "The presidency is not a good place to make new friends," Jack said. "I'm going to keep my old friends."

The Peace Corps — once an idea that seemed, spontaneously, to create itself — was now in the process of becoming a reality. Not sure exactly how the logistics of the visionary but also highly practical project might work, Kennedy put it in the hands of Sargent Shriver. As the founding director, Shriver got it off the ground, with the first volunteers overseas by the end of the year in countries such as Ghana and Tanganyika, Colombia and Ecuador. "The president is counting on you," he told one early group on the eve of their departure. "It's up to you to prove that the concepts and ideals of the American Revolution are still alive. Foreigners think we're fat, dumb, and happy over here. They don't think we've got the stuff to make personal sacrifices for our way of life. You must show them."

But then, Washington bureaucratic jealousy threatened the enterprise. Shriver sought help from Vice President Johnson, named by JFK to chair the advisory council. "You put the Peace Corps into the Foreign Service," he told Shriver, "and they'll put striped pants on your people when all you'll want them to have is a knapsack and a tool kit and a lot of imagination. And they'll give you a hundred and one reasons why it won't work every time you want to do something different. If you want the Peace Corps to work, friends, you'll keep it away from the folks downtown who want it to be just another box in an organizational chart."

Like a high priest in cowboy boots, Johnson knew the secrets of life and death in the capital. Thanks to him, the Peace Corps remained independent.

Having first talked about it when she entered the White House, Jackie Kennedy now wanted to start making good on her desire to redecorate the Executive Mansion. To help her, she asked her friend Rachel "Bunny" Mellon, married to the Pittsburgh banking heir and philanthropist Paul Mellon, whose high-patrician style she admired. According to Bunny, "When he became president, Jackie changed — she became just as royal as could be. She said, 'Will you come now? Jack's president. Will you come now and help me fix up this house? It's terrible. And don't call me "First Lady" ever, because I just work here. This is a job. I've got to do it for Jack.'"

But in addition to her work with Jackie on the public and private rooms, Bunny Mellon made another singular and lasting contribution to the Kennedy-era White House. In this case, it was Jack himself who asked for her expert knowledge. Knowing her to be a celebrated garden designer and horticulturalist, he requested that she renovate the Rose Garden, which he could see from his Oval Office window and called "a mess."

Established in 1913 by Mrs. Woodrow Wilson, it continues to this day to be the scene of ceremonial events. The layout Bunny Mellon created for JFK, often following his specific instructions, comprises the admired Rose Garden layout still seen today.

On April 12, 1961, the Soviet cosmonaut Yuri Gagarin orbited the earth. It was the first time in human history that man had gone beyond our planet's atmosphere. Having beaten the United States into space with their first unmanned craft, the satellite *Sputnik 1,* back in 1957, the Russians once again had surpassed us. That first victory had come on President Eisenhower's watch, but this one was on Kennedy's.

But April, the "cruelest month," held further setbacks, ones that would leave even more serious political scars. On April 17, more than 1,400 anti-Castro Cuban exiles — trained, equipped, transported, and given limited air cover by the CIA — landed on a Cuban beach bordering an inlet now known as the Bay of Pigs on the island's south side. The disembarking Cubans had been assured by Agency officials they'd have full U.S. military support were they to encounter trouble on landing, but this turned out to be a false promise.

As Kennedy famously quoted at the time, "Victory has a hundred fathers; defeat is an orphan." The best way to look back with full understanding at the debacle known as the "Bay of Pigs" is to get an idea of how it appeared going forward.

There were several factors contributing to the pressure put on the new president to approve this ostensibly secret plan. Kennedy had himself called for such an action during the campaign, having gotten a tip-off from, if not others, Governor John Patterson of Alabama, who knew his National Guard units were helping the CIA invasion effort. He felt another spur to action. Once he'd taken the oath of office, and had it confirmed that the operation was already well into its planning stages, he understood that to back off and shut down the preparations would paint him as a soft-liner.

Driving him the hardest were his new colleagues. Somehow, the people directing "Operation Zapata," the invasion's CIA code name, fully believed their plan could succeed. They were encouraged by the success Allen

Dulles, the brother of the late John Foster Dulles, President Eisenhower's secretary of state, had had in pulling off what was regarded as a similar scheme back in 1954, when a coup d'état had been stage-managed in Guatemala.

Richard Bissell, Dulles's chief of operations, had slyly arranged, while Kennedy was still a candidate, to meet him at a Georgetown party, and the two Ivy Leaguers had hit it off. Not only was Bissell a persuasive and convincing supporter of Operation Zapata, but so were key Kennedy people, such as Secretary of Defense Robert McNamara and National Security Advisor McGeorge Bundy.

But what really clinched it for those men sitting safely in faraway Washington was the escape hatch many were led to believe was built into the plan: if the exiles found themselves unable to hold a beachhead once they landed, they could then retreat to the Escambray Mountains only eighty miles away, where they'd be able to join up with counterrevolutionary forces hiding out. Unfortunately, it was a *very* long eighty miles, across nearly impassable swamp — and getting even to that point meant eluding a Castro force vastly larger than the exile group. Obviously — had he known, and he *should* have known this — instead of signing off on it, Kennedy should have shut Zapata down while it was still possible.

Instead, there on the sands of that Cuban

bay, every member of the invading Brigade 2506 — mostly middle-class professionals recruited in Miami with little idea how to defend themselves against Fidel's soldiers — was captured or killed. Quickly, in the aftermath, Kennedy asked for the resignations of both Dulles and Bissell. "In a parliamentary government, I'd have to resign," JFK told Bissell. "But in this government, I can't, so you and Allen have to go."

In the end, even from this distant vantage point, nothing is perfectly clear about that ill-conceived CIA operation except for the fact that, once it was launched, it was bound to fail.

It's hard to say just why Kennedy went along with his advisors, most of whom seem to have either had their heads in the sand or were otherwise enacting agendas of their own. Yet what does a president have such military and intelligence experts for if not to listen to them? JFK had been in office only three months, and however quick a study he was, he was still learning on the job. He was also used to being entirely his own boss, his own skipper, his own engine of accomplishment — from the Muckers to *PT 109* to his extraordinary campaigns. The scope and scale, the sheer bulkiness of the apparatus around him made a difference to his sense of maneuverability. Now he'd signed on, not just to an operation, but to a government. He was surrounded by a government establishment he himself had no hand in forging.

But the contradictions buried in the Bay of Pigs scheme echoed Kennedy's own. It was the old "two Jacks" problem. He was an idealist pursuing a new foreign policy he hoped would transcend the Cold War. He was also a Cold Warrior who had promised in the recent campaign to back "fighters for freedom" against Fidel Castro. Here he was caught going down the one road while signaling the other.

Just a month earlier, at a White House reception for Latin American diplomats, Kennedy had delivered his "Alliance for Progress" speech. In it he'd vowed to abandon the gunboat diplomacy engaged in by the "Goliath of the North" for generations, as the United States intervened at will in countries such as Cuba. This declaration of Pan-American mutual respect would be tarnished by U.S. efforts to overthrow Castro. Only too aware of the hypocrisy it revealed, Kennedy insisted that the Cuban invasion be carried out in the absence of direct U.S. military action, on the principle of what's known in dark diplomacy as "plausible deniability."

To achieve this goal, Kennedy had instructed the CIA's Bissell, whose baby the operation really was, to see that it was carried out with the minimum of "noise." For this reason he ordered the landing point shifted from Trinidad, a busy port city, to the desolate Bahía de Cochinos. As a result, the invasion inevitably lost what chance it might have had of triggering a countrywide rebellion, with citizens coming out to join the "liberators."

Kennedy's conflict in purpose continued as he sought to reconcile his aggressive Cold Warrior stance, which had seen him denouncing the Truman administration's "loss" of China, with his newly emerged recognition of postwar nationalism. The incredibly tricky challenge of toppling a despot on foreign soil by supporting an invasion was dealt another blow when Kennedy called off two of the planned air strikes in the midst of the operation. For the anti-Castro force to hold the beachhead, the small Cuban air force needed to be knocked out of action. In the event, it suffered only limited damage.

By the third day, the battle was lost. The mountains with their promise of sanctuary were little more than a mirage, real but impossible to reach. The eyes of the world were watching as Castro rounded up the poorly served and even more poorly supported surviving combatants, who would not return home to Florida for twenty more months, not until the United States bartered for their freedom with more than $50 million worth of medicine and baby food.

In the aftermath, there was certainly enough blame to go around, as JFK ironically suggested. But that mattered little in the face of such headlines as the one that ran in *the New York Times* on April 21: "CUBA SAYS SOVI-ETS SCARED OFF U.S.; Asserts Washington Feared 'Superior' Russian Arms."

The question must be asked: What *was* Kennedy thinking? Why did he sign off on an invasion offering so slender a possibility of success? What about the thought he never seemed even to take into account: What would success actually look like? Could anyone seriously imagine the people of Cuba overthrowing Fidel Castro — or attempting to — upon hearing news of a 1,400-man invasion force landing on a remote beach? And given the strong chance of the mission's failure, how did he imagine the United States would then appear to the world, both in Latin America and around the globe?

Those questions having been put on the table, there are others equally important. Why didn't Dulles or Bissell tell JFK he was compromising the invasion by changing the landing area, and that the air strikes — all of them — were essential? Why had they maintained that there would be a widespread Cuban uprising against Castro? Why did they lie in saying the members of Brigade 2506 could escape into the mountains if they failed to secure a beachhead? Bissell, the chief instigator, would later admit to having misled Kennedy into believing that option was a viable one. But why hadn't General Lyman Lemnitzer, chairman of the Joint Chiefs of Staff, spoken up to warn the president that the invasion plan was a fool's game? Why had Secretary of State Dean Rusk not expressed his own doubts about the Cuban people's willingness to embrace a general revolt? Far more important, why hadn't Kennedy asked the right questions, and made sure to have the solid answers such a risky undertaking demanded? Beyond the human toll, the collateral damage, after all, would be to his administration's credibility.

To his credit, Kennedy kept disaster from becoming calamity. He decided at the most critical moment to cut his losses, refusing to send in U.S. forces, and that may have been the crucial decision of the entire episode. He took charge — far too late, admittedly — but with executive firmness. He told the military and the intelligence brass that the United States would not openly attack the island of Cuba. He would let those men meet their fate on the beach rather than commit his country to possible direct confrontation with the Soviet Union. Who knew how many Russians were on the island, how many would be killed by a U.S. air attack on Castro's forces?

The Bay of Pigs cast a long shadow over the Kennedy White House, but the value of the early lessons it provided for Kennedy cannot be underestimated. One of them involved one of his very first presidential acts. "I probably made a mistake in keeping Allen Dulles on," the president told Arthur Schlesinger just two days later. "It's not that Dulles is not a man of great ability. He is. But I have never worked with him and therefore I can't estimate his meaning when he tells me things. We will have to do something about the CIA. I must have someone there with whom I can be in complete and intimate contact — someone from whom I know I will be getting the exact pitch. I made a mistake in putting Bobby in the Justice Department. He is wasted there. Bobby should be in the CIA. It's a helluva way to learn things, but I have learned one thing from this business — that is, that we will have to deal with the CIA."

In a statesmanlike gesture, he soon met with Richard Nixon, who hawkishly urged him to "find a proper legal cover and go in." Nixon's idea was to use the defense of our naval base at Guantánamo as a possible excuse. Hearing this, Kennedy pointed to the inherent danger in that plan. "There is a good chance that if we move on Cuba, Khrushchev will move on Berlin," he said. The former vice president, always touched by any sign of respect from Jack, came away ready to rally support for him. "I just saw a crushed man today," Nixon told his allies after the encounter, asking them to resist taking easy shots at the demoralized president.

President Eisenhower was more hard-nosed, wanting to know why Kennedy had called off the air strikes. When the younger man said it was to conceal the country's role in the operation, Ike was contemptuous. The very concept was obviously contradictory. Here was the United States offering training, equipment, transportation, and air cover to a military operation in which it intended to deny involvement. "How could you expect the world to believe that we had nothing to do with it?" When Kennedy said he feared how the Russians might retaliate in Berlin, Ike's response was to tell his successor that the Soviets didn't react to what we did. Rather, they "follow their own plans." The general, now a partisan proud of his presidential service, refused to allow that Soviet strength and belligerence had grown toward the end of his watch. The new president had to.

Accustomed to success, Jack took the defeat hard. For the first time, witnesses actually saw him in tears. Yet, recognizing that he'd backed a military effort requiring greater resources than he was ready to commit and greater risks than he, in the end, wanted to take, he accepted the responsibility. "I'm the responsible officer of the government," JFK assured reporters and the country.

The American people decided they liked

the fact that Kennedy, whatever his failings heading into the disastrous mission, had acquitted himself as a true commander in chief at its conclusion. The record shows that he gained his highest job approval rating — scoring 83 percent in a Gallup poll — in the weeks thereafter.

Close friends such as Red Fay could see the toll it had taken. "In the months that followed, no matter how you tried to avoid touching on the subject, by one route or another it seemed to find its way back into the President's conversation." Even on vacation in Hyannis Port, it obsessed him, much to the distress of Jackie, who was ready to put the nightmarish scenes on that Cuban beach that haunted her husband behind them.

One of those Cape Cod evenings provided an outpouring Fay never forgot. It was when Jack outlined for him what he believed in: "I will never compromise the principles on which this country is built," JFK told him, "but we're not going to plunge into an irresponsible action just because a fanatical fringe in this country puts so-called national pride above national reason." Then he went on, "Do you think I'm going to carry on my conscience the responsibility for the wanton maiming and killing of children like our children we saw here this evening? Do you think I'm going to cause a nuclear exchange — for what? Because I was forced into doing something that I didn't think was proper and right? Well, if you or anybody else thinks I am, he's crazy."

When his host reached for his crutches, Fay understood he was finished with him for the evening. "He started up the stairs, straining with every step. He stopped me in the middle of the stairs and looked down at me, his face still inflamed. 'By God, there will be no avoiding responsibility — nor will there be any irresponsibility. When the decisive time for action arrives, action will be taken.' Turning, he lifted himself painfully up the rest of the stairs and to his room."

Meeting with the leaders of the Cuban Revolutionary Council, the main exile group, Jack spoke of his own wartime losses, even sharing a photograph of his brother Joe. One of the leaders, who'd lost his son in the invasion attempt, said the exiles had been "taken for a ride." He suggested Kennedy had been taken for one as well.

With the wounds from the Bay of Pigs still smarting, another Communist threat suddenly loomed on the horizon. It presented the likelihood of a far more dangerous crisis. Premier Nikita Khrushchev, who'd been making dark utterances for several years about changing the balance of power in Berlin — a city that had become such a symbol — demanded a showdown with President Kennedy in Vienna in early June.

Before heading to the summit in Austria, JFK took his first foreign trip, to Ottawa, where he and Jackie were welcomed by Prime Minister John Diefenbaker. Fifty thousand people turned out to watch the Kennedys' arrival. After addressing jointly both houses of Parliament, Jack took part in a tree-planting ceremony. As he lifted a silver shovel of dirt, he suddenly wrenched his weak back so painfully that he grabbed his forehead in anguish. Upon his return to Washington, he needed his crutches — which he used now only in private, in front of family and friends — to walk from the helicopter landing pad on the South Lawn to the White House.

Jack Kennedy had spent the past decades stoically rising above extreme physical discomfort, and he wasn't about to change, having now reached the White House. Less than two weeks after their return from Canada, the First Couple flew off to France, where one of the highlights was a luncheon at the Elysée Palace hosted by President Charles de Gaulle. Throughout her stay, beautiful Jackie, with her fluent French and stunning wardrobe, was an unqualified success, both fascinating and delighting the French public. People would remember that her husband joked to the traveling press corps, "I'm the man who accompanied Jacqueline Kennedy to Paris, and I have enjoyed it." But fewer will know that de Gaulle, an entirely formidable figure, had been captivated enough by her on a trip to Washington the previous year to have commented, "If there were anything I could take back to France with me, it would be Mrs. Kennedy."

The two leaders got along surprisingly well. During the war, de Gaulle had headed the Free French, symbolizing their country's resistance to the Nazi occupation. With regard to the American's coming engagement with Khrushchev in Vienna, de Gaulle was both thoughtful and candid. Urging Kennedy to keep his priorities in perspective, the French president expressed doubts about the ultimate sustainability of the Soviet system. He put little faith in their economic model, and so the Russian tide, he predicted, eventually would recede from Europe. Until that happened, the West, he reminded JFK, must stand firm. The greater threat, he predicted, would come decades later from China.

De Gaulle, like Kennedy, was able to put himself in the other man's shoes. Yet even as he could see beyond the immediate conflict to three decades down the road, de Gaulle recognized that such foresight little helped the predicament now. His practical advice, when it came to dealing with Khrushchev over the fate of Berlin, was to avoid even the *appearance* of negotiating. To do so would mean playing the Soviets' game.

Yet, as Eisenhower had been, de Gaulle was somewhat out of step with the times when it came to assessing the Russian mood. It had been one matter to not take the Soviets seriously when Russia, despite its immense size, seemed to lag behind the West. Now, just sixteen years after the war had ended, leaving devastation and demoralization in its wake, the Soviets were gunning their engines, trying to race ahead of the European powers and the United States. Their numerous gains — from their first-in-space status to their successful backing of "wars of liberation" in Africa, Asia, and Latin America — had left them confident, ready to flaunt their new standing vis-à-vis the West.

Moreover, if the size and power of the Soviet military forces weren't sufficiently frightening, the fact that the Soviet defense system had come to include a sizable nuclear arsenal surely was. What was bringing President John Kennedy to Vienna with such uncertainty — and foreboding — was Khrushchev's announced intention to sign a separate treaty between the Soviet Union and East Germany that would have the effect of stranding the city of Berlin 110 miles within the Russian-allied German Democratic Republic. Berlin, split by the Allies into sectors at the end of the war, had become the main escape route for millions fleeing west to escape Communist dictatorship. Ambassador Llewellyn Thompson told the president that the Soviet leader was so personally committed to a solution to the Berlin problem that the chances for either war or an "ignominious" retreat by the West were "close to fifty-fifty."

Kennedy's arrival in Vienna resembled a campaign stop of the year before. As they had in Paris, adoring crowds greeted the American First Couple at the airport. Khrushchev — who'd become first secretary of the Russian Communist Party in 1953 after the death of Josef Stalin and consolidated his power, ascending to premier five years later — had taken the train west from Moscow. He arrived to no fanfare. The glamour of Jack and Jackie Kennedy, and their excited reception, undoubtedly stirred resentment.

The meetings were scheduled for alternating sessions in the Soviet and American embassies. On the first day Khrushchev took the role of teacher, lecturing Kennedy on the case for socialist inevitability. Kennedy was no match for his ideological fervor. Both Ken O'Donnell and Dave Powers would write in their joint memoir how the bull-necked Soviet leader paced circles around his slender, youthful listener, "snapping at him like a terrier and shaking his finger."

That vivid description also paints a picture of Jack Kennedy having to endure the far outer limits of his comfort zone. When Evelyn Lincoln asked the president how the meeting had gone, "Not too well" was his reply.

Khrushchev's performance was a far cry from an American politician's usual encounters — except, perhaps, his use of the filibuster. But it seemed to have the effect the Soviet premier desired. Kennedy believed he meant business. Nixon and all the others back home could sound off about the need to call the Soviets' bluff. Nikita Khrushchev looked and sounded nothing like a bluffer.

The second day turned out to be worse. Khrushchev, having had his ideological warm-up, was now ready for the main event. JFK had come to Vienna hoping to build on what he saw as a recent major diplomatic breakthrough. In April, the United States and the USSR had reached an agreement that each would stop supplying military aid to Laos, a little landlocked kingdom north of Thailand and Cambodia and west of Vietnam. Its significance lay entirely with its central Indochinese location. Kennedy hoped that he and Khrushchev could jointly see the Laos cease-fire as a starting point for broader negotiations.

Unfortunately, Khrushchev himself was there to talk about Berlin, and only Berlin. The Soviet Union, he reiterated, was planning to sign a treaty with East Germany that gave it total authority to control access to West Berlin. What this meant — and Khrushchev made it sharply specific — was that the

Americans, the British, and the French would have to end their historic shared occupation of the divided city. The Russians had been edging up to this land grab, then backing away, for several years. This time, however, they seemed ready to proceed.

"The USSR will sign a peace treaty, and the sovereignty of the GDR will be observed," Khrushchev said in a formal pronouncement. "Any violation of that sovereignty will be regarded by the USSR as an act of open aggression. If the U.S. wants to start a war over Germany, let it do so."

Kennedy argued, to no avail, for the opposite approach. Instead of heightening Cold War tensions, why not try to lessen them? If Berlin was going to change, why not see it as a model for the future and not as a relic of the past? He tried to interest the Russian in a topic that meant more to him than just about anything else: a treaty over nuclear testing. He tried everything he could think of that might touch the man who was his opponent. He even invoked their shared losses in World War II. For, in the same way Jack mourned his brother Joe, so Khrushchev grieved, still, for his downed fighter-pilot son. But all the efforts the American made to light some spark of commonality between them produced no results.

Desperate, Kennedy requested a third meeting. In the last encounter with Khrushchev, he tried separating the two issues, suggesting that the Soviets might sign a treaty with East Germany while still allowing open access to West Berlin. That way, peace, at least, could be maintained. But the whole idea of the USSR-GDR agreement was to shut down the steady drain of East German workers through the city. Again, Khrushchev dug in his heels.

The new East German government, he said, would have full authority to deny access. Any effort to resist by either America or its allies would be met with the full force of the Red Army, which greatly outnumbered American and allied forces. When Kennedy pushed Khrushchev to acknowledge the right of the United States to continue to have access to West Berlin, Khrushchev held firm. "It is up to the U.S. to decide whether there will be war or peace."

At this final session Kennedy's companion made it clear, if it wasn't already, that his decision was "irrevocable" and "firm." In the end, all Jack was able to offer in reply to Khrushchev's threat of war was this grim prediction: "If that's true, it's going to be a cold winter." He left Vienna and returned to Washington, crushed by the experience. The Bay of Pigs had tainted him, he saw, allowing Khrushchev to treat him so contemptuously.

Jack Kennedy now understood he *had* to find a way to convince Khrushchev he was someone who would fight. But, even before that, he needed to understand exactly why the Soviet leader had talked to him that way, hectoring him. Was Khrushchev, in fact, crazy? He hadn't thought so, but what else explained why he was talking about war between two countries armed with nuclear weapons? "I never met a man like this," he told *Time*'s Hugh Sidey. "I talked about how a nuclear exchange would kill seventy million people in ten minutes, and he just looked at me as if to say, 'So what?' My impression was that he just didn't give a damn if it came to that."

To Ken O'Donnell he spelled out his own deeper belief, one he'd never share with a reporter, that not even Berlin was worth the possibility now threatened. "It will have to be for much bigger and more important reasons than that. Before I back Khrushchev against the wall and put him to a final test, the freedom of all Western Europe will have to be at stake." It fell to Lem Billings to record that Jack Kennedy had told him he'd "never come face to face with such evil."

Jack knew the order of battle for any conflict over Berlin. The United States had 6,500 troops in the city, for a combined American, British, and French force of 12,000. The Soviets had 350,000. Once the first shot was fired, the choice he'd be facing would be Armageddon or Munich. Long his greatest fear, it was now what he saw before him. Worse

492

still, his adversary refused to acknowledge their mutual humanity.

He heard the voices — the chorus was always there — that exhorted him to "stand tough," the voices that encouraged him to ignore the signals he was getting from Khrushchev in favor of a different party line. "Our position in Europe is worth a nuclear war, because if you are driven from Berlin, you are driven from Germany. And if you are driven from Europe, you are driven from Asia and Africa, and then our time will come next. You have to indicate your willingness to go to the ultimate weapon." Hadn't he said that, himself, to a Milwaukee radio interviewer during the campaign?

So, he knew how to talk like a war hawk. But what did it actually mean — words like that, all the threats and gun-cocking — if you're the first American president to come into office aware of your enemy's rival nuclear stockpile? It's one thing to use words such as *appeasement* and *surrender* and *vital principle* with regard to Berlin when someone else is making the decisions.

It was the old "Munich" argument — the one that had so obsessed him that he'd written a book about it — adapted to the nuclear age. The Berlin conflict would endure through much of the summer. As the months went on, Kennedy seemed sapped of initiative. "He's imprisoned by Berlin," members of the cabi-

493

net told Sidey. "That's all he thinks about."
On June 21, he would suffer another flare-up
of his Addison's disease, with his temperature
spiking to 105 degrees. For several days he
was sick in bed, ministered to by Jackie and
Lem.

On July 25, Kennedy gave a pivotal speech
on the conflict in Europe. "We cannot and
will not permit the Communists to drive us
out of Berlin, either gradually or by force.
. . . We will at all times be ready to talk, if
talk will help. But we must also be ready to
resist with force, if force is used upon us." He
spoke of West Berlin as a "showcase of liberty,
a symbol, an island of freedom in a Communist sea." But he also made concessions.
Suggesting that it might be possible to remove
"irritants" from the conflict, he then made a
conciliatory statement about Soviet security
concerns regarding Germany, the country
that cost it 20 million lives in World War II.

Throughout the speech, he made a point of
referring to "West" Berlin. The message was
that his country did not care what the Soviets
and East Germans did in the rest of the city.
They had a free hand in that regard. Five days
later, Senator William Fulbright, chairman of
the Foreign Relations Committee, told a Sun-
day-morning TV audience that it was in the
Russians' power to shut down the West Berlin
escape route if they wished. They could end
their problem without war. It was an assess-

ment of American policy, quickly cheered by the East German government, that Kennedy never denied.

On August 3, the Soviets made their long-threatened move on West Berlin. Fortunately for the world, the Soviets and East Germans had found a solution to stop the tide of refugees to the West — a wall. To the man in the White House, it came as a secret relief. "Why would Khrushchev put up a wall if he really intended to seize West Berlin? There wouldn't be any need of a wall if he planned to occupy the whole city. This is his way out of his predicament. It's not a very nice solution, but a wall is a hell of a lot better than a war."

Chapter Fourteen
Zenith

I felt I was walking with destiny and all my past life had been but a preparation for this hour and for this trial.
— Winston Churchill, May 10, 1940

Jack Kennedy's victories had taught him essential lessons. He recognized the edge a candidate receives when he's made the earliest start and kept at it. He realized the importance of the vital energy gained by building a trusted team. He discovered the power derived when a politician grasps the nature of the times and wields that understanding.

But failures also offer education. The Bay of Pigs taught him something more critical: When the stakes are the highest and most desperate, there must be both clarity and completion. Know the enemy *and* your goal, and hold fast to what you're attempting. Should any oppose your course, fight them with all your resolve.

Throughout the summer of 1961, Jack Kennedy had managed to sustain his hopes for a ban on nuclear arms testing to which the Soviets would agree. At the very heart of his presidency was his mission to keep his country from nuclear war. It would be, he knew, a battle from which no winners could emerge. In 1946, the young journalist John Hersey had published in *the New Yorker* his account of the survivors of the attack on Hiroshima; no one who'd read it would ever forget it.

We'd agreed, as had the Soviets, to halt nuclear testing in 1958. Yet, in July, a Gallup poll had indicated that public support for the resumption of U.S. nuclear testing stood at two to one. The other side, exhibiting its greater aggression, suddenly showed its hand. August brought Moscow's shocking announcement of its unilateral decision to resume nuclear testing in the atmosphere. Kennedy's reaction — "fucked again!" — was deep and personal. Even before this horrifying news hit the headlines, Americans had gotten reports that the milk drunk by Russian children across the country contained detectable traces of radioactivity. Had the Russians treacherously been testing underground all along, even if they'd sworn not to? And was this a clue? And, if so, what were we going to do about it?

Over the next three months the Soviet Union would go on to conduct thirty-one such tests, including the exploding of the largest bomb in history — 58 megatons, four

33

President Kennedy with the Joint Chiefs (L to R): Gen. David M. Shoup, Marine Corps; Gen. Thomas P. White, Air Force; Gen. Lyman Lemnitzer, chairman; Kennedy; Adm. Arleigh Burke Navy; Gen. G. H. Decker, Army

34

James Meredith with U.S. Marshals after enrolling in the University of Mississippi, October 1, 1962

35

Sargent Shriver, Peace Corps Director

thousand times more powerful than the one dropped over Hiroshima in 1945. Despite partisan pressure to respond by resuming U.S. testing, Kennedy resisted. He persisted in believing in the possibility of a comprehensive ban on all forms of nuclear arms testing, atmospheric and underground as well. "Mankind must put an end to war — or war will put an end to mankind." Yet as the leader of the Free World, he couldn't allow the Soviets to proceed without a U.S. response. With this in mind, the president instructed Defense Secretary McNamara to begin testing underground.

The United States had tested its first nuclear weapon at the White Sands Proving Ground in New Mexico in July 1945, a month before the U.S. fighters flew off to drop the atomic bombs on Hiroshima and Nagasaki. Those attacks, of course, brought about the Japanese surrender and ended World War II. Seven years later, the United States tested the first hydrogen bomb in the isolated Marshall Islands in the western Pacific in early November 1952. It was one of the last acts of the Truman administration before the election on November 4 ushered in the Eisenhower era.

Truman himself had presided over the dawn of the nuclear era by signing off on the Hiroshima and Nagasaki missions. Other peacetime nuclear explosions — military tests of new, far deadlier weapons — followed on his watch. Then, under President Eisenhower, the number doubled or even tripled. For a dozen years, from 1946 to 1958, the Marshall Islands, a U.S. Trust Territory until 1986, bore the brunt of America's experimentation. For the Soviets, the testing of their nuclear weapons secretly in their vast territory had begun in 1949. They had selected sites in remote Kazakhstan and later in Novaya Zemlya, a chain of islands in the Arctic Ocean at Russia's northern edge.

The history of the Cold War is written in the long lists of these many tests. During this period, our allies France and Great Britain were intent on developing their own nuclear arsenals. But distinctions such as "atomic" and "hydrogen," "nuclear" and "thermonuclear" mean little to the average citizen. Americans accepted the basic contradiction. The United States could keep the Soviets from aggression in Europe by the threat of nuclear retaliation. At the same time, neither side would dare use nuclear weapons, knowing the other would as well.

Even after Kennedy issued the directive for underground nuclear tests, he continued to be pressured by his own experts. They wanted more. In November, the National Security Council delivered a blunt assessment: "If we test only underground and the Soviets tested in the atmosphere, they would surely pass us in nuclear technology." Still, Kennedy persisted in trying to negotiate. Following a further failure to bring the Soviets around to the American position, he let it be known that the United States was now prepared to begin atmospheric testing again. Though he did nothing beyond indicate American willingness to resume, it was a necessary step in getting to the negotiating table. With it came a new pressure: Prime Minister Harold Macmillan of Britain, considered by JFK a personal as well as an official friend, urged the United States to put off any such activity for six more months.

As 1962 began, Kennedy hadn't given up on his hope of bringing the Russians around to his idea of a peaceful rivalry, not a nuclear one. What he cared about, above all, was making sure the nuclear genie got put back in the bottle; for him, arriving at a mutual test ban would be the first step. "A journey of a thousand miles begins with one step," he liked to quote.

Nothing mattered more to him.

In February he and Prime Minister Macmillan jointly wrote a letter to Khrushchev, calling for a "supreme effort" to stop the arms race and avert a nuclear apocalypse. Kennedy, in a phone call with Ben Bradlee not long after sending it, shared his frustration with what he called this "hard-boiled" conflict over nuclear weapons testing between the United States and the USSR, but also the "soft-boiled" one with the British.

Kennedy's national security team now voted unanimously to resume atmospheric testing. But with the next round of international peace talks scheduled for March in Geneva, he wanted to delay the announcement. It would get in the way, he felt, of offering Khrushchev another chance.

It didn't matter. Once again, his approaches were refused, his aims thwarted — and, as a result, he saw himself gradually pushed toward brinkmanship. At this point, with the Russians intransigent and any attempts at persuasive diplomacy a failure, Jack felt it was time to present his case to the country. On March 2, speaking on television and radio for forty-five minutes, he made the case for deterrence, explaining the strategic necessity.

He wanted to explain to millions of worried Americans why he'd agreed to resume atmospheric testing. "For all the awesome responsibilities entrusted to this office, none is more somber to contemplate than the special statutory authority to employ nuclear weapons in the defense of our people and freedom." He needed to test, he said, in order to maintain the country's deterrent strength. "It is our hope and prayer that these . . . deadly weapons will never be fired." Red Fay, at the White House for dinner that night, recalled how deeply delivering the speech had affected his friend. "It was about 9:30 when the President

503

finally arrived. Jackie had placed me so that when he came in, I'd be sitting on his left. He was flushed . . . really worn from the whole experience. Everybody sensed that he was very tense. His hands shook. . . . Everybody else, because of his tension, all started to talk among themselves. He directed his conversation to me and said, 'God, I hope you've been enjoying yourself over here, because I've been over there in that office, not knowing whether the decision I made . . .' " His voice trailed off, and Fay was left to imagine the agonizing weight of the responsibility that he felt.

Kennedy had dark forebodings. "Ever since the longbow," he would tell a trusted visitor to the oval office, "when man has developed new weapons and stockpiled them, somebody has come along and used them. I don't know how we can escape it with nuclear weapons."

Still Kennedy clung to the fading notion he might be able to shift the two-power rivalry between the United States and the Soviets to peaceful pursuits. He understood that the real contest between the USA and the USSR was over authority in the "Third World." The rising peoples of Africa, Asia, and Latin America were looking to see who was winning, which system — democracy or Communism — best suited their needs and their hopes.

The ability to conquer space mattered greatly in this quintessential Cold War struggle to be top gun. The way to win was by looking like a winner. Unfortunately, through 1961 the Soviets had held the competitive edge. The launch of *Sputnik* four years earlier in 1957 had thrown America off stride, and the flight of Yuri Gagarin in April 1961 had done the same again, making the Russians seem invincible by virtue of their superior technology.

But on February 20, 1962, the balance of power, when it came to achievement in space, was restored. On that day, John Glenn became the first American to orbit the earth, circling the globe three times in *Friendship 7.* A marine among the original seven American astronauts picked by the National Aeronautics and Space Administration in 1959, Glenn met with President Kennedy at the White House both before and after the flight. Even space — *especially* space — isn't free of politics, John Glenn well understood. Kennedy knew "we were actually superior to the Soviets and that that's what we were out to prove."

Glenn's triumphant space flight proved the boost NASA needed. What it had lacked before were bragging rights. "I think one reason my flight got so much attention was that we sort of turned the corner in public opinion at that point." In fact, conquering space offered an unprecedented thrill for the American public. Suddenly it seemed as if all things extraordinary were possible under the young president's leadership. The dark shadows cast by the unchecked arms race were forgotten for the moment. Yet, however urgent the question of nuclear disarmament was, it was far from the only crisis facing John F. Kennedy.

In the fall of 1961, Walter Heller, who chaired the president's Council of Economic Advisers, came to tell him that it was crucial to the economy that steel prices get brought under control. Because the industry's high prices drove up costs across the board, they had the effect of crippling America's ability to compete with foreign producers.

Kennedy acted. To keep American steel in the game, Kennedy went in and won an agreement from the United Steelworkers to cut back their wage demands. In March 1962, industry executives and top union officials gathered at the White House and emerged from the meeting having agreed to defer increases. While the president had no right to tell the steel companies how much to charge, the deal was clear: labor would keep down salaries, the executives would hold back on prices. Afterward, JFK called both sides to thank them for making concessions in the national interest. The union men, when he talked to them, seemed especially pleased to hear the president praising them for their sacrifice.

Then came trouble. Roger Blough, chairman of United States Steel, requested a meeting. From across the cabinet table he handed

Kennedy a press release. His company was raising the price of steel 3.5 percent. "Mr. Blough," JFK said, "what you are doing is in the best interest of *your* shareholders. *My* shareholders are every citizen of the United States. I'm going to do everything in the best interest of the shareholders, the people of this country. As the president of the United States, I have quite a bit of influence."

Blough, Jack realized, had already released the announcement. "You have made a terrible mistake," he said. "You have double-crossed me."

To Ken O'Donnell, it was a shocking episode. "These guys felt they were so powerful they could stiff the president of the United States without consequences." He also saw how livid his boss was. "He was white with anger." Big steel had betrayed its workers and "made a fool of him." Discussing it with Ben Bradlee, Jack explained he wasn't about to take a "cold, deliberate fucking."

The president's credibility was now on the line because he'd acted as broker. Labor leaders, he knew, would never trust him again. The steel industry, meanwhile, assumed, "wrongly, he could not or would not do anything." O'Donnell, who'd watched him at work in Massachusetts, knew what sort of surprise they were in for. "You find out about these guys in these steel companies, where they have been on vacation, who they have been with on vacation," he instructed.

His instincts told him where the corporate chiefs were vulnerable. "I don't think U.S. Steel or any other of the major steel companies wants to have Internal Revenue agents checking all the expense accounts of their top executives," Kennedy told Red Fay, who, before becoming undersecretary of the navy, had himself been a Republican businessman. "Too many hotel bills and nightclub expenses would be hard to get by the weekly wives' bridge group out at the Country Club."

The next day, Attorney General Robert Kennedy announced that, under the antitrust laws, a grand jury investigation into the steel industry's pricing had been ordered. Subpoenas to produce documents were served on U.S. Steel. Defense Secretary Robert McNamara instructed the Pentagon to purchase steel "where possible" from companies that had not raised prices. Later that day, in a press conference, Kennedy addressed the issue: ". . . the American people will find it hard, as I do, to accept a situation in which a tiny handful of steel executives whose pursuit of private power and profit exceeds their sense of public responsibility can show such utter contempt for the interests of 185 million Americans." By the next night, eight steel companies that had announced price hikes canceled them.

The president's response to the pullback

was to congratulate the steel companies for honoring the public good. "Kennedy's style of politics: you never paint a guy into a corner," O'Donnell later observed. "You give the other fellow as much credit as you can. So, he wants a statement thanking the steel companies for realizing their commitment to the United States Government was more important than their commitment to their stockholders."

But the swords were sheathed only when the mission was accomplished. America's competitiveness was restored, but revenge had also been extracted. Robert Kennedy later confessed the rough tactics employed. "We looked over all of them as individuals . . . we were going to go for broke . . . their expense accounts and where they'd been and what they were doing. I picked up all their records . . . I told the FBI to interview them all, march into their offices the next day! We weren't going to go slowly. . . . So, all of them were hit with meetings the next morning by agents. All of them were subpoenaed for their personal records. I agree it was a tough way to operate, but under the circumstances, we couldn't afford to lose."

When the action settled, Jack Kennedy didn't like being left alone. If no one else happened to be around for the evening, he'd ask Dave Powers — now, like Ken O'Donnell, a presidential special assistant — to stay and have supper with him. They'd then spend the evening together until it was time for Dave to escort him to his bedroom. When he was finally ready to sleep, it'd be: "Good night, pal. Will you please put out the light?"

What's curious — and fascinating — are the fixed orbits JFK assigned to this circle of friends. He always exhibited great fondness for his "Irish mafia" of O'Donnell, O'Brien, and Powers, but they were never part of his social life. With the exception of Powers, who'd join him when nothing else was going on, these men formed an indispensable support team that could be dismissed at sundown. The same went for Ted Sorensen, who'd spent those four years with him in close quarters day after day, flying around the country. They'd become so attuned that Sorensen was practically an alter ego, yet he was never invited for an evening out with his boss.

Novelty and turnover mattered in Jack's personal world. And, naturally, there were rules. Chuck Spalding liked to say that nobody got as much as forty-eight hours with him. If you bored him, you got less. Anyone ever imagining he was an equal colleague soon knew better. Even social friends might step across invisible boundaries and pay the price. Ben Bradlee was "banished," to use his word, for several months in 1962 for daring to mention to another reporter how sensitive Kennedy was to critical reporting. Proving Bradlee to be right, Jack gave him a protracted cold shoulder — a kind of grown-up's "time out" — until eventually the Bradlees were returned to his good graces.

In the White House, he didn't leap up at dawn like some presidents, but read the newspapers in bed over breakfast. He regularly went for a swim before lunch, took a nap afterward, and then would have another swim before dinner. Kennedy was far from the healthiest president on record, but, clearly, he wanted to come across as that. In photographs, especially, he projected a smiling vitality. When it came to his ongoing medical problems — above all, the intractable back pain — he didn't complain. Nor did he explain.

As a married man, he'd decided not to forgo his bachelor pleasures. It seems not to have occurred to him. Lem had been right to try to warn Jackie at the wedding. But one of his affairs had an abrupt ending not of his own choosing. In March of 1962, he was visited by J. Edgar Hoover. The FBI, which had kept tabs on him during his Inga Arvad days, had now been chronicling his current relationship with a woman "of interest" to the Bureau. "Information has been developed that Judith E. Campbell, a freelance artist, has associated with prominent underworld figures Sam Giancana of Chicago and John Roselli of Los Angeles. Went on to note the phone calls back and forth between the White House and

Campbell." President Kennedy broke off the liaison with Campbell, who'd been introduced to him by Frank Sinatra, later that day.

His affair with the free-spirited Washington socialite Mary Meyer was very different. This was a relationship of equals. Divorced at the time of their relationship, she'd been married to a top CIA strategist, Cord Meyer, and was the sister of Tony Bradlee. So well did Jack segment his life, he could be good friends with her brother-in-law at the same time he was sleeping with her. He'd regularly see Meyer, who was legendarily attractive and also unpredictable, at Georgetown and White House parties. Sometimes he'd even be the one inviting her to White House functions. "She'd be difficult to live with," he once noted to pal Ben. But, then, he didn't have to.

Now that they'd been settled in the White House for more than a year, Jack had grown accustomed to being no longer able to avail himself of the absences necessitated by the campaign trail. His response was to start arranging his time to avoid being alone socially — even alone with Jackie, it seems — for any extended period. He used New York overnights, Palm Beach weekends, campaign trips, and Jackie's summer-long departures to the Cape for "girling" with pals Chuck, Torby, or George Smathers invited along for company. If they went away together for a weekend, he invariably asked one or more of his pals along. Whether it was the Virginia hunt country, Camp David, Hyannis Port, or Palm Beach, he made a point to start calling around Tuesday to fill up the guest list. His nature seemed to render him unable to look forward to a weekend alone with his wife, or even a dinner, without the addition of outside company.

Rachel "Bunny" Mellon was the close friend who helped Jackie restore the White House, close enough to have Jackie confide in her.

"Jackie knew that he had this . . . feeling. But she sort of said, 'Well, Jack's got these girlfriends.' She never griped about it, she said he could do what he wants."

Part of it, she believed, was that Jackie had a very "old world" view of men.

"She was a Bouvier and, how can I put it, I think she was strange enough not to be small. It was her fault to marry Jack Kennedy. I mean, she was attracted by him. She was fascinated by him. Regular, decent kind of guys, they would come down the road. She didn't care who, but she married him. She married him because he was different."

The presidency offered Jack the chance to act on his old schoolboy's love of heroes. In August, he invited General Douglas MacArthur to visit. Jack was entranced by the old soldier, respectful even when the eighty-two-year-old wartime general showed what the years and

Korea had done to him. He told of his recommendation that his infantrymen each be issued "some kind of cartridge that would clear ten or fifteen yards in front of him." He was talking about nuclear weapons carried in holsters! "If you could get me this type of atomic cartridge so that every soldier will have that," he told of his frustrated efforts to win production of this new serviceman's hardware, "one hundred men could stop a division." Awestruck at the preposterous idea, Kennedy was true to form. He asked for details. "Let's say that the cartridge would be fired, let's say, at some man, or group of men, coming across a field at a hundred and twenty yards. It would hit one man and what? You just explode in a puff?"

It must have occurred to the young president how much war had changed. Here was a revered military hero, a general for the ages, who'd come back to liberate the Philippines and win the war in the Pacific. Here was the genius behind the Inchon Landing in the Korean War, totally unaware of the menace posed by a minor nuclear explosion. Kennedy, the junior officer from World War II come back to lead his country, could not afford such anachronistic thinking, even if it survived among the top military men who now commanded the services.

At the University of Mississippi as that fall semester began, a new student was under extraordinary scrutiny. The air force veteran James Meredith was seeking admission. He would be the first African-American to enroll — and in a rigidly segregated state, it wasn't going to happen without trouble.

Washington efforts to end discrimination were another issue on the Kennedy administration's agenda. The main task up to this point, however, had been to encourage government contractors to hire more minorities. But even more radical social change was on the minds of civil rights leaders, and across the South, the educational system at all levels was under assault. Ernest Green and eight other African-American students had made history by integrating Little Rock's Central High School in 1957. In early May 1961, the first Freedom Riders — seven black, six white — had begun courageously riding buses throughout the South, challenging the rules of segregation.

Now it was Ole Miss's turn to join the late twentieth century, however unwillingly.

On September 10, the U.S. Supreme Court ruled in favor of Meredith. Supported by the NAACP — the pioneering civil rights organization founded in 1909 by W. E. B. Du Bois, among others — Meredith petitioned the university to admit him. The school continued to refuse, making it increasingly clear that the federal government might need to use force. As the crisis escalated, President Kennedy feared he was heading for a showdown, not just with one school or even one state, but with the entire South.

Here is the recorded conversation between Kennedy and Mississippi governor Ross Barnett:

Kennedy: Can you maintain this order?

Barnett: Well, I don't know. That's what I'm worried about. I don't know whether I can or not. I couldn't have the other afternoon.

Kennedy: You couldn't have?

Barnett: There was such a mob there. It would have been impossible. There were men in there with trucks and shotguns and all such as that. Certain people were just enraged. Would you be willing to wait awhile and let the people cool off on the whole thing? It might be . . . two or three weeks, it might cool off a . . .

Kennedy: Would you undertake to register him in two weeks?

Barnett: You know I can't undertake to register him myself.

Governor Barnett continued to be intransigent. His stance put him in a long succession of Southern governors such as Orville Faubus, who'd summoned the Arkansas National Guard to "protect" Central High. "I won't agree to let that boy get to Ole Miss," Barnett told Attorney General Kennedy. Jack and Bobby both were hoping they'd get James Meredith into Ole Miss without using federal troops, but Jack was also determined not to be caught unprepared. Aware of the shellacking he'd taken over the Bay of Pigs, what he intended to avoid was trusting anyone to share his agenda when their own was what mattered to them.

Jack was now involved in checking out every detail, scanning the aerial photographs of the university's campus and ascertaining such details as where military helicopters might land. When two thousand demonstrators, students and nonstudents alike, showed up on September 30 to protest Meredith's registration, Kennedy, on the phone with Barnett, pressed him either to take charge or defer to the president. The university president was evasive and came across as increasingly unstable.

The problem was whom they could trust to protect Meredith. As the day wore on, the U.S. marshals guarding him were being attacked by the crowd. Governor Barnett, claiming he couldn't control the Mississippi state troopers — in fact, he'd secretly taken them off duty — refused to guarantee Meredith's further safety. Kennedy had federalized the Mississippi National Guard but was reluctant to rely on them; he'd also positioned U.S. Army backup in Memphis.

By late that night, the hostilities had increased to a level of violence that saw two men — one a journalist from Agence France-Presse — killed. Military intervention was urgently needed. There was now little option but to summon the waiting troops and pray they arrived in time. Nicholas Katzenbach, the deputy attorney general representing the Justice Department at the campus, confessed to his boss Bobby Kennedy his doubt that the marshals could hold off the rioting protesters until the U.S. soldiers appeared.

If they didn't manage to arrive in time, Katzenbach worried "neither Meredith nor any of those men have a chance." Moreover, the reliability of the Mississippi National Guard remained a real question. In Ken O'Donnell's words, "we knew that most of the National Guard members were students, former students, or else ninety percent in sympathy with the mob." When the president issued the order to the marshals to protect Meredith at all costs, it was with the knowledge that it might be their last. In Washington, all they could do now was sit and wait. Kennedy and his advisors were on tenterhooks. Some of them feared the next news they'd hear was that Meredith was dead and Katzenbach a prisoner being held by out-of-control students and townie hooligans.

Kennedy was responsible for all the lives that hung in the balance. It was critical that the army not fail him. Yet, here again, as in the Bay of Pigs operation, Kennedy discovered the difference between command and control. Those troops stationed in Memphis, it turned out, had yet to be mustered. When the soldiers finally landed at the Rebels' football field, it was quickly evident they weren't mobilizing fast enough. Communicating with them by phone, staying on top of their positions minute by minute, Jack began issuing orders as their commander in chief. As they at last made their way onto the central campus, their presence had an immediate effect. By dawn on October 1, the situation was stabilized. That day, James Meredith became the first black student at the University of Mississippi.

It had been a very long night.

In the aftermath, JFK felt pretty unforgiving toward the military. "They always give you their bullshit about their instant reaction and their split-second timing, but it never works out. No wonder it's so hard to win a war." And he had even harsher thoughts about the local officialdom. It was simply incredible to John Kennedy that not a single elected Mississippi authority had stepped in to attempt to restore civil order. The siege of Ole Miss — like his experience as skipper of the foundering *PT 109* — had forced him to assume a lone command and grab tight his own destiny. What it also had done was give him the satisfaction of enforcing, to the best of his abilities and with all the conviction he had, the law of the land.

To be the American president at this moment in history was to sense the edge of the precipice. Jack Kennedy's deepest fear was that he might somehow take the step that would send the United States toppling over it. And when he looked out at the world beyond Washington, what he saw was a single place — West Berlin — that, in the flash of an instant, could provide the setting. The balance between the two superpowers was now so precarious that a single stumble there would be all that it took.

The German Democratic Republic, or East Germany, as it was commonly known, was determined to take back full control of its capital, the largest city in Germany. In pursuit of this aim — a land grab completely unacceptable to the Free World — the German Communists had their Russian patron's full support. In July, Premier Khrushchev had once again thumped his chest, demanding the end of "the occupation regime in the West Berlin."

The American, British, and French troops billeted there since the end of World War II were to be replaced by a newly organized police force, Khrushchev insisted. This constabulary's members would be recruited from the three Western powers, as well as from neutral and Warsaw Pact countries. Four years down the road, the new force would be composed entirely of East Germans.

The Soviet leader sent word to Kennedy that he would put off pressing his demands until after the American midterm elections in November. As Khrushchev made clear, this was just a temporary reprieve. Alluding to West Berlin as the "bone in my throat," he wasn't about to let it remain there. Rumors of an increased Soviet military presence on the island of Cuba were also disturbing the peace of mind at the Kennedy White House.

Khrushchev, very certain that he had the upper hand and meaning to keep it, had Interior Secretary Stewart Udall, who was visiting Moscow, flown to his Black Sea dacha. There the startled American was entrusted with a warning to pass on to the president. "We will not allow your troops to be in Berlin." He then added an even more specific threat that he wished relayed. "War over Berlin," he said, "would mean that within the space of an hour, there would be no Paris and no France."

Then, having issued this horrifying message, he told Udall that he wanted to meet the president at the United Nations General Assembly meeting in New York in the second half of November. The main topic would be Berlin.

With the Americans continuing, nervously, to monitor Russian activity in Cuba, the Soviet leader once again issued an ultimatum. He sent JFK a letter bluntly informing him that any U.S. attack on Cuba would bring a retaliatory strike at West Berlin. The Russian behavior was so provocative as to be puzzling. Two days later, Kennedy told his close friend David Ormsby-Gore, now British ambassador to the United States, and Secretary of State Dean Rusk that he thought Khrushchev might actually be encouraging him to invade Cuba so he could grab West Berlin. Why else would he be tying the two together?

Suddenly it came, the real threat of war over Berlin. It came in a fight, once again, over Cuba. A bit after eight a.m. on Tuesday, October 16, 1962, McGeorge Bundy carried to Jack Kennedy the news that the latest U-2 spy flight had brought back photographic evidence of Soviet offensive missile sites under construction in western Cuba. Kennedy quickly called his brother, who now hurried to the White House, studying the photos even before the president did.

Though running the Justice Department, Bobby had decided to moonlight in the area of intelligence. He'd done so because of the numerous dissatisfactions with the ill-conceived Bay of Pigs scenario. He was now running the administration's secret anti-Castro operation himself. Code-named "Operation Mongoose," this enterprise involved an array of secret plots to topple the Cuban dictator, all doomed to be pathetically unsuccessful.

In the Senate, Kennedy was already under attack from two Republicans — New York's Kenneth Keating and Indiana's Homer Capehart — with both insisting on the fierce reality of those now verified Soviet missile installations. "Ken Keating will probably be the next president!" Jack commented as he looked at the three large photographs Bundy had carried to him. The Republicans who had been mounting the attacks may have lacked hard evidence, but at the moment it didn't matter. They were right.

Squeezed between his soon-to-be-gloating critics on the right and the Soviets, whom he now realized had deceived him, Kennedy was suddenly in an extremely tight spot with little breathing room. The wily Khrushchev had made use of the delay he initiated for the American election to arm his Cuban allies with nuclear weapons — SS-24 Scalpels, medium-range ballistic missiles with a range of a thousand miles — able to reach well into the United States.

The only question on which the CIA had no intelligence at that moment was how rapidly the weapons on that site could be equipped with nuclear warheads. Summoned to the

White House, the top cabinet officials and military advisors began to weigh in, making their case for immediate action to destroy the missiles. Such a response, Kennedy was told, would entail either an air strike on the missile sites alone or else a full-scale invasion.

The latter option, General Maxwell Taylor, chairman of the Joint Chiefs of Staff, told him, would mean an involvement of up to 150,000 troops — a hundredfold increase on the ragtag Bay of Pigs invaders. Attacking Cuba was serious military business, and for the Joint Chiefs, what they'd been lobbying for all along. As he listened to his people, one thing was clear: the overall consensus in the room held that the least delay would allow the Soviets the time needed to ready the missiles for use.

Kennedy now assembled an expert panel to decide on what steps to take. The purpose of this group, called ExComm — for Executive Committee — was to keep all intelligence regarding the Soviet missiles at San Cristobal limited to a smaller group than the National Security Council.

"Virtually everyone's initial choice, at that first October 16 meeting, was a surgical air strike against the nuclear missile sites before they could become operational," said O'Donnell. "U.S. bombers could swoop in, eliminate the sites, and fly away, leaving the problem swiftly, magically ended. But further questions — JFK always had further questions — proved that solution illusory. First, no cruise missiles or smart bombs existed in those days to assure the precision and success of the strike. The air force acknowledged that it could be certain of eliminating only sixty of the missiles, leaving the others free to fire and destroy us."

With each question he now asked, Kennedy gained more knowledge. It would be highly risky to send bombers over Cuba unless its surface-to-air missile sites were destroyed, along with its antiaircraft sites, its fighter planes, and its bombers, which might head off to Florida. But an invasion would pit American fighting men against Cubans defending their homeland, a recipe for long casualty lists on both sides, a guarantee of a bitter occupation. It would also mean killing countless numbers of Russians.

Time was of the essence. But so was taking the time — even if it was in short supply — to weigh all the options. Every so often, JFK would leave the room during the deliberations, allowing the others to express themselves more freely. One statement that must have played and replayed in his head was General Taylor's "It'll never be one hundred percent, Mr. President." In other words, an air strike could never be guaranteed to wipe out all the missiles. But Berlin was also central to his thinking. Any attack on Cuba could give Khrushchev his chance. He was only too aware that, back in 1956, when the British, French, and Israelis had gone to war with Egypt, it gave the Soviets the opportunity to crush the Hungarian revolution. If Khrushchev was attempting the same ploy this time, using a U.S. attack on Cuba as a pretext for rolling through West Berlin, Britain and France might well blame the Americans for this mortal breach in the West's defense.

By Thursday, Bobby was starting to have second thoughts of his own about a raid on Cuba. The issue of America's moral standing had become part of the debate. After one meeting he passed a note to Sorensen: "I now know how Tojo felt when he was planning Pearl Harbor." It was a serious consideration. Despite the photographic evidence, there would be many around the world who would regard any military strike against Cuba as aggression, pure and simple. For the United States to attack such a tiny neighbor would wind up in the history books as a classic example of imperialism.

Friday marked the fourth day since Bundy had shown the president the surveillance pictures. Now the stakes were raised even higher, with new aerial photographs revealing more sites in Cuba, ones serving intermediate-range missiles. Such weapons could travel nearly three thousand miles, all the way to New York. The hawks were now screaming for action. The most ferocious was the air force chief of staff, General Curtis LeMay, the former head of the Strategic Air Command, who, during World War II, had led brutal incendiary attacks over Japan.

Kennedy challenged LeMay's thinking. Might not an American attack on Cuba quickly start a nuclear chain reaction? We attack their ally, they grab for Berlin. Then, confronted by the overwhelming force of the Red Army, the only resort of the United States would be to use tactical atomic weapons right there in the middle of Europe. The next escalation, involving an exchange of each side's nuclear arsenals, was not, after that, hard to imagine.

This was all unfamiliar language to the cigar-smoking LeMay, who'd entered the air corps in 1929. His interest was simply spelling out the strategic facts. The United States enjoyed a huge advantage in intercontinental missiles. Why weren't we playing our strength? A naval blockade of Cuba, the only alternative to an attack on the missile sites, would be a sign of weakness. It would be like "appeasement at Munich," LeMay said. He'd dared — though he may not have entirely realized what he was doing — to imply that Jack Kennedy was his father's appeasing son.

Yet, to his credit, Kennedy realized to whom he was talking, understood the mindset of what he was confronting in this frightening moment. LeMay was telling him that the smart move for the United States was to engage in a nuclear test of strength, as if it were an arm wrestle. We lose tens of millions but we end up winning the test of strength, since the Russians will get the worst of whatever planetary horror is inflicted. "You're talking about the destruction of a country," Kennedy said simply. That led to the following exchange:

LeMay: You're in a pretty bad fix at the present time.

Kennedy: What did you say?

LeMay: You're in a pretty bad fix.

Kennedy: Well, you're in there with me. Personally.

Tapes of the discussions among the Joint Chiefs after their civilian commander left the room show them united against the president. "You pulled the rug right out from under him," Chief of Staff General David Shoup of the marines applauded LeMay. The military men agreed that anything short of an all-out invasion was "piecemeal."

Kennedy, fortunately, knew whom he was dealing with. He knew that LeMay and others in the high strategic command leaned toward a "first strike" option, especially in the case of a Soviet move on Berlin. This meant an "obliterating" nuclear attack on all Communist countries, three thousand weapons aimed at a thousand targets. "And we call ourselves human," Kennedy said after a briefing.

Out campaigning in Chicago, fulfilling his obligation to attend a Democratic fund-raiser for Mayor Richard J. Daley, Jack received a call from Bobby. His brother didn't mince words. The time had come to make a decision, he said. Flying back to D.C. on *Air Force One,* Jack warned Pierre Salinger: grab your balls.

A phalanx of powerful men now was allied against him. The Joint Chiefs, McGeorge Bundy, John McCone, Douglas Dillon — all supported an air strike. Here was the Establishment — intelligence, military, and finance — mutually agreeing that the best move was to send in the bombers. And other influential voices were about to join the chorus. On Monday, Senator Richard Russell of Georgia, chairman of the Armed Services Committee, stood by LeMay, urging an air strike followed by an all-out invasion. The time for the showdown with the Soviets had arrived. Yet, still, Kennedy persisted in disagreeing.

Here was a perfect affirmation of the Founding Fathers' reasoning, which had led them to place ultimate constitutional authority in the hands of the person elected by the American people. As the French statesman Georges Clemenceau more recently had observed, "War is far too important to be left to the generals." Thus, even after hearing the expert arguments, Kennedy rejected the air-attack option, ordering instead a blockade on all offensive weapons headed to Cuba, a suggestion earlier made by Dean Rusk. He would announce it three days later in a nationally broadcast address.

"This government, as promised, has maintained the closest surveillance of the Soviet military buildup on the island of Cuba," he told American listeners, the aerial photographs in hand. "Within the past week, unmistakable evidence has established the fact that a series of offensive missile sites is now in preparation on that imprisoned island. The purpose of these bases can be none other than to provide a nuclear strike capability against the Western Hemisphere."

The missiles had to go, Kennedy declared, decreeing a naval blockade of all ships carrying offensive weapons or missile-firing equipment to Cuba. Any such vessel would be stopped and turned back. "It shall be the policy of this nation to regard any nuclear missile launched from Cuba against any nation in the Western Hemisphere as an attack by the Soviet Union on the United States, requiring a full retaliatory response to the Soviet Union." He then recited the Cold War canon: "The 1930s taught us a clear lesson: aggressive conduct, if allowed to go unchecked and unchallenged, ultimately leads to war."

Now began the waiting. During this period he distracted himself, as usual, by having his buddies to dinner at the White House. "I think the pressure of this period made him desire more to have friends around," recalled Charlie Bartlett. "I think I was over there for dinner three times in the week . . . just small groups, which he would break up about nine thirty and go back to the cables."

He shared what he could. On one of those nights, Bartlett was climbing into bed around eleven thirty when the phone rang. Kennedy told him, "You'd be interested to know I got a cable from our friend, and he says that those ships are coming through, they're coming through tomorrow." To hear such information gave his listener a very clear notion of what kind of pressure Jack was under. Bartlett realized "it was on that kind of a note that he had to go to sleep. But I must say that the president's coolness and temper were never more evident than they were that week."

Under the careful supervision of Robert McNamara, the navy enforced the blockade without attacking the Soviet ships, which retreated from the Cuban sea channels. Within the Department of the Navy, however, it was an unpopular decision. That's because, as Red Fay explained it, his friend was stepping all over what the navy brass saw as the right of a captain to run his own ship. "The President said, 'Any communication with any skipper of our ship when coming in contact with a Russian ship, I will make the decision as to exactly what he is to say, when he's to say it, and how he's to say it.'" He was running the operation, but it wasn't what they wanted to hear.

Nor was the young president's operation like any they'd known before. He wasn't fighting a war but acting to prevent one, signaling to the other side the terms on which peace could be maintained.

Two letters arriving from Premier Khrushchev marked the beginning of the conclusion to the crisis. They were sent to the U.S. embassy in Moscow on consecutive days, October 26 and 27. The first letter proposed the removal of missiles and Soviet personnel in exchange for a promise not to invade Cuba. The second asked for the added concession of the removal of Jupiter missiles from Turkey.

The text of the second letter, sent on the following day, was broadcast on Moscow radio at the same time it was delivered to the U.S. embassy.

Kennedy resolved to answer Khrushchev's first letter, agreeing not to invade Cuba. He then instructed Bobby to tell the Soviet ambassador, Anatoly Dobrynin, in confidence that the Jupiter missiles in Turkey would be withdrawn later. Bobby gave Dobrynin a timetable of one day to accept.

Arriving at the Justice Department, Dobrynin was taken aback by Bobby's conduct. In the past he'd come to expect the same rough treatment the president's brother had meted out to Mike DiSalle and other resistant Democrats two years earlier. He had prepared himself to be castigated for the Soviets' deception. Instead, he came face-to-face with an upset young father trying desperately to prevent a nuclear war. "He didn't even try to get into fights," the envoy cabled his superiors in Moscow. The United States would remove the missiles from Turkey, as Khrushchev had requested, within four or five months, Bobby assured him, but couldn't let it look like a concession. "He persistently returned to one theme: time is of the essence and we shouldn't miss the chance."

Still, the entire perilous and exhausting adventure wasn't going to be over, Bobby told Dobrynin, until the Russian missiles were actually removed from Cuban soil. That was "not an ultimatum, just a statement of fact." Khrushchev *must* commit to doing so. It worked. Within the week, Kennedy had won the Soviet leader's agreement. The crisis had ended. A country that had lived for days with the prospect of nuclear war could now breathe easy.

Though Curtis LeMay would call the decision to not invade Cuba "the greatest defeat in our history," it was a minority view. "If Kennedy never did another thing," said the British prime minister, Harold Macmillan, "he assured his place in history by this single act."

It was later learned that the Soviets had deposited in Cuba a disturbing cache of nuclear weapons in early October, well before the Kennedy administration had the photographic evidence that spurred it into action. There were ninety nuclear warheads in all. Thirty of them possessed sixty-six times the explosive power of the bomb dropped on Hiroshima. There was an equal number of warheads with the firepower of the Hiroshima atomic bomb, plus an assortment of other, smaller ones.

Would Khrushchev have fired them? Here's what he said afterward in his memoirs: "My thinking went like this: If we installed the missiles secretly, and then the United States discovered the missiles after they were poised and ready to strike, the Americans would think twice before trying to liquidate our installations by military means. I knew that the United States could knock out some of our installations, but not all of them. If a quarter or even a tenth of our missiles survived — even if only one or two big ones were left — we could still hit New York, and there wouldn't be much of New York left. I don't mean to say everyone in New York would be killed — not everyone, of course, but an awful lot of people would be wiped out . . . And it was high time that America learned what it feels like to have her own land and her own people threatened."

But if America had attacked those missile sites, killing the Soviet soldiers and technicians there to deploy them, Khrushchev had in mind another target: West Berlin. "The Americans knew that if Russian blood were shed in Cuba, American blood would surely be shed in Germany."

The bitter coldness of that statement would have surprised the American president only in tone. It's precisely what Kennedy had on his mind when everyone else was thinking Cuba. It's hard to imagine any other president — let alone the youngest one ever elected — resisting the pressures the way Jack Kennedy had managed to. Despite the many buddies he relied upon, despite his brother's indispensability, despite the curiosity about the world that drove him, the Bay of Pigs had taught him whom he could best rely upon: himself.

Bobby Kennedy offered the sharpest assessment of what his brother had done. "The final lesson of the Cuban missile crisis is the importance of placing ourselves in the other country's shoes. During the crisis, President Kennedy spent more time trying to determine the effect of a particular course of action on Khrushchev and the Russians than on any other phase of what he was doing. President

Kennedy understood that the Soviet Union did not want war."

It was his detachment that saved us. Another man would have reacted with force to the Soviet treachery. He would have shared in the righteousness of the cause, been stirred to attack by the saber rattling. Jack resisted. He was not moved by the emotion of others around him. He knew his course and stayed to it. Thank God. The boy who had read alone of history's heroes was now safely one of them. He had done it not by winning a war, but by averting one far more horrible than any leader in the past could have imagined.

CHAPTER FIFTEEN
GOALS

Blessed are the peacemakers.
— Matthew 5:9

Politicians are, at different times, driven by grand notions and near necessity. Speak of the next election when they're dreaming loftily, and you risk being dismissed as a hack. Speak of high purpose when they're hearing the footsteps of a rival, and you invite instant dismissal.

Jack Kennedy was both an original and a consummate politician. Yet his stewardship of priorities still resembled those of a college student. With a number of classes on his schedule, he gave most of his attention to some, did the best he could with others, and let a few slide. It's common enough. He was always most committed to what interested him. What made all the difference was the love of history that never failed to engage him.

In the first two years of his presidency, he had been making history. His accomplish-

President Kennedy in West Berlin

36

37

"I have a dream." Dr. King in Washington, DC, August 28, 1963

Caroline and John Jr. in the Oval Office

38

ments were linked in a singular way to what he most highly valued: his commitment to the Peace Corps, to peaceful competition in science and space travel, to containment of nuclear arms, to civil rights. But he also needed to be reelected. He began his third year in office pushing for a tax cut. It was an attempt to court a constituency that was resisting him: a previous year's poll had shown that 88 percent of businessmen viewed him as hostile to their interests. However, many of them didn't even go for his idea of a tax cut. The view then from Wall Street and Main Street both was that balanced budgets were the best thing for business.

Kennedy had campaigned on just such a principle, only to grow concerned over time that the economy simply wasn't growing as it should. His chief economic advisor, Walter Heller, believed tax cuts would stimulate spending and investment, thereby increasing employment. Eisenhower's commitment to fiscal conservatism had spiked the jobless rate in the fall of 1960, hamstringing Nixon's quest to succeed him. Looking ahead to November 1964, Kennedy wanted that rate heading downward — and believed a slash in taxes would do the trick.

He also sought to correct the unfairness he saw in the tax code. Why, for example, had H. L. Hunt, the oil baron, paid just $22,000 in taxes the previous year? Why had J. Paul

Getty, another ridiculously wealthy oilman, forked over only $500? When Ben Bradlee told him he paid the same amount, Kennedy said it made his point. "The tax laws really screw people in your bracket." Hearing this, Bradlee suggested it would surely help the cause of reform if he'd release the figures on those oilmen's tax levels. Kennedy paused before replying. "Maybe after 1964." All he wanted at the moment was a tax cut that would juice the economy enough to get it moving before voters had their next chance to weigh in at the polls.

President Kennedy delivered three epochal addresses in June of 1963. The first was the commencement address at American University. It became known as his "Peace" speech. In it he spoke of his desire for a limited nuclear test ban treaty with the Soviet Union. The Cuban Missile Crisis, he knew, had been a terrifyingly close call.

"What kind of peace do I mean? Not the peace of the grave or the security of the slave. I am talking about genuine peace, the kind of peace that makes life on earth worth living, the kind that enables man and nations to grow and to hope and to build a better life for their children — not merely peace for Americans, but peace for all men and women — not merely peace in our time, but peace for all time."

He was calling on the Soviet Union to join

with the United States to prove that peace was possible, conflict not inevitable. "The problems of man are man-made; they can be solved by man. And man can be as big as he wants. No problem of human destiny is beyond human beings. Man's reason and spirit have often solved the seemingly unsolvable — and we believe they can do it again." With these words, he revealed that his highest commitment was not to arms control alone but to human hope.

Kennedy then expressed thoughts new to an American president, ideas especially startling coming from a man who'd once been a committed Cold Warrior. What he pointed out was the obvious but unspoken fact that the peoples inhabiting the two countries, the USA and the USSR, are not that different in their needs and dreams. "For in the final analysis, our most basic common link is that we all inhabit this small planet; and we are all mortal." He went on to offer a gesture of respect that was even more unexpected. "As Americans, we find Communism profoundly repugnant as a negation of personal freedom and dignity. But we can still hail the Russian people for their many achievements — in science and space, in economic and industrial growth, in culture and in acts of courage."

He continued, powerfully, to make his case. "Among the many traits the peoples of our two countries have in common, none is stronger than our mutual abhorrence of war. Almost unique among the major world powers, we have never been at war with each other. And no nation in the history of battle ever suffered more than the Soviet Union suffered in the course of the Second World War. At least twenty million lost their lives. Countless millions of homes and farms were burned or sacked. A third of the nation's territory, including nearly two thirds of its industrial base, was turned into a wasteland — a loss equivalent to the devastation of this country east of Chicago.

"The one major area of these negotiations where the end is in sight, yet where a fresh start is badly needed, is in a treaty to outlaw nuclear tests. The conclusion of such a treaty, so near and yet so far, would check the spiraling arms race in one of its most dangerous areas. It would place the nuclear powers in a position to deal more effectively with one of the greatest hazards which man faces in 1963, the further spread of nuclear arms. It would increase our security — it would decrease the prospects of war. Surely this goal is sufficiently important to require our steady pursuit, yielding neither to the temptation to give up the whole effort nor the temptation to give up our insistence on vital and responsible safeguards.

"To make clear our good faith and solemn convictions on the matter, I now declare that the United States does not propose to conduct nuclear tests in the atmosphere so long as other states do not do so. We will not be the first to resume. Such a declaration is no substitute for a formal binding treaty, but I hope it will help us achieve one. Nor would such a treaty be a substitute for disarmament, but I hope it will help us achieve it."

Finally came the radical commitment: "Our primary long-range interest in Geneva, however, is general and complete disarmament — designed to take place by stages, permitting parallel political developments to build the new institutions of peace which would take the place of arms."

What Kennedy had said would quickly become known to the men and women of the Soviet Union — but only because Nikita Khrushchev had dictated that it be so. According to a *New York Times* piece three days later, headlined "Russians Stirred by Kennedy Talk About Cold War," the Communist daily *Izvestia* had published the speech in full. Reported the *Times,* "The decision to make the speech available to the Soviet people through the government newspaper was interpreted here as an indication that the speech had made a favorable impression in the Kremlin."

The story then quoted a Soviet intellectual: "The speech and its publication in *Izvestia* show that there can be mutual understanding." While a young woman worker was "overheard to ask a friend: 'Have you read the Kennedy speech? It is all about peace.'"

The previous month, however, most Americans had witnessed something they wanted no one in the world to see. It had been in their newspapers and on their television sets. The incident had occurred in Birmingham, Alabama, in early May, when Eugene "Bull" Connor — the unrepentantly racist commissioner of public safety, just elected for his sixth term — had unleashed dogs and ordered fire hoses turned on peaceful African-American civil rights demonstrators.

Now, on June 11, the day after Kennedy's American University speech, two black students, Vivian Malone and James Hood, had attempted to enroll at the University of Alabama. Their way was blocked by order of Governor George C. Wallace, who'd campaigned on a promise to do just that. Watching the eleven o'clock news two weeks earlier with Jackie and the Bradlees, the president had grown solemn at clips of Wallace promising — in the face of a federal court order — personally to "bar the door" against any attempts at desegregation. "He's just challenging us to use the marshals . . . that's going to be something."

He'd once met Wallace — whose recent campaign slogan had been "Segregation now — Segregation tomorrow — Segregation forever" — and was disgusted by the man. "Make him look ridiculous. That's what the president wants you to do," Attorney General Robert Kennedy instructed his deputy, Nicholas Katzenbach.

There in Tuscaloosa, flanked by an enormous contingent of National Guardsmen — his earlier experience at Ole Miss had taught him about strength in numbers — Katzenbach instructed Wallace to allow the two students to be admitted. When the governor remained immovable in the door of Foster Auditorium, the commander of the Alabama Guard, General Henry Graham, told him to "stand aside," which Wallace then did.

Thanks to a documentary shot at the time by Robert Drew, we can see much of what happened next. Titled *Crisis: Behind a Presidential Commitment,* it shows Kennedy standing in the Oval Office and asking his top aides — Ken O'Donnell, Larry O'Brien, Ted Sorensen, Pierre Salinger, and his brother Bobby — to join him around a small coffee table. Kennedy assumed the captain's seat, in this case a rocking chair. He did so with a subtle, two-thumbs-up gesture as if he were still a young skipper calling his crew to quarters. General Graham's success, acting on his behalf, obviously had energized Kennedy. At that moment he made the call to deliver a major speech that night, giving Sorensen only three hours to prepare it.

In his State of the Union that January, President Kennedy had affirmed that the "most precious and powerful right in the world, the right to vote . . . not be denied to any citizen on grounds of his race or color. In this centennial year of Emancipation, all those who are willing to vote should always be permitted." He'd followed it by endorsing a push for voting rights, backing an end to all discrimination in hiring and supporting full access to public accommodations. Now, with his own deepening conviction heightened by the confrontation in Alabama he'd just seen on television, he was ready to further speak his thoughts.

Calling civil rights "a moral issue . . . as old as the Scriptures and . . . as clear as the American Constitution," he framed it in the context of the Cold War. "Today we are committed to a worldwide struggle to promote and protect the rights of all who wish to be free. And when Americans are sent to Vietnam or West Berlin, we do not ask for whites only. We preach freedom around the world, and we mean it."

The commonsense truths he spoke that night were framed in the idiom of everyday American conversation.

"It ought to be possible, therefore, for American students of any color to attend any public institution they select without having to be backed up by troops.

"It ought to be possible for American consumers of any color to receive equal service in places of public accommodation, such as hotels and restaurants and theaters and retail stores, without being forced to resort to demonstrations in the street, and it ought to be possible for American citizens of any color to register to vote in a free election without interference or fear of reprisal.

"It ought to be possible, in short, for every American to enjoy the privileges of being American without regard to his race or his color. In short, every American ought to have the right to be treated as he would wish to be treated, as one would wish his children to be treated. But this is not the case.

"If an American, because his skin is dark, cannot eat lunch in a restaurant open to the public; if he cannot send his children to the best public school available; if he cannot vote for the public officials who represent him; if, in short, he cannot enjoy the full and free life which all of us want, then who among us would be content to have the color of his skin changed and stand in his place? Who among us would then be content with the counsels of patience and delay?"

Martin Luther King, Jr., declared that the speech he'd heard represented "the most sweeping and forthright ever presented by an American president."

But it was one thing to speak eloquently in one's own language, and another to confront an audience on foreign land. Driving through the streets of West Berlin later that month, on June 26, Ben Bradlee watched Kennedy struggling to rehearse the German sentences he intended to use in a speech. Bradlee knew his friend was no linguist. In fact, Jack was secretly taking French lessons, having resented Bradlee's own fluency, which he'd gained years before as a press attaché with the American embassy in Paris. "Two thousand years ago the proudest boast was '*civis Romanus sum.*' Today, in the world of freedom, the proudest boast is '*Ich bin ein Berliner.*' "

Twenty-two months earlier, the East Germans had stepped back from the edge of conflict and constructed the Berlin Wall, taking the city — and the watching world — by surprise. Overnight, the twelve-foot concrete-and-barbed-wire symbol of totalitarianism had taken shape as a scar on the landscape of European history. More than a hundred miles long, one section of the Wall divided East and West Berlin, while a much larger one encircled the American, British, and French sectors, cutting them off from the rest of East Germany. Where once there had been reasonably free passage between the halves of the politically bifurcated city, now there were checkpoints and guards with guns.

Kennedy tackled the problem of addressing the beleaguered West Berliners straightforwardly. He and his country stood for democracy, and everything else derived from that simple reality. "There are many people in the world who really don't understand, *or say they don't,* what is the great issue between the Free World and the Communist world. Let them come to Berlin. There are some who say that Communism is the wave of the future. Let them come to Berlin. And there are even a few who say that it is true that Communism is an evil system, but it permits us to make economic progress. *Lass' sie nach Berlin kommen!* Let them come to Berlin. Freedom has many difficulties, and democracy is not perfect, but we have never had to put a wall up to keep our people in to prevent them from leaving us. All free men, wherever they may live are citizens of Berlin, and, therefore, as a free man, I take pride in the words *'Ich bin ein Berliner.'* "

A million Germans lined the parade route, with 300,000 jamming into the square fronting West Berlin. Two thirds of the population had come out to greet JFK. His speech that day was — for both his listeners and for all those who lived in that time — the greatest of the Cold War. Seeing the Wall itself affected the president physically, shocking him probably even more than he'd expected. He looked "like a man who has just glimpsed Hell," Hugh Sidey observed.

Jack called the time he spent in Berlin and then in Ireland, where he flew next, the happiest days of his life. There, in the country of his ancestors, the first Irish-Catholic American president was welcomed with near ecstatic enthusiasm. Accompanied by his sisters Eunice Shriver and Jean Smith, he made a stop in Dunganstown in County Wexford, site of his Kennedy roots, and then, in Galway, was honored with the Freedom of the City. At the port town of New Ross, he told the crowd gathered to hear him, "When my great-grandfather left here to become a cooper in East Boston, he carried nothing with him except two things — a strong religious faith and a strong desire for liberty. I am glad to say that all of his grandchildren have valued that inheritance."

In England, before going to Birch Grove, Harold Macmillan's residence, to meet with the prime minister, he traveled to Derbyshire to visit the grave of his sister Kathleen. The current Duchess of Devonshire remembers how the presidential helicopter affected one resident of the small rural village: "The wind from that machine blew my chickens away, and I haven't seen them since," the woman complained. At St. Peter's Church there, Jack went to the gravesite and, carrying some flowers for his sister, carefully and painfully went down on his knees to pray.

The fact that Jack Kennedy achieved this historic hat trick — the "peace speech" on nuclear arms, the epic address on civil rights, and the *"Ich bin ein Berliner"* moment — while enduring chronic back pain enhances the nobility of it all. You can see in the documentary footage of the Oval Office scene during the Birmingham crisis a tinge of the torture in the careful way Kennedy carries himself, the deliberate way he rocks his chair. There's nothing easy in his manner.

For ten days in July, Averell Harriman, who'd been the U.S. ambassador in Moscow in the 1940s, negotiated with Nikita Khrushchev a treaty to ban the testing of nuclear weapons in the atmosphere. During those negotiations, recalled Ted Sorensen, "Khrushchev told Harriman that more than anything else, Kennedy's 'Peace Speech' — which the chairman allowed to be rebroadcast throughout Russia and to be published in full in the Moscow press — had paved the way for the treaty."

The treaty outlawed nuclear testing by the USA, USSR, and Great Britain in the atmosphere, outer space, and underwater. On July 25, 1963, envoys from the three powers signed the document, making it official. John Kennedy considered this his greatest achievement.

David Ormsby-Gore, the British ambassador in Washington, traced Kennedy's determination to secure the treaty and his courage in pursuing it to his good friend's own biography. "With all human beings, one of the things that gives confidence is to have been in extreme peril and come well out of it, perhaps on some occasions to have been near death and come back from the brink. I have always noticed that people who have had that kind of experience have a sort of calm; not quite a detachment from life, but a calm attitude to anything that life can throw at them, which is rather significant. Of course, he had had the experience on more than one occasion of being faced by death."

During that summer, as Jack had been traveling, Jackie Kennedy had remained at home pregnant, expecting to deliver her third child in September. Their second, John Fitzgerald Kennedy, Jr., born right after the 1960 election, was now twenty months old. Caroline was almost six. On August 7, Jackie gave birth, five weeks early, to a boy whom they named Patrick. Never strong to begin with, two days later he began to fail. The father held his tiny fingers for two hours as the infant tried to breathe. He was holding them when Patrick died. "He put up quite a fight." Then, "He was a beautiful baby."

Afterward, the president went to his room, having asked to be given time alone. Through the door, Dave Powers could hear him sobbing. Later he would kneel beside Jackie's bed and tell her about the son he'd loved that they now, together, had lost.

There was never a good time to try to come to grips with the situation in Vietnam, and Kennedy had been delaying it. Within days of taking office, he'd signed a national security directive stating that it was our country's policy to "defeat Communist insurgency" in South Vietnam. By 1963 there were twelve thousand U.S. "military advisors" there. However, JFK had resisted calls from South Vietnam's president, Ngo Dinh Diem, to send in combat troops, seeing no merit to that idea. Fully aware that there were gung ho American officers hoping he'd upgrade our status there from "advising" to actually fighting, he had no intention of letting that happen.

"I can remember one particular case," Red Fay recalled. "We were out, I believe it was off of Newport. I think the Blue Angels had just flown over. The president was sitting in his swivel chair in the back of the *Honey Fitz,* and the phone rang next to him. There were some marines that wanted to lead their unit into combat. The situation, they thought, was ideal for an attack, and so, therefore, they wanted to lead it. And, evidently, the standing orders of the president at that time were that our advisors over there were not there to lead Vietnam troops into battle. Fay heard his old navy buddy make it crystal clear that he wanted that order enforced to the *letter.*

But he couldn't abandon Saigon to the Communists and expect to win a second term. He couldn't afford to be the president who "lost" South Vietnam, just as he'd accused Harry

Truman of doing with China. The problem was President Diem. A Roman Catholic, Diem had enjoyed strong support from American Catholics, including Kennedy, since taking command when Vietnam was divided at the Geneva Convention in 1954. Diem was now conducting a campaign of repression against the country's Buddhist majority. In June a seventy-three-year-old Buddhist monk had lit himself on fire in a main Saigon thoroughfare, having moments earlier handed a statement to reporters. "Before closing my eyes to Buddha, I have the honor of presenting my word to President Diem, asking him to be kind and tolerant toward his people and to enforce a policy of religious equality."

President Kennedy realized he could no longer support a regime that was fighting the Communist guerrillas *and* Buddhist monks. Besides this, the Diem government was viewed as hopelessly corrupt, totally under the control of Diem's brother and sister-in-law, the notorious "Dragon Lady," Madame Nhu. Feeling stymied, he had the idea to name his onetime political rival Henry Cabot Lodge as U.S. ambassador. There were clear advantages to this. Lodge lacked any sentimental feelings toward Diem. He was arrogant enough to act decisively. Most important, he wanted a victory, personally as well as nationally. He had the added advantage, for Kennedy, of making the hellish situation in South Vietnam bipartisan.

Something had to be done. Diem and his brother Nhu were leading the country's special forces in raids on Buddhist pagodas in Saigon and other cities, arresting monks and nuns alike. Lodge now represented a group within the Kennedy administration who wanted to back a military coup to topple Diem. The leader of that faction was Averell Harriman, who'd proven himself to Kennedy by winning Khrushchev's agreement in July to the limited nuclear testing ban.

On August 24, Kennedy approved a cable to Saigon authorizing American support for a military coup against President Diem. It was a cold decision, certainly a stark shift in loyalty. Kennedy had been a backer of Diem from the earliest days of the country's division, and had been a supporter of the American Friends of Vietnam, a lobbying group. Now he was approving his former ally's overthrow. Inside his administration, his decision was never truly cleared by either McNamara or Rusk, and it met with disfavor from Lyndon Johnson.

The cable said: "U.S. Government cannot tolerate situation in which power lies in Nhu's hands. Diem must be given chance to rid himself of Nhu and his coterie and replace them with the best military and political personalities available. If, in spite of your efforts, Diem remains obdurate and refuses, then we must face the possibility that Diem himself cannot be preserved. You will understand that we cannot from Washington give you detailed instructions as to how this operation should proceed, but you will also know we will back you to the hilt on action to achieve our objectives." It was precisely what Lodge wanted: a death warrant.

August was also the month of the extraordinary, epoch-making March on Washington, with its unforgettable "I have a dream" speech delivered with Moses-like fervor by Martin Luther King, Jr., to the crowd of 250,000. The president had done what he could to stave off the possibility of conflict at the event. His efforts had helped swell the numbers of marchers, especially whites, because he'd encouraged Walter Reuther to bring his UAW members. He'd taken steps to accommodate the crowd, reducing the chances of discord by making sure there was both food and bathroom access. And, sensibly, he drew the route from the Washington Monument to the Lincoln Memorial — not to the gates of the White House.

Meeting with the leaders after the speech, Kennedy immediately quoted the most memorable line to show his admiration: "I have a dream," he repeated.

Ben Bradlee accompanied Kennedy when he went the following month to visit Jackie at her mother's house in Newport, where she'd been staying since the loss of their infant boy. It was the Kennedys' tenth wedding anniversary. "This was the first time we'd seen Jackie since the death of little Patrick, and she greeted JFK with by far the most affectionate embrace we had ever seen them give each other. They were not normally demonstrative people, period."

Also in September, Jack attended the Harvard-Columbia football game. He left at halftime to head off for a secret visit to the grave of his lost son, Patrick. He told Ken O'Donnell to make sure no press people were around. When he got to the grave in Brookline, he knelt down and prayed.

It's always difficult to penetrate another person's religious beliefs. This would be especially the case with someone as complex as Jack Kennedy.

Back in his younger years Jack would stay in his pew during Communion because he wasn't in a state of grace. Now, as president, he'd go to mass weekly, but also to confession. When a priest once signaled he'd recognized his distinctive accent, he had a way to evade detection. In future visits to the confession booth, he took a place in line among the Secret Service agents, assuming the confessor would not be quite sure who was telling him what.

When it came to family and loss, his faith regularly showed itself. Mark Dalton was always touched, he said, when Jack stopped by a church to light a candle for Joe Jr. There were often times when friends would catch him losing himself briefly in reveries about the older brother who'd so much paved the way for him. Dave Powers, who saw Jack off to bed so many nights, said that the president would kneel and pray before retiring. One wonders whether he ever echoed St. Augustine's famous prayer: "Give me chastity and continence, but not just now."

Ted Sorensen offered this moral verdict on Jack. "An American President, commander in chief of the world's greatest military power, who during his presidency did not send one combat troop division abroad or drop one bomb, who used his presidency to break down the barriers of religious and racial equality and harmony in this country and to reach out to the victims of poverty and repression, who encouraged Americans to serve their communities and to love their neighbors regardless of the color of their skin, who waged war not on smaller nations but on poverty and illiteracy and mental illness in his own country, and who restored the appeal of politics for the young and sent Peace Corps volunteers overseas to work with the poor and untrained in other countries — was in my book a moral president, regardless of his personal misconduct."

On October 4, Jackie left on a Caribbean cruise aboard Aristotle Onassis's yacht, the *Christina.* The trip offered her a chance to regain her spirits. Jack took her absence as a chance to get to know his children better, and put in time as their babysitter. Pictures taken in the Oval Office show John Jr. peeking out from under the front of his father's desk.

In late October, Kennedy was pounding away for passage of the civil rights bill. At one point, he called Mayor Richard Daley to put pressure on a Chicago congressman who was holding up the measure. Their conversation, packed with old-school politics, was picked up on the White House taping system:

Kennedy: Roland Libonati is sticking it right up us.

Daley: He is?

Kennedy: Yeah, because he's standing with the extreme liberals who are gonna end up with no bill at all. I asked him, "If you'll vote for this package which we got together with the Republicans, [it] gives us about everything we wanted," and he says, "No."

Daley: He'll vote for it. He'll vote for any goddamned thing you want.

Kennedy: (laughs) Well, can you get him?

Daley: I surely can. Where is he? Is he there?

Kennedy: He's in the other room.

Daley: Well, you have Kenny. Tell Kenny to put him on the wire here.

Kennedy: Or would you rather get him when he gets back to his office? That's better. Otherwise, he might think . . .

Daley: That's better. But he'll do it. The last time I told him, "Now look it. I don't give a goddamned what it is. You vote for it, for anything the president wants and this is the way it will be and this the way it's gonna be."

Kennedy: We have a chance to pull this out. Billy [Green] in Philadelphia got Toll. If you can get Libonati.

Using the muscle of his political pals, the same bosses who helped get him to the White House, Kennedy nailed down Democratic members of the House Judiciary Committee. By November, he had gotten it out of the committee, though stymied by the segregationist chairman of the Rules Committee, who refused to bring it to the House floor.

On November 2, Ngo Dinh Diem was killed in the military coup that the United States had signed off on in August. When he learned of the death, and the brutal manner of it, Kennedy bolted from the room in horror. Hearing the coup leader's claim that Diem had taken his own life, Kennedy rejected it outright. He never believed that a fellow Roman Catholic would commit suicide. Ted Sorensen would later say: "Perhaps he should have guessed that, in that part of the world, the overthrow of Diem by the South Vietnamese army could well lead to Diem's death. But I could see from the look of shock and dismay on JFK's face when he heard the news of Diem's assassination that he had no indication or even hint that anything more than Diem's exile was contemplated."

After retreating from the cabinet room, Jack called up Mary Meyer, his sometime mistress and friend. Not wanting to be alone, he spent the rest of the day with her.

Back at his desk after the weekend, he dictated a memorandum of what had happened.

"Monday, November 4, 1963. Over the weekend the coup in Saigon took place. It culminated three months of conversation about a coup, conversation which divided the government here and in Saigon.

"Opposed to the coup was General Taylor, the attorney general, Secretary McNa-

mara to a somewhat lesser degree, John Mc-
Cone, partly because of an old hostility to
Lodge, which causes him to lack confidence
in Lodge's judgment, partly as a result of a
new hostility because Lodge shifted his station chief. In favor of the coup was State,
led by Averell Harriman, George Ball, Roger
Hilsman, supported by Michael Forrestal at
the White House.

"I feel I must bear a good deal of responsibility for it, beginning with our cables of early
August in which we suggested the coup. In
my judgment that wire was badly drafted; it
should not have been sent on a Saturday. I
should not have given my consent to it without
a roundtable conference at which McNamara
and Taylor could have presented their views.
While we did redress that balance in later
wires, that first wire encouraged Lodge along
a course to which he was in any case inclined."

On the tape, the listener can hear the voices
of John Jr., who was almost three, talking with
his father. Caroline, six, joins in at the very
end:

Kennedy: You want something? Say something. Hello.

John: Hello.

Kennedy: Why do leaves fall?

John: Because it's winter.

Kennedy: No, autumn.

John: Autumn.

Kennedy: And why does the snow come on the ground?

John: Because it's winter.

Kennedy: Why do the leaves turn green?

John: Because it's winter.

Kennedy: Spring. Spring.

John: Spring.

Kennedy: And why do we go to the Cape? Hyannis Port?

John: Because it's winter.

Kennedy: It's summer!

John: It's summer.

Kennedy: Say your horses . . .

Caroline: Your horses.

"I was shocked by the death of Diem and Nhu," Kennedy continued his dictation.

"I'd met Diem with Justice Douglas many years ago. He was an extraordinary character. While he became increasingly difficult in the last months, nevertheless over a ten-year period he'd held his country together, maintained its independence under very adverse conditions. The way he was killed makes it particularly abhorrent. The question now is whether the generals can stay together and build a stable government, or whether . . . the intellectuals, students, et cetera, will turn on the government as repressive and undemocratic in the not too distant future."

The following day he gave Maxwell Taylor, the chairman of the Joint Chiefs, a clear signal of his intentions in Vietnam, offering what he viewed as the limits of American commitment in-country. "He is instinctively against introduction of U.S. forces," Taylor would report. Jack made a similar comment to Arthur Schlesinger. "They want a force of American troops. They say it's necessary in order to restore confidence and maintain morale. But it will be just like Berlin. The troops will march in, the bands will play, the crowds will cheer, and in four days everyone will have forgotten. Then we will be told we have to send in more troops. It's like taking a drink. The effect wears off, and you have to take another."

Yet his exact thoughts about Vietnam remain a mystery. What we do know is his early understanding of the fighting. Motivated by nationalism, the Viet Minh had fought the French, and he'd grasped what was at stake. Why would he make a different assessment of the Viet Cong war against the pro-American Diem? Ken O'Donnell said Kennedy told him he was determined to get out once the election-year politics were behind him. But it's not that simple. Ted Sorensen believed his boss could never have the cynicism about war and human lives that the conflict in Vietnam would turn out to mandate. "I do not believe he knew in his last weeks what he was going to do."

At about this same time, Kennedy called members of the House Rules Committee to the White House. He was interested in getting their insider knowledge about why his legislation, which included the Civil Rights bill, was stalled. Tip O'Neill remembered being asked to come for a drink afterward when Jack spotted him stranded without a ride. The two of them chatted about the old days. Jack was curious about how some of his old boys were doing, the ones who'd been with him in the beginning. He asked about Billy Sutton, Mark Dalton, Joe Healey, John Galvin, and the others. He asked Tip to make sure Billy had a job up in Massachusetts.

The Kennedys spent the Veterans Day weekend with the Bradlees down at their friends' new getaway in Virginia. Jack told Ben he didn't like what he'd heard about Dallas, where he was soon headed, about the way Adlai Stevenson had been spat on, heckled, and jeered when giving a United Nations Day speech there. He felt, he told his friend, that the "mood of the city was ugly." In a front-page editorial, the *Dallas Times Herald* had pronounced the city "disgraced. There is no other way to view the storm-trooper actions of last night's frightening attack on Adlai Stevenson." Governor John Connally called the affair "an affront to common courtesy and decency." And Mayor Earle Cabell pointed out that the demonstrators were "not our kind of folks." Jack allowed White House photographers to take pictures of the family that weekend. One film shows Jackie rehearsing with John Jr. a salute he was practicing, perhaps for when he joined his father that Monday at the Tomb of the Unknown Soldier.

The following Thursday, Jack had invited the film legend Greta Garbo to the White House. Lem Billings had met her on a recent European trip and was thrilled at the prospect of introducing her to his pal. Jack, meanwhile, ever the practical joker, had hatched a plan. The evening was arranged so that Garbo would arrive before Lem, giving Jack a chance to chat with her and lay the groundwork for his scheme.

Kennedy's idea was to convince her to act as if she'd never before set eyes on Billings. The pair of them carried it off for a quite some time before finally taking Lem out of his misery. It is a perfect example of Jack's taking the time, as he often did with his closest friends, to give them a little trouble. Though mildly sadistic — Lem devoted himself to trying to get Garbo to remember the various outings they'd had together, only to have her stare at him blankly — the prank also showed, in an odd way, that Jack cared. And cared enough — he, a president of the United States — to concoct a scheme that was at once so silly and yet so intimate. He'd done such things all his life.

It was a dinner to remember: Jackie, Jack, and Lem — and Garbo. But it would always be a sad memory for Lem. It had taken place on November 13, 1963.

That month, Kennedy hosted his first major campaign meeting for 1964. Included were Bobby, Ted Sorensen, Ken O'Donnell, and Larry O'Brien. It was the same team that had met in Palm Beach and later in Hyannis Port in 1959. Once again, his brother-in-law Steve Smith was to take charge, overall. The effort would be run from the White House, and the theme would be "peace and prosperity."

Kennedy looked forward to running against Senator Barry Goldwater. He was convinced that the conservative Arizonan was just too candid for a presidential candidate and would quickly self-destruct. His bigger worry was

Governor Nelson Rockefeller of New York. Told that "Rocky" liked him, Kennedy said it didn't matter. Politics would change that. "He'll end up hating me. That's natural," he said, remembering, perhaps, his own change of heart over Nixon.

President Kennedy was confident. But he also knew that he needed Texas and, perhaps, Georgia — not easy states to get in his corner, given the growing rage of white Southerners against him for his strong stand on civil rights. The polling showed that two thirds of them were deeply hostile, not an easy situation for a man looking to nail down Southern support. It was going to be a tough election. He needed to begin raising money and rousing those yellow-dog Democrats who'd been raised with the party and might still be won over.

Jack spent the next weekend in Palm Beach with Torby Macdonald, now in his fifth term as a Massachusetts congressman. It was a bachelor party fueled by enough bonhomie to induce JFK to croon "The September Song" with extra feeling. That Monday, November 18, he traveled with George Smathers to Miami and Tampa to deliver speeches denouncing Castro and his regime.

"A small band of conspirators has stripped the Cuban people of their freedom and handed over the independence and sovereignty of the Cuban nation to forces beyond the hemisphere. This, and this alone, divides us. As long as it is true, nothing is possible. Once this barrier is removed, everything is possible."

With the trip to Texas ahead of him, Kennedy worried about the South. "I wish I had this fucking thing over with," he complained to Smathers. He also told him, "You've got to live each day like it's your last day on earth."

On November 22, having spent the night in Fort Worth, he agreed to meet outside, before breakfast, with a good crowd of union people. Despite the early morning drizzle, the crowd was warm and enthusiastic. Inside, as the business leaders sipped their coffee, he gave a tough speech on Vietnam. "Without the United States, South Vietnam would collapse overnight."

Whatever concerns he had in the long run, whatever hesitation kept him from committing combat troops, he had those eighteen thousand "advisors" there on the ground. He was also thinking about an exit strategy. The day before, he'd asked his national security aide Michael Forrestal to "organize an in-depth study of every possible option we've got in Vietnam, including how to get out of there."

On the way from Fort Worth to the airport later that morning, Jack grilled Congressman Jim Wright and Governor John Connally about the strange difference in politics between the city he'd just left and the one he was about to enter. Why is Fort Worth so Democratic and Dallas so angrily right-wing? It was his usual curiosity abetted here by fresh reason to wonder. After all, he'd just been given a hero's welcome by the people of one city but remembered only too well Richard Nixon carrying Dallas with 65 percent in 1960. Now, there was the pall cast by the recent ugly treatment of Adlai Stevenson.

While Wright laid some of the blame on the conservative press, especially *the Dallas Morning News,* Connally offered a more sophisticated assessment of the difference between the two Texas cities. He said it could be traced to their different economies. Fort Worth was still a cowboy town. Dallas, on the other hand, was a white-collar town where people worked in high-rise office buildings. They identified with the folks on the floor above them, not the guy or woman working next to them in the stockyard or factory. They voted like their managers because they wanted to join them. This explained the shift of the city to the Republicans, a change that Connally understood and that was a precursor of his own ambitions.

Jack was just trying to figure it all out. He was out there in the American landscape, doing what he'd come very much to love, perhaps even more than the public service it allowed. He was on the road, doing the work of an American politician. He had goals, and he needed to be president to reach them.

Chapter Sixteen
Legacy

He was acutely responsive to the romance of history in the making, to the drama of great events; and to national sentiment.
— David Cecil, *Young Melbourne*

On a cold Friday night in late November 1963, Teddy White of *Life* magazine traveled through a driving rainstorm from New York to Cape Cod. When he arrived at Hyannis Port, he was received at the main house, Joseph P. Kennedy's. He found the president's widow fully composed despite the horror of the week before. Chuck Spalding was there, Dave Powers and a few others, but they quickly left the guest alone with the woman who had so earnestly invited him.

White would remember her appearance vividly. She wore trim slacks and a beige pullover sweater. Yet it was her eyes he most recalled. "They were wider than pools." She was, of course, beautiful. Her voice, as she spoke to him, was low, and what she said seemed to

39

Bobby, Jack, Joe Sr., Teddy, and Joe Jr.

40

41

At the London embassy

42

43

44

Sister Kathleen "Kick" Kennedy

45

offer almost total recall.

Jacqueline talked and talked for nearly four hours. Her companion was mesmerized and could barely write fast enough. The story that ran in *Life* was a careful selection from what she told him. He'd been summoned in a situation of the utmost distress as a respected journalist. But he was also a friend, and his instinct was to protect this woman whom he cared about when he dictated on deadline during those first hours of Saturday morning. She was listening to his every word as he called it in, he would confess years later, and she'd pushed hard for the idea of Jack Kennedy's presidency being like Camelot.

Not surprisingly, what was left out of White's story was far more fascinating than the narrative she'd designed. Her monologue had been simultaneously art and accident, and White was an expert assembler of information. But when you see his actual notes, the raw material, what you find is telling.

The piece quotes her as saying to White that "men are a combination of good and bad." Yet it isn't, in fact, how she'd phrased it. "Comb. of bad and good" is what sits there in White's scribbled notes. Why would he transpose it for the magazine? Why did he transcribe it correctly later on? "His mother never really loved him," she said, and that, too, is in the typescript of the handwritten interview, but again, not in the article. "She likes to go around talking about being the daughter of the mayor of Boston, of how she's the ambassador's wife. She didn't love him," Jackie had repeated.

She wanted to explain Jack Kennedy, not as a president, not as a husband, but as a man. It may not have been what she thought she intended, but it was what gripped her. "History made him what he was. He sat and read history." She mentioned his scarlet fever. "This little boy in bed, so much of the time. All the time he was in bed, this little boy was reading history, was reading Marlborough. He devoured the Knights of the Round Table. And he just loved that last song."

She was talking about *Camelot* now, the musical that was a hit on Broadway. The final song was the reprise of "Camelot," and in it was the image that soon came to haunt a nation: "Don't let it be forgot that once there was a spot / for one brief shining moment that was known as Camelot."

Here are more of White's raw notes, jotted quickly as he tried to keep up with her: "History is what made Jack. He was such a simple man. He was complex, too. He had that hero, idealistic side, but then he had that other side, the pragmatic side. His friends were all his old friends. He loved his Irish mafia." She knew his compartmentalized way of living better than anyone.

She also said this: "And then I thought, I

mustn't think that bad way. If history made Jack that way, made him see heroes, then other little boys will see." In the shock of tragedy, she was telling her husband's story, as she put it, both the "bad and good."

Aided and abetted by Jackie Kennedy, White produced a thrilling evocation of the fallen president, bringing home the immense loss. Around the world, everyone old enough to this day remembers exactly where they were when they heard the news of the assassination. When the story ran, the readers of *Life,* and then millions more, accepted his widow's vision; they took to their hearts the notion of Camelot — that vanished, shining place presided over by a noble, merry hero.

It was her gift to him. She'd wanted only two monuments to her husband. First, there would be an eternal flame to mark his grave at Arlington National Cemetery. She told White about how, driving across Memorial Bridge to Virginia at night, you can see the Lee Mansion lit up on the side of the hill from "miles and miles away." When Caroline was little, she said, that immense white building had been one of the first things she recognized. Now, below it, there would be the small twinkling light for her father.

The other commemoration she requested was quite different. She'd clearly given it careful thought. NASA's *Apollo 5* mission was set for takeoff in January 1964. The president had mentioned the launch in recent speeches. She asked that her husband's initials be placed on a tiny corner of the great Saturn rocket where no one would even see them.

To White, she also talked about Jack's last look at life, that instant when the end came, out of nowhere during that Dallas motorcade. "You know when he was shot, he had such a wonderful expression on his face," she told him. "You know that wonderful expression he had when they'd ask him a question about one of the ten million gadgets they have on a rocket, just before he answered? He looked puzzled."

I think we know that expression. It was a look he gave when he'd conjured up a witty answer at a press conference. It was the startled but pleased expression of a guy who's just figured something out. His friends as far back as Choate knew it well and remembered it.

Jacqueline Kennedy had come a long way that week. A short piece of film recently unearthed shows us a slender, dark-haired young woman — seemingly no more than a girl — racing to catch up to a gurney. She is a woman chasing after her love.

Within hours she'd assumed the reins of command, designing and staging a magnificent funeral. It was Lincolnesque with its horseless rider, the boots of the lost hero turned backward. There were the drums, relentless, insistent, hammering their bleak

579

reality. Soldiers die to the sound of drums.

"Jackie was extraordinary," Ben Bradlee would write after watching her from close up that weekend. "Sometimes she seemed completely detached, as if she were someone else watching the ceremony of that other person's grief." Still at the age Jack had been when he married her, she was observing the whole scene as if, really, she weren't a part of it.

Jack had, as Arthur Schlesinger described it, "to an exceptional degree, the gift of friendship." As Jim Reed, his navy friend, put it: "each of us had a certain role we were cast into, whether we knew it or not." The night they lost their leader, Ken O'Donnell, Dave Powers, and Larry O'Brien had headed up Wisconsin Avenue to Gawler's Funeral Home to pick out a coffin. The Irish mafia, the men Jack loved, were doing what their people do. The Irish are good with death. That Saturday night — the day after the horror — Dave delighted Jackie with stories of her husband before she knew him, of his endless climbs up the stairs of those wooden "three-deckers" in the old 11th Congressional District. Dave said he'd hoped that Jack would have one day come to *his* wake up in Charlestown.

Ken O'Donnell would be haunted by what he saw as his role in the tragedy. Before Jack had given anyone else a job, he'd handed him his: to protect him. It was impossible to forget that he, Ken O'Donnell, had been in charge of the Secret Service covering his friend, and he'd been the one urging Jack to make the trip to Texas.

I would get to know some of these men who'd been part of Jack's story. Billy Sutton was one, the first guy hired, just off the train from the army. One day in the 1980s, I walked into a back room in Speaker Tip O'Neill's suite of offices up in Boston. There was this little fellow sitting at a table. Moment by moment he would transform himself. One instant, he'd be Adlai Stevenson, gravely addressing the General Assembly. Next, he'd be Rose Kennedy, her voice high and churchy. It was as if she were standing there before me. No wonder Jack had called Billy his "firecracker."

Tip O'Neill, as you can tell from this book, was rich in stories, each shining with a love of the game that bonded him and Kennedy.

Jack's closest friends have helped me answer that question he himself gave for the reason people read biography. What was *he* like? Once, when I got Charlie Bartlett remembering his friend, he took his glasses off to dry his eyes as he thought back. Here's what Charlie himself wrote in November 1963, upon first hearing the news:

"We had a hero for a friend — and we mourn his loss. Anyone, and fortunately there were so many, who knew him briefly or over long periods, felt that a bright and quickening impulse had come into their life. He had uncommon courage, unfailing humor, a penetrating, ever-curious intelligence, and over all a matchless grace. He was our best. We will remember him always with love and sometimes, as the years pass and the story is retold, with a little wonder."

Chuck Spalding and Jack had been buddies since the year before the war. It was a matter of "chemistry," Chuck said. When I asked him my question, "What was he like?" he said he'd answer by way of a story. It was back when he and his then-wife, Betty, were getting ready to go through divorce, not a good time for them. Still together, though, they were out on the dock one day when Jack joined them for a sail. Spotting their two faces, he said, "Ah, the agony and the ecstasy." That's what one of his closest lifetime pals said Jack Kennedy was like.

I loved hearing Sally Fay, Red's daughter, speak of the joy in her house each time the phone rang and it was Jack Kennedy. "The most charming man I ever knew," George Smathers told me. His old Senate pal was thrilled when I told him how Jack explained liking him, saying the reason was because "he doesn't give a damn." Ben Bradlee, a good friend of mine as well, described Jack as having an "aura of royalty about him."

Robert Kennedy carried on, we know, never stopped trying to keep his brother's spirit alive, until he, too, was stopped. Teddy surprised everyone. Jack had said his kid brother wanted to spend his life "chasing girls in the South of France." But it didn't happen that way. Jack was once asked to pick the greatest senators in history. Of course, he could only look backward. Had he been able to look forward, he might well have included his youngest brother.

Daniel Patrick Moynihan, who served Kennedy as assistant secretary of labor, was the one who said, "There's no point in being Irish if you don't know the world's going to someday break your heart." He carried on Jack's plan to make Pennsylvania Avenue, the presidential inaugural route, a corridor of grandeur. "Make it like Paris," he'd said. Pat once remarked to me, in a very personal way, his feeling about the events of November 1963: "We've never gotten over it." Then, looking at me with generous appreciation, he added, "You've never gotten over it." I saw it as a kind of benediction, an acceptance into something warm and Irish and splendid, a knighthood of the soulful.

In a 2009 national poll, people were asked to say which American president deserves to be added to Mount Rushmore. It's a good question, because it really gets to heroic stature. Who should be there with Washington, Jefferson, Lincoln, and, especially the old "Rough Rider" himself, Teddy Roosevelt? They chose

John F. Kennedy.

In July 1969, a fellow volunteer of mine sat on a hillside in Swaziland with a group of local villagers looking at the night sky. He wanted them to sit and watch with him. Finally it arrived overhead, what they were looking for: a small light moving in the distance. It was his countrymen heading to the moon. That Saturn rocket Jack so loved had done its job; so had his Peace Corps.

Twenty years later, the Berlin Wall came down. I was there on a drizzly night that November with the beaten-down East Germans, waiting for the Brandenburg Gate to open. When I asked what "freedom" meant to him, a young man answered, "talking to you." Jack Kennedy would like to have heard that, deserved to, I think. The Iron Curtain was being ripped aside. Communism was in its death throes. The Cold War was ending without the nuclear war we so feared. We had gotten through it alive, those of us who once hid under those little desks of ours.

Thanks to him, I'd say. He'd come a long way from the kid who caused trouble at boarding school, from being Joe Kennedy's son. In the time of our greatest peril, at the moment of ultimate judgment, an American president kept us from the brink, saved us really, kept the smile from being stricken from the planet.

He did that. He, Jack Kennedy.

ACKNOWLEDGMENTS

The person I owe most for this book's completion is my son Michael Matthews. At a critical juncture, he transformed a mountain of historic material — chapter themes, interview transcripts, oral histories and citations from other sources — into coherent notes. He has a beautiful historic sense.

I want to thank Michele Slung for an editing and literary craft that gave shape and life to my narrative.

I owe my TV producer Tina Urbanski for her role at every stage of *Jack Kennedy.* Taking on this project amid the schedule of six television programs a week is a chore no one can accomplish alone.

I want to thank Helen O'Donnell for providing me with the vast oral history recorded by her father with correspondent Sander Vanocur. Kenneth O'Donnell was at Jack Kennedy's side from that first senate race in 1952 to the end. His sharp political mind is well on display here. It took a reporter of Vanocur's moxie to ask him just the right questions, and ask them he did.

I want to thank the inimitable Vincent Virga for the design and selection of the photographs that give this book its artistic completion. He is a visual choreographer. I want to thank U.S. Congressman Edward Markey of Massachusetts and Mark Johnson, a teacher of history, for reviewing my manuscript with sharpness and intelligence.

In an important way, this book emerges from my decades of real-time interest in Jack Kennedy. It benefits, of course, from the foundation of research I did for *Kennedy & Nixon.* Two other books have provided sturdy scaffoldings: Nigel Hamilton's *JFK: Reckless Youth,* the best-ever work on Kennedy's early life, and Robert Dallek's *An Unfinished Life,* which reveals for the first time his full medical history.

I need to credit Jon Meacham, author of *Franklin and Winston,* for the inspiration on how to craft this biography from the perspectives of those around him.

Jack Kennedy lived his life in a golden circle of friends and close associates. By bringing together their firsthand memories, I've sought to bring to life the man at their center. For the first-person accounts in this book I interviewed many witnesses to the life of Jack Kennedy: Letitia Baldridge, Charles Bartlett, Benjamin Bradlee, Mark Dalton, Fred and

Nancy Dutton, Red Fay, Paul Ferber, John Glenn, Lester Hyman, Peter Kaplan, Patrick Lucey, Rachel "Bunny" Mellon, Thomas P. "Tip" O'Neill, Jr., Dave Powers, Terri Robinson, Tazewell Shepard, George Smathers, Ted Sorensen, Chuck Spalding, Billy Sutton, Bill Wilson, Christopher Lawford, and, especially, Ambassador Jean Kennedy Smith.

For those I could not interview — Torbert Macdonald, James Reed, and Rip Horton — I depended on the oral histories archived at the John F. Kennedy Library. I owe the personal accounts of Lemoyne Billings to the excellent *Jack and Lem: The Untold Story of an Extraordinary Friendship* by David Pitts, as well as the wonderful chapter on the Jack-Lem relationship in *Best of Friends* by David Michaelis.

I benefitted greatly from Thomas P. O'Neill's *Man of the House,* Lawrence F. O'Brien's *No Final Victories,* Red Fay's *The Pleasure of His Company,* Ben Bradlee's *Conversations with Kennedy,* Ted Sorensen's *Counselor,* Deirdre Henderson's *Prelude to Leadership: The European Diary of John F. Kennedy: Summer 1945,* and Arthur Schlesinger's *Journals.*

Other books on John F. Kennedy are essential to any understanding of him. *Jack: The Struggles of John F. Kennedy* by Herbert Parmet, *Kennedy* by Theodore Sorensen, *President Kennedy: Profile of Power* by Richard Reeves, *Mrs. Kennedy* by Barbara Leaming, and *A Thousand Days* and *Robert F. Kennedy and His Times* by Arthur Schlesinger.

I need to thank Lorraine Connelly and Judy Donald of Choate Rosemary Hall for the great help in understanding Jack's early years; David McKean, Tom Putnam, Laurie Austin and Maryrose Grossman of the John F. Kennedy Library and Christopher Peleo-Lazar who did the excellent research there for me.

I also want to thank Phil Griffin, President of MSNBC; *Hardball* executive producer John Reiss; Nancy Nathan, executive producer of *The Chris Matthews Show;* and the committed production teams of both programs.

I want to express my strong gratitude to Jennifer Walsh of William Morris Endeavor for her tremendous professional talent in bringing this project to completion. At Simon & Schuster, I want to thank Nicholas Greene, Jonathan Evans, Nancy Singer, Alexis Welby, Emer Flounders, Rachelle Andujar, Jackie Seow, Elisa Rivlin and Richard Rhorer. Most vital of all, I want to express my esteem for Editor-in-chief Jonathan Karp as editor, friend, pathfinder.

For *Jack Kennedy,* like all the projects and hopes before, I thank Kathleen, to whom this book is dedicated, for forming the loving world in which this project was undertaken and completed.

NOTES

The sources for this book include my interviews for *Kennedy & Nixon,* published in 1996 (Simon & Schuster). In a number of cases — Charlie Bartlett, Ben Bradlee, Ted Sorensen — I returned to the same people for fresh interviews that centered on Jack Kennedy himself. With the passage of time, many of those I interviewed earlier — Billy Sutton, Dave Powers, Mark Dalton, Paul "Red" Fay, George Smathers, and the warmhearted Tip O'Neill — have died. I treasured the opportunity to know them and benefit from their generous accounts of life with Jack. I was able to add to their memories with new interviews with Jean Kennedy Smith, John Glenn, Rachel Mellon, and others.

An extremely powerful resource for this book is the extraordinary collection of taped interviews with Kenneth O'Donnell made available to me by his daughter Helen. I refer to his sourcing as KOD. He was Jack Kennedy's political strategist from the first Senate race in 1952 to the end. He offers a colorful account that gives this book a spine and spring it would not have otherwise. His leads a long list of oral histories (abbreviated herein as "OH"), most of them archived at the John F. Kennedy Library, that cover the man's life from his teenage years onward.

The key documents exhibited in this volume include a binder of chapel notes kept by George St. John, who was headmaster in the years Jack Kennedy attended Choate. Also vital to me are the scribbled and typed notes Theodore H. White kept of his historic interview with Jacqueline Kennedy on the night of November 29, 1963.

A far more expansive source for me is the collection of great books written about John F. Kennedy, works I have come to respect enormously. Each section of this book relies on these remarkable efforts that have come before. Together they provide a scaffold for the new material I have been able to assemble and develop. I want to give full credit to the part these earlier works, some of them truly majestic, played in building the story of Jack Kennedy's rise from rich kid to national hero.

Chapter One: Second Son

The greatest achievement in chronicling Jack's younger years is *JFK: Reckless Youth* (New York: Random House, 1992) by Nigel Hamilton. It is a treasure trove of research up to and including his first political race. He did more than anyone to unearth the great story of Jack and his "Muckers Club" at Choate.

There were two other valued sources for this early chapter. The first is Robert Dallek's *An Unfinished Life: John F. Kennedy, 1917–1963* (Boston: Little, Brown, 2003), which reveals Jack Kennedy's medical history. The second is David Pitts's equally revealing *Jack and Lem: John F. Kennedy and Lem Billings: The Untold Story of an Extraordinary Friendship* (Cambridge, MA: Da Capo Press, 2008), which tells the wondrous story of Kennedy's friendship with LeMoyne Billings, his Choate roommate and lifelong companion. I have relied here as before on Herbert Parmet's *Jack: The Struggles of John F. Kennedy* (New York: Dial Press, 1980). Barbara Leaming alerted me in *Jack Kennedy: The Education of a Statesman* (New York: W. W. Norton, 2006) to the power of Winston Churchill in young Jack's imagination and ambition.

Joseph Kennedy's handsome eldest boy: Parmet, p. 31.

Jack Kennedy, almost as soon as he got to Choate: Examples of JFK's early, wry sense of humor appear in Hamilton, pp. 83–84, 93.

What happened to Jack when: Robert Kennedy's recollection of his brother's illnesses appears in his foreword to the 1964 edition of John F. Kennedy's *Profiles in Courage*

(New York: Harper, 1956), p. 8.

So it was in the sickbed: Reading King Arthur and Sir Walter Scott, Leaming, p. 17.

Leukemia was one of the grim possibilities: Dallek, *An Unfinished Life,* p. 77.

"Ratface": Joan Meyers, ed., *John Fitzgerald Kennedy — As We Remember Him* (New York: Atheneum, 1965), p. 15.

"Gee, you're a great mother": Rose Kennedy, *Times to Remember* (Garden City, NY: Doubleday, 1974), p. 93. Francis Kellogg, a classmate of Jack's, responded to a Choate class survey and wrote: "I remember clearly one thing which surprised me during my four years at Choate: to the best of my knowledge, I do not believe Jack was ever visited during those four years by either his mother or father."

Chilly and restrictive: Choate's English influence, Parmet, p. 29.

Perhaps because he suddenly: JFK's going to church, Hamilton, p. 146.

At night, he knelt next to his bed: David Michaelis, *The Best of Friends: Profiles of Extraordinary Friendships* (New York: Morrow, 1983), p. 137.

He understood, too: Parmet, p. 33.

While at the Catholic school: Leaming, p. 21.

Soon he was getting: Ralph "Rip" Horton, John F. Kennedy Library Oral History Program.

There would come over his face: Maurice A.

Shea, John F. Kennedy Library Oral History Program.

Lem was a big kid: Pitts, p. 8.

With all the strength of: Kennedy and Billings meeting at the *Brief,* Michaelis, p. 132.

He would confide in Lem: LeMoyne Billings, John F. Kennedy Library Oral History Program.

Jack was willing to divulge: Lem's family background, Pitts, p. 9.

"God, what a beating I'm taking": Hamilton, p. 111.

As Joseph Kennedy, Sr., wryly observed: "As Dad liked to say, with some exasperation, Lem Billings and his battered suitcase arrived that day and never really left . . ." This is taken from Edward Kennedy's published eulogy, May 30, 1981.

Next came Ralph: Parmet, p. 34.

The rest followed: Shea OH.

Yet there is another: Story of the "Muckers Club," Hamilton, pp. 122–32.

Troublemaking by kids: Public Enemies Number One and Two, Michaelis, pp. 131–32.

Strategically astute: Muckers as "wheels," Class of 1935 survey conducted in 1985, courtesy of Choate Rosemary Hall Archives. Robert Beach, a classmate of Kennedy's, recalled in a class survey that "the main thesis was that we were such 'wheels' your father couldn't kick us out."

Jack, Lem, and one of the girls: The barn story,

Michaelis, pp. 138–40.

Jack wanted "Most Likely to Succeed": Shea OH.

In this long-ago microcosm: Tip O'Neill with William Novak, *Man of the House: The Life and Political Memoirs of Speaker Tip O'Neill* (New York: Random House, 1987), p. 76.

Headmaster George St. John kept a number of loose-leaf binders over the years containing selected choral hymns and sermon notes. Choate archivist Judy Donald allowed me to study and copy from an early page in the binder that contained the essay written by Dean LeBaron Russell Briggs of Harvard, who was St. John's mentor and lifelong hero. It's from this essay, marked "Dean Briggs Essay," that St. John would recite the "Ask not" lines once or twice a year (more on this in Chapter Thirteen notes).

Tom Hawks, a bank president, was a '35 classmate of Jack's. He wrote in a class survey taken in 1985 how angry he was at hearing those familiar words in Jack's January 20, 1961, inaugural address. "What bugged me most was the way he plagiarized (the Head) in his inaugural address. I boil every time I hear the 'ask not' exhortation as being original with Jack. Time and again we all heard the Head say that to the whole Choate family. Jack did not even have the decency to give him credit — and now it is engraved in marble at his final resting place."

Chapter Two: The Two Jacks

The blood-count roulette: Kennedy's health diminished at Princeton, Hamilton, pp. 144–45.

Back he went to: JFK's stay at Peter Bent Brigham Hospital, Pitts, p. 45.

he spent the remainder: Parmet, p. 43.

Interestingly, he followed: Ibid., p. 159.

Jack's new friend was: Jack and Torby as friends and roommates, Torbert Macdonald, John F. Kennedy Library Oral History Program.

Now at Harvard: JFK placed poorly in Harvard freshman student election, Rose Kennedy, p. 186.

But then he chalked up: Chairman of the Smoker, Macdonald OH.

"It was a leadership activity at Harvard": Said Harvard classmate Jimmy Rousmaniere about the Smoker, Parmet, p. 50.

During his sophomore: Besting Joe Sr. by being accepted to Spee Club, Hamilton, pp. 205–9.

Demonstrating what we might: Joe Sr.'s group of Boston friends as described by Ralph Pope in ibid., p. 207.

According to Joe's tutor: John Kenneth Galbraith said Joe Sr. was "slightly humorless," ibid., p. 165.

And more than that: Observations of JFK's

inquisitive mind at Harvard, Parmet, p. 49.

As Jack started to make: Meeting Lem Billings at the Stork Club, Pitts, p. 48.

Only in his "Gov": Initially only serious about government classes, Hamilton, p. 175.

Before an injury sidelined him: Macdonald practices throwing passes with JFK, Parmet, p. 45.

After spending Jack's freshman year: Pitts, p. 65.

Jack showed himself willing: Ibid., p. 54.

"Hi yah, Hitler!": Dallek, *An Unfinished Life,* p. 51.

His friend even snuck Jack: Description of Macdonald trying to keep JFK in shape for the swim team is detailed in Parmet, p. 47.

Jack knew the valor Britain: As late as May of 1963, Jack Kennedy recited verbatim Churchill's lines about Raymond Asquith, surprising Asquith's sister, Violet Bonham Carter, Leaming, pp. 431–32.

Even in front of them: "decadent," ibid., p. 57.

When the Nazis invaded: Macdonald OH.

"I don't think he really": Macdonald on JFK, Hamilton, p. 242.

"The failure to build up": Parmet, p. 68.

"I do not believe necessarily": John F. Kennedy, *Why England Slept* (New York: W. Funk, 1940), p. xxiii.

Why England Slept: On donating the British royalties, Michael O'Brien, *John F. Kennedy: A Biography* (New York: Thomas Dunne

Books, 2005), p. 105.

"Democracy is finished in England": Joseph P. Kennedy quote, Evan Thomas, *Robert Kennedy: His Life* (New York: Simon & Schuster, 2000), p. 33.

"He loved his youth": John Buchan, *Pilgrim's Way: An Autobiography* (New York: Carroll & Graf, 1984), p. 60.

Chapter Three: Skipper

In this chapter I have relied on the accounts of Jack's navy exploits in Robert Donovan's *PT 109: John F. Kennedy in World War II* (New York: McGraw-Hill, 1961), p. 39.

Look back at Raymond Asquith: On the life and death of Asquith, Buchan, pp. 49–60.

Jack and Lem Billings were: Pitts, p. 83.

In fact, the navy had turned: For a chronology of JFK's struggles to enter the military, the intervention of Joe Sr.'s former London attaché, Captain Alan Kirk, and his entry into Naval Intelligence, Hamilton, pp. 405–6.

His specific distraction: Inga Arvad's background, Doris Kearns Goodwin, *The Fitzgeralds and the Kennedys* (New York: St. Martin's Press, 1987), pp. 729–30.

"Her conversation was miles": Hamilton, pp. 684–85.

"He had the charm that makes birds": Leaming, pp. 122–23.

Struck by the beautiful: Goodwin, pp. 731–32.

They maintained surveillance: FBI surveillance on Inga Arvad, Pitts, p. 85.

Hoover's agents bugged: Pitts, pp. 85–86.

"They shagged my ass back down": Geoffrey Perret, *Jack: A Life Like No Other* (New York: Random House, 2001), p. 98.

Now, more than ever: Goodwin, p. 734. "He had become disgusted with the desk jobs . . . and as an awful lot of the fellows that he knows are in active service, and particularly with you in fleet service, he feels that at least he ought to be trying to do something."

"If you can find something you really believe in": Inga wrote to Jack, Leaming, p. 131.

"I want to go over": Author interview with Paul Ferber.

"I have applied for torpedo boat school": Pitts, pp. 95–96.

Bulkeley was looking: The makeup of the PT officers, Goodwin p. 747.

He and Joe had: Harvard intercollegiate sailing team, O'Brien, *John F. Kennedy,* p. 80.

After they completed: JFK orders to stay stateside, Goodwin, p. 749.

This time, political rescue: Senator David I. Walsh, Dallek, *An Unfinished Life,* p. 89.

Even going at half speed: Goodwin, p. 748.

"I'm rather glad to be on my way": Jack letter to Lem, Pitts, p. 96.

"I had been praising the lord": Ibid., pp. 96–97.

Lieutenant (JG) Kennedy found: United with

fellow officers in South Pacific, Hamilton, p. 534.

"Do you realize that if what you did": Red Fay quote, ibid., p. 516.

One day Bill Battle: Visiting the chaplain, William Battle, John F. Kennedy Library Oral History Program.

"Jack was a big letter writer": Johnny Iles quote, Goodwin, p. 751.

But Jack would join other: Account of going to church near Sesape Island, Donovan, p. 39.

"Getting out every night on patrol": Letter from JFK to parents, Goodwin, p. 752.

"That laugh of his": Red Fay quote, Hamilton, p. 629.

"There was an aura around him": Jim Reed quote, ibid., p. 544.

"Get acquainted with this damn war": JFK to Johnny Iles, ibid., p. 518.

"Just had an inspection by an Admiral": Letter to Inga, Dallek, *An Unfinished Life,* p. 93.

"His back was troubling him, he wasn't well": Jim Reed quote, Hamilton, p. 629.

Jack Kennedy often slept with a plywood board: Johnny Iles quote, ibid., p. 518.

In another officer's: Recalling Jack's corset, Joan and Clay Blair, Jr., *The Search for JFK* (New York: Putnam, 1974), pp. 179–81.

"I've been shafted": Dick Keresey quote, Kennedy Library Panel, June 27, 2005.

"What's the purpose of having the conflict": Red Fay recalled, Hamilton, p. 629.

"We'd sit in a corner and I'd recall": Blair, p. 191.

"He had a way of really picking": Goodwin, p. 752.

"He loved sitting around talking": Hamilton, p. 543.

There were twelve crewmen: Description of Jack's command vessel, thirteen men including JFK on *PT-109,* Donovan, p. 128.

"Lenny, look at this": JFK tells executive officer, ibid., p. 210.

"Sound general quarters!": JFK quote, ibid., p. 212.

"Who's aboard?": JFK quote, Goodwin, p. 758.

"You go on": Pappy McMahon quote, Hamilton, p. 578.

When dawn came: Goodwin, p. 759.

Each man was well aware: Japanese treatment of prisoners, Donovan, p. 160.

"There's nothing in the book": Maguire account, ibid., p. 158.

Their skipper's solution: Ibid., p. 162.

"The rest of you can swim together": Ibid., p. 162.

As McMahon floated on his back: McMahon's account of JFK saving his life, ibid., p. 166.

Plum Pudding Island: Ross description, Hamilton, p. 582.

And when he went to stand: Vomiting source, Donovan, p. 165.

"George Ross has lost his life": Red Fay's pre-

maturely eulogizing JFK, ibid., pp. 169–70.

"The next morning we heard": Jim Reed quote, Hamilton, pp. 575–76.

"How are we going to": JFK quote, Donovan, p. 170.

Hanging his .38 pistol: Going on patrol, ibid., p. 172.

Kennedy reached his destination: Out on patrol, ibid., p. 177.

He arrived at noontime: Ibid., p. 177.

"Barney, you try it tonight": Ibid., p. 177.

The day after that: Ibid., p. 181.

There, they came upon: Finding canoe, water, crackers, Goodwin, p. 760.

Exhausted, Ross fell asleep: Hamilton, pp. 587–88.

This time he was greeted: Donovan, p. 191.

NAURO ISL NATIVE: Goodwin, p. 760.

"On His Majesty's Service": Ibid., p. 761.

"As a captain": Dick Keresey quote, Keresey, "Farthest Forward," *American Heritage* 49, no. 4 (July/August 1998).

Jack had his own account: Letter to Inga, Hamilton, pp. 616–17.

"proven himself on foreign soil": Hometown booster quote, Red Fay, *The Pleasure of His Company* (New York: Harper & Row, 1966), pp. 156–57.

"On the bright side": Letter from JFK to his parents, Hamilton, p. 611.

"We have been having a difficult time": Letter from JFK to Lem, Pitts, p. 99.

At the same time he got off a letter: Jack letter to Lem's mother, ibid.

Before leaving the South Pacific: Describe getting crew members back to States, Hamilton, p. 646.

"chronic disc disease": Thomas Fleming, "John F. Kennedy's PT-109 Disaster," *Military History Quarterly,* February 8, 2011.

"His skin had turned yellow": Macdonald description, Hamilton, p. 655.

"extremely heroic conduct": Parmet, p. 121.

"That wound was a savage wound": Ibid., p. 122.

"I'll never forget Jack sitting": Spalding quote, Hamilton, p. 640.

That August, Joe Jr. was killed: Ibid., pp. 659–60.

Jack, up at Hyannis Port: Ibid., p. 662.

"clenching and unclenching his fists": Ibid., p. 660.

A month later, another terrible: Leaming, pp. 161–62.

"greatest campaign manager": Author interview with Billy Sutton.

Chapter Four: War Hero

This chapter benefits from a diary Jack Kennedy kept of his travels through Europe in 1945 and the early weeks of his race for Congress. It was published and edited by Deirdre Henderson as *Prelude to Leadership: The European Diary of John F. Kennedy, Summer*

1945 (Washington, DC: Regnery, 1995). The jotted-down notes contained here are priceless clues to Jack's postwar thinking, also a wonderful clue to his studious approach to his new career in politics. I cite it as *Diary*.

The topic is Jack Kennedy's first race for Congress. Here again, as in preceding chapters, I have relied on Nigel Hamilton's remarkable reporting.

"It was written all over the sky": Hamilton, p. 543.

"I think there was probably a serious side to Kennedy": Ibid., p. 623.

All of the other old troubles continued: Parmet, p. 151.

Curley, now, was about to abandon: Joe Sr. used former Boston police chief Joseph Timilty as his go-between, Hamilton, p. 674.

His father wrangled him a job: Parmet, p. 131.

"from the point of view of the ordinary GI": Diary, p. 85.

"I'm not talking about Bohlen": Author interview with Paul Fay.

"We must face the truth that the people": JFK letter to war buddies, Arthur M. Schlesinger, Jr., *A Thousand Days: John F. Kennedy in the White House* (Boston: Houghton Mifflin, 1965), p. 88.

"Either wittingly or unwittingly": Hamilton, p. 703.

"He asked every sort of question": Barbara

Ward Jackson, John F. Kennedy Library Oral History Program.

"We have suffered the loss of nearly 8 hundred thousand young men": Diary, p. 3.

"The clash may be finally and indefinitely postponed": Ibid., pp. 7–8.

"Mr. Roosevelt has contributed greatly to the end of Capitalism": Ibid., p. 10.

"People did not realize what was going on in the concentration camps": Ibid., p. 58.

But he predicted the Red Army's treatment: Ibid., p. 56.

"scared the hell out": Hamilton, p. 722.

"He made me speak into it": Horton OH.

"I've made up my mind": Hamilton, p. 689.

"He was never pushed off": Ibid., pp. 702–3.

"A lot of stories have been written": Ibid., p. 673.

When Jack asked Torby Macdonald: Macdonald OH.

"I tell you, Dad is ready right now": Hamilton, p. 679.

"Although Jack shammed indifference": Fay, pp. 2–4.

"I had never lived very much in the district": Presidential recordings, John F. Kennedy Library.

"He was very clear about his decision": Charles Bartlett, John F. Kennedy Library Oral History Program.

"A reporter is reporting what happens": Presidential recordings, John F. Kennedy Library.

Writing his stump speech himself: Ibid. "The first speech I ever gave was on 'England, Ireland, and Germany: Victor, Neutral, and Vanquished.' It took me three weeks to write and was given at an American Legion post."

"For all Irish immigrants": Ibid.

"I had in politics, to begin with": Ibid.

"Says I'll be murdered": Diary, pp. 79–80.

In politics you don't have friends: Ibid., p. 80.

"The one great failure of American government is the government of critics": Ibid., p. 83.

The shrewd first hire was Billy Sutton: Billy Sutton, John F. Kennedy Library Oral History Program.

The person most surprised by this was his father: Goodwin, p. 828.

The fact that he was a returning: Dave Powers in the Flying Tigers, Bart Barnes, "JFK Aide David Francis Powers Dies at 85," *Washington Post,* March 28, 1998.

"I think I know how you feel": Jack's appearance before a group of Gold Star Mothers, Goodwin, p. 823.

Not surprisingly, the daily slog of introducing: Sutton OH.

"I couldn't believe this skinny": O'Neill, p. 73.

"wasn't looking healthy": Sutton int.

"skeleton": Mark Dalton description of JFK, Hamilton, pp. 747–48.

"My father thought I was hopeless": John F. Kennedy's January 5, 1960, interview with Ben Bradlee.

"This impatience that he passed on": Spalding quote, Hamilton, p. 690.

"even though I was a Republican": Red Fay quote, ibid., p. 745.

"My God": JFK had forgotten to file his nomination papers, Fay, p. 147.

Kennedy pulled off other escapades: Joe Russo newspaper ad, *Boston* magazine, June 1993.

Tip O'Neill recalled a far more daunting: O'Neill, p. 77. "During the campaign, the Kennedys flooded the district with copies of that article [John Hersey's on *PT-109*] and sent reprints to every returning veteran. Using the mails to send out campaign literature was a new and expensive proposition. Normally, a volunteer would give it out on the street or hang a flyer on your door. Naturally, the Hersey article served as a good reminder that only one of the candidates has much of a war record."

Jack's father and mother: Tea party at Hotel Commander, Goodwin, p. 830.

Kennedy was starting: O'Neill, p. 76. "Jack Kennedy, of course, was a Democrat. But looking back on his congressional campaign, and on his later campaigns for the Senate and then for the presidency, I'd have to say that he was only nominally a Democrat. He was a Kennedy, which was more than a family affiliation. It quickly developed into an entire political party, with its own people, its own agenda, and its own strategies."

"He was probably the first": Hamilton, p. 756.

"I guess I'm the only one": Peter Collier and David Horowitz, *The Kennedys: An American Drama* (New York: Summit Books, 1984), p. 153.

"Womanpower": O'Neill, p. 78.

"They would scream": Fay quote, Hamilton, p. 767.

"My chief opponents": Presidential recordings, John F. Kennedy Library.

"We were constantly": Reardon quote, Hamilton, p. 757.

"Remember, we were all": Billings quote, ibid., p. 769.

"fighting conservative": Diary, p. 10.

"What about Communism?": Hamilton, p. 774.

Chapter Five: Cold Warrior

Jack Kennedy knew well before: Parmet, p. 147.

Besides, he'd formed: Joseph P. Healey, John F. Kennedy Oral History Program. "I know he had felt a particularly warm regard and feeling for Senator Saltonstall, who had been very helpful to him in his years in Washington."

"Don't you think": Sutton OH.

"Stop 'n' Shop": Sutton int.

Richard Nixon had just beaten: Roger Morris, *Richard Milhous Nixon: The Rise of an American Politician* (New York: Holt, 1990), p. 293.

"So you're the guy": Sutton int.

"How's it feel?": Ibid.

"John wanted to know": Author interview with Mark Dalton.

"People have always said": Ibid.

"Listen to this fellow": Ibid.

"I'd like you to meet Richard Nixon of California": Ibid.

In the coming years Jack would be: Author interview with Ambassador Jean Kennedy Smith.

" 'Kennedy is courageous' ": Mark Dalton, John F. Kennedy Library Oral History Program.

"I told him that day": Sutton OH.

"You can imagine": Dalton OH.

McKeesport debate: *McKeesport Daily News,* April 17 and 25, 1947; July 21, 1960.

"So many people said": Mary Davis, John F. Kennedy Library Oral History Program.

"And then I remember": Kay Halle, John F. Kennedy Library Oral History Program.

"He was very particular": Sutton OH.

"I would say that": Davis OH.

"I got a call from": Healey OH.

"I guess I'm going": Ibid.

"My strong reaction": Parmet, p. 183.

"lived for some ten years": Healey OH.

"Curley was crooked": Author conversation with Thomas P. O'Neill, Jr.

"I don't know whether": Edmund S. Muskie, John F. Kennedy Library Oral History Program.

"I'm going to debate": Dalton int.

"I was never so": Davis OH.

"At the hearing": Author interview with Timothy J. "Ted" Reardon.

"He was not feeling well": Davis OH.

"Emaciated!": Author interview with George Smathers.

For a bon voyage: Jonathan Aitken, *Nixon: A Life* (London: Weidenfeld and Nicolson, 1993), p. 136.

"That American friend": Leaming, p. 192.

On those nights: Davis OH.

"He was someone": Ibid.

"Thinking about girls": Sutton int.

"He did have a lot": Davis OH.

"He used to enjoy": Bartlett OH.

Confiding that he voted: Ted Sorensen, *Counselor: A Life at the Edge of History* (New York: Harper, 2008), pp. 146–47. Ted Sorensen reveals that in *Profiles in Courage* Kennedy was referring to Smathers and "decided, for reasons of senatorial courtesy, not to identify in his opening chapter the name of the fellow senator 'who acknowledged to him one day during a roll call that he voted with the special interests on every issue, hoping that, by election, all of them added together would constitute nearly a majority that would remember him favorably while the other members of the public would never know about it, much less remember his vote against their welfare.' I see no reason for anonymity now: It was his close friend, the late Senator George Smathers of Florida. Maybe Smathers was joking when he said that; maybe not."

"because he doesn't give a damn": Bartlett OH.

"deeply preoccupied by death": Smathers int.

"Quick": Ibid.

"It was a bright, shining day": Reardon int.

"Unless I'm very mistaken": Joseph W. Alsop, John F. Kennedy Library Oral History Program.

"He used to turn green": Ibid.

Billy Sutton recalls: Sutton OH.

"Did you ever read": Dalton OH.

"As I look back": Ibid.

"Another day I can": Ibid.

"He was in terrible pain": Goodwin, pp. 742–44.

"He always heard the footsteps": Collier and Horowitz, pp. 207–9.

One of those who thrilled: Kenny O'Donnell background, Thomas, p. 50.

"took on the American Legion": KOD.

"When we've got the map": Kenneth P. O'Donnell and David F. Powers with Joe McCarthy, *"Johnny, We Hardly Knew Ye": Memories of John Fitzgerald Kennedy* (Boston: Little, Brown, 1973), pp. 77–79.

"the Russians, by their actions": General Lucius D. Clay quote, Perret, p. 156.

Back home, the pursuit: Nixon's exposure of

Hiss, account of Hiss case, drawn from Stephen E. Ambrose, *Nixon: Volume I: The Education of a Politician 1913–1962* (New York: Simon & Schuster, 1987), pp. 169–72, and Allen Weinstein, *Perjury: The Hiss-Chambers Case* (New York: Random House, 1997), pp. 5–7.

For denying that: Parmet, p. 245. In February 1952, a speaker at an anniversary evening at Kennedy's Harvard club told the gathered alumni how proud he was that their college had never produced "a Joseph McCarthy or an Alger Hiss." Kennedy jumped to his feet. "How dare you couple the name of a great American patriot with that of a traitor!" Angry, he left the dinner early.

"The responsibility for the failure": Congressional Record, January 29, 1949.

"a sick Roosevelt": Parmet, p. 210.

"Isn't this something": Bill Arnold, *Back When It All Began: The Early Nixon Years* (New York: Vantage Press, 1975), p. 14.

Jack wanted what Nixon now had: George Smathers, John F. Kennedy Library Oral History Program. "I think Jack was that competitive. When I won, he figured he could do it. And at the same time in 1950 when I won my race — my big race was in the primary in May — Nixon ran for the Senate in California against Helen Gahagan Douglas. . . . And I think all of that worked on Jack and started him with the idea that when the time came he would run."

"This rivalry developed": Dalton OH.

"I think the thing": Sutton OH.

"I'm up or out": Lawrence O'Brien, *No Final Victories: A Life in Politics — from John F. Kennedy to Watergate* (Garden City, NY: Doubleday, 1974), p. 17.

"I'm going to use": Smathers int.

Chapter Six: Bobby

Whichever happened: Healey OH. Joseph Healey: "I remember him saying to me flatly that regardless of what was going to happen in terms of what the then incumbent governor of Massachusetts, Paul Dever, was planning to do, that he was not going to run for another term as congressman. He said to me one day, and I think that these are his exact words, 'I would rather run for governor or the Senate and lose and take the shot, than to go back and serve another term as congressman.'"

"I've decided not to run": O'Neill, p. 105.

"pain in the ass": Collier and Horowitz, p. 155.

As Jack traveled with his brother: Schlesinger, *A Thousand Days,* p. 120.

More important: Getting to know RFK on Indochina trip, Arthur M. Schlesinger, Jr., *Robert Kennedy and His Times* (Boston: Houghton Mifflin, 1978), pp. 90–93.

As Jack was flown from Tokyo: Addison's complications and evacuation to Okinawa,

612

Collier and Horowitz, p. 156, and Bobby Kennedy's foreword, *Profiles in Courage,* pp. xv–xvi.

"worms": Referring to members in Congress, O'Brien, *No Final Victories,* p. 17.

He'd already begun spending: KOD.

"if he was going to get anywhere": Charles Spalding, John F. Kennedy Library Oral History Program.

"So, I think, he made": Ibid.

When I was in Boston last week: Meet the Press, December 2, 1951.

"You can never defeat the Communist": Ibid.

"unconscious of the fact": Boston Globe, November 20, 1951.

The very first recruit: O'Brien, *No Final Victories,* pp. 11–14.

One day on Capitol Hill: Ibid., p. 18. ". . . [O]n a Sunday in March we had dinner at Kelly's Lobster House in nearby Holyoke. Kennedy was not long in getting to the point. 'Larry, I'm not going to stay in the House,' he told me. 'I'm not challenged there. It's up or out for me. I'm definitely going to run for state-wide office next year. I don't know many people in western Massachusetts and I'd like your help.' 'What are you running for?' I asked. 'I don't know yet,' he admitted. 'I want to run against Lodge, but if Dever makes that race I'll run for governor.'"

Larry O'Brien: "Republicans were respectable.

Republicans didn't get thrown in jail like Jim Curley . . . ," ibid., p. 29.

"Larry, I don't look forward": Ibid., p. 27.

"For the Kennedys": Jack Newfield, *Robert Kennedy: A Memoir* (New York: Dutton, 1969), p. 42.

"He called me and said": KOD.

"lace-curtain": Ibid.

"He started getting our attention": Ibid.

"Lodge, killing off Walsh": Ibid.

Mark Dalton: Campaign manager of 1946, O'Brien, *John F. Kennedy,* p. 193.

Therefore, the first thing: KOD. O'Donnell: "I had said to Dalton, look we need to name a secretary or leader in each community to be a Kennedy man and then that person can form committees and set up events, but we can't be sitting in this office doing it from 10 Post Office Square. Well, Mark Dalton would not even ask either the father or candidate if we could begin to do it, he was too afraid of them. I had nobody to get any action from. I would tell this [to] Dalton, Dalton would agree and say he would ask the old man or Jack, but he never would. He'd go to Morrissey, who'd bury it and nothing ever happened."

He wouldn't fire Dalton: Dalton OH. "The major thing at the time which came as a very grave disappointment and a very grave blow to me was that a release had been prepared by John Galvin announcing that I was the campaign manager of John Kennedy's campaign for the Senate. John Kennedy never spoke to me, but John Kennedy would not issue that release."

If Dalton was too weak: KOD. "I had told Bobby you got to come up here, this is just chaos. Dalton can't handle it, he's got to go and you've got to take over."

"We arrived at the Ritz": Healey OH.

a smart combination: The teas, Parmet, p. 250.

As David Powers would note: KOD. Dave Powers, as said to Sander Vanocur, saw that "the success of these receptions was because the only thing these poor working ever get in the mail was a bill. He said when some of these people got an invitation to have tea with the Kennedys, they were amazed. It was great, because these are all very poor people."

"You're talking two or three": Ibid.

X-rays taken of Jack's spine: X-rays are available for December 14, 1944, and November 6, 1950, medical records of Dr. Janet Travell at the John F. Kennedy Library.

"I must say": Bartlett OH.

"The whole operation": KOD.

"I knew the Kennedys well enough": Ibid.

He phoned Bobby: Ibid.

Bobby hated what: Ibid. "He [Bobby] had no intention of coming up. He gave me the devil. He was really mad, he wanted me to do it, but it had to be him. It had to be someone with the authority to take on the father."

Now that Bobby seemingly: Ibid. In a car ride meeting in mid-April, "he [Kennedy] threw Frank Morrissey out of the car . . . it was Bob Kennedy, the congressman, and myself and I had really, this was the closest I'd really seen him, in my life to this moment, or had substantive discussion with him. I recollect he was irritated and as I look back I think he was irritated because he felt I had in a sense been telling tales out of school to his brother, who was reporting to his father, perhaps instead of telling him, who I really worked for."

"As far as I'm concerned": Ibid.

"That was the day that Bobby": Ibid.

"Bobby, as I recall": Ibid.

"He got in the car": Dalton int.

"He didn't like the building": KOD.

"I decided that I could": Dalton OH.

"I didn't become involved": Schlesinger, *Robert Kennedy and His Times,* p. 94.

This was, just for the record: Bobby's work on 1946 campaign, ibid., p. 64.

"Yes, Dad": Thomas, p. 60.

"Our secretaries were making": O'Brien, *No Final Victories,* p. 36.

At their April 6 meeting: KOD.

"Lodge was always on the popular side": Horton OH.

"Lodge's Dodges": Ted Reardon took down

616

the leather loose-leaf binder from the top shelf of his closet to show me it. It was nearly a half century since it had been put to very good political use.

"The major credit belongs": Healey OH.

"Any decision you wanted": KOD.

"How much money": Ibid.

"Don't give in to them": Ibid.

"Nobody went to one": Ibid.

"The 'tea party' technique": Fraser OH.

The reason, according to O'Donnell: KOD.

"We appreciated the fact": Ibid.

"We'd be in those homes": Ibid.

"kicked the living hell": Matthews, p. 88.

Here Joe Kennedy: Ibid., p. 87.

"buy a fuckin'": Ibid.

"100 percent": Ibid.

"Well, for Christ's sake": Alastair Forbes, John F. Kennedy Oral History Program.

"I told them I'd go up": William F. Buckley, Jr., *Boston Sunday Globe,* September 30, 1962.

"Dear Dick: I was tremendously": Letter courtesy of Richard M. Nixon Library and Birthplace.

"was the man": Parmet, p. 250.

"a Joseph McCarthy or an Alger Hiss": Ibid., p. 245.

"You and your . . . sheeny friends": Ibid., p. 251. Transcript, Mutual Broadcasting Network, February 6, 1951, Pre-Presidential Papers, Box 95, John F. Kennedy Library.

"He didn't have to": O'Neill, p. 119.

"the Rabbi": Parmet, p. 248.
"You can't stop a whispering": KOD.
"They have problems": Ibid.
In October he made: Ibid.
"He was in intense pain": John Galvin, John F. Kennedy Oral History Program.
"handsomest": United Press International report in *Boston Globe,* July 2, 1952.
"'It looks like Eisenhower's'": Macdonald OH.
"John Barry, a well-known writer": KOD.
"Well, all hell broke loose": Ibid.
"Finally, he got so frustrated": Ibid.
"That guy must never sleep": Robert Caro, John F. Kennedy Oral History Program.
"The senator-elect got up": KOD.

Chapter Seven: Magic

"Mary, now don't be silly": O'Neill, pp. 117–18.
"They were all experienced": Davis OH.
"If you work for a politician": O'Brien, *No Final Victories,* p. 40.
"I'd go down to his office": Smathers OH.
"His mind was on bigger things": Ibid.
"ability to write in clear": Sorensen, *Counselor,* p. 96.
"Jack had the ability": Reardon int.
"he was soft on Senator Joe McCarthy": Sorensen, *Counselor,* pp. 98–99.
"He was much the same": Ibid., pp. 102–3.
"Few could realize": Ibid., p. 109.
"During my first year": Ibid., pp. 103–4.
"I do not remember": Ibid., p. 102.

"The thing to remember": Author interview with Charles Bartlett.

"Black Jack" Bouvier: Leaming, pp. 4–5.

Jackie, who'd spent: Ibid., pp. 5–8.

While he was wooing her: Ibid., pp. 8–9.

"Jack appreciated her": Dallek, *An Unfinished Life*, p. 193.

"Jackie was certainly very": Forbes OH.

"There was this beautiful girl": Bartlett int.

"Well, she knew what": Ibid.

"I gave everything a good deal": Fay, p. 160.

In fact, with an eye: O'Donnell and Powers, p. 95.

"They haven't seen you since": KOD.

"I said, 'God, she's a fantastic-looking woman' ": Red Fay, John F. Kennedy Oral History Program.

"Almost across the street from": Fay, p. 152.

"I want to tell you": Ibid., p. 153.

"Torby Macdonald stood up": Fay OH.

"There were only a few political": KOD.

"She was terribly young": Pitts, p. 137.

Chuck Spalding had his own telling: Spalding OH.

"This would be a helluva": Thomas Reeves, *A Question of Character: A Life of John F. Kennedy* (New York: Free Press, 1991), p. 114.

"When Jack and Jacqueline": Fay, p. 151.

"they spoiled him": Bartlett int.

"He saw her as a kindred spirit": Collier and Horowitz, p. 233. Based on interview with Lem Billings.

Chapter Eight: Survival

"The story circulated": KOD.

"I knew Jack was serious": O'Neill, p. 90.

"After he had been in the Senate": Sorensen, *Counselor,* p. 145.

Kennedy had come upon accounts: John Quincy Adams story, Kennedy, *Profiles in Courage,* 29–50.

"If we do not stand firm": Remarks of Senator John F. Kennedy at Boston College, Chestnut Hill, Massachusetts, February 1, 1953.

He also challenged the Republicans': Parmet, p. 282. "Under these circumstances, we must ask how the new [Secretary of State Jim Foster] Dulles policy and its dependence upon the threat of atomic retaliation will fare in these areas of guerilla warfare. At what point would the threat of atomic weapons be used in the struggles in Southeast Asia — in French Indochina — particularly where the chief burden is carried on the one side by native communists and on the other by the troops of a Western power, which once held the country under colonial rule?"

"To pour money, material": JFK speech on the Senate floor, April 6, 1954.

"My good friends": Joseph R. McCarthy in response to Edward R. Murrow, CBS, April 6, 1954.

"The reason why we find": Joseph R. McCarthy speech, Wheeling, West Virginia, February

9, 1950.

"not fit to wear that uniform": McCarthy quote, Zwicker hearing, February 1954.

A close friend of Bobby's: Sorensen, *Counselor,* p. 152.

"Senator McCarthy and Mr. Cohn": Schlesinger, *Robert Kennedy and His Times,* p. 113.

"He was told to sit down": KOD.

"political suicide": Ibid.

"to avoid the vote": Ibid.

"I was in the Bellevue bar": Ibid.

"JFK knew that if he voted": Sorensen, *Counselor,* p. 152.

According to the historian: Dallek, *An Unfinished Life,* p. 196. "He could not bend down to pull a sock on his left foot and he had to climb and descend stairs moving sideways."

"I don't understand Jack's": Bartlett int.

"This is the one that kills": O'Brien, *No Final Victories,* p. 45.

"They said the best thing": Galvin OH.

"empty suit": Sorensen, *Counselor,* pp. 127–28.

" 'sometimes party asks' ": Ibid.

Late that summer: KOD.

"Furcolo told him": Ibid.

"We'd been building up": Ibid.

On October 10: Dallek, *An Unfinished Life,* p. 196.

"I kept pushing and": KOD.

"the only wrong political move": Powers and O'Donnell, pp. 85–86.

The back operation: Dallek, *An Unfinished Life,*

p. 196.

The odds made by the political wise guys: KOD.

"the doctors didn't expect him": Evelyn Lincoln notes.

"That poor young man is going to die": Conversation with Rex Scouten, Aitken, p. 137.

"The doctors don't understand": Evelyn Lincoln notes.

"The tenor of his voice": KOD.

"feared the wrath": Sorensen, *Counselor,* p. 154.

"You know, when I get downstairs": Parmet, p. 310.

Junior Chamber of Commerce dinner: Schlesinger, *Robert Kennedy and His Times,* pp. 115–16.

When the senator died: Ibid., p. 173.

"In January 1955, Bobby": Fay, p. 159.

Oil painting and Monopoly: JFK's oil painting described, Rose Kennedy, p. 127; Monopoly playing, Jean Kennedy Smith int.

"I think we hit it off": Peter Lawford, John F. Kennedy Oral History Program.

"I don't think anybody ever": Ibid.

"He was really ill": Ibid.

"He was enormously well read": Fraser OH.

"I think the whole concept": Bartlett OH.

"Kennedy played an especially serious role": Sorensen, *Counselor,* p. 146.

The theme and the bulk: Ibid., p. 38.

nowhere as well read: Author interview with

Ted Sorensen.

"Where else, in a non-totalitarian society": Kennedy, *Profiles in Courage,* p. 7.

the prospect of forced retirement: Ibid.

"One senator, since retired": Sorensen, *Counselor,* pp. 146–47.

"He must have been getting": Ormsby-Gore quote, Lord Harlech, John F. Kennedy Oral History Program.

"Shut that door!": Martin Dowd interview.

"Larry and I got a call": KOD.

Chapter Nine: Debut

Onions was a John McCormack guy: Parmet, pp. 347–51, 354.

For Jack to woo: Ibid.

"Anybody who's for Stevenson": O'Donnell and Powers, p. 109.

"You're either going to get": Schlesinger, *Robert Kennedy and His Times,* p. 131.

"We argued that Onions shouldn't be allowed": O'Brien, *No Final Victories,* p. 50.

"He and his millions": Parmet, pp. 347–51, 354.

To camouflage the effort: Ibid., p. 359.

"You know, about the Catholic vote": Finnegan quote, Sorensen, *Counselor,* p. 160.

The applause in the hall: Parmet, p. 356.

"I didn't even know Senator Kennedy existed": Edmund Reggie, John F. Kennedy Oral History Program.

Kennedy and Sorensen then: Parmet, p. 359.

The knock on Vice President: Ibid., p. 372.

"Call Dad and tell him I'm going for it": Schlesinger, *Robert Kennedy and His Times,* p. 132.

Bellowing what an "idiot": Joe Sr. to Jack, O'Donnell and Powers, p. 140.

"Just talk about the war stuff": Smathers int.

"If we have to have": Parmet, p. 362.

"America is not ready": Schlesinger, *Robert Kennedy and His Times,* p. 132.

"troubled": Eleanor Roosevelt quote, Matthews, p. 108.

"My name is Mary Jones": KOD.

"After Stevenson had thrown": Bartlett OH.

"Texas proudly casts its fifty-six": Robert Dallek, *Lyndon B. Johnson: Portrait of a President* (New York: Oxford University Press, 2004), p. 96.

"I'm going to sing 'Dixie'": JFK quote, Collier and Horowitz, p. 181.

"The second ballot was already under way": Reeves, p. 466.

"He's not our kind of folks": Oklahoma governor quote, Sorensen, *Kennedy,* p. 89.

"He hated to lose anything": O'Donnell and Powers, p. 142.

"I've learned that you don't": JFK quote, ibid., p. 144.

"It was too damned close": Kennedy interview with Ben Bradlee, January 5, 1960.

"Magic": Nickname given to Jack by Jackie, Parmet, p. 194.

"She wasn't the carefree": Pitts, p. 142.

Chapter Ten: Charm

"Kefauver has never done": Stevenson to Schlesinger, Arthur M. Schlesinger, *Journals: 1952–2000* (New York: Penguin Press, 2007), p. 8.

"I know I'll never be more": JFK to Fay, Perret, p. 238.

"For Christmas that year": Sorensen, *Counselor,* p. 172.

"The smaller states": Ibid.

"It was more than a list": Ibid., p. 175.

"When we said good-bye": Ibid., p. 174.

"Those early trips were": Ibid., p. 178.

Many of their stops: Ibid.

By late 1959: KOD.

"My main job, in those early months": O'Brien, No Final Victories, p. 60.

"I introduced myself as a representative": Ibid.

"I paid a courtesy call": Ibid., p. 61.

"Senator Kennedy has every": Ibid., pp. 61–62.

"As I moved from state": Ibid., p. 62.

"I don't think anybody realizes": Bartlett OH.

"He was urged to accept": Sorensen, *Counselor,* p. 160.

"As hard as it is": Ibid., pp. 186–87.

Kennedy's physical condition: Medical records of Janet Travell at the John F. Kennedy Library.

For everything that ailed him: For a list of Kennedy's treatments in 1955, see Dallek, *An Unfinished Life,* pp. 212–13.

The cortisone he took: Sutton int. More than

save his life, the cortisone he had taken during the 1950s had transformed his face, fleshing out his features until they coalesced into the radiant handsomeness, the familiar JFK image, that would linger in the nation's fantasy years later. Billy Sutton, who had lived with Kennedy those early years in Washington, would remark that he never looked better than he did in those months of running for president against Richard Nixon.

"In the late 1950's": Sorensen, *Counselor,* p. 106.

"In retrospect, it is amazing": Ibid.

"On the political circuit": Ibid.

"best suited to fanatics, egomaniacs": Ibid., p. 187.

It was still the age: Dallek, *An Unfinished Life,* p. 225.

"Senator Kennedy, do you have": Ralph Martin and Ed Plaut, *Front Runner, Dark Horse* (Garden City, NY: Doubleday, 1960), pp. 461–62.

"You could go to the A&P Store": Hubert Humphrey, John F. Kennedy Oral History Program.

While the stillbirth: Pitts, pp. 150–52.

"to promote Senator John F. Kennedy as a man of intensive": Sorensen, *Counselor,* p. 145.

"Careful spadework": Rose Kennedy quote, Laurence Leamer, *The Kennedy Women: The Saga of an American Family* (New York: Vil-

lard Books, 1994), p. 467.

"who was on the committee": Ibid.

"Things don't happen": Ibid.

"The most powerful single force": JFK on Senate floor, July 2, 1957.

"The war in Algeria": "Facing Facts on Algeria" speech, p. 3.

In the same year he gave: Taylor Branch, *Parting the Waters: America in the King Years, 1954–63* (New York: Simon & Schuster, 1988), p. 221.

"Well, I wondered why more people": Forbes OH.

"always greatly interested": Smathers OH.

"I remember very late": Forbes OH.

July 19 — Jack Kennedy called up around noon: Schlesinger, *Journals,* p. 56.

"I think he genuinely thinks he was wrong about it": Ibid., p. 58.

"All his golfing pals are rich men he has met since 1945": Ibid.

"He won't stand by anybody": Ibid.

"No one who has Addison's disease ought to run for President": Ibid.

The Senate Select Committee: Schlesinger, *Robert Kennedy and His Times,* pp. 147–60.

"If the investigation flops": O'Donnell and Powers, p. 132.

The result of this rout: KOD. On the 1958 elevating of O'Donnell and O'Brien in eyes of Joe Sr.: "We had had some disagreements with him during the campaign. Mr. Ken-

nedy has never been noted for his willingness to brook disagreements from someone
whom he considered young kids who are
hardly wet behind the ears. In addition, his
sources of information about our conduct
during the campaign had not always been
friendly to us . . . The test had always been
the score at the end of the game as far as he
was concerned . . . He was very profuse in
his congratulations to both of us. He could
not have been warmer, kinder, or more
grateful now that everything had turned
out."

The Rackets Committee managed: Schlesinger,
Robert Kennedy and His Times, pp. 147–60.

"Would you tell us anything": RFK interrogates
Giancana, ibid., p. 165.

"We shall not flag or fail": RFK banner, Thomas,
p. 83.

*"John F. Kennedy had clearly done his home-
work":* Pierre Salinger, John F. Kennedy
Library Oral History Program.

*"was not only good in terms of defending the
union":* KOD.

"I think that his performance": Muskie OH.

"the Presidency is the source of action": Kennedy Transcript, January 5, 1960, Bradlee,
16.

The image remains suspended: Photo of RFK
and JFK in the Rackets Committee, courtesy of John F. Kennedy Library.

Jack Kennedy made few new personal friends:

Ben Bradlee, *Conversations with Kennedy* (New York: Norton, 1975), p. 21.

"Nothing in my education": Ben Bradlee, *A Good Life: Newspapering and Other Adventures* (New York: Simon & Schuster, 1995), p. 206.

"the mines": Ibid.

Chapter Eleven: Hardball

Ken O'Donnell's oral history provides the dominant source for the Kennedy presidential campaign's hardball tactics. It gives a strategist's look at the methods used to organize what was a breakthrough political effort. Where not otherwise identified, this chapter is based on O'Donnell's account.

"Together, the two of them": O'Neill, p. 86.

"There's nothing there in 1960": Bartlett OH.

" 'wounded tiger' ": Salinger OH.

It was Salinger's first exposure: Ibid. "John F. Kennedy had the exterior façade of such an easygoing nature, and yet with this one remark he revealed something to me that I was later to find in him in other situations."

"At Palm Beach, the senator was in full command": Sorensen, *Kennedy,* p. 120.

"The truth of the matter is that Brown": Frederick Dutton, John F. Kennedy Library Oral History Program.

"There was no bullshit to the man": Author interview with Pat Brown.

"His complete familiarity with California politics": Dutton OH.

"Mike, it's time to shit or get off the pot": Dallek, *An Unfinished Life,* p. 247, from Abraham Ribicoff Oral History, Columbia University.

"just another pretty boy": Ben Bradlee, *Conversations with Kennedy,* pp. 17–18.

"I always had a feeling": Bartlett int.

"He hated the liberals": Author interview with Ben Bradlee.

"You have no idea": Author interview with Joan Gardner.

"did make it out there": Ralph Martin, *A Hero for Our Time: An Intimate Story of the Kennedy Years* (New York: Macmillan, 1983), p. 221.

"I worked with him on the Hill": Ibid.

"Had dinner with Jack and Jackie": Bartlett int.

The official handout opened: Candidate's biography that was stapled to prepared remarks, courtesy of John F. Kennedy Library.

"I asked him what he considered": Schlesinger, *Journals,* p. 63.

"You think I'm out here": Reeves, *A Question of Character,* p. 159.

Hubert Humphrey: Robert Caro, *Master of the Senate* (New York: Knopf, 2002), p. xiii.

"He was campaigning": Author interview with Governor Pat Lucey.

"effective presentation of a celebrity": Patrick Lucey Oral History, John F. Kennedy Library.

Using Lou Harris's polling data: Author interview with Louis Harris.

"Shall I wear this blue overcoat?" Bartlett OH.

"I have great respect for the Polish people": Fay, p. 17.

Probably his most famous stunt: Craig Shirley, *Rendezvous with Destiny: Ronald Reagan and the Campaign that Changed America* (Wilmington: ISI Books, 2009), p. 424.

"On the day Wisconsin voters went to the polls": Bradlee, *Conversations,* pp. 16–17.

thousand-dollar contribution he'd delivered from his father: Arnold, p. 21. A March 3, 1960, note from Rose Mary Woods to Vice President Nixon recalls the Kennedy campaign contribution, also Nixon's "flabbergasted" reaction.

"In all fairness to myself": Pitts, p. 160.

"Kennedy is, of course, Roman Catholic": Cronkite's broadcast on primary night is included in the Robert Drew documentary *Primary.*

"It means that we've got to go": O'Donnell and Powers, pp. 159–60.

"When the question of West Virginia": Bradlee, *Conversations,* p. 26.

"He knew that if he dropped": Pitts, p. 161.

"The reversal was, of course": Salinger OH.

Around this time: O'Neill int.

"Give Me That Old Time Religion": Humphrey quote, Dallek, *An Unfinished Life,* p. 253.

"pretty well avoided the religious": Billings

quote, Pitts, p. 161.

"Nobody asked me if I was a Catholic": O'Donnell and Powers, pp. 166–67.

"Young man, I should tell you": Battle OH.

"I believe West Virginia brought": Salinger OH.

had been in the "wor-ah": Bradlee int.

Ben Bradlee knew: Ibid.

"basic strategy was a psychological one": Salinger OH.

"We were running the campaign": Ibid.

"They went through West Virginia": Author interview with Charles McWhorter.

"I'd give my right testicle to win this one": Bartlett OH.

"If Jack were beaten in West Virginia": Macdonald OH.

"The Kennedys asked us to sweat": Bradlee, *Conversations,* p. 27.

"Kennedy ignored Jackie": Ibid., p. 28.

Chapter Twelve: Charisma

"We talked to the governor": KOD.

The Kennedy treatment: Dallek, *An Unfinished Life,* p. 247.

Even with this agreement: Dutton OH.

"I'm not running a popularity contest": Schlesinger, *Robert Kennedy and His Times,* p. 213.

After West Virginia he was convinced: Author interview with William J. Green III.

"I could tell, as Governor Lawrence": KOD.

"It was still the last moment": Moynihan OH.

"This organization, this Kennedy-for-President": Horton OH.

"God, why won't he be satisfied": Bill Blair, John F. Kennedy Library Oral History Program.

Eleanor Roosevelt would arrive: Author interview with Lester Hyman.

"riverboat gambler": Bradlee, *Conversations,* p. 18.

"He was having throat problems": Ibid., pp. 30–31.

"six regions, and every region was manned": KOD.

"looked like an impartial newspaper": Salinger OH.

"It was the goddamndest thing": Robin Cross, *J.F.K.: A Hidden Life* (Boston: C. E. Tuttle, 1992), p. 78.

"I wasn't any Chamberlain-umbrella": Robert Dallek, *Lone Star Rising: Lyndon Johnson and His Times, 1908–1960* (New York: Oxford University Press, 1991), pp. 573–74.

"We seized on the opportunity": Salinger OH.

"There were a few rough Irishmen": KOD.

"I was really digging at Johnson pretty hard": Salinger OH.

With Lyndon Johnson's arrows: KOD. "Adlai called Daley and said to Daley, 'I have a lot of support in the convention and I am going to place my name before the convention. I would like to know from you how many votes I can count on out of the Illinois delegation?' Mayor Daley said, 'Well, Governor, you know I have always been for you. I supported you for the governorship. However, it is too late now, I think you are making a mistake. In answer to your question, Governor, in all candor the answer is none. You will not get one vote from the Illinois delegation.'"

Despite some packing of the galleries: Bradlee, *Conversations,* p. 31. "At first glance it looked as if everyone on the floor was screaming and waving something. But a careful look showed most of the delegates sitting quietly, half-hidden by demonstrators."

"operation was slick": Author interview with John Ehrlichman.

"If Kennedy wants Johnson": Dallek, *Lone Star Rising,* p. 575.

" 'Well, I'd just as soon' ": Salinger OH.

"It was a case of grasping": Schlesinger, *Journals,* p. 75.

"Don't worry, Jack, in two weeks": Joe Sr. to JFK, Bartlett OH.

"They sat rapt, then content": Theodore White, *The Making of the President, 1960* (New York: Atheneum, 1961), p. 178.

"I took the telegram to him": Pierre Salinger, *P.S.: A Memoir* (New York: St. Martin's Press, 1995), p. 89.

"meeting of 150 ministers": Account of the organized religious campaign to defeat Kennedy drawn from Shaun A. Casey, *The Mak-*

*ing of a Catholic President: Kennedy vs. Nixon
1960* (New York: Oxford University Press,
2009), pp. 146–49.

"It was night and we were late": William At-
wood, "In Memory of John F. Kennedy,"
Look, December 31, 1963.

"ten times after we got": KOD.

"In the end, he alone made": Ibid.

"meanest, nastiest-looking": Author interview
with Robert S. Strauss.

"to satisfy this audience": KOD.

The loud daily barking: Richard Reeves, *President Kennedy: Profile of Power* (New York:
Simon & Schuster, 1993), p. 41.

Jack's ongoing transformation: Sutton int.

"I wonder where Dick Nixon": Author interview
with Dave Powers.

"Kennedy took the thing": Author interview
with Don Hewitt.

"He was nervous": Harris int.

Bill Wilson had been a young: Author interview
with Bill Wilson.

"He and I were standing there": Hewitt int.

"The design was that we attack": Wilson int.

Once the two men were: Description of candidate rehearsal based on CBS recording of
the event.

"Nixon looked awful off camera": Salinger OH.

"Ted Rogers, who was Nixon's": Wilson int.

"Five minutes to airtime": Ibid.

"erase the assassin image": White, p. 285.

"That son of a bitch": Fawn Brodie, *Richard*

Nixon: The Shaping of His Character (Cambridge, MA: Harvard University Press, 1983), p. 427.

"What the hell is this?": Wilson int.

"I had the impression that": Schlesinger, *Journals,* p. 88.

"He was likely to get himself": Dean Acheson, John F. Kennedy Library Oral History Program.

"There was hardly a place": The account of Martin Luther King's arrest and the Kennedys' effort to free him is drawn from Harris Wofford, *Of Kennedys and Kings: Making Sense of the Sixties* (Pittsburgh: University of Pittsburgh Press, 1992), p. 16.

"Last week, Dick Nixon hit": Fay, p. 60.

"He's a filthy, lying son of a bitch": Goodwin, p. 105.

"Nixon wanted the presidency so bad": Fay, 9.

"They're much more concerned": KOD.

"I was beginning to panic now": Ibid.

"It started out like gangbusters": Salinger OH.

"Ohio did that to me": JFK quote, White, p. 21.

"All those people now say": KOD.

"Nebraska has the largest Republican": Horton OH.

"Does this mean you're president": Matthews, p. 179.

"What am I going to tell the press?": Salinger OH.

"I want to repeat through this wire": Telegram courtesy of Richard M. Nixon Library and

Birthplace.

"Mr. O'Donnell, the president has": KOD.

"Nixon was, in my opinion": Author interview with Herb Klein.

"I think we are in enough trouble in the world today": Richard Nixon, *Six Crises* (New York: Simon & Schuster, 1962), p. 404.

"It was the difference between": Klein int.

"He had done it by driving home": Time, November 16, 1960.

"He wisely decided to concentrate": Schlesinger, *Journals,* p. 93.

"I know there is a God": Jack Kennedy quoted these from Abraham Lincoln during a speech in Muncie, Indiana, on October 5, 1960.

Chapter Thirteen: Landing

urgent phone calls were placed: Bradlee, *Conversations,* pp. 33–34.

President-elect Kennedy put a pair of Republicans: Schlesinger, *A Thousand Days,* pp. 131–36.

McNamara, showing no lack of toughness: Ibid., p. 133.

Looking to the liberal faction: Reeves, *President Kennedy,* pp. 26–27.

Now, as always, concessions needed to be made: Bartlett OH. "I always had the feeling that the decision on Bobby was not made by the President-elect, but I think by his father. I think he took his father's position on it. I never had the feeling that Bobby had any great burning desire to be attorney general, that this was really almost forced upon him."

"I think I'll open the front door": Bradlee, *Conversations,* p. 38.

"I think he hadn't really thought": KOD.

Kennedy's "spokes of the wheel": Ibid. "Roosevelt wanted them competing amongst themselves for what was best for him; at least in reading, this is what I gathered and the president gathered. President Kennedy did not want that; he did not want fighting amongst his staff. He did not want jealousy and infighting; he realized that there would be some competing for presidential favor, that is human nature. But, this was not a goal."

There was little camaraderie: Parmet, p. 47.

Ben Bradlee, the Washington sophisticate: Bradlee int.

"The president-elect was a complex": Wofford, pp. 67–68.

You'd see him sitting: Clifford quote, KOD.

"I remember he told me": Bartlett OH.

"'I'm going to keep the White House white'": Sally Bedell Smith, *Grace and Power: The Private World of the Kennedy White House* (New York: Random House, 2005), p. 173.

Kennedy and Ted Sorensen working on inaugural speech in Palm Beach: Thurston Clarke, *Ask Not: The Inauguration of John*

F. *Kennedy and the Speech That Changed America* (New York: Henry Holt and Co., 2004), pp. 23–27.

To some who'd once been at Choate: Hearing President Kennedy's historic call to "Ask not what your country can do for you; ask what you can do for your country," several of his Choate classmates recalled headmaster George St. John's use of a quite similar phrase. These included some of his Class of '35 classmates, at least one of whom charged plagiarism in a survey taken by the school in 1985. Putney Westerfield, Choate '47, volunteered this account to me:

"For five years I attended compulsory chapel five evenings a week after dinner. Usually the headmaster would quote from the Bible, or literature, or political figures, and make a point concerning how a Choate student should think or act. It was in this context that he would say, once every year or two: 'Ask not what your school can do for you; ask what you can do for your school.' Sometimes it might be mundane, like, 'Be well-dressed and don't smoke cigarettes when on the train to New York or Boston for vacations.' Or: 'Pick up a paper carelessly thrown on the grass.' Or the campaign for a Christmas gift to each member of the school's support staff. It took many forms.

"Listening to the inaugural address in

1961 I immediately related the two 'Ask not's.

"Many years later, when St. John's 'quote books' (three volumes of them) were found, there was a quotation from Harvard dean LeBaron Briggs who wrote: 'The youth who loves his alma mater will always ask not "What can she do for me?" but "What can I do for her?"' Clearly this was the inspiration source for George St. John who knew Briggs from his own Harvard days in the late 1890s. In 1911, as headmaster, he asked Briggs to give the commencement address at Choate."

In *Counselor*, on p. 29, Ted Sorensen cited St. John as the "most credible theory" on the derivation of the "Ask not" exhortation. For whatever reason, he was not able to get Choate administrators to produce St. John's "quote book" for him. On a visit to Choate in 2010, archivist Judy Donald showed me the "quote book" that contained the Briggs essay. It was right there on an early page of St. John's looseleaf binder, right below the hymns to be sung that day.

"greatly exceeded the boldest": Schlesinger, *A Thousand Days*, p. 114.
"The positions of the USA, Britain, and France": Ibid., p. 303.
During those early weeks: Mary Van Rensse-

laer Thayer, *Jacqueline Kennedy: The White House Years* (Boston: Little, Brown, 1967), pp. 103–6.

Lem Billings arrived on Friday: Pitts, pp. 191–92.

He joined the couple, too: Ibid., p. 212.

"What would you do now": Fay OH.

"Listen, Redhead": Ibid.

But, clearly, the president: Pitts, p. 184.

for Rip Horton to: Horton OH.

"The presidency is not a good place": Pitts, p. 184.

"The president is counting on you": The account here of the early organization of the Peace Corps is taken from Wofford's *Of Kennedys and Kings.*

"When he became president, Jackie changed": Author interview with Rachel Mellon.

"Victory has a hundred fathers": Schlesinger, *A Thousand Days,* p. 289.

The disembarking Cubans had been assured by Agency officials: An "Official History of the Bay of Pigs Operation," revealed in 2011, said the CIA task force in charge did not believe it could succeed without becoming an open invasion supported by the U.S. military. The task force met on November 1960 to prepare a briefing for President-elect Kennedy. It failed to share with him its assessment that an invasion plan limited to the brigade of Cuban exiles could not succeed. The revelation came through a Freedom of Information request by the National Security Archive.

"Operation Zapata": Jim Rasenberger, *The Brilliant Disaster: JFK, Castro, and America's Doomed Invasion of Cuba's Bay of Pigs* (New York: Scribner, 2011), pp. 138–40.

Background on Guatemala coup: Ibid., pp. 61–62.

Kennedy and Bissell meet during campaign: Harris int.

Bundy and McNamara support Zapata: Rasenberger, p. 159.

But what really clinched it: Ibid., pp. 136–40.

"In a parliamentary government": Thomas Powers, *The Man Who Kept the Secrets: Richard Helms and the CIA* (New York: Knopf, 1979), p. 115.

landing point shifted from Trinidad: Rasenberger, p. 139.

Castro rounded up: Ibid., pp. 323–25.

Prisoner exchange: Ibid., pp. 361–78.

"I probably made a mistake": Schlesinger, *Journals,* 112.

"How could you expect the world": Reeves, *President Kennedy,* p. 103.

For the first time: Ibid, p. 95.

"I'm the responsible officer": Schlesinger, *A Thousand Days,* p. 290.

83 percent in a Gallup poll: Dallek, *An Unfinished Life,* 386. (That April 1961 number would be the highest in his administration.)

"In the months that followed": Fay, p. 171.

Even on vacation in Hyannis Port: Ibid.

"I will never compromise the principles": Ibid., pp. 172–73.

The French president expressed doubts: KOD.

His practical advice: Ibid.

even the appearance *of negotiating:* Ibid.

"snapping at him like a terrier": O'Donnell and Powers, p. 296.

"Not too well": Leaming, p. 309.

He tried everything: KOD.

Kennedy requested a third meeting: Dallek, *An Unfinished Life,* p. 402.

"If that's true, it's going to be a cold winter": Reeves, *President Kennedy,* p. 171.

"I never met a man like this": Hugh Sidey, "The Presidency," *Time,* October 15, 1984.

"It will have to be for much bigger": JFK to O'Donnell, Dallek, *An Unfinished Life,* p. 430.

"never come face to face with such evil": Pitts, p. 220.

"Our position in Europe": Ibid., p. 55.

"He's imprisoned by Berlin": Hugh Sidey, *John F. Kennedy, President* (New York: Atheneum, 1964), p. 218.

On June 21, he would suffer: Leaming, pp. 321–22.

"showcase of liberty, a symbol": Kempe, p. 423.

Five days later, Senator William Fulbright: Reeves, *President Kennedy,* p. 204.

"Why would Khrushchev put up a wall": Kempe, p. 379.

Chapter Fourteen: Zenith

We'd agreed, as had the Soviets: Leaming, p. 337.

"fucked again!": David Halberstam, *The Best and the Brightest* (New York: Random House, 1972), p. 84.

"If we test only underground": Dallek, *An Unfinished Life,* p. 462.

With it came a new pressure: Leaming, pp. 378–80.

"A journey of a thousand miles begins with one step": Reeves, *President Kennedy,* p. 551.

"hard-boiled . . . soft-boiled": Bradlee, *Conversations,* pp. 52–53.

Kennedy's national security team: Leaming, pp. 378–80.

"we were actually superior to the Soviets": Author interview with John Glenn.

In the fall of 1961: Dallek, *An Unfinished Life,* p. 482.

Afterward, JFK called both sides: KOD.

His company was raising the price of steel: Ibid.

"what you are doing is in the best interest": Fay int.

"You have made a terrible mistake": Reeves, *President Kennedy,* p. 296.

"These guys felt they were so powerful": KOD.

"cold, deliberate fucking": Bradlee, *Conversations,* p. 76.

"wrongly, he could not or would": KOD.

"You find out about these guys": Fay int.

"I don't think U.S. Steel or any other": Dallek,

644

An Unfinished Life, p. 486.

"where possible": Fay int.

"the American people will find it hard": Dallek, *An Unfinished Life*, p. 485.

"Kennedy's style of politics": KOD.

"We looked over all of them as individuals": Robert F. Kennedy, John F. Kennedy Library Oral History Program.

"Good night, pal": To Dave Powers, Smith, p. xiv.

He always exhibited great fondness: Bradlee, *Conversations*, p. 148.

Even social friends might step: Ibid., pp. 114–15.

He regularly went for a swim: Nancy Tuckerman and Pamela Turnure, John F. Kennedy Library Oral History Program. Nancy Tuckerman: "Yes, twice a day."

"Information has been developed": Perret, p. 346.

He'd regularly see Meyer: Bradlee, *Conversations*, p. 54.

Washington efforts: "Summary of Civil Rights Progress," Box 63, Papers of the President, John F. Kennedy Library.

On September 10, the U.S. Supreme Court: KOD.

"I won't agree to let that boy get to Ole Miss": Ibid.

Jack and Bobby both were hoping: Ibid.

Jack was now involved in checking: Ibid.

When two thousand demonstrators: Dallek, *An*

Unfinished Life, p. 515.
"neither Meredith nor any of those men": KOD.
"we knew that most of the National Guard": Ibid.
Kennedy was responsible: Reeves, *President Kennedy,* pp. 359–64.
"They always give you their bullshit": Ibid, p. 363.
"the occupation regime": Letter from Khrushchev to JFK, July 5, 1962, ibid., p. 41.
"bone in my throat": Ibid., p. 168.
"We will not allow your troops to be in Berlin": From State Department, *Foreign Relations of the United States: Cuba, 1962–1963,* pp. 1045–57.
he told Udall that he wanted to meet: Frederick Kempe, *Berlin 1961: Kennedy, Khrushchev, and the Most Dangerous Place on Earth* (New York: Putnam, 2011), p. 493.
He sent JFK a letter: Leaming, pp. 378–80.
Suddenly it came: Ibid., p. 413.
Kennedy now assembled: Sorensen, *Counselor,* p. 286.
"Virtually everyone's initial choice": Ibid., pp. 288–89.
If Khrushchev was attempting: Dallek, *An Unfinished Life,* p. 554.
"I now know how Tojo felt": Schlesinger, *Robert Kennedy and His Times,* p. 507.
Might not an American attack on Cuba: On January 15, 1992, the *New York Times* reported that the Soviet Union had 43,000 troops in

Cuba during the 1962 Cuban Missile Crisis, not 10,000 as was reported by the Central Intelligence Agency. This was according to Robert McNamara, who had just returned from a conference on the crisis in Havana. He said Soviet officials had told him that Moscow had sent short-range nuclear weapons to Cuba and that Soviet commanders there were authorized to use them in the event of an American invasion.

Grab your balls: JFK to Salinger, Salinger, p. 115.

"I think the pressure of this period": Bartlett OH.

"You'd be interested to know": Ibid.

"'Any communication with any skipper'": Fay OH.

He then instructed Bobby: Sorensen, *Counselor,* p. 302.

"the greatest defeat in our history": LeMay quote, Dallek, *An Unfinished Life,* p. 571.

"If Kennedy never did another thing": Macmillan quote, O'Donnell and Powers, p. 284.

There was an equal number of warheads: Michael Dobbs, *One Minute to Midnight: Kennedy, Khrushchev, and Castro on the Brink of Nuclear War* (New York: Knopf, 2008), p. 98.

"My thinking went like this": Nikita Khrushchev, *Khrushchev Remembers* (Boston: Little, Brown, 1970), p. 494.

"The final lesson of the Cuban missile crisis":

Robert Kennedy, *Thirteen Days: A Memoir of the Cuban Missile Crisis* (New York: W. W. Norton, 1969), p. 95.

Chapter Fifteen: Goals

"The tax laws really screw people": Bradlee, *Conversations,* p. 218.

"The decision to make the speech available": New York Times, June 13, 1963.

"The speech and its publication in Izvestia *show":* Ibid.

"He's just challenging us": Bradlee, *Conversations,* p. 195.

"Make him look ridiculous": Dan T. Carter, *The Politics of Rage: George Wallace, the Origins of the New Conservatism, and the Transformation of American Politics* (New York: Simon & Schuster, 1995), p. 149.

"most precious and powerful right in the world": Public Papers of the Presidents: John F. Kennedy: 1963, p. 14.

"the most sweeping and forthright ever": Martin Luther King, June 20, 1963, Box 97, President's Office Files at John F. Kennedy Library.

Driving through the streets: Bradlee, *Conversations,* pp. 95–96. "Just before his trip to Berlin in June, 1963," wrote Bradlee, "he spent the better part of an hour with the Vreelands (Frederick 'Frecky' Vreeland, a young foreign service officer and the son of *Vogue* editor Diana Vreeland, and his wife) before he could master 'Ich bin ein Berliner.' "

In fact, Jack was secretly: Ibid., p. 84. "For some reason it bugs Kennedy that I speak French."

A million Germans lined the parade route: Michael Beschloss, *The Crisis Years: Kennedy and Khrushchev, 1960–1963* (New York: Edward Burlingame Books, 1991), pp. 604–8.

"like a man who has just glimpsed Hell": Hugh Sidey, Reeves, *President Kennedy,* p. 535.

Jack called the time he spent in Berlin: Sorensen, *Counselor,* p. 325.

"When my great-grandfather left here to become a cooper in East Boston": President Kennedy to the people of New Ross, Ireland, June 1963, John F. Kennedy Library.

"The wind from that machine blew my chickens away": Duchess of Devonshire, *The House: A Portrait of Chatsworth* (London: Papermac, 1987), p. 222.

During those negotiations: Sorensen, *Counselor,* p. 327.

On July 25, 1963, envoys from the three: Leaming, p. 435.

John Kennedy considered this his greatest achievement: Sorensen int.

"With all human beings, one of the things": Ormsby-Gore quote, Lord Harlech OH.

"He put up quite a fight": Leaming, p. 298.

"defeat Communist insurgency": Reeves, *President Kennedy,* p. 50.

"I can remember one particular case": Fay OH.

He had the added advantage: Schlesinger, *A Thousand Days*, pp. 988–89.

The leader of that faction: Ibid., p. 985.

Now he was approving his former ally's: Leaming, p. 309.

"U.S. Government cannot tolerate situation in which power lies in Nhu's hands": Reeves, *President Kennedy*, pp. 562–63.

August was also the month of: Schlesinger, *A Thousand Days*, pp. 972–73; Schlesinger, *Robert Kennedy and His Times*, pp. 350–52.

"This was the first time we'd seen Jackie": Bradlee, *Conversations*, p. 206.

He left at halftime: O'Brien, *John F. Kennedy*, p. 779.

In future visits to the confession booth: Fay, pp. 222–23.

light a candle for Joe Jr.: Dalton OH.

There were often times when friends: Ibid.

president would kneel: Dave Powers int.

"An American President, commander in chief": Sorensen, *Counselor*, p. 123.

On October 4, Jackie left: Leaming, p. 314.

"Perhaps he should have guessed that": Sorensen, *Counselor*, p. 354.

After retreating from the cabinet room: Leaming, p. 323.

"Over the weekend": Presidential recordings, John F. Kennedy Library.

"He is instinctively against introduction": United States State Department, *Foreign Relations of the United States: Vietnam, 1961*, pp. 532–33.

"They want a force of American troops": Schlesinger, *A Thousand Days*, p. 547.

"I do not believe he knew": Sorensen, *Counselor*, p. 359.

At about this same time: O'Neill, p. 177.

"mood of the city was ugly": Bradlee, *Conversations*, p. 237.

"disgraced. There is no other way": Time, November 1, 1963.

The following Thursday, Jack had invited: Pitts, pp. 205–6.

He was convinced: Bradlee, *Conversations*, p. 190.

"He'll end up hating me": Reeves, *President Kennedy*, p. 465.

Jack spent the next weekend: Barbara Leaming, *Mrs. Kennedy: The Missing History of the Kennedy Years* (New York: Free Press, 2001), pp. 326–27.

"A small band of conspirators": JFK speech to the Inter-American Press Association, November 18, 1963, John F. Kennedy Presidential Library and Museum.

"organize an in-depth study": William J. Rust, *Kennedy in Vietnam* (New York: Da Capo Press, 1985), pp. 4–5.

While Wright laid some of the blame: Author interview with Jim Wright.

Chapter Sixteen: Legacy

"They were wider than pools": Theodore White's notes on his interview with Jacqueline Ken-

nedy are at the John F. Kennedy Library.

Within hours she'd assumed the reins: Tuckerman/Turnure OH.

"Jackie was extraordinary": Bradlee, *Conversations,* p. 244.

"to an exceptional degree": Schlesinger, *A Thousand Days,* p. 78.

"each of us had a certain role we were cast into, whether we knew it or not": Jim Reed, John F. Kennedy Library Oral History Program.

"We had a hero for a friend": William Manchester, *The Death of a President: November 20–November 25, 1963* (New York: Harper & Row, 1967), p. 446.

"chemistry": Author interview with Chuck Spalding.

"The most charming man I ever knew": Smathers int.

"aura of royalty about him": Bradlee int.

"chasing girls in the South of France": Bartlett int.

"There's no point in being Irish if you don't know the world's going to someday break your heart": Moynihan, said to columnist Mary McGrory.

In a 2009 national poll: National survey conducted for CBS's *60 Minutes* and *Vanity Fair,* published in January 2010.

PHOTO CREDITS

Associated Press: 1, 14, 21, 24, 29, 30, 32, 34

JFK Presidential Library and Museum: 2, 7, 12, 23, 28, 31

John Morse/JFK Presidential Library and Museum: 3

Courtesy Choate Rosemary Hall Archives: 4

Princeton University Archives: Department of Rare Books and Special Collections, Princeton University: 5

The John F. Kennedy Library Foundation: 6, 10, 11

Author's collection: 8, 9

Courtesy Sutton Family: 13

Dave Powers/JFK Presidential Library and Museum: 15

McKeesport Heritage Center: 16

Courtesy Richard Nixon Foundation: 17

Getty Images: 18

Tony Frissell, Library of Congress: 19

The Lowenherz Collection of Kennedy Photographs, Friedheim Library, Archives and Special Collections, Peabody Institute of

Johns Hopkins University, Orlando Suero,
  photographer: 20
Courtesy Reardon Family: 22
Newsweek: 26
Courtesy Sorensen Family: 27
Associated Press/Bill Allen: 33
Peace Corps: 35

ABOUT THE AUTHOR

Chris Matthews is the host of MSNBC's *Hardball* and NBC's *The Chris Matthews Show.* His bestselling books include *Hardball; Kennedy & Nixon; Now, Let Me Tell You What I Really Think;* and *American: Beyond Our Grandest Notions.* Go to www.jackkennedybook .com for more.

The employees of Thorndike Press hope you have enjoyed this Large Print book. All our Thorndike, Wheeler, and Kennebec Large Print titles are designed for easy reading, and all our books are made to last. Other Thorndike Press Large Print books are available at your library, through selected bookstores, or directly from us.

For information about titles, please call:

(800) 223-1244

or visit our Web site at:

http://gale.cengage.com/thorndike

To share your comments, please write:

Publisher
Thorndike Press
10 Water St., Suite 310
Waterville, ME 04901